West German
Balance-of-Payments Policy

William Pollard Wadbrook

The Praeger Special Studies program—
utilizing the most modern and efficient book
production techniques and a selective
worldwide distribution network—makes
available to the academic, government, and
business communities significant, timely
research in U.S. and international economic, social, and political development.

West German Balance-of-Payments Policy

The Prelude to European Monetary Integration

PRAEGER SPECIAL STUDIES IN INTERNATIONAL ECONOMICS AND DEVELOPMENT

Praeger Publishers   New York   Washington   London

PRAEGER PUBLISHERS
111 Fourth Avenue, New York, N.Y. 10003, U.S.A.
5, Cromwell Place, London S.W.7, England

Published in the United States of America in 1972
by Praeger Publishers, Inc.

Library of Congress Catalog Card Number: 76-151959

Printed in the United States of America

The political unification of Europe may soon be achieved by way of the monetary integration of the continent. This momentous possibility has awakened a new and more urgent worldwide interest in European affairs. The present study is intended to be useful to students and practitioners of "political economy" in all its forms, as an introduction to the backgrounds of the European monetary-integration movement. This introduction is accomplished through a detailed case-study of German international financial policy and its motivations over the past decade, especially in the cardinal problem area of international economic adjustment. The emphasis is on those motivational elements which have been fundamental to German's past policy, and so promise to influence the future. A fuller orientation to the aims and methods of this study has been incorporated in the first chapter.

Two technical points about the presentation may be made here. First, the necessarily large number of citations has suggested the maximum convenient use of abbreviations in the notes. Full details of this arrangement are given in the List of Abbreviations preceding the text.

The second technical point concerns three terminological usages. While the application of each is made fully clear in the text, the reasons for their introduction may be explained here.

Throughout the study, the ordinary concept of balance-of-payments equilibrium is often referred to as a "compatibility" of numerous relationships as between economies. The advantages of this synonym appear to be three: it emphasizes the fact that international equilibrium may be measured by one or another payments-balance accounting concept, but does not consist thereof; it reminds the reader of the complexity of the simultaneous equations whose solution is the equilibrium; it points up the diversity of the elements which are harmonized in equilibrium, and which can produce disequilibrium by their shifts. By doing these things, this conception of equilibrium facilitates an easier and more unified explanation of undervaluation, exported inflation, and the workings of the direct international price-transmission effect of disequilibrium.

v

In several places, contrary to general practice, "real" and "structural" economic elements are distinguished. This is merely for elegance of logical division and brevity of reference. Any other rubrics would have served as well; the two chosen seemed to cry out for an economical and useful distinction.

In Chapters 4 and 5, the liquidity effect of balance-of-payments surplus is said to be offsetable on the "exchange level" and on the "monetary-base level." Exchange-level offsets are merely Machlup's "corrections" of the payments balance; monetary-level offsets are reabsorptions of the monetary effect of the surplus through domestic financial policy. The phrases were chosen for their symmetry, to emphasize the line of exposition-by-residuals followed in the text.

All translations from German sources are my own.

Finally, I hasten to express here my gratitude to Professor George N. Halm and Professor Don D. Humphrey of the Fletcher School of Law and Diplomacy for their inspiration and patient guidance as teachers; to my wife Elizabeth Anne and my small daughters Catherine Clare and Paula Susanna for their constant help and comfort; to Consul Johann W. von Mallinckrodt for his cheerful assistance and advice; to Miss Carol Steiman and Mrs. Earline Walling for their efficient editorial aid; and to the Boston University Grants-in-Aid Program for its generous support of the physical production of the manuscript for this work. Of course, no one except myself is responsible for errors or other shortcomings in the present study.

CONTENTS

LIST OF TABLES, FIGURES, AND EQUATIONS

LIST OF ABBREVIATIONS

AP   Federal Republic of Germany, Bundesbank, <u>Auszüge aus Presseartikeln</u>

AR   Federal Republic of Germany, Bundesbank, <u>Annual Report</u>

BB   Deutsche Bundesbank

BR   Federal Republic of Germany, Bundesministerium für Wirtschaft, Wissenschaftliche Beirat

BRD   Federal Republic of Germany

CDU   Christian Democratic Union

DDR   German Democratic Republic

DM   Deutsche Mark

EEC   European Economic Community

EPU   European Payments Union

FR   Federal Republic of Germany, Bundesministerium für Finanz, "<u>Finanzbericht</u>" (Finance Report)

GATT   General Agreement on Tariffs and Trade

GER   <u>German Economic Review</u>

IBRD   International Bank for Reconstruction and Development

IFS   <u>International Financial Statistics</u>

IMF   International Monetary Fund

JEC   United States, Congress, Joint Economic Committee

JG   Federal Republic of Germany, Sachverständigenrat zur Begutachtung der gesamtwirtschaftlichen Entwicklung, <u>Jahresgutachten</u>

MR   Federal Republic of Germany, Bundesbank, <u>Monthly Report</u>

NATO	North Atlantic Treaty Organization
OECD	Organization for Economic Cooperation and Development
OECDS	Organization for Economic Cooperation and Development, Economic and Development Review Committee
OECD3	Organization for Economic Cooperation and Development, Economic Policy Committee, Working Party Three
QES	Economist, Quarterly Economic Survey (Germany)
SG	Federal Republic of Germany, Sachverständigenrat zur Begutachtung der gesamtwirtschaftlichen Entwicklung, Sondergutachtung
SPD	Socialist Party of Germany
SS3	Federal Republic of Germany, Bundesbank, Supplements to Monthly Reports, Series 3
UK	United Kingdom of Great Britain and Northern Ireland
US	United States of America

Note: The foregoing list explains all abbreviations used in the text, in the Bibliography, and in the notes. Since this study must often discuss points raised in the German payments-balance policy debate, it is very fully annotated, not always in order to cite authority for the substance of a statement made in the text, but often merely to indicate by whom, where, and approximately how often such a statement was made in the course of the debate itself. To avoid a needlessly cumbrous citations apparatus, therefore, the following plan is followed. In each chapter of the present study, the first citation of any given work is in the full traditional footnote form. In all other instances, citations in the notes are made by the bibliographical alphabetizing word or name (or by one of the abbreviations above) alone, followed immediately by the page reference. Where the alphabetizing name of several authors is the same, first initials are cited; in the one case where first initials are also identical, a full first name is cited. Where several works of one author are cited in the notes, the first nominative noun (or, failing this, the first grammatically dominant word) in each title is cited after the author name. However, long German compounds are in some cases cited only by the smallest gender-determining element capable of independent meaning.

West German
Balance-of-Payments Policy

1

THE
POLICY CHALLENGE:
GERMANY'S
PAYMENTS–BALANCE
SITUATION

INTRODUCTION

The Inquiry and its Significance

Background of the Inquiry

The recent great interest in international monetary affairs has focused on two growing needs: general reforms and regional integration. Springing from partly parellel, partly quite divergent developments in the industrialized West, both movements face the same fundamental problem, that of the mutual adjustment of national economic policies and structures.

The other two problems often ascribed by reformers to present international monetary arrangements, viz., inadequate liquidity and an undesirable composition of reserves, are basically related to the same adjustment problem.[1] For certainly, confidence in the composition of world monetary reserves could not be threatened if any given stock of liquid assets could be made to serve for all demands without steady augmentation. And the "scarcity" of world liquidity would not cause concern if the adjustment process ensured an adequate exchange and distribution of the existing stock. Liquidity and adjustment are substitutes.[2] Thus the speed and efficiency of the adjustment process ultimately determines the urgency of the liquidity and confidence problems. Yet world monetary reform has thus far dealt much more readily with the latter problems than with the former.

Regional monetary integration efforts encounter the adjustment problem in an almost exactly reversed logical setting. Here the difficulty is not to create an international monetary system capable of

stimulating, guiding and facilitating the adjustment of national structures and policies. The integrationists' problem is rather to ensure
that national structures and policies are in fact capable of a harmonious
adjustment, before imposing on them a monetary system that presupposes such a capability.

In both cases, the underlying difficulties involve individual national structures, policies and reactions to the payments balance. An
investigation into the national-policy bases from which spring the attitudes of important individual nations to the international adjustment
process, therefore, can reveal the basic conditions which any future
international monetary arrangements must accommodate or control.
For this purpose, of course, it is important for such an investigation
to seek out those fundamental motivational elements which will outlive
today's rapid psychological and institutional changes.

For over a decade, it has been practically impossible to discuss
the general problem of balance-of-payments adjustment without touching on the case of the world's second largest trading nation, the Federal
Republic of Germany.*[3] Conversely, it has been equally impossible
to discuss the national economic policy of this, the world's most for-
eign-trade-dependent country, without reference to its ongoing payments-balance problems and payments-balance debate.[4] And indeed
that debate has been carried on, so far as it has been aimed at motivating substantive policy decisions, overwhelmingly in terms of domestic and national goals and interests.[5]

Nature of the Inquiry

The present study proposes to investigate both the nature of
German balance-of-payments policy from March 1961 through June
1971, and the sources of this policy in German economic structure
and German national and domestic policy goals. This effort will be
aimed at a clear understanding of the mainsprings of past policy, as
a prerequisite for a judgment of the present, and predictions and
prescriptions for the future.

It cannot be the direct aim of such a study as the present, either
to extend abstract theory on the one hand, or to analyze exhaustively
concrete German economic structures on the other. Even in the narrower context of balance-of-payments policy formulation, this work

---

*In the present study, the simple term "Germany" always refers
to the Federal Republic of Germany. This convenient usage is not
intended to convey any prejudgment on any question affecting the whole
German nation.

cannot be primarily concerned with the international debate over the adjustment problem, except as this is reflected in the specifically German policy situation. This is consonant with the emphasis here laid on national adjustment policies as the root of international monetary problems. Finally, the analytical purpose of this study opposes a chronological recital of events for its own sake.

Such concentrated analysis of policy formulation in a single country in no way excludes more general applications of this study. On the contrary, the sharper and the more analytical the work's focus, the greater its value as a representative case-study of the international financial position of an important industrialized nation.

Concentrated study of the internal springs of German balance-of-payments policy holds important lessons for further discussion on other levels as well. The German experience, central and weighty in itself, has been complicated politically by Germany's economically open and geopolitically exposed situation, and enriched theoretically by traditional German "thoroughness" and modern German sensitivity to questions of social order. In addition, several unique features of the German policy agencies afford sidelights on the development of institutional arrangements for foreign economic policy formulation.

The Period Under Review

The present study draws upon the experience of the period from March 1961 through June 1971. This choice of period offers several advantages. It is long enough to be representative of continuing economic and social trends through several governmental administrations. At the same time, it coincides with the period of most "fully German" postwar economic policy, which saw the removal in 1961 of the last direct and institutionalized foreign influences on policy-making.6 This period also coincides with the postwar era of currency convertibility. Finally, the period chosen embraces three dramatic and very characteristic attempts to meet German payments-balance problems, the upvaluation of 1961, the floating and restabilizing of the DM in 1969, and the floating of the DM in 1971.

Method

In the present study, the attempt is made to explain, in terms of what was done and why it was done, a course of policy actually adopted. In a strict sense, of course, this is not possible, for it would require both an exposition of the full range of potential alternative outcomes, and a full understanding of all relevant goal priorities and of the political strength of those holding them. In this study, the scope and permutations of both these variables of the decision-making calculus must be narrowed. However, the method often adopted of reducing the "explanation" of policy to a single regression formula has here been rejected as sacrificing too much, both in depth and in breadth of understanding, to obtain a merely statistical probability.[7]

The full meaning of an economic policy choice can be understood only in terms of its alternatives. The most significant German balance-of-payments alternatives can be isolated by a preliminary discussion of the German payments balance seen as the indicator of problems and choices. The remainder of this chapter therefore develops the meaning of the German balance-of-payments as a poser of alternatives. What market-mechanical effects will result from it if no measures are taken? Alternatively, what causal conditions are discernible against which corrective measures could be directed?

Chapter 2 develops the goals side of Germany's policy choices. To avoid later lengthy excursions into politics and sociology, the several more or less standard economic and political goals are here supplemented with a discussion of well-attested partial or interest-group goals. The nature, balance-of-payments implications and political support of each goal is indicated. Chapter 2 also introduces some of the institutional protagonists in the German balance-of-payments policy debate, with an outline of their relevant internal organization, external connections, and public intellectual position on payments-balance policy.

Chapters 3, 4, and 5 pass in review the adjusting and non-adjusting policy measures open to Germany, surveying their effects on national goals, analyzing their tools or means of impact on the payments-balance mechanics, reviewing the domestic debate on each of these points, and summarizing the German experience with the use of each tactic.

In the light of the preceding discussion, Chapter 6 first isolates the most appropriate statistical indicators of recent German payments-balance policy, seen as a combination of the various classes of measures discussed in the study. The overall policy strategy is then characterized, and its impacts on goals are then presented as an explanation of the policy's adoption. On this basis, Chapter 7 assesses Germany's present payments-balance situation and intentions, and applies all the study's findings to predictions and prescriptions for the future.

CONCEPTS OF PAYMENTS-BALANCE
EQUILIBRIUM

The Concept of Payments-Balance Policy

Since policy is a choice among alternative responses to a problem, an understanding of the balance-of-payments policy actually adopted in Germany in recent years must be based on a careful examination of the real options that existed. This examination in turn demands careful conceptualization of the possible states of the payments balance, and careful formulation both of the causal areas open to intervention by active policy measures and of the expectable effects of a policy of non-intervention in the situation. There is thus no room in such an investigation for a payments-balance policy goal as such: the balance of payments is rather seen as an indicator of underlying causes and of expectable effects.

The cause-and-effect mechanisms which define the policy options spring from fairly simple and basic assumptions about mass behavior, on the one hand, and from constraints on behavior of a specific institutional or "structural" nature, on the other. The former, less understood, patterns are not normally considered usefully alterable by measures acceptable in liberal societies. The latter, more external, guides to behavior are changeable by policy measures to varying extents. Thus, some of these institutions are technically or politically difficult to alter, and so form a species of policy framework within which more easily-made changes can produce their effects. The changes most easily effected by governmental authorities may be called policy tools.

Thus, in a fundamental sense, there are no wholly mechanical, policy-free balance-of-payments processes or outcomes. Every state of the balance-of-payments in fact presupposes some market-structuring decisions. What will in this study be called policy responses to Germany's balance of payments must therefore be identified against a given complex of such market-structuring measures, and the latter must be specified.[8]

For these purposes, certain pre-existing "normal" conditions can be taken for granted. The very notion of a balance of international payments, first of all, presupposes some degree of openness of economies, compatible with international transactions, and at the same time it presupposes less-than-perfect international markets. During the period under review, Germany's economy was indeed unusually open, as its international trade indicates.*[9] Again, since more than one currency is involved in international payments, the regime governing their rate of exchange must be specified as a departure point for policy responses. Pegged exchange rates, defended by central-bank trading in foreign and domestic currencies, was virtually the only regime operated by Germany during the period under review, and will here be taken as the policy-"normal" case. Also taken as analytically "normal" are stability of trade and exchange controls, of administrative barriers, and of subsidies, bounties and taxes on tradable goods.[10]

Thus, "non-intervention" in the payments-balance situation does not imply the total dismantling of the framework of trade and exchange regulation, but simply the absence of measurable departures from these "normal" states.

Payments-Balance Accounts,
Equilibrium, and Adjustment

Construction of the Payments-Balance Document

The document reflecting the state of a nation's "payments balance" is actually designed to record all international transactions involving exchanges of economic value, whether or not these involve sales or formal payments. The entries are arranged in an accounting format, as debits and credits, according to their tendency to generate inpayments or outpayments.

An overall balance-of-payments document is therefore always in accounting balance, since it is able to record, in some category (including credit and gifts), all actual and known international payments and all the virtual or inferable payments which balance these. To the extent known transactions do not balance, a residual item is added to the document.

The significance of the state of the balance of payments therefore must consist in the proportions of the various categories of recorded

---

*R. Triffin (Gold and the Dollar Crisis [New Haven, 1960], p. 486) describes the openness (or international integration) of an economy in terms of a high percentage of Gross National Product generated by foreign trade, stable trade and exchange restrictions, and an industrial structure complementary to those of its trade partners. A high degree of economic interaction between foreign-trading and non-foreign trading sectors of the economy is a further feature of openness.

payments. Since the balance-of-payments document is meaningful for policy chiefly as an indicator of potential problems and their solutions it can be understood only by investigating the causes and effects of the proportions of its categories.

Autonomous Payments-Balance Items

From the causal viewpoint, the balance of payments can be broken down conceptually into autonomous and compensating items. Autonomous accounts are those regarded as resulting from transactions motivated otherwise than by the state of the balance of payments itself, i.e., either by the usual market mechanisms within the normal policy framework, or by non-payments-balance-oriented government policy decisions. Compensating accounts are those resulting, either automatically or through a conscious payments-balance-policy decision of the government, from the state of the remaining accounts.[11]

Evidently, policy measures to control the state of the compensating items would be unnecessary if all the autonomous items were in balance. Overall and lasting balance in autonomous accounts thus broadly conceived (under fixed exchange rates) could be called a priori indicative of long-run equilibrium in the balance of payments. Movement toward this state of equilibrium could be called adjustment. In discussing such purely accounting indicators of adjustment, the various compensating items should thus be accorded very different analytical weights.

Payments-Balance-Induced Items

Obviously, the accounts directly and strongly influenced by the state of the other payments-balance accounts, for instance through exchange-rate speculation, cannot be treated as permanent flows of payments when payments-balance policy measures are under consideration. Again, accounts which are mechanically and residually implied by the net balance of other transactions, such as spontaneous increases in monetary claims on foreigners, cannot normally be regarded as stable elements when a projected move toward equilibrium is being contemplated. More circuitous feedback impacts on the payments balance, as illustrated by several well-known international-income-multiplier models,[12] must also be allowed for in quantitative treatments of concrete policy proposals.

Policy-Induced Items

All international transactions under government control, as to which the government has reasonable medium-term policy leeway, at least at the margin, must be correspondingly discounted in analyzing a nation's underlying payments balance. Such a discount must be applied to almost all direct government transactions, including central-bank operations, and to private payments affected by temporary manip-ulations of the trade, tariff or tax frameworks.13

The distinction between autonomous and compensating balance-of-payment accounts, while fairly clear conceptually, cannot always be drawn in practice.14 This is partly because of shortcomings in the keeping of the statistics themselves, and partly because of the impossibility of drawing a firm a priori line between balance-of-payments-induced and non-balance-of-payments-induced market incen-tives.15 Even after the institutional facts in each case have been throughly sifted, it is often impossible to determine the most suitable breakdown of these accounts. Inevitably, then, a certain amount of arbitrariness exists in the disignation of autonomous, induced, and policy-determined items within concrete payments-balance accounts.

The concept of payments-balance equilibrium and adjustment used in the present study is, to the extent possible, based on the autonomous compensating distinction as applied to the actual items of the German balance of payments. The proper applications can be developed and supported only by thorough discussion, in the ensuing pages, of Ger-many's specific institutional structure and payments-balance composi-tion. Even then, obscurities must remain: utter clarity on this point would require entering the minds of the public and the government pol-icy-makers.16 Where statistical and definitional consistency is needed (as in Chapter 6), an arbitrary line will at times need to be drawn.

Theoretical Economic Significance
of International Equilibrium

Equilibrium as Compatibility

International adjustment has been defined as the process whereby long run payments-balance equilibrium is approached. Payments-balance equilibrium has been identified in terms of accounting balance among the autonomous transactions generating inpayments and outpay-ments. Autonomous transactions have in principle been isolated as those not directly induced by the state of the payments balance, or by artificial policy measures designed to produce balance.

The underlying and essential meaning of such abstract statisti-cal equilibrium is that the various real, market-structural, and fi-nancial variables of a nation are compatible with those of the trading world at large.*

---

*Some of the import of this statement, which is directly quanti-fiable only under heroic restrictions, is developed by R. Nurkse,

If all domestic markets were perfect, this compatibility would mean
that the world division of labor would be properly based on national
factor endowments, tastes and technology, and hence would produce the
textbook gains of trade.[17] International payments equilibrium, as indirect measure of this efficiency, thus represents a worthwhile goal
even prescinding from national objectives which might favor it.

This overall compatibility of economic variables in several
countries, which is conceivable in terms of complex simultaneous
equations, can be visualized in highly simplified form as an equality
of the purchasing power at home and abroad of a given national currency,[18] or as the compatibility of export price-cost ratios of the trade
partners, viewed in conjunction with their differing income distributions,
differing "degrees of monopoly" and differing social-power relationships.[19] These latter conceptualizations of basic international equilibrium are, however, not clearly measurable, so that the payments-
balance indicator of equilibrium remains the most useful.

The mechanics of the adjustment process, and the tendency of
international payments disequilibrium, if not counteracted by policy,
to force a mutual adjustment of real national economic structures,
will be discussed later in this chapter.

Equilibrium and the Gains of Trade

The theoretical gains of trade, stemming from efficient world
division of labor, are of two chief kinds, those of efficiency and those
of welfare.* Efficiency gains derive from producing with the most
appropriate resources available and from the scale economies of producing for wider markets. Welfare gains stem from consumers' wider
choice and from effective income shifts from world producers to world
consumers.**

The degree to which textbook gains of trade are realized today
is not directly measurable amongst the many allocational and distributional distortions of the real world.[20] Rapid technological advances
in industrialized nations have increased the wealth gap among the

———————————————

Conditions of International Monetary Equilibrium (Essays in International Finance #4) (Princeton, 1945).

*Ignoring the "demonstration" and "fraternization" benefits
which have been claimed for trade.

**These last gains are not strictly necessary in logic, but do
follow from the more likely assumptions about configurations of functional marginal utilities of income and of price elasticities in exporter
nations vis-à-vis customer nations.

world's many countries, aggravating divergences of interests and the
felt need for international economic barriers. Irresistible technological
drives toward market concentration have produced inflexible domestic
industrial structures, which are subject to crises if not controlled and
guided. This in turn has produced interventionist states dominated by
powerful economic interest groups. The resulting macrofinancial
manipulation of nominal incomes, together with fiscal rechanneling
of perhaps a third of the real income of the typical industrial nation,
produce efficiency and welfare distortions which easily prevent, counteract and obscure any potential gains from trade.[21]

As a result of domestic and international constellations of interests, misunderstandings and inadequate measurements, therefore,
world-welfare and efficiency effects of trade are normally ignored
(except as propaganda) in everyday national policy decisions. International transactions are looked upon as a "vent for surplus", i.e., for
the surplus produced by inflexible industrial structures, or as a means
for gaining a national "presence" in the world through aid, direct investment and the like. Payments-balance equilibrium is on the other
hand at times desired as a gesture toward one's trade-dependent military and political allies, or at best as a means of avoiding retaliatory
protectionism abroad.

At the same time, international incomes gaps raise political
risks parallel to capital scarcity and so discourage efficiency-in-
creasing capital flows to developing countries.[22] Amongst developed
countries, capital movements are a favorite target of payments-balance corrective measures (Chapter 4).

Common Payments-Balance
Concepts Compared

In view of the breadth, complexity and national diversity of the
payments-balance determinants, and given the strong forces making
for government payments-balance intervention, it is not surprising
that confusion exists with regard to the most appropriate analytical
presentation of the payments balance. All of the many proposed
presentations are attempts to put policy-induced and grossly feedback-
induced accounts "below the line", i.e., to show these accounts as
compensating items to an underlying autonomous balance.[23] Where
the line is to be drawn depends on how deeply the determinants are
traced, and how dynamically government's broad activities are treated.
A review of the chief payments-balance concepts, ordered according
to how many items are put "below the line", will elucidate the con-
troversies over the placement of individual accounts.

The "official settlements", "overall", or "regular transactions" balance of international payments is conceived of as compensated by official international reserve movements. This definition has been used by the United States Department of Commerce and occasionally by the German Bundesbank and the German federal government.24 There exists, however, "no agreed or always usable definition of international reserves."25 In particular, the net liquid assets of banks and other firms are subject to management or even appropriation by the monetary authorities.

The "liquidity" balance attempts to take account of this fact by (in principle) putting public and private liabilities to foreigners and foreign assets of under one year's term "below the line". However, in United States usage, privately held short-term assets, and government-owned short-term assets denominated in non-"reserve" currencies, remain "above the line" as autonomous exports of capital. The well-known Lederer-Bernstein debate concerned the classification of these latter items.26 The critical point in such a controversy is the stimulus behind the acquisition of these assets and the directness of its connection with the United States balance of payments. Under either the Bernstein or the Lederer definition, in any case, the resulting balance is a managed balance.

The "basic" or "genuine performance" balance, often cited and approved by the Bundesbank,27 is viewed as compensated by international reserves and short-term capital movements, thus obviating a Lederer-Bernstein-type dispute. Short-term capital movements thus placed "below the line" include the balance-of-payments statistical residual (including trade credit), and direct financial credit to firms. Yet, as the Bundesbank admits, the probably large effects of balance-of-trade movements on trade credit cannot be determined. Still more problematical is the inclusion "above the line" of unilateral government transfers in this "specially fair measure": in the year 1965, for example, the German "genuine performance balance" showed a deficit of 5.5 billion DM, while the unilateral outpayments alone amounted to 5.8 billion DM.28

The Organization for Economic Cooperation and Development takes account of such difficulties in its "balance on non-monetary transactions," which is defined as compensated by international reserve movements, "monetary" short-term capital movements, and "monetary" public-sector transactions.29 What this concept gains in definitional clarity and consistency it loses in statistical measurability. Are long-term government capital exports and government unilateral transfers, as in development aid programs, to be considered compensating flows? Usually, the relevant governments do not so consider them, as they are said to represent "long-term, basic policy decisions." However, it is equally possible to view government-controlled capital exports as connected with payments-balance policy.

To accommodate this possibility, at least definitionally, it is necessary to take a further step toward logical completeness, but away from statistical distinctness. Haberler's balance, for instance, is compensated by all "accommodating capital movements."[30] Haberler's examples of accommodating capital movements include inventory changes, government prepayment of debt, government imports as a result of exchange-offset agreements, and Roosa-type bonds.

Virtually the same balance was called "basic" by Germany's Council of Experts for the Evaluation of Economic Trends,* which saw in it the "long-run criterion" of balance-of-payments equilibrium.[31] Nearly this same balance, compensated by international reserve movements and short-term capital movements including all "special transactions" of whatever form, is advanced by Mosse as his "complicated model."[32] Official lending, development aid gifts, contributions to international agencies and international central-bank operations are in this model also seen as compensatory. This kind of ad hoc balance has had many users.[33]

The inclusion of long-term capital movements amongst the autonomous accounts often draws criticism. Portfolio investment, particularly that denominated in currency foreign to the holder, is very often long-term in form only. Shifts in international interest-rate differentials can quickly lead to reversals of such long-term items.[34] On the other hand, much short-term credit is arranged on the understanding that it will be renewed. Elimination of this problem would require retreating to the balance on goods, private services, and private remittances. Even remittances by foreign workers could be regarded as an item resulting from a persistent goods-and-services surplus and international real-interest advantage. The resultant import of financial capital without real capital (goods) finds an outlet in the import of labor.

Finally, it has been pointed out that the payments-balance accounts alone cannot by themselves reflect all the necessary elements of full international equilibrium.[35] Logically, full equilibrium anywhere in an interconnected system requires equilibrium in all the individual markets. Even a full economic equilibrium might not take account of the unsatisfied goals of policy makers, e.g., full employment.

---

*The Council of Experts for the Evaluation of Economic Trends is hereafter referred to as the Council of Experts.

There is thus in effect no one a priori correct definition of payments equilibrium, while there are dozens of defensible and usable
a posteriori definitions, depending on the aims of analysis and the
institutional situation.36 But adequate definition is still not adequate
measurement. A payments-balance account which is highly responsive
to policy measure, for example, nevertheless normally embraces
transactions which would have been insensitive to such measures.

It must be concluded that no amount of refinement of the available
international-payments figures can in the abstract provide a true autonomous balance. Even an approach to the theoretically desirable indicator
is possible only after a thorough sifting of the institutional facts of
each case. The resulting ad hoc definition will still remain merely a
plausible point of departure for analysis.

Over and above the conceptual and statistical difficulties, a
policy-apologetic element appears at times to enter into the discussion
of the ideal payments-balance indicator. The Bundesbank and other
German commentators have, for example, over the years attempted to
draw conclusions about Germany's long-run payments position from
almost every conceivable balance, including the current-account balance, a useful definitional concept without special meaning for equi-
librium.37 Short-term capital movements, however persistent, have
normally been treated as unessential in the Bundesbank's publications.38
Yet long-term capital exports, no matter how temporary and artificial,
have usually been treated as "realities" which must be taken into ac-
count.39

Government unilateral transfers have regularly been counted
as autonomous in German discussions, despite abundant evidence that
official circles made every effort to encourage capital outflows for
payments-balance reasons.40 Finally, German spokesmen often pointed
out that United States and British troop-stationing outlays in Germany
might be an unreliable source of invisible export earnings, even though
in reality the impact of these receipts on official reserves is already
in large part nullified by intergovernmental arrangements.41 Most
recently there has been a movement within the Bundesbank to recon-
sider the Bank's existing "misleading" payments-balance concepts.42

CAUSES OF GERMAN
PAYMENTS-BALANCE DISEQUILIBRIUM

Causal Situation and Causal Elements

As analyzed above, balance in a nation's autonomous international payments is logically equivalent to the adjustment of that nation's total economic structure and policy to those of the trading world. The cause of autonomous-account imbalance thus lies in an incompatibility as between countries of their respective relations among tastes, factor endowments, methods, market structures, and policy aims and measures. The incompatibility itself, through purchasing-power, price-cost or interest-rate differentials, produces the imbalance observed in the autonomous accounts.

Separately discussing the various elements which can become incompatible in this sense will not necessarily lead to the discovery of a single "cause" of the incompatibility as a whole.[43] Such separate discussion can, however, produce a list of areas in which to look for corroborative evidence of the existence of basic disequilibrium, and in which remedial action can be taken.[44] This approach also points up the importance of the non-financial elements in the cause and cure of disequilibrium.[45] Without attention to these, any judgment on the role of the financial-policy variables is impossible.[46] The adjustment elements will be discussed from the German point of view, as possible net contributors to a situation of balance-of-payments surplus.[47]

The areas where incompatibility may arise can be divided into the "real," the market-structural, and the financial. And this abstract notion of a complex fundamental equilibrium has recently received practical support from policy-makers in the "economist"-monetarist debate over European monetary integration.* A situation of full adjustment or equilibrium could be illustrated by a complex set of equations describing the compatibility of all supply, demand and policy factors in all countries with the long-run elimination of non-autonomous international payments. Somewhat more simply, the factors involved in adjustment within one country can be summarized and arranged as follows:

$$(I)\, \Delta R \cdot \frac{\Delta M}{\Delta R} \cdot \frac{\Delta i}{\Delta M} \left(\left[\frac{\Delta(I+C)}{\Delta i} \cdot \frac{\Delta Y}{\Delta(I+C)} \cdot \frac{\Delta T}{\Delta Y} \right] + \frac{\Delta F}{\Delta i} \right) = \Delta B$$

$$\quad\ (1)\quad\ (2)\quad (3)\quad\ (4)\qquad\ (5)\qquad\ (6)\quad (7)$$

Where: R = effective monetary base
        M = money stock
        i = level of interest-rate pattern
        I = expenditures on real capital goods
        C = expenditures on consumption

---

*For example, from Finance Minister Wittveen of the Netherlands (AP [1970], #80, p. 12; see also Chapter 7).

Y = nominal (i.e., money) national income
T = autonomous goods-and-services balance
F = autonomous net international capital flow
B = total autonomous balance

Subdeterminants of the various numbered members of the equation shown can be listed as follows:

1. Legal reserve requirements of banks; net central bank credit

2. The public's marginal requirement for currency as a proportion of its money; excess reserves (and vault currency) of banks

3. In the Keynesian system, the demands for money for transactions balances and for asset balances

4. Expectations as to the marginal efficiency of capital, including the relation of wages to productivity of labor, the state of competition in the product and labor markets, and the relative price elasticities of demand for consumption goods and producers' goods

5. The marginal propensity to spend domestically out of income (which is the complement of the marginal propensities to import, to save, and to "pay taxes")

6. Trade controls; exchange restrictions; relative national tastes; comparative national technological methods; comparative international market structures

7. International capital-market structure; domestic capital-market conditions.

Many of these subdeterminants can themselves readily be subdivided into still more refined considerations. This analytical ordering of adjustment factors is, however, not strictly followed in the present study, as the apparent clarity, exactness and logic of such formulations as equation (I) do not in every case survive detailed discussion.

Real Causal Elements

The Fundamental Elements

In an abstractly theoretical view of the capitalist economic system, the most basic "real" elements of all economic life might be listed as tastes, available technological possibilities, and national productive-resource endowments. This listing rests on two propositions.

First, under markets workable enough to justify capitalism's existence, these three elements are sufficient to determine, in the gross, the behavior of the entire economic system, Second, under these theoretical market structures, the three elements just mentioned could be considered as being themselves not fully determined by the workings of the economic system.

In the more realistic view appropriate to a study of actual policy, however, the three listed factors cannot be assigned so unique a position. Where markets are not perfectly flexible, tastes, technology and resource endowment cannot fully determine the system's behavior; and indeed they themselves fall increasingly under the influence of the system's workings. At this stage of the discussion, therefore, it may be helpful to consider certain still more fundamental factors, particularly such as influence the workability of markets. The advantage for this study of founding analysis on economically irreducible factors lies in the increased probability that the basic trends derivable from such factors will survive the thorough-going changes of institutions and attitudes now at work in Germany, Europe and the world, and will thus provide useful policy guides for the future.

Two such fundamental and irreducible factors appear to influence Germany's economic situation at virtually every step. These are the pace of technological progress common to the whole capitalist world, and Germany's historically and geographically determined geopolitical position in Middle Europe.

The Technological Imperative to Large Scale. The second and third quarters of our century have been strongly marked by the economic, social and political effects of the relationship economists call "scale economies", viz., the larger the productive operation (within as yet undefinable limits), the lower the feasible unit cost of its product. The resulting impact stems from an accelerating series of industrial revolutions, characterized by specialization of labor, interchangeable parts, assembly-line production, and automation. There is no reason whatever to anticipate a deceleration of such technological change.*

In common with all industrialized nations, Germany has obeyed a technological imperative to increase the scale of production, since

---

*The explanation usually given for the exponential pace of technological change is convincing. The higher the existing state of technological development, the more tools and possible tool permutations exist; the more specialists exist to deal with and experiment with these tools; and the more channels of communication exist among these centers of change.

the productive units that are slow to do so are normally vulnerable
through their higher costs. The impacts on industrial society of this
expansion of scale have been manifold. The chief purely economic
results of the movement have been three: concentration in the product
markets, countervailing political organization of concentration in the
labor (and agricultural) markets, and a unique and cumulative advantage
for producers with access to the larger markets. As a few large-scale
firms came to dominate each important market, the welfare and stability benefits associated with free competition were correspondingly
reduced.48 Ever-increasing government intervention to maintain
incomes, economic activity, and social balance became indispensable.
The resulting interest-group state has been unable to reduce the economic and political power positions of the concentrated industries,
unions, and farm organizations.49

It has likewise proved impossible thus far for the interest-group
state to redistribute incomes down the income scale. Lawyers and
lawmakers alike are, for several reasons, more amenable to the requirements of the favored groups. As a result, the overall tax systems
of modern states are in effect sharply regressive. As long as this is
the case, most true social reforms must inevitably be fiscally deficitary. In the absence of such reforms, literally intolerable imbalances
of incomes, environments, and opportunities are able to arise without
finding any equilibrating outlet in either the economic or the political
system. Even the resulting physical explosions, as in the United States,
have been far from producing a significant effort to redress the balance.
On the contrary, in the political as in the economic field, interests
seem likely to outlast systems.

Since the modern industrial state has succeeded neither in reducing nor in regulating market power, its necessary interventions normally constitute subsidies to unregulated market power. Given the
sharp overall regressiveness of the tax systems, fiscally supported
programs for arms, agricultural support, international aid and international financial compensation are not usually unwelcome to a majority
in decisions-making circles. Social-reform or income-redistribution
programs, on the other hand, are normally defeatable on the grounds
of their deficitary nature. Finally, increasing state intervention, by re-
distributing incomes so as to support or compensate the power maneuvers of the market groups, and also by diminishing popular faith in the
"fairness" of the resulting income distribution, continually worsens the
market behavior of the power groups. It will be shown in what follows
that all of these byproducts of modern technology have a bearing on both
the German payments-balance policy challenge and its policy response.

Germany's Geopolitical Position. The second basic factor in Germany's economic situation is Middle-European geopolitics. The

case could be made that the whole dynamics of German history since the Migration of Nations has been shaped by the geopolitical significance of the North European Plain. Here it will be sufficient to point to the geopolitical context of the rise and fall of the National Socialist state. Obviously, the resulting physical destruction, human dislocation, territorial truncation, inflation, occupation regime and border-state status have had continuous influence on postwar Germany's economic institutions and psychology. It is in the light of these influences that Germany's more traditional or theoretical basic economic factors may be briefly considered.

The Traditional Real Elements

The real elements which may depart from international compatibility are national tastes, national factor endowments, and the technological methods actually employed. It has been suggested that long periods of autarky and war may have altered German tastes so as to lower German income- and price-elasticities of demand for imports relative to those of other nations. This proposition, though not properly testable, appears plausible. To the extent that it is true, chronic payments surplus would be avoidable only if the other elements of international compatibility as a whole had been shifted somewhat during the same period toward a deficit-generating setting.

Germany's factor-endowment proportions have undergone some change since World War II. In spite of sizable territorial losses, Germany's resource base is still remarkably good, and may not have suffered much proportionally vis-à-vis major trading lands like Great Britain, which have had decolonization and depletion difficulties.

In the forties the capital-to-labor balance certainly swung toward labor abundance, due to the destruction of capital and the influx of refugees.[50] In the sixties population growth slowed, due to the erection in 1961 of the east-German wall and to the effects on natural birth contingents of two wars and the depression. Population increased twenty-five percent in the fifties, against around five percent in the period under review; after 1956, increases in hours worked practically ceased, and the work force of German nationality fell numerically after 1965.[51] The population of employable age has itself fallen in the later sixties.[52] At the same time investment had added increasingly to the capital stock.

The expectable shift of income shares to labor has begun,[53] but may well have been retarded by the steady importation of labor from lands with relatively low marginal productivity of labor, by the disciplined attitudes of the labor force carried over to very recent years from various earlier experiences, and by the export of real capital represented by the steady balance-of-trade surpluses (and also by the policy of encouraging financial capital export, for which see Chapter 4). The upshot of these contradictory movements is indecisive, but it is likely that Germany is more capital-rich today than in the fifties, and that its price-cost structure does not yet fully reflect the shift. This would tend to make Germany a relatively low-cost country. This conclusion is strengthened by reference to the composition of Germany's trade.

As has just been indicated, it is likely that the methods applied in Germany today are more labor-intensive than the native factor endowment would warrant.[54] Widespread war destruction did offer the chance to design and build a more modern, lower-cost and less import-dependent plant. But, perhaps due to insufficient scale of markets, much investment appears to have been capital-saving rather than labor-saving. Investment-goods production, also, in which Germany is top-heavy, is said to require a smaller proportion of imported inputs than does consumption-goods production. The faster technical progress in the postwar era seems thus to have lowered the imported-goods input component while raising the imported-labor component.[55] This substitution of labor inputs for goods inputs probably favors German costs, since the labor inputs are from low-wage areas.[56] The flexible buffer of foreign labor also permits a specially large lag to develop between shifts in factor endowment and shifts in technology.* Europe's growing relative backwardness in developing and exploiting advanced technology will be discussed in Chapter 7. The existence of this entire situation may also be evidenced by the now-rising percentage of investment goods in German imports.[57]

The net tendency of all these shifts in "real" elements is probably to lower German costs relative to those abroad, and to raise the German payments surplus. This suggests that, if a surplus is not to arise, market-structural and financial elements should have shifted to foster balance-of-payments deficit.

Market-Structural Causal Elements

Market-structural elements can create balance-of-payments surplus by changes on the international or the domestic level which

---

*However, since the imported labor has generally thrust native labor up the income scale, encouraging psychological resistance to a reversal of the process, a rise in the entire wage pattern could result from too free a reduction of this buffer.

alter the effectiveness of existing supply and demand in forming an appropriate price. Market-structural considerations in the product, factor, and exchange markets will be treated in order.

Structural Causal Elements in Product Markets

As suggested by the preceding discussion, Germany's domestic goods market is dominated by large firms. It is said that forty firms control sixty percent of the nation's capital stock, while eight financial groups control forty percent of its industrial capital.[58] Expectably, prevention and regulation of concentration has been as ineffective in Germany as in most other modern industrial states. The present cartel law was debated in the Bundestag for five years before its passage. For seven years thereafter, the only penalty ever assessed under it was a two-hundred-mark fine.[59] A currently planned amendment to German antitrust legislation contemplates the rather belated introduction of preventive control of mergers.[60]

The progressive truncation of German domestic markets, and post-collapse subsidies to recovery, left postwar Germany with a disproportionately large heavy industry, which must turn to the wide export markets in order to enjoy modern economies of scale.[61] The suppression of Germany's arms-industry demand has added to heavy industry's need for world markets. Two decades of export surpluses have, by creating biases in the self-finance and the bank finance of firms, further shifted Germany's industrial structure toward export dependence. This dependence is indicated by the export industries' position as the leading investing sector.[62] The same large-scale and hence export-prone industries were for some time also encouraged by a turnover-tax system which favored concentration.

At the same time, it has been held that German industries as a whole may be currently passing through an internationally optimal stage of concentration, due to a high prewar degree of concentration relatively arrested by Germany's collapse and occupation.[63] They would thus be concentrated enough to reap most of the scale economies required to compete internationally, while competitive enough to maintain German alertness to delivery, quality, price shading, and selling effort in general.[64]

All these conditions tend to channel German resources into the supply of exports. On the demand side, a relatively skewed income distribution coupled with a more-than-usually regressive tax structure reduces domestic demand for exportable goods and so for German resources in general. The one area in which Germany might be expected to display a structural balance-of-trade weakness is food imports, due to the loss of "breadbasket" areas, the gain of refugees,

and a somewhat inefficient tenure structure in agriculture. This
problem has, however, been partly masked by an internationally
acceptable agricultural protectionism, and partly alleviated by a
program to restructure agricultural production.[65]

Germany's export tradition (or mystique) is thus well grounded,
and in turn underlies a quite conscious drive to maintain and expand
the German market position.[66]

The price- and income-elasticities of demand for German
goods on the international market have doubtless shifted considerably,
over the postwar period, due precisely to Germany's postwar effort
to recover from entire political and economic isolation. Trade contacts
had to be renewed from almost nothing, and export-trade contacts
were naturally stressed in the recovery drive. German governmental
postwar export-expansion programs, while not perhaps unusual by
recent standards, have grown considerably over the postwar period
as government and trade-organization resources permitted (Tables
A3411, A3412). Special rediscount facilities for export credit form
an important though more disguised part of these programs.

As German economic strength and political position were restored,
too, Germany's foreign aid came to be systematically aimed at projects
tied to German exports. (See Chapter 4 below). The worldwide postwar emphasis on industrialization favored the investment-goods-
oriented German export industries, perhaps more than those of most
great exporting lands. International integration and the reduction of
tariffs and quantitative controls, both worldwide in the fifties and
within the Common Market in the sixties, probably aided German industry similarly, since the more sensitive and integrated markets for
capital goods would be more responsive to the opening of economies
than would the consumers'-goods markets.

These relationships throw light on Germany's attitudes toward
trade barriers, and on its leading position in the drive for European
integration. One direct effect of this drive is the German taxpayer's
effective subsidization of German agricultural exports through the
Common Market agricultural support program.[67]

Private entities as such have also entered into the German
export mystique. German automobile firms, for example, early called
for a conscious policy of industrial concentration in order to meet the
United States threat.[68] The causes and effects of the entrenchment of
Germany's export industries, and of their interest in regional integration, will be discussed on later pages.

Another quasi-structural item on the export side of the balance-of-payments accounts is tied to the presence in Germany of NATO troops (Tables A2). The expenditures of these troops seem to be fairly inelastic to relative prices or incomes, based as they are on a combination of geopolitical considerations, domestic power relations in the countries involved, and the way of life of military units and personnel abroad.[69] The "troop money"[70] accounted for about sixty percent of Germany's cumulative basic surplus from 1961 through 1970, and was responsible for much of the external political pressure on Germany regarding the balance of payments. This weighty item must be considered in assessing every phase of the German payments situation over the period under review.

In certain non-trade accounts, on the other hand, Germany shows significant structural deficits. The largest of these by far, the travel deficit, ranks second only to that of the United States, and for similar reasons. Relative to averages in the world at large, Germany is a country small in area but high in population density and per capita income. Germany's specific location, too, contributes to making the travel item quite insensitive to normally expectable swings of incomes and prices.[71] Despite some rise in unemployment, for example, fifty-one percent of Germans were expected to vacation abroad in 1971.[72]

On the whole, relative shifts in market-structural elements of postwar German goods markets seem also to have contributed to a German balance-of-payments surplus. Logically therefore, the burden of maintaining equilibrium has had to be borne by further elements, to be discussed immediately below.

Structural Causal Elements in Factor Markets

The markets for the productive factors land (or natural resources) and physical capital, so far as they have international significance, are indistinguishable from the product markets. The basic structure of the German labor market and its meaning for the payments balance have been sketched above in connection with Germany's factor endowment. The labor situation in Germany gives rise to one quasi-structural payments-balance account characteristic of this period, the remittances of foreign workers. This deficit item was relatively sensitive to the influence of income differentials, since the very number of such workers, as well as their rate of earnings, depended drastically on the level of economic activity. Prolonged periods of high tension in the labor market, on the other hand, can involve a reduction of remittances, as foreign workers begin to feel secure enough to bring their families with them to Germany (as in 1964 especially). German industrialists have expressed the feeling that these workers, numbering around two million in 1971, must be counted in any discussion of unemployment.[73]

Inappropriate capital-market structure can contribute to an autonomous balance-of-payments surplus by not translating an inflow of funds from a balance-of-trade surplus readily enough into an export of capital.*

These results may be expected if international capital markets are unresponsive to international interest-rate differentials, or if domestic German interest rates are not responsive to the existing supply and demand within Germany.

The international integration of the German capital market presents no special problem in this regard. Capital movements have been quite elastic and indeed increasingly elastic to international interest-rate differentials. (As long as exchange rates are stable, real relative international interest differentials as a percentage of capital do not depend on the relative rates of inflation in the countries involved.)

Domestic imperfections of the German capital market can prevent actually existing liquidity from forming an interest rate low enough, relative to foreign countries', to reverse inflows of funds from a current-account surplus. Household saving is relatively quite high in Germany, entailing relatively reduced domestic demand.[74] Domestic-oriented firms are thus especially dependent on "outside" financial markets. Much saving, however, never reaches the transparent, price-forming sectors of the capital market, and so is less effective in moderating interest rates.[75] Considerable saving is at once reinvested in self-finance by firms. This is especially true in the export industries, which are thus relatively advantaged, particularly in recession.

For tax reasons and by a tradition of maintaining high liquidity, much saving of large institutional savers--insurance and social security--is lent in the form of earmarked bank accounts which are rather insensitive to capital-market interest rates. Interbank agreements restricting bank-portfolio transactions also narrow the direct access of non-banks to the money and capital markets.[76] Fiscal-policy expedients have recently entailed the net decapitalization of the social-security institutions, further narrowing the supply of savings in the capital market (Chapter 5). Subsidized forms of bank

---

*Paradoxically, Germany's poor capital-market structure also hampered payments-balance-oriented restrictive financial policies by too readily transmitting their effects to long-term markets.

saving--for housing and the like- have also been disproportionately
large (Chapter 6). Bank time and savings accounts have been very
popular with all classes of savers: savings accounts continued to
grow even when their net interest was zero.[77] Various cartel-like
anti-disintermediation devices, such as tied deposit interest rates,
have helped determine this traditional preference. All these deposited
funds are relent by the banks in the money market or are invested
speculatively in the securities market.[78]

On the side of demand, government investment and government-
subsidized housing investment tend to absorb the narrow supply and
bid up interest rates. Until quite recently, the government could be
characterized as inexperienced in borrowing. The result was an
inconsistent borrowing tempo, careless placement, and half-hearted
price support of outstanding issues.[79] Since the proceeds of government borrowing are usually held in the Bundesbank, thus cutting
commercial-bank reserves, and since the capital market is heavily
dependent on the banks, government borrowing can have a double-
edged effect on capital-market interest rates. Until recently, too,
Germany's unusually variegated and independent governmental entities
were practically uncoordinated in their debt management.[80] Over the
early sixties, government investment rose as a percentage of total
investment, with special emphasis on building, particularly of roads.[81]
These factors all tended to raise the uncertainties and at the same
time the demand in the German capital market, and so to keep interest
rates above the otherwise expectable level. However, the Council of
Experts doubted that government debt alone fundamentally harmed
the capital market;[82] the experts placed chief blame for this on the
Bundesbank's policies. (See Chapters 3 and 5.)

The German government subsidizes much borrowing, especially
for residential construction, through tax benefits, partial loans, and
interest subsidies.[83] From 1956 to 1966 total German housing units
rose by over twenty-eight percent.[84] In 1965, government subsidy
programs cheapened around one seventh of the whole volume of loans
transacted on the open capital market, and one third of all housing
finance between 1958 and 1966.[85] Despite constant remonstrances
by the Bundesbank, the government seems addicted to the interest-
subsidy idea: even after the serious collapse of the capital market
in 1966, the Bundesbank had to object to the proposal of further
interest subsidies in the second anticyclical government investment
program (Chapter 5) of 1967.[86]

As it were by compensation, German governments subsidized
much saving as well--nearly twenty percent of all financing in the
early sixties.[87] The property-formation aids to lower income groups
established in 1970 also very largely took the form of interest subsidies
on small savings.

While German savers are typically seeking unusually liquid forms of saving, German firms and goverments normally seek long-term lending as a substitute for equity funds.[88] Throughout the period under review, there has existed the need for long-term projects to recover from war, to keep abreast of world technical progress and the ever-increasing scale of operations, to replace increasingly scarce labor, and to meet the intensified capital needs of progressive industrialization.

The result of all these structural factors seems to be internationally high capital-market interest rates relative to money-market interest rates.* Yet it is particularly difficult for the authorities to reduce these rates in view of the peculiar way in which German banks intermediate between the two markets.**[89] Several of the factors already mentioned tend to make German firms heavily dependent on bank credit for outside finance. Equity capital is not sought by many firms, which are unwilling to disclose their affairs or surrender control to outsiders.[90] A less independent accounting profession and less stringent legal disclosure provisions make savers much less confident in taking up equity offerings.[91] High emission costs and relatively high taxes on emissions make equity finance more than sixty percent dearer than outside capital.[92] The resulting dependence on bank credit makes German industry more cycle-sensitive and so makes the German economy more dependent on foreign demand.[93]

This situation also makes the open capital market overly dependent on the money market.[94] Since any drop in interest rates reduces securities-price expectations, the speculatively handled bank securities are the first assets dropped from bank portfolios when monetary policy is tightened, and the last to be added in times of monetary ease. This behavior multiplies the impact of monetary policy on the market. Through much of the sixties, accordingly, the authorities' emphasis on monetary-policy measures in the campaign for price stability has had

---

*This fact could be viewed as creating structurally differing sets of international interest-rate differentials in the two markets. This would give color to the Kindleberger-Salant thesis that the United States payments-balance situation represented voluntary acquisitions of long assets in Europe and sales of short assets to Europeans simply as a response to expectable differences in capital-market structures (E. Despres, and C. P. Kindleberger, "The Dollar and World Liquidity--A Minority View," The Economist [5 February 1966]).

**The banks' percentage of the supply of capital has been from forty to sixty-five percent in the period under review.

a serious effect on confidence in the capital market, which may be chronic enough to be called structural.[95] (The evolution and the effects of monetary-policy measures will be further discussed in Chapters 3 and 5.) This kind of damage to the capital market has been reinforced by the abrupt and retroactive application of controls on the foreign supply of capital, e.g., the "coupon" tax, or withholding tax on fixed-interest payments abroad on German securities.

Additionally, since securities issued on the German market by non-German issuers were exempted from the coupon tax, German corporations have used foreign subsidiaries to borrow funds from foreigners, thus creating a parallel DM market whose interest rates tend to be assimilated to those of the Euro-dollar market, and so to escape the influence of domestic German supply and demand. This compartmentalization of the DM market has further narrowed it. The allocation of capital by banks may be distorted by reason of the institutional connections between banks and firms.[96] The "big three" banks, which survived the Occupation attempt to break them up, grant around one third of all short-term credit and one half of all middle-term credit.[97] In addition, the Capital Market Committee, an association of the chief issue banks, controls access to the capital market, at times using its powers to reduce foreign demand in Germany's market.[98]

It appears that the German capital market was in the early sixties structurally imperfect relative to those of the great foreign financial centers, and thus was not able to translate inflows of funds effectively into lower interest rates. Conversely, payments-balance-oriented efforts to brake rising German income and price levels quickly drove up capital-market interest rates, tending to cause a surplus on capital account and one-sidedly to squeeze non-exporting industries, which are dependent on the open capital market for funds. The sensitivity of world capital to such international discrepancies in credit conditions has grown markedly over the sixties (Chapter 4). Attempts to seal off capital inflows through discriminatory taxes have further weakened the capital market, as described above.

Structural Causal Elements in Exchange Markets

Changes in exchange-market structure, similarly to those in other markets, can affect the payments balance either by altering the sensitivity of the exchange rate to the existing market supply of and demand for foreign currencies, or by altering the sensitivity of payments flows themselves to the exchange-rate price.

A significant example of the latter type of change over the past half dozen years has been the increased sensitivity of large corporate funds to anticipated exchange-rate shifts and to international interest-rate differentials. Corporate financial managers were sensitized to these factors by the succession of exchange crises during the sixties, by the United States payments-balance program, and by the growth of the Euro-currency markets. As a result, all international economic policy today must reckon with a greater volume and responsiveness of short-term capital movements and with a greater proneness to purely speculative considerations. The growing international integration of exchange markets thus left virtually no room for any other shifts in market forces over the period studied.

The sensitivity of the exchange rate to real supply and demand forces can in one sense be regarded as altered over the past several years by the growing official recognition of various schemes for greater exchange-rate flexibility. This development will be explored fully in Chapter 3. During most of the period under review, however, the exchange rate was rendered largely insensitive to market forces by a fully accepted system of fixed and officially defended exchange rates.

The impact of the supply of and demand for DM on the price of the DM was effectively nil, as long as the exchange rate was defended by the Bundesbank, which readily supplied DM against offerings of gold and foreign exchange.

The German exchange-rate parity was originally set in 1948 by non-specialists, in hopeless economic circumstances, and with no way of determining a proper rate.[99] It is evident that the rate selected was based on the traditional pre-World War I and interwar rate, apparently with the basic intention of maintaining Germany's vitally needed exports.[100] In the world-wide Korea crisis the German central bank managed to hold changes in the German price level well below those of Germany's trade partners.[101] This development put the DM in an undervalued position, which the changes noted in the sections above, associated with recovery from war, accentuated. Thereafter, and until late 1969, this original parity had been modified only once, to open the period under review, under great buying pressure on the DM, which was not thereby relieved. The presumption is therefore strong that this exchange-rate adjustment away from undervaluation was not sufficient to offset the other elements shifting to foster payments surplus. The proposition will be further investigated in considering exchange-rate manipulation as a policy option during the period under study (Chapter 3).

It seems probable that the net postwar relative movement of all Germany's real and structural elements has been in favor of chronic balance-of-payments surplus. This would argue that basic equilibrium could only be expected if Germany's financial elements, narrowly conceived, had moved in favor of payments deficit.

Financial Causal Elements

Financial Reaction Functions

The financial elements in the payments-equilibrium constellation include both the market-mechanical financial reaction functions (often called the liquidity functions) and the macrofinancial policies of the government and monetary authorities. With all else constant, in other words, the balance of payments could be altered either through a change in the monetary base supplied to the financial system or through a change in the habitual responses of the financial system and of the economy to the availability of a changed monetary base. The financial reaction functions are in part merely formalizations of the real and market-structural elements already discussed, and in part depend on indirect effects of such elements within the financial institutions themselves. Given the financial reaction functions conceptualized in this way, it is a residually--and trivially--true proposition that Germany has in fact experienced too little monetary expansion in recent years to produce fundamental payments-balance equilibrium.

The monetary base is essentially universally-accepted currency issued by the central bank, or binding claims on the central bank to issue such currency. Changes in this ultimate cash contribute to change in a nation's payments balance in the following way. Since the purpose of currency is to mediate payments too small or too risky to warrant the costs of non-currency transactions, its almost exclusive function, once issued, is to form a fraction of the aggregate money holdings of those who make or receive money payments. In the gross, this currency-drain fraction is fairly stable, depending as it does on the efficiency of the information machinery connected with non-currency payments: greater efficiency would reduce the unit cost or the risk of non-currency transactions, and so reduce the relative usefulness of currency.

Accordingly, an entity forming part of the non-currency payments machinery, such as a deposit bank, which can make a sufficiently large amount of trustworthy promises to pay currency on demand, will find that only a fraction of these promises is redeemed, while the rest is passed from one owner to another through the non-currency payments system. Conversely, the deposit-banking system will attract to itself all outstanding currency beyond the desired fraction corresponding to the existing stock of deposits and currency together. A banking system acquiring either additional currency or the monetary authorities' promise to issue additional currency (i.e., a reserve deposit) is thus in a position to issue its own promises to pay (i.e., commercial-bank deposits) up to a multiple of the newly available monetary authorities' currency.

Since these deposits in the banking system are accepted as money, they can be lent at interest, and normally (since very little administrative cost is involved) at a profit. However, in any given state of demand for money, increasing amounts of it can be lent only at progressively lower rates of interest. This is because the economy's willingness to hold money is inversely related to the rate of return on substitute forms of liquidity.

If all other independent influences are constant, therefore, when the monetary authorities' credit institution, the central bank, makes the new loans or buys a greater volume of assets, a competitive financial system can be expected to lower its interest rates and to lend more, thus increasing the stock of acceptable money. The money thus lent would be spent largely on investment projects. This would occur because in any limited period a higher volume of money can be profitably invested in capital goods at lower marginal rates of return. Thereafter, this spent money would circulate normally, creating incomes. The increase in incomes would represent some combination of higher average prices on the one hand, and higher employment, transactions volume, and output on the other.

Higher domestic prices will change international price differentials in such a way as to stimulate imports and discourage exports. Higher real output and incomes, on the other hand, will raise the percentage of foreign goods in the national budget, because of changed substitution elasticities, both on the taste side and on the technology side. Both of these results will tend to reduce the trade-balance surplus, and restore basic balance.

Lowered interest rates, due to the net influx of funds entailed by the original export surplus, will also tend toward readjustment, by stimulating outflows of capital. A definitive capital export, whether denominated in domestic or in foreign currency, eventually requires the purchase in the exchange market of the foreign currencies, and so tends to balance the autonomous accounts.

It is obvious from this schematic scenario that the reaction of the economic system to increases in the monetary base could be described in terms of reaction functions, and that these are themselves largely determined by the real and market-structural elements already described. The financial reaction functions, in sequential order of their activation by changes in the monetary base, can be summarized as the marginal deposit-expansion ratio, the marginal income-velocity of money, and the marginal propensity to import net (and/or to demand for domestic use exportable goods or their underlying productive resources).

The marginal deposit-expansion ratio of a banking system links inputs of new monetary base to the creation of new money stock. It depends logically on two sub-ratios (of whose sum it is the reciprocal): marginal cash drain to the public, and marginal excess-reserve ratio. From 1961 to 1966, the marginal cash-drain and marginal excess-reserve ratios in Germany (seasonally adjusted) were sensibly stable.[102] There have been no marked changes in banking technical efficiency or market structure which might alter the cash drain; and there have been no such marked changes in financial markets in general as would cause a change in the banks' negligible excess reserves.[103] Banks developed "genuine" excess reserves only for a few weeks in connection with each of the speculative exchange crises of 1968 and 1969. The "expectable" cash-drain ratio has been around .3.*

Therefore the observed changes in the money stock have depended almost entirely on monetary policy (i.e., on the supply of reserve money and the legal reserve requirements), the interplay of which determines the monetary base. The non-policy components of the banking system's marginal deposit expansion ratio, taken alone, have not influenced the balance-of-payments in either direction.

The average income-velocity of money (preceding footnote) links changes in the stock of money to changes in monetary income. In

---

The marginal cash-drain ratio of German banks is difficult to measure, partly because of problems in the concept of monetary assets and partly because of probably abnormal shifts in recent years among the classes of monetary assets (see Chapter 6). Marginal cash drain as applied to all monetary assets with banks, as catalogued by the Bundesbank, MR (Dec 69), p. 2, has varied over the sixties between extremes of .09 in 1964 and .02 in 1968. As applied to "money stock," recorded by the Bundesbank and by the International Monetary Fund (IMF, Statistics, Germany, Line 34), marginal cash drain was fairly stable around a value of .33 through 1965. The cumulative marginal cash drain from 1966 through the second quarter of 1969 was .26, but the individual ratios for 1966, 1967 and 1968 were much lower, averaging below .20. Although a declining trend, due to steady modernization of financial practices, is very probable, these extremely low ratios probably reflect abnormal shifts into deposit moneys, due to the freeing of deposit interest rates after 1966 and to the generally high interest-rate pattern associated with recession and exchange problems. In this study, the marginal cash-drain ratio is measured against "money stock" and its long-run "expectable" value is taken to be trending downward from around .33. In the text below the same" money stock" figure is used to calculate the income-velocity of money, by a comparison of its annual-average money figure with the GNP.

Germany during the first half of the sixties this ratio remained quite stable on an annual basis (at around 6.5), with perhaps a slight upward trend, reflecting ongoing improvements in the efficient use of money.104 In 1966 this ratio moved noticeably above the trend, reflecting intensified working of money in response to the sharp tightening of the money supply by the Bundesbank. In 1967 the average ratio again fell somewhat below the trend, reflecting the sluggish response to monetary and fiscal recovery efforts in the 1966/1967 slump.105

In the most basic Keynesian analysis, the income-velocity of money reflects marginal propensity to spend domestically, marginal efficiency of capital, and demand for money balances. As the real and structural factors influencing these variables have already been touched upon, only the gross quantitative results will be noted here.

The marginal propensity to consume domestically can be viewed as unity less the marginal propensities to save and import. The German marginal propensity to save has been high in the postwar period. In the first half of the sixties, money/household-disposable-income fell slightly, as the rise in per capita real income caused a rise in household saving;106 but there was little change in money/Gross-National-Product, as firms continued to replenish liquid balances from their low point after the currency reform.107 Rather than falling as this need was more satisfied, however, the marginal propensity to save has even risen further in the sixties. Only such violent blows to confidence as the Suez crisis have noticeably retarded this trend.108 This situation may reflect the spread of more expensive and more discretionary consumption objectives.109 Perhaps the subsidies to household expenditures and the rising export surplusses have also promoted saving. Much of the substance and the official atmosphere of postwar German monetary policy has probably also been encouraging to savers. While the German marginal propensity to save has thus risen somewhat, the marginal propensity to import has remained in the high twenty percents with proportionately large annual variations due to the degree of synchronization of world economic cycles.110 During most of the sixties, on the other hand, the marginal tax burden has risen slowly. The net effect on the marginal propensity to spend domestically has been small.

High household savings would seem to threaten demand and hence the marginal efficiency of capital; but the export bias in industry has enabled saving to be high without corresponding harm to the marginal efficiency of capital. It has already been noted that a variety of conditions in the capital market have encouraged a demand for monetary and near-money financial assets.

All of this suggests the underpinning of the structurally stable (though cyclically sensitive) income-velocity of money observed. This being so, the past decade does not appear to display any marked per-manent shifts in the factors of the German liquidity functions, other than those discussed above, by which monetary policy affects the bal-ance-of-payments accounts. This does not, however, demonstrate that there has been no shift of these functions relative to those abroad. For this reason, conclusions on the intentions behind Germany's macro-financial policy must await a later chapter.

The foregoing discussion thus finds a net preponderance of Germany's real, structural and liquidity-preference elements either shifted relative to those abroad so as to bring about basic payments disequilibrium, or else at least neutral in their payments-balance effects. This would indicate that stable balance-of-payments equi-librium could only have been expected in Germany if financial policy itself had moved toward ease relative to that of other countries.

Financial Policy

It has already been suggested that a priori international com-parisons of financial policy to determine their payments-adjustment compatibility, in the sense used here, are not possible. The kind of policy compatibility intended here is obviously not identity, even of general direction. If, however, the foregoing discussion is generally correct, it would appear that an international comparison of percentage changes in effective monetary base (i.e., reserve money adjusted for changes in the reserve requirement), would meet the case. That is, this procedure would be adequate to close the circle of the present discussion of the setting of German balance-of-payments policy, it cannot substitute for a thorough investigation of the policy options open to Germany, nor can it prove conclusively at this stage that Ger-many was following a deliberately conceived policy of undervaluation. Such a quasi-tautological procedure can obviate the difficulties of a comparison of national price or cost movements, which, as indicated above, are distorted by differing original degrees of employment, different Phillips curves, and indeed different possibilities for spill-over of excess demand into the balance of payments itself.*

---

*Boarman (p. 114) makes this comparison and shows that the German export surplus grew even in periods when German cost of living was rising faster than that of its trade partners. This would not be surprising in any case, in view of the foregoing analysis of real and market-structural shifts. But Boarman's comparison-base year of 1951, during Germany's successful bid to stay behind the world "Korea inflation," may very well be misleading.

A cursory comparison of the indicated figures for the United States, Britain, France, Italy and Germany will show that German monetary policy, in the sense just indicated, has itself tended toward international payments surplus rather than deficit.111

The discrepancy of German monetary elements was accentuated during the sixties by the lack of complete coordination of world economic cycles after 1958.112 In the recession of 1966/1967, Germany fell away markedly from the world demand cycle, causing the international incompatibility of payments-balance elements to grow disproportionately and preventing full restoration of payments balance in the recovery of 1968.113

Thus, Germany's basic balance-of-payments disequilibrium is evidenced in the indications derivable from the entire procedure, here followed, of progressively isolating causal elements as a series of analytical residuals. These indications already make it clear that Germany's international payments problem is very much a structural one, and not simply a matter of fundamentally subjective "demands for reserves" on the part of financial authorities.114

Another source of evidence for Germany's basic surplus position is the continuing market-mechanical effects of surplus, observable despite their being obscured by policy offsets. These mechanical effects also induce the genuinely challenging policy problems associated with payments surplus. While payments-balance disequilibrium is, as previously noted, in principle an indicator of real disadjustment of national economies and of consequent physical and welfare inefficiencies, international disequilibrium is in practice rarely a live policy issue merely in terms of the substantive, underlying disalignment of monetary and real elements, or even in terms of surplus or deficit in the autonomous balance alone. Disequilibrium is in fact most often measured and discussed in terms of the various observable market-mechanical effects, discussed in the following pages, which flow from the substantive and accounting imbalances.

EFFECTS OF GERMAN
PAYMENTS-BALANCE DISEQUILIBRIUM

General

Basic payments-balance surplus, such as Germany's, has several expectable market-mechanical effects and concomitants. Strictly speaking, the former phenomena are direct effects of the surplus itself, while the latter are, with the surplus, coeffects of the same fundamental cause, viz., international incompatibilities among the causal elements already discussed. For present purposes, however, they may all be spoken of as "effects" of the basic surplus situation.

All of these mechanical effects tend to raise domestic price and income levels as against foreign, and so to resolve the underlying incompatibility and to restore balance in the autonomous payments-balance accounts. Balance-of-payments disequilibrium thus has an inherent tendency to adjust itself; this indeed is the etymological definition of disequilibrium, that it is not a state of final rest for the system. The effects of underlying incompatibility are indeed its most reliable indicators, since they in fact flow from it in the ways developed below.

Again, each of these effects in the surplus country can be looked upon as a way of importing foreign inflation, actual or potential. Such potential, or "ex ante," inflation need not show up in the actual price levels of the inflationary countries:[115] the expression refers to the existence in a country of an overly large money supply relative to the real and structural conditions of that country, such that inflationary pressures are dissipated by a balance-of-payments deficit instead of by rises in domestic price levels.[116]

Another common quality of these effects is their lagged operation. Evidently, a condition of basic disequilibrium could never arise if the resultant readjustment mechanisms worked without a lag. Because a basic disequilibrium will thus adjust itself only over a measurable period of time, none of the market-mechanical effects of basic surplus, for example, can "keep up with" (i.e., maintain payments balance in the face of) a continuous source of disturbance to equilibrium, e.g., continuous foreign inflation or potential inflation from monetary expansion.

The Direct International Price-Transmission Effect

The most basic concomitant of an autonomous payments-balance surplus is the direct international price-transmission effect, which may be referred to hereafter simply as the price effect. This effect flows directly from the general incompatibility of causal elements, in the following way. Consider a nation and its potential trade partners, before any trade among them is possible. Take the general "socio-economic structure" of each nation as given in the medium run. This structure includes the legal, psychological and other institutional relationships which produce the nations' medium-term expressed patterns of tastes, general technological methods, and market structures in the broadest sense. Such an assumption of medium-term

stability is compatible with the self-perpetuating properties of institutions in general. The assumed structures imply given "pre-trade"
equilibrium relationships of unit prices to unit costs in each nation.
These ratios are related to the "functional" (i.e., labor/property)
sharing of income, which has been (imperfectly) observed to be remarkably stable over time. The cost-price ratios also reflect the level of
"normal profits", which in an oligopolized economy is logically arbitrary, as it in effect is the visible measure of existing socio-economic
structural barriers to market mobility, or in other words of the
existing "degree of monopoly."

Average unit production costs in terms of each country's currency
are likewise given by factor endowments, technological possibilities,
and the structure of factor markets. A hypothetical equilibrium pre-
trade average export price is thus given for each country competing
in exports on the international market.[117] Speaking from this ex ante
standpoint, there is every reason to believe that these prices will be
different in each country.[118]

Where national economies are open, if the rate of exchange of
the currencies is not free to move to equalize all world export prices
in terms of any given currency,[119] competition in international markets
will tend to raise the prices actually charged by the lower-cost countries above their given ex ante levels (as these countries' exporters
try to maximize profits), and will tend to depress the prices actually
charged by the higher-cost countries (if they are to be able to sell at
all). Since the bargaining positions of these two classes of exporters
differ in obvious ways, the tendency will be for higher-cost sellers
to charge near their given pre-trade minimum prices (or to withdraw
from the export market), allowing the lower-cost sellers to charge
above their given minimum prices.

In the lower-cost countries, the resulting export profits, which
(ex hypothesi) exceed what longer-run domestic economic and social
conditions permit, will eventually be dissipated in wage rises in the
export industries.[120] An analogous process will take place in the
import-competing industries. [121] To the extent that these classes of
industries are large in proportion to the economy or costs are a high
proportion of prices, general wage and price rises will soon follow.[122]
Such general price rises can require and "justify" (in terms of the
nominal value of loan collateral) an increase in commercial credit.[123]
The resulting pressure on the banking system eventually poses to the
monetary authorities the choice of "meeting the needs of trade" by
lending to finance further expansion, or of halting an inflation which
was "no one's fault," at a point in time at which the resulting burden
of inflation-redistributed incomes is uncertain. The inflationary
tendency thus generated will tend to reduce the balance-of-payments
surplus, as outlined on an earlier page.[124]

Halting this kind of imported inflation by general financial-policy absorption of liquidity is possible, if at all, only at cost of the most intolerable repression of demand in non-international-trading industries, so as to lower the acceptable average cost-price ratio far enough to halt wage rises also in the international-trading industries, despite the ever-increasing markets and profits of the latter. The greater the economic weight of international-trading industries in a nation, the harder this will be.

By definition the international economy is not as well integrated as the individual national markets. Therefore the adjustment process provided by the direct international price-transmission effect described here will be considerably lagged behind the initial onset of disequilibrium. If the source of disequilibrium is continuous, e.g., an ongoing monetary expansion abroad,* the price-transmission mechanism working alone will permit a permanent lag in adjustment, involving progressive disadjustment of real and market-structural elements, since the first impact of the continuing source of disequilibrium is on the demand facing, and on the income of, international-trading industries. In one sense, indeed, the income and liquidity effects, to be described below, are alternative adjusting mechanisms, which can occur only to the extent that the direct price-transmission effect falls behind the original disequilibrium.[125]

According to the German Council of Experts, the medium-term price development in Germany has been determined almost exclusively by "international conditions."[126] Among these determining conditions the direct price-transmission effect has been "dominant" and "decisive."[127] However, mere parallel development of world export prices, as adduced by the Council, cannot prove the lines of causality, in view of the tautological connection between the price effect and the other balance-of-payments effects. No more can any temporal sequence of wage and price rises in the trade-goods industries be made to demonstrate the process. In addition, the price parallels themselves are inexact and erratic. Specially interesting is the fact that the percentage rise in German export prices often lags behind that of German domestic prices, depending on the periods chosen.

Yet, it may be countered that, even if German export prices were (as they are not) stable, Germany would still be importing inflation by the direct price-transmission mechanism.[128] This is because a stable German domestic price level would require falling export

---

*Since mid-1966, even the realized foreign price levels have outpaced the German analogs (JG [1968], Section 104 ff.).

prices.[129] As real incomes rise, well-known sectoral differences in productivity growth require that the unit costs of services rise faster than those of the social product in general. Now the proportion of services in the German Gross National Product exceeds that in German exports. Therefore the costs of domestic-oriented output rise faster than those of exports. Thus to keep the domestic purchasing power of the DM stable, export prices in DM must fall.[130]

The Income Effects

International incompatibility of basic economic elements causes not only the direct international price-transmission effect but also the recorded payments surplus itself. Such a surplus has three distinguishable effects on incomes. First, it puts new income and liquid wealth at the disposal of exporters. All else remaining constant, such an accretion of income or wealth, working through income expectations, marginal propensities to spend out of income, and asset-portfolio liquidity preferences, will tend to raise the expenditures of exporters and so of the whole economy.[131] Since the real goods corresponding to this net new income have gone abroad in conjunction with the payments surplus, the new expenditures will tend to drive up prices. Thus this situation, too, tends to redress the basic international balance. (For a more complex model of the readjustment effects of change in net export incomes, see J. Williams.)

Besides the general effect on incomes and spending, a payments surplus results in a different sectoral distribution of income than would payments balance. Both export industries and import-competing industries tend to gain proportionally at the expense of industries not directly connected with foreign trade. These industries are thus made less dependent on outside sources of funds for expansion. Additionally, to the extent that the economy is not fully open, the increased income of the favored sectors tends to be absorbed mainly by property incomes in the first instance.

This last result may be designated as the "functional" income effect of payments-balance surplus. In general, the property-income share of national income rises with the trade surplus as a percentage of income, unless domestic investment or capitalists' consumption sink, or labor's saving rises, since:[132]

$$(\text{II.1}) \quad I^d/Y + T/Y + C^K/Y - S^L/Y = Y^K/Y$$

Yet neither a rise in the trade surplus nor the expectable rise in property incomes seems likely to raise labor's saving. To the extent that prices rise in relation to costs as a result of the export boom, for example, labor's average propensity to save should be damped. Capitalists' consumption, on the other hand, is not likely to sink, but may indeed rise. It could fall only if capitalists' marginal propensity to consume fell, or if interest rates rose and found a response in higher saving. Depending on its origin, finally, the trade surplus may raise demand and so the incentive to invest domestically, and may also bring to firms the liquid means to invest. Where, as in Germany, export-oriented firms are also the investment leaders, and these same firms are specially prone to self-finance, raising the profits of these firms will tend to raise investment. With constant marginal propensity to save, a higher investment ratio implies a higher property-income share, since

$$(III.1) \quad \frac{S^K/Y^K - I/Y}{S^K/Y^K - S^L/Y^L} = \lambda$$

(There are hints of this relationship from the Council of Experts, JG [1964], Section 250.) Offsetting the liquidity effects of a trade-balance surplus by the export of capital does not alter this outcome in the least.[133]

To the extent that a payments-balance surplus adjusts itself through its inflationary effects, on the other hand, there is still an appreciable chance of an income shift to property, since product prices are by and large freer to move than are collectively-bargained wages.

Because the income effects of payments surplus have general, sectoral and functional aspects, it is relatively difficult for policy to offset their inflationary, adjustment-fostering impact. Merely re-absorbing the equivalent of the net new incomes by general financial-policy measures will almost never fully offset this inflationary effect. It would persist even without any net new overall incomes at all, due to the rise in community marginal spending out of income, resulting from the income redistribution effected by specifically export-connected earnings coupled with a general monetary reabsorption. Empirical evidence of the working of the income effect as such is difficult to document in Germany.

The Liquidity Effect

The most obvious effect of autonomous payments imbalance, if uncorrected, is the accumulation by the surplus country of international reserves, either in the form of various liquid assets denominated in foreign currencies, or of gold which is guaranteed in terms of foreign currencies. This much indeed follows from the definition of autonomous imbalance. Under the fixed-exchange-rate system, if the new foreign earnings of the surplus country's exporters are not desired in that form by their recipients, or by the rest of the public, the monetary authorities will passively buy these earnings to keep the price of their own currency down to parity.

The monetary authorities are legally constituted the sole issuers of liabilities which can serve as acceptable hand-to-hand cash. In making a net addition to their assets through the purchase of foreign-exchange earnings, the monetary authorities pay by means of this cash, or by a promise to pay cash on demand.[134] The mechanics of such expansion of the monetary base have already been described in detail. The expectable effects are higher prices, lower interest rates, and a tendency to payments-balance adjustment.

The above processes can be called the liquidity effect of the balance of payments.[135] As will be shown, Germany received a large volume of potential additions to its monetary base from its autonomous payments balance in the period under review.

The Payments-Balance Policy Challenge

So long as basic payments-balance surplus exists, its effects and concomitants produce not only mechanical tendencies toward adjustment, but also the immediate impacts or policy challenges of the balance of payments. For Germany, these problems include: a part of the cost of reduced world productive and distributive efficiency; progressive bias in firms' self-finance and in bank finance in favor of international-trading industries; the export of potential growth through "involuntary lending" (the holding of excessive international reserves acquired by the export of real goods);* a tendency to become export-dependent in real structure and a "helpless creditor" financially; political and economic pressures from deficit countries; and price inflation. The implications of these problems will be developed in connection with the discussion of available policy responses. It will be found that the responses themselves entail further major problems.

Even at this stage of the investigation, no exact magnitude can be calculated for the challenge presented to policy-makers by Germany's basic payments balance. As defined in principle in an earlier part of the present chapter, the basic payments balance is essentially

---

*On various concepts and calculations of "needed" and "excessive" reserves, see Jenkis 19 ff.

that balance with which the policy-makers would be confronted in the absence of any positive measures of their own, i.e., under a "normal" set of framework-setting policies. While this principle is sufficiently clear, it is in practice impossible to distinguish autonomous, induced and policy components of a real-life stream of international payments. Accordingly, the expedient has here been followed of describing structural tendencies toward payments surplus which are reflected in various accounts of the payments balance. A detailed (if still rough) breakdown of Germany's actual international payments into autonomous and policy-induced accounts must await a full discussion of the possible policy tactics with their tools and their actual effectiveness.* Paradoxically then, a situation of basic payments imbalance has here been imputed to Germany, without its being possible to document the exact magnitude of the challenge. According to the Council of Experts, however, true international equilibrium was not achieved in 1970.[136] And obviously, there existed a fundamental disequilibrium in the eyes of most German authorities and of the International Monetary Fund for a considerable period prior to the 1969 revaluation. Before examining, in Chapters 3, 4 and 5, the range of possible policy responses to the payments-balance challenges, it will be convenient to complete the picture of Germany's balance-of-payments situation by discussing in the following chapter the range of German payments-balance-connected goals and interests.

NOTES

1. F. Machlup and B. G. Malkiel, eds., International Monetary Arrangements: The Problem of Choice (Princeton, 1964), p. 24 ff.

2. G. N. Halm, Toward Limited Exchange-Rate Flexibility (Essays in International Finance #73) (Princeton, 1969), p. 11.

3. M. Friedman, and R. V. Roosa, The Balance of Payments: Free vs. Fixed Exchange Rates (Washington, 1967), p. 73, 93, 94; F. A. Lutz in American Enterprise Institute, International Payments Problems (Washington, 1966), p. 21, 22; R. Triffin, The World Money Maze (New Haven, 1966), p. 81; M. Michaely, Balance-of-Payments Adjustment Policies (New York, 1968).

---

*Even this procedure is a very imperfect substitute for knowing all the relevant functional relationships in all the economies involved in Germany's payments intercourse.

4. O. Veit, Grundriss der Währungspolitik (Frankfurt, 1961), p. 608; G. Schmölders, Finanzpolitik (Berlin, 1965), p. 474.

5. Financial Times (27 May 1969), p. 3.

6. The Bundesbank Law of 1957, the Foreign Trade and Payments Law of 1961 and the Credit Institutions Law of 1961 each removed the last vestiges of Occupation control in its respective field.

7. W. Dewald, and H. G. Johnson, "An Objective Analysis of the Objectives of American Monetary Policy, 1952-1961," D. Carson, ed., Banking and Monetary Studies (Homewood, 1963); M. W. Keran, and C. T. Babb, "An Explanation of Federal Reserve Actions (1933-1968)," Federal Reserve Bank of St. Louis, Review (July, 1969).

8. Federal Republic of Germany, Sachverständigenrat zur Begutachtung der Gesamtwirtschaftlichen Entwickling, Jahresgutachten (1964), Section 20; JG (1968), Section 193.

9. JG (1964), Section 1-8.

10. J. M. Fleming, Guidelines for Balance-of-Payments Adjustment under the Par-Value System (Essays in International Finance #67) (Princeton, 1968), p. 8.

11. J. E. Meade, The Theory of International Economic Policy, Vol 1: The Balance of Payments (New York, 1961), p. 9 ff.; J. Vanek, International Trade: Theory and Economic Policy (Homewood, 1962), p. 26 ff.; G. Haberler, A Survey of International Trade Theory (Princeton, 1961), p. 30.

12. W. Salant, E. Despres, L. D. Krause, and A. M. Rivlin, The United States Balance of Payments in 1968 (Washington, 1969); R. Rhomberg, and L. Boissoneault, "Effects of Income and Price Changes on the United States Balance of Payments," International Monetary Fund Staff Papers (March 1964).

13. L. Yeager, International Monetary Relations (New York, 1966), p. 46.

14. JG (1968), Section 87; J. Robinson, "Exchange Equilibrium," Economia Internazionale (1950), p. 401.

15. R. Mossé, "Die Messung der Zahlungsbilanzsalden mit besonderer Berücksichtigung der Kontroverse Bernstein-Lederer," Weltwirtschaftliches Archiv (1968), p. 198; F Machlup, "Adjustment,

Compensating Corrections and Financing of Imbalances in International Payments," R. E. Baldwin and others, eds., Trade, Growth, and the Balance of Payments (Chicago, 1965); F. Machlup, "Three Concepts of the Balance of Payments and the So-Called Dollar Shortage," Economic Journal (March 1950); L. A. Hahn, Ein Traktat über Währungsreform (Tübingen, 1964), p. 101.

16. Mossé, p. 205.

17. J. Bhagwati, "The Pure Theory of International Trade: A Survey," A.E.A. and R.E.S., Surveys of Economic Theory (Vol. 2) (New York, 1965), Sections 6, 7; B. Ohlin, Interregional and International Trade (Cambridge, 1933), Parts I, II.

18. G. N. Halm, International Monetary Cooperation (Chapel Hill, 1945), p. 127 ff.

19. E. M. Bernstein, "Strategic Factors in Balance of Payments Adjustment," International Monetary Fund Staff Papers (August 1956), p. 154 ff.

20. F. A. Lutz, The Problem of International Economic Equilibrium (Amsterdam, 1962), p. 31.

21. A. Predöhl, Das Ende der Weltwirtschaftskrise (Hamburg, 1962), p. 70.

22. Federal Republic of Germany, Bundesbank, Auszüge aus Presseartikeln (1970), #86, p. 14.

23. Meade, Chapter 1.

24. BRD, Bundestag Proceedings (25 Sep 1968).

25. International Monetary Fund, International Reserves and Liquidity (Washington, 1958), p. 5.

26. G. Haberler, Money in the International Economy (Cambridge, 1965), p. 7; W. Lederer, The Balance on Foreign Transactions: Problems of Definition and Measurement (Special Papers in International Economics #5) (Princeton, 1963); United States, Bureau of the Budget, Review Commission for Balance-of-Payments Statistics (Bernstein Commission), The Balance of Payments of the United States (Washington, 1965).

27. Federal Republic of Germany, Bundesbank, Annual Report (1965), p. 101.

28. AR (1965), p. 98.

29. Organization for Economic Cooperation and Development, Economic Policy Committee, Working Party Three, The Balance of Payments Adjustment Process (Paris, 1966), p. 23n.

30. Haberler, Money, p. 13.

31. JG (1964), Section 20; see also JG (1969), Section 235.

32. Mossé, p. 199, 219.

33. JG (1966), Section 156; JG (1968), Section 193; Fleming, Guidelines, p. 8.

34. C. P. Kindleberger, Balance-of-Payments Deficits and the International Market for Liquidity (Essays in International Finance #46) (Princeton, 1965).

35. R. N. Cooper, "The Balance of Payments in Revue," Journal of Political Economy (August 1968), p. 379-395.

36. W. Lederer, "Measuring the Balance of Payments," United States, 86th Congress, 2d Session, Joint Economic Committee, Sub- committee on International Exchange and Payments, Factors Affecting the United States Balance of Payments (Washington, 1962), p. 83; C. P. Kindleberger, International Economics (Homewood, 1958), p. 501; F. Machlup, International Payments, Debt and Gold (New York, 1964), p. 140 ff.; T. Scitovsky, Money and the Balance of Payments (Chicago, 1969), p. 81.

37. Federal Republic of Germany, Bundesbank, Monthly Report (June 1970), p. 8.

38. MR (Nov 1970), p. 9.

39. Berliner Bank, AP (1969), #61, p. 8; MR (June 1970), p. 8.

40. MR (Sep 1970), p. 39; also see note 8 in Chapter 4.

41. AP (1969), #61, p. 8.

42. AP (1970), #28, p. 8.

43. Haberler, Money, p. 18-20.

44. OECD3, p. 12, 27, 43; Fleming, Guidelines, p. 20.

45. P. Boarman, Germany's Economic Dilemma (New Haven, 1964), p. 192; Arbeitsgemeinschaft Deutscher Wirtschaftswissenschaftlicher Forschungsinstitute, Die Internationalen Währungsprobleme in der Weltwirtschaft der Gegenwart (Supplement to Zeitschrift für Angewandte Konjunkturforschung #14) (Berlin, 1967), p. 71.

46. The OECD's Working Party Three, for example (OECD3, p. 42), at one time presented it as a policy guide that demand and money should be "neither excessive nor deficient."

47. For a similar approach, see C. P. Kindleberger, "Germany's Persistent Balance-of-Payments Disequilibrium," R. E. Baldwin and others, eds., Trade, Growth, and the Balance of Payments (Chicago, 1965); and Scitovsky, Money.

48. G. Stigler, The Theory of Price (New York, 1952), p. 50 ff.

49. Jelle Zijlstra, President of the Board, Bank for International Settlements, AP (1970), #40, p. 2; SPD spokesmen in the Bundestag, AP (1970), #74, p. 3; AP (1970), #37, p. 6; AP (1970), #83, p. 8; JG (1970), Section 204 ff.

50. K. Blessing, Die Verteidigung des Geldwertes (Frankfurt, 1960), p. 37; Organization for Economic Cooperation and Development, Economic and Development Review Committee, Survey (Germany) (1965), p. 6.

51. German Economic Review (1963), #2, p. 195; JG (1964), p. 83; AR (1969), p. 25; JG (1966), Section 80.

52. AR (1969), p. 5.

53. See JG (1965), Section 92. Between 1960 and 1967, dependent workers increased four percent, gross wages per worker rose sixty-seven percent, disposable wages per worker rose sixty-five percent, and the property-income share in national income fell twenty-three percent. This shift of incomes agrees, with an understandable lag, with such series as investment as a percentage of Gross National Product compared with population growth modified by employment rates. The Council of Experts attributes falling profit rates to the end of reconstruction (JG [1968], Section 196).

54. JG (1968), Section 196.

55. H. W. Jenkis, Die Importierte Inflation (Schriften zur Wirtschaftswissenschaftlichen Forschung #15) (Meisenheim, 1966), p. v.

56. JG (1964), Section 53.

57. JG (1965), Sections 20, 21.

58. Deutsches Wirtschaftswissenschaftliches Institut (East Berlin), Berichte, Heft 14, p. 2; BRD, Bundestag, Bericht über die Ergebnis einer Untersuchung der Konzentration in der Wirtschaft (Drucksache 2320, 4. Wahlperiode) (Bonn, 1964), p. 4.

59. Vorwärts (23 November 1964), p. 13; GER (1964), #1, p. 16-24.

60. Schiller, AP (1971), #8, p. 9.

61. JG (1964), Sections 4, 7, 8, 10, 33.

62. Boarman, p. 90.

63. GER (1964), #1, p. 16-24.

64. JG (1966), Section 28; Boarman, p. 203-204.

65. GER (1964), #2, p. 112.

66. H. Wallich, Mainsprings of the German Revival (New Haven, 1965), p. 244.

67. JG (1968), Section 83.

68. W. Hitzinger, Die Europäische Automobilindustrie (Kiel, 1965), p. 15.

69. JG (1964), p. 147.

70. Hahn, Traktat, p. 42n.

71. MR (Dec. 1969); A. S. Gerakis, "Effects of Exchange-Rate Devaluations and Revaluations on Receipts from Tourism," International Monetary Fund Staff Papers (November 1965), p. 366.

72. German Tribune (9 July 1970), p. 3.

73. MR (Sep 1970), p. 39.

74. JG (1964), Section 181; AR (1967), p. 31.

75. OECD3, p. 35.

76. G. Gutman, H. J. Hochstrate, and R. Schüter, Die Wirtschaftsverfassung der Bundesrepublick Deutschland (Stuttgart, 1964), p. 1967
ff.; E. Brehmer, Struktur und Funktionsweise des Geldmarkts der
Bundesrepublik Deutschland seit 1948 (Kieler Studien) (Tübingen, 1964),
p. 41 ff.; Blessing, Verteidigung, p. 44.

77. JG (1965), Section 113.

78. Blessing, Verteidigung, p. 239-240, 262-263.

79. JG (1965), Section 134.

80. MR (Oct 1967), p. 5; JG (1966), Section 181 ff.

81. JG (1964), Section 53.

82. JG (1966), Section 179.

83. MR (Jan 1965), p. 34; MR (Apr 1966), p. 3.

84. MR (Jan 1967), p. 38.

85. MR (Apr 1966), p. 3; Federal Republic of Germany, Bundesministerium für Finanz, Finanzbericht (1969), p. 229 ff.

86. MR (July 1967), p. 4.

87. JG (1964), Section 53.

88. JG (1967), Section 493.

89. MR (June 1965), p. 4.

90. JG (1965), Section 247. Available figures on capital structure of German firms are quite general, yet it appears that export-
oriented industries are less dependent on outside financing than the
average firm (MR [Apr 1970], p. 21 ff.; MR [Aug 1970], p. 30-31).

91. AP (1971), #8, p. 9.

92. JG (1967), Section 493; AP (1970), #75, p. 3; AP (1970), #75,
p. 5.

93. JG (1967), Section 484-485.

94. German banks combine investment-banking and commercial-
banking functions. Suggestions that these functions be split have been

rebuffed, on the ground that trends in Britain and France are in the opposite direction.

95. JG (1967), Section 213.

96. Brehmer, Struktur, p. 77.

97. Veit, Grundriss, p. 603; Gutman, p. 42, 172; R. Loehr, The West German Banking System (n.p., 1952), p. 52-60, and primary sources cited there.

98. AP (1970), #73, p. 2; AP (1970), #86, p. 14.

99. Arbeitsgemeinschaft, p. 72.

100. W. Gatz, "Gründe und volkswirtschaftliche Wirkungen der D-Mark-Aufwertung," Weltwirtschaftliches Archiv (1963), p. 380 ff.; Loehr, p. 38 ff.

101. Binder in Arbeitsgemeinschaft, p. 74; OECDS (1965), p. 6.

102. MR (Apr 1966), p. 30; W. Schmidt, "The German Bundesbank," Bank for International Settlements, Eight European Central Banks (London, 1963), p. 77.

103. Bundesbank, AP (1971), #10, p. 1; AR (1968), p. 50.

104. This ratio was calculated by comparing Gross National Product and the unadjusted average annual "money stock" according to IMF, Statistics, Germany, Lines 34 and 99a.

105. This experience agrees with Friedman's observation that the dominance of changes in money stock over changes in velocity is more important secularly than cyclically (M. Friedman, and D. Meiselman, "The Relative Stability of Monetary Velocity and the Investment Multiplier in the United States 1897-1958," Commission on Money and Credit, Stabilization Policies [Englewood Cliffs, 1963], p. 330).

106. AR (1965), p. 47.

107. JG (1966), Sections 163-169.

108. Blessing, Verteidigung, p. 116.

109. JG (1964), Section 75.

110. AR (1969), p. 5; AR (1969), p. 79.

111. IMF, Statistics, Germany, France, Italy, United Kingdom and United States, Line 14.

112. JG (1967), Section 27.

113. JG (1968), Section 80.

114. Emminger, AP (1970), #38, p. 3; M. Barrett, "Activation of the Special Drawing Rights Facility in the International Monetary Fund," Federal Reserve Bank of New York, Monthly Review (February 1970), p. 45.

115. R. G. Hawtrey, The Art of Central Banking (New York, 1933), p. 11.

116. Hahn, Traktat, p. 34; Jenkis, p. vii; O. Emminger, Währungs-politik im Wandel der Zeit (Frankfurt, 1966), p. 78; O. Veit, Reale Theorie des Geldes (Frankfurt, 1966), p. 343.

117. W. Stützel, "Ist die schleichende Inflation durch monetäre Massnahmen zu beeinflussen?" (Beihefte zur Konjunkturpolitik #7) (Berlin, 1960), p. 24.

118. L. A. Hahn, Fünfzig Jahre zwischen Inflation und Deflation (Tübingen, 1963), p. 205; Hahn, Traktat, p. 34.

119. JG (1964), Section 159.

120. JG (1964), Section 39; Hahn, Jahre, p. 119; JG (1970), Section 303.

121. And a converse process will take place in the higher-cost countries, depressing costs, unless downward price inflexibility and consequent social tensions force an expansionary financial policy or an exchange-rate devaluation. In any case, factor prices in terms of any one currency will tend to converge. As factor prices are leveled, the nations with the higher structural cost-price ratio will logically gain the international competitive advantage. This means that nations would be forced to compete in terms of their acceptable profit rates, and not in terms of their tolerable degrees of monopoly. Note that in this simple analysis there are two distinct factors entering into final international prices of trading nations: their average unit production costs and their normal cost/price ratios. As trade causes the international differential in the first to approach zero, it is clear that the differential in the second must also disappear if goods are to trade at identical prices internationally.

122. Haberler, Money, p. 25; JG (1966), Section 35; JG (1969), Section 293.

123. Hawtrey, Art, p. 127 ff.

124. See also the explanation in AR (1969), p. 19.

125. JG (1966), Section 210.

126. JG (1964), Section 237; JG (1966), Section 207 ff.; JG (1967), Section 429 ff.; JG (1968), Section 227 ff.

127. JG (1967), Section 457 ff.; JG (1966), Section 208 ff.

128. Federal Republic of Germany, Sachverständigenrat zur Begutachtung der Gesamtwirtschaftlichen Entwicklung, Sondergutachten (1967), Section 8.

129. JG (1967), Section 447.

130. JG (1964), Section 35.

131. Vanek, Part II, Ch. 7; Kindleberger, Economics, Ch. 16; R. I. McKinnon, and W. E. Oates, The Implications of International Economic Integration for Monetary, Fiscal, and Exchange Rate Policy (Studies in International Finance #16) (Princeton, 1966), p. 29 ff.

132. AR (1968), p. 27; Schiller, AP (1969), #66, p. 1.

$$(\text{II. 2}) \quad I^d + T + C^K - S^L = Y^K$$
$$(\text{II. 3}) \quad I^d + T + C^K + (C^L - Y^L) = Y^K$$
$$(\text{II. 4}) \quad I^d + T + C^L + C^K = Y^K + Y^L$$
$$(\text{II. 5}) \quad I + C = Y$$

Where Y = national income = $Y^K + Y^L$

K = received, or spent, by capitalists

L = received, or spent, by labor

C = consumption expenditures = $C^K + C^L$

I = investment expenditures = S

I^d = investment at home

S = saving = $S^K + S^L$

T = balance-of-trade surplus = $I - I^d$

The logical and practical caveats propounded after Equation (IV) in Chapter 2 are applicable to the above formulations also.

133. $$(\text{III. 2}) \quad \frac{S^K Y}{Y^K} - I = \frac{S^K Y^L}{Y^K} - S^L$$

(III. 3) $S^K Y - I Y^K = S^K Y L - S L Y K$

(III. 4) $S^K Y - S Y^K = S^K Y L - (S Y^K - S^K Y K)$

(III. 5) $S^K Y = S^K Y L + S^K Y K$

(III.6) $Y = Y$

The logical and practical caveats propounded after Equation (IV) in Chapter 2 are applicable to the above formulations also.

134. R. Sayers, <u>Modern Central Banking</u> (Oxford, 1958), p. 292.

135. For further discussion of these relations, see R. A. Mundell, "Capital Mobility and Stabilization Policy under Fixed and Flexible Exchange Rates," <u>Canadian Journal of Economics</u> (November 1963).

136. AP (1970), #91, p. 1.

2

THE POLICY AIMS:
GERMANY'S GOALS,
INTERESTS,
AND
POLICY INSTITUTIONS

MACROECONOMIC GOALS AND
PAYMENTS-BALANCE POLICY

General

The purpose of this study is to gain an understanding of a course of payments-balance policy actually adopted and pursued in the recent past. As a national-level case study, aimed at international-level decisions based on the real motivations of national policy, this study must dispense with the convenient assumption that national governments necessarily work for a common national weal. Here, therefore, in agreement with most ancient and modern political economists, a relatively "hard-nosed" and unidealized view of policy motivation will be taken.[1]

Chapter 1 indicated that the payments balance is not an end in itself. The formulation of a policy response to the payments balance cannot, therefore, be explained wholly in terms of the announced balance-of-payments goals, which are merely the publication or the rationalization of the underlying policy. The actual policy line can best be explained by resolving the "balance-of-payments goal" into those other goals toward which the payments balance is instrumental.[2] Real-life choices which have actually been made must ultimately be explained in terms of real-life goals actually held by decision-makers. Some of these goals are not always clearly announced, and must in effect be deduced from indirect evidence.

This can be done by examining a range of a priori plausible goals; tracing their interrelations, their connection with the great imperatives of Germany's world situation, and their impact on policy organs;

showing the public support they have received; and indicating both the logical relations of each to balance-of-payments policy and the rationalizations of these relations formulated during the policy debate. Standard, announced macroeconomic goals, more tacit national objectives, and some important group interests will be discussed in the present chapter.

The standard macroeconomic goals are growth, employment and price stability. Although these are normally agreed goals from the community standpoint, and announced as such, they do not fully explain the actual policies pursued, because of their too-general formulation, their own mutual conflicts, and the opposition of interests. Still, since public-opinion surveys have indicated that economic questions are the first preoccupation of the German citizen, it is to be expected that much of the policy debate will have been conducted in terms of the macroeconomic goals.

Alongside the standard macroeconomic objectives, there exists an important class of goals relating to the whole society's shape and position which are more or less agreed among the decision-makers, but which are not usually announced explicitly among the economic goals. For historic and geopolitical reasons, goals of this class are especially prominent in today's Germany; they will here be treated under the rubrics of social order and geopolitical position.

Finally, the non-agreed goals held by parts of the community may be called interests. Such goals are extremely varied, and will here be reduced to functional and sectoral income-distribution goals, and the outlook of the financial managers themselves. The factors leading to the modern "interest-group state" have already been noted. Policy is politics, and things financial, resting on many conventions, are especially close to the realm of social psychology and social power. And this is nowhere more true than in Germany, in whose history the interconnections of finance and politics have become especially visible.[3]

It will be easier to relate all levels of policy motivation to the policy measures actually taken, if the policy-making organs with the most direct influence on international payments are next discussed, and thereafter, the ways in which these organs are motivated to follow various goals are indicated. In the final section of the present chapter, therefore, the German Federal Bank (hereafter called the Bundesbank), the Council of Experts for the Evaluation of General Economic Trends (hereafter called the Council of Experts), and the federal government's economic cabinet are briefly described and evaluated in their payments-balance policy roles.

The Growth Goal

A need for economic growth, measured in terms of per capita national income, is felt by all modern societies, for a series of closely related reasons. With the weakening of the pure market mechanisms, the growth of overall income is an important lubricant in the resulting semi-political struggle over income distribution. Market imperfections can also lead to errors in today's large-scale economic decisions; steady growth can over-ride the distortions thus produced, and so maintain jobs, which are the only fully system-conformed source of income and demand. These advantages of growth are crucial in the near revolutionary social conditions in many industrial countries today.[4]

Again, unwillingness to control population growth raises, even on a strictly pecuniary basis, the per capita social costs of crowding and of never-adequate planning.

Further, since adaptability is held out as one of the chief strengths of a market system, while markets are losing their guiding sensitivity, it becomes as important ideologically as practically to maintain a large proportion of added production, within which a margin of flexibility is possible.[5] As was noted in Chapter 1, too, a large proportion of investment to income implies (all other independent factors unchanged) an increased property-share of national income.

Finally, in a world of nation-states, each country must grow in per capita industrial production in order to maintain itself, politically and economically, in competition with rival states. The Federal Republic must not only compete economically with the OECD states, but also ideologically with the German Democratic Republic, which is the world's eighth nation in per capita industrial production, and which boasts a growth rate fully comparable to that of the western German state. As is to be expected, then, support for economic growth in principle is general in Germany. Recently, Chancellor Brandt expressed the increased emphasis of his government on growth with the words, "This Administration is also aware that we can only assure social and political stability in a growing economy."[6]

Despite all of this, there has been a remarkable undercurrent of misgiving about growth-oriented policy, and particularly about expansive anticyclical policy to preserve steady growth rates.[7] The main objection to such measures has been their inflationary tendency, not least because of the latter's effect on Germany's international competitiveness.

The debate over Germany's growth goal may be discussed in terms of the implications for the accumulation and for the allocation of capital. This general viewpoint is especially appropriate in German conditions. It has been noted that the composition of the German factor endowment is shifting. With a stationary or declining work-force, growth depends on labor productivity, which in turn depends on capital deepening and efficient structural change.[8]

The export bias of Germany's economic structure, and the modern weakening of market guidance of economic structures every-where, were discussed in Chapter 1. In the light of these factors, the key policy question for the overall level of German investment concerns the flexibility of the nation's industrial structure. If that structure will readily adapt itself to relative demands, a policy of maintaining steady high domestic demand (i.e., a policy of expansive anti-cyclical measures as needed) is a feasible way to maintain investment and growth. If that structure can be altered only with extraordinary lags, such a policy, by raising the domestic price level, will reduce the demand facing German exporting and import-competing industries, and so retard growth.

In fact, the Council of Experts found that investment in Germany is demand-sensitive, and specifically that investment is closest related to the ratio of capacity to new orders.[9] The relatively large share of outside (bank) financing in the capital structure of German firms causes relatively small drops in demand to be reflected in bigger drops in profits as a percentage of owned capital.[10] The implication is that steady demand is indeed required for investment and growth.

On the other hand, attitudes toward growth through productivity have seemed ambivalent. The Bundesbank, for example, while recognizing the demand-sensitivity of German growth rates, often pictures high demand as leading to significant misallocations of capital.[11] This notion may have special applicability to Germany, in which self-finance of firms is a strong tradition and the capital-allocating role of the capital-market cannot have been extremely strong or accurate. However, the question of structural flexibility raised above is not resolved until the distinction is made between demand of foreign and of domestic origin. The present study takes the view that large, and therefore export-oriented, productive units are vital to Germany's competitiveness, and so represent for it "indispensible constituent parts of the modern economy."[12]

In this connection, the Bundesbank has repeated throughout the period studied the conviction that export competitiveness is desirable and, once lost, cannot easily be regained.[13] In support of this the

Bank has cited the experiences of the United States and Britain. Yet, if such a reversal of circumstances is really so difficult, a world-wide inflexibility of economic structures is implied. This would mean that low domestic demand produces export-biased structure, while high domestic demand would impair export competitiveness. Such a loss of competitiveness and consequent tendency to basic payments imbalance, in the Bundesbank's eyes, has led to slow and unsound growth in other countries,[14] and would in Germany's case be disastrous for the process of private productive investment, because of the export bias in industry, the weakness of the capital market, and the German predilection for self-finance.[15] Remedies or palliatives for similar situations abroad have involved far-reaching government intervention in economy and society,[16] an eventuality which German policymakers consistently abominated.[17] Genuine growth, the Bank maintained, must have a "real basis" in private saving.[18]

This view was shared point for point by Chancellor Erhard and by President Herman Abs of the German Bank Association.[19] Erhard drove the question back to a more fundamental point by asserting that private saving means middle-class saving, and that the middle class forms the strength of the nation, and the safeguard of its freedom.[20]

Steady high demand is also seen by the Bundesbank as leading to "hoarding of labor," i.e., retaining temporarily unneeded employees to avoid difficulties due to a later tight labor market.[21] This practice, if widespread, would tend to lower labor productivity. Finally, good times lead in the Bundesbank's eyes to lax labor discipline.[22] Although such assertions are seldom accompanied by specific evidence, this phenomenon too, may be specially important in Germany, to the extent that mutually reinforcing attitudes of labor and management are still guided by older conceptions of their economic, social and political relations.[23]

If labor productivity is lowered by these processes, the squeeze on profits will eventually bring on a cut in investment and a recession, which the Bundesbank, in the light of all the foregoing, tends to see as a purging experience. The drop in investment does not hurt growth in the long run, argues the Bundesbank, but will rather put subsequent growth on a sounder basis allocation-wise.[24]

After the 1966/1967 recession the Council of Experts was in a position to rebut the Bundesbank propositions and to illustrate its own contention that measured labor productivity (much relied on in the Bundesbank's presentations) is demand-sensitive. In the recession, productivity rose by only two percent, this due mostly to a good harvest.[25] As demand and capacity utilization fall, labor productivity must fall sharply unless firms can cut their labor forces fast enough to stay "ahead" of the process.[26] Yet with the growth of white-collar work, a larger proportion of firms' workers have become difficult to remove in response to demand shifts.[27] As to labor "discipline," this must in any case rise with the laying off of such "undisciplined" elements as the healthy and the like.

Further, the poor profits experienced in recessions almost always are traceable to a shrinkage of the spread between average revenue and average plant costs per unit of output, i.e., to the fall in demand and the consequent underutilization of capacity.[28] The emphasis of this assessment is in striking contrast to that of the Bundesbank's continuing notion of recession as a quasi-automatic purge of over-investment.[29]

A further set of relationships has been operative in Germany. In a closed system in which no firms enjoyed preponderating market power, a rise in real wages could force the pace of labor-saving innovation. In Germany, where active recruitment of workers from countries with a lower labor productivity is highly developed,[30] tendencies toward higher real wages are partly dissipated through imported labor, thus tending to maintain labor-intensivity in German industry and so to depress labor productivity.

Finally, the Council challenged the Bundesbank notion of good times as a cause of slowed increases in productivity, by pointing to the loss of capital productivity and to the intensification of maintenance activity when demand is weakened, both of which indicate that productivity is supported by high demand.[31] Thus there exist objective grounds for the Council's 1970 proposition that the government must make a choice between price stability and growth with high employment.[32]

Both of these lines of reasoning on the relationship of demand to growth are plausible; they are in fact compatible. Indeed, during the latest surge of inflation, former Council Chairman Giersch warned of the distorting effects of inflation on investment.[33] The Bundesbank reasoning is in one sense more long-run and the Council's more short-run in nature. However, when due weight is given to the issue of foreign as against domestic demand, and to the possible replacement of the latter by the former in times of recession, the effect of tolerating or even precipitating domestic demand fluctuations appears, under current German circumstances, favorable to the export industries, thus causing a capital misallocation, which in turn perpetuates the tendency to payments-balance surplus.

It seems inconsistent in the German case to deplore both the misallocation of investment and the loss of international competitiveness attendant on inflation. Given German economic and financial structure, "adequate" international competitiveness itself fosters a growing bias in investment. Perhaps the answer may lie, less in rebalancing domestic and foreign-trading industries, than in permitting a redefinition of these groups, for example as a result of European integration.

Export surpluses further entail the danger of expending real resources to acquire an unproductive hoard of international reserves. The opposing policy of maintaining steady domestic demand is in the very long run less likely to foster these effects on growth.

In spite of the possibility of an abstract reconciliation of their views, the Council of Experts and the Bundesbank have entertained quite different opinions as to the desirable strength of anticyclical policy (Chapter 5). The Council's view in effect stresses growth through domestic-oriented industries, while the Bundesbank's tends to favor growth through foreign-oriented industries.

In the "test case" of 1966/1967, the government decided, in effect, that recession did not constitute a structural purge, and so should be combated by increasing domestic demand.[34] Economics Minister Schiller expressly denounced the "moral purge" view of recession.[35] The economic-growth goal formulated by Minister Schiller was put at a three-and-a-half percent per year increase in real output.[36]

The Employment Goal

Steady full mass employment is endangered by the same features of modern industrial society that endanger steady economic growth. Apart from the desirability of using all resources effectively for growth, full employment finds general support everywhere as a matter of social policy.[37] Employment is not only the sole income-distribution method fully conformable to present concepts of incentives; it is also the only alternative to a mass leisure for which neither society nor individual appears to have been adequately prepared.

Germany shares these common concerns, aggravated by the physical and psychological nearness of the rival system in the eastern German state and by the country's traditionally deep right-left split. It would hardly be prudent for a West German government of today to reckon with much leeway in this area. The Schiller quantification of the macroeconomic goals during the Kiesinger government called for four fifths of one percent unemployment.[38] The Brandt government, for its part, repeatedly announced a philosophy of excluding large-scale involuntary unemployment as an acceptable byproduct of cyclical-policy measures.[39] Despite much disapproving partisan discussion of an "employment guarantee" which can derail all market-conformed economic-policy tools, the Brandt position may be a rather bold acknowledgment of existing social and economic realities, in some ways parallel to the philosophy of the Ostpolitik.*[40]

In this connection, it is of interest to consider whether employment rates constitute an independent economic goal, to which an independent policy tool should be assigned, and which can be visualized independently of the inflation rate and thus of the payments balance. This question relates to the stability of the factors entering into the statistical relation, known as the Phillips curve, between inflation rate and unemployment rate.

Significant Phillips-curve relationships logically require a closed system and an intermediate degree of oligopoly in the economic structure. In an open system, inflation can worsen the trade balance and so conceivably decrease, rather than increase, employment. Under perfect competition, there need be no trade-off between inflation and unemployment; and under a high degree of market power, virtually all attempts to stimulate employment and output by means of increased monetary demand would be dissipated in price and wage rises.

Thus in an open, non-dominant system such as Germany's, under fixed exchange rates, an autonomous set of Phillips-curve relations cannot operate. Indeed, any variations in the significance of this trade-off which stem from purely domestic economic structure, would occasion merely subsidiary departures from the Phillips curve of the world economic system as a whole. Thus payments surplus and deficit, through the wage "leeway" generated by direct international price transmission effects and by income effects, set the lower and upper limits for German wages, which are in this way tied to wages and inflation rates abroad.[41]

It is safe to say that growing economic concentration and social disequilibrium, especially in such a dominant economy as that of the United States, has recently worsened the world-system inflation/unemployment trade-off (or rather, increased the shiftability of the trade-off curve) so far as to impair the concept's predictive significance. The Council of Experts has also expressed the feeling that the international Phillips curve is presently unfavorable.[42]

---

*"Ostpolitik" is used in the present study to designate the Brandt government's more conciliatory policy toward eastern Europe.

Germany's own Phillips-curve factors have also tended to a worsening or dissolving of the trade-off. Here may be cited the cessation of the influx of refugees, the political gains of the Social Democrats, the "demonstration effect" of events abroad, and the structural shrinkage of Germany's work-force. Against these facts, however, must be set the use of around two million foreign workers and the declining prevalence of relatively labor-intensive methods in Germany.

All of these considerations imply a net weakening of usable Phillips-curve relationships. Thus any policy justifications which treat the rate of employment as a covariable with price levels--such as those at times given for the central bank's tight-money policies-- are assuming a non-existent closed German system, or are assuming some form of insulation from the international system, such as flexible exchange rates.[43] Yet the Economics Ministry calculations,[44] which conclude that price stability is endangered by over four percent per year real growth and that employment is endangered by under two and a half percent per year real growth, seem to imply a usably stable Phillips curve. The Council of Experts, on the other hand, feels that employment has been too steady for too long for any such calculation to be possible.[45]

Thus the policy measures calculated to insure steady growth are also desirable for full employment. The same key question concerning the flexibility of German economic structure is fundamental to the choice of an appropriate strategy in this area. The relationship of employment level to changes in price level is not stable enough for policy calculations. Due to Germany's heavy dependence on exports, the relation between the rates may not even always be a positive one. Clearly, however, an export boom can support full employment as well as it can growth.

The Price-Stability Goal

Price stability is strictly interpreted in Germany. Economics Minister Schiller's quantified goals included a maximum one-percent per year difference between nominal and real Gross National Product, while the Finance Ministry, the Bundesbank and the Council of Experts have opted for yet more stringent versions of price stability.[46]

Article 80 of the Basic Law in effect made currency stability the chief goal of German economic policy. This priority was announced with great consistency and emphasis by all policy organs throughout the period under review.[47] The Brandt government's equal emphasis on employment stability in the most recent months caused some questioning of its dedication to price stability. Nevertheless, the long

primacy of price stability in German policy has several enduring
bases.

The German people are highly stability-conscious.[48] For example, a 1970 poll showed that seventy-six percent of the population
preferred (at least in the abstract) price stability to economic growth,
while only four percent voiced the reverse priority.[49] It has indeed
been that this consciousness is extreme, even pathological.[50] Partly
this sensitivity is of a piece with postwar German involvement with
notions of social order. The revolutionary effects of inflation were
emphasized in the writing of the leading German social-order pub-
licist, Walther Eucken, who made price stability one of the almost
metaphysical principles of a free social order.[51]

Recent German history has in fact illustrated the ruinous social
consequences of extreme inflation.[52] Two major inflations have taken
place in Germany in this century, both associated with fiscal deficits
and a dependent central bank.[53] The worldwide Korea boom reawakened German fears of inflation.

It may well be argued likewise that the inflation of the twenties,
seen as a cause of the political events of the thirties, and the inflation
throughout the already unpleasant forties, in contrast to the startling
success of the stabilized fifties, have made the German people hyper-
conscious of inflation. This reaction, coupled with a certain ration-
alistic national tendency to anticipate (and thus precipitate) the fullest
logical implications of a situation, suggests that even creeping inflation would in Germany not only have its "standard" economic and
social effects magnified, but would also carry uniquely German
political connotations. In Germany's current political and geopolitical
environment, this is a sobering possibility.* On the other hand, precisely this possibility makes it wise for the monetary authorities to
sound the inflationary tocsin less urgently, and to begin to establish a
more reassuring psychological tone in their pronouncements.

Many Germans doubtless had unforgettable experiences of inflation. Many more have been subjected to a constant barrage of
denunciation of inflation and exhortation to avoid it.[54] The unvarying
tone of the Bundesbank's warnings throughout the sixties is but the
most responsible example of the weighty propaganda against inflation
which has never slackened in postwar Germany.[55] A cynic might be
tempted to question whether such an "extreme" attitude as the

---

*According to Finance Minister Alex Möller, inflation has always
"radicalized the unemployed masses" (AP 1970, #32, p. 2).

Germans'--whether plausibly justifiable or not--could be or would be maintained without its being in the direct and tangible interest of some identifiable group.

As has been noted in the discussion of the growth goal, much is made in some German circles of the allocative and distributive evils of inflation and of their possible impact on discipline, efficiency and growth.[56] Yet when increased effective demand seemed called for to avoid irreplaceable growth losses during the 1966/1967 recession, roughly the same circles showed little zeal for absolute-maximum growth potential, urging the sacrifice of marginal growth possibilities in favor of, once again, price stability. This apparent inconsistency stems from a fundamentally consistent fear of the social consequences of inflation.

Thus, a related line of thought sees inflation cutting voluntary saving, with state saving replacing middle-class saving as the backbone of growth.[57] This socialization, according to former Chancellor Erhard, would be "explosive."[58] The predicted drop in private savings rates would also, in this view, reduce the individual's feeling of self reliance, and so usher in the welfare state.[59] Many observers similarly see German stability policy as basically social policy.[60] Thus, "one of the most pressing social-policy tasks" is to keep the confidence of the savers.[61] However, in fact German saving has not declined, but rather risen with the recent rise in nominal interest rates.[62] Further debate on the social-order implications of inflation will be analyzed in a subsequent section.

Again, under German conditions inflation means a forced real adjustment of the export industries. The spector of lost international competitiveness continually haunts German policy-making.[63] If export-industry readjustment were slow in taking place, the self-financing profits of this leading investment sector could indeed be impaired.[64]

All of these considerations closely link the price-stability goal to the goals of growth and a liberal social order.[65]

The acceleration of world inflation in the past three or four years, associated very largely with increased social and foreign-policy problems of the United States, has added a new impetus to the struggle for price-stability. The September 1970 annual meeting of the IMF in Copenhagen furnished the occasion for a visibly concerted burst of anti-inflationary "moral suasion" from the world financial community.[66] Not only was inflation deplored as the top-priority problem, but three less usual notes were sounded from all sides with increasing frequency.

First, the domestic (allocation and distribution), rather than the international (payments-balance), evils of inflation received predominant emphasis.[67] This is consistent with the facts that a world-wide inflation is not necessarily directly harmful to individual countries' payments balances, and that an accelerating inflation threatens to become more obvious even in its subtler (or less measurable) domestic effects.

The second new strand in the anti-inflationary drive was represented by the unprecedented frequency with which calls for price and/or wage freezes or controls were heard and acted upon. Nearly every peripheral country of Europe introduced such measures in the fall and winter of 1970/1971, and nearly every core country, including Germany, heard weighty counsel in favor of doing likewise.[68] It cannot be denied that these events evidence a rapid erosion of confidence in the automatic equilibrating mechanisms of the market.

The third novelty in the post-Copenhagen anti-inflationary campaign confirms this inference. Within a few months nearly every authoritative voice in the world financial community had been raised in favor of a long-term, institutionalized incomes policy, as a primary economic-policy tool. Such suggestions were heard from the Secretary-General of the OECD, the Bank for International Settlements, the International Monetary Fund, and from the heads of numerous central banks, including the Chairman of the Federal Reserve Board and the Governor of the Bank of England.[69]

The last-named authority fairly epitomized the entire movement in declaring that a modern society cannot "expect to maintain a fully employed, fully informed and increasingly well-off democracy, in which the development of wages and prices is left entirely to the operation of market forces." Even intervention by monetary and fiscal policies, said the Governor, can achieve price stability only at the cost of very large-scale unemployment. "Over the longer run," he continued,

> I believe that Government will have to set about devising
> a fair and workable incomes policy and developing the
> understanding and acceptance of it throughout society.
> This will be easier if we have the right framework of in-
> dustrial relations. . . .[70]

This speech contained both elements of the new attitude: distrust of markets even when guided by macrofinancial measures, and the call for longterm institutionalized incomes-political measures, to be developed by government and "sold" to the public.

As noted on a succeeding page, Germany has if anything been ahead of other nations in considering a formal incomes policy. In the recent discussion, however, President Klasen of the Bundesbank, while calling some form of incomes policy "unavoidable," was notably hesitant to suggest specific steps beyond the traditional macrofinancial tools and labor-property-government "concerted action." [71] Professor Norbert Kloten of the Council of Experts called for a more elaborate form of concerted action. [72]

The goal of price stability is obviously related to the payments balance. An internationally low price level, on the one hand, implies a payments surplus, while all the mechanical effects of surplus, on the other hand, tend toward inflation. In 1968 and 1969, the Bundesbank saw the payments balance as the chief cause of inflation. [73]

Goal Conflicts and Priorities

It is well known that the macroeconomic goals conflict in some degree, and several conflicts have been noted in preceding sections. The Economics Ministry's 1969 "calculable" goals presupposed such conflicts. [74] In relation to the payments balance, growth and employment can be maintained by a policy of undervaluation. But undervaluation will erode price stability and bias industrial structure further toward export dependence. Consequent payments surpluses may cause an "export of growth" through "involuntary lending" in the form of international-reserves holdings. On the other hand, growth and employment can also be had by substituting domestic for foreign demand. But this requires at least temporarily accelerating inflation to readjust price levels, and thereafter keeping abreast of foreign inflation. Such an inflation might distort allocation, stunting growth, and would certainly shift income from the currently most influential representatives of the German "middle class." This is an example of the impact of goals beyond the standard macroeconomic three. The trends which have already been noted in the modern industrial state tend to accentuate the goal conflicts and to make system-conformed resolutions more difficult.

In cases of conflict, goal priorities, express or implicit, must come into play. Several conclusions about German goal priorities can be drawn. Many policy pronouncements, including the 1967 Stability Law itself, indeed proceed explicitly from the assumption that all three goals can be reached. Often, of course, such optimistic pronouncements are no more than disingenuous pleas by labor or property against making any special effort in a given direction, since any determined effort toward one goal usually endangers the others. By and large, however, policy makers realize that the conflicts and choices are real.[75] In normal circumstances, thus, some degree of all goals simultaneously is striven for, and even inflation has, in reality, constantly been "accepted" by the authorities. In case of acute conflict, the official ideology calls for a priority, even an "absolute priority," on price stability. Bundesbank President Blessing made it quite clear that he would sacrifice both employment and growth to price stability.[76] The Brandt government, on the other hand, under a motto of "stability and growth," has at times come close to implying that price stability can be sacrificed to the other two goals.

The German monetary authorities were faced unequivocally with the choice between unemployment and possible inflation only once in the period under review, viz., during the 1966/1967 slump. At that time, the authorities' actions indicated that the employment goal was quite secondary, while their statements indicated that this goal was not seriously taken up until price rises had entirely subsided.[77] The highest unemployment rates of the sixties were described as "the progressive normalization of the situation on the labor market,"[78] and the Bank announced a policy of credit relaxation on the "expectation" that wage rises would be contained.[79] In the midst of these same difficulties, the political arm of government was reshuffled, and its attitude toward the policy choice become more flexible. (See the discussion in Chapter 5.) More recently, Economics Minister Schiller, a member of the Kiesinger and of the Brandt governments, has stated that, for him, unemployment is "no permissible economic policy tool."[80]

Although most of the Bundesbank's statements indicate a conviction that wage rates react to the monetary milieu, i.e., that employment and price levels form essentially one goal,[81] there are passages which betray the feeling that wage movements are largely independent of monetary policy--because of labor-market imperfections.[82] It is this latter feeling which might explain general support of provisions in the 1967 "Stability Law" (Chapter 5), calling for "concerted projections" of economic conditions by all economic decision-making groups. Yet the Bank later concluded that incomes policy really means wages policy which in turn really means monetary policy.[83]

Faced with the same stability-employment conflict, the Council of Experts anticipated the Kiesinger and Brandt governments in choosing employment on growth grounds.

The announced goal of overall external payments balance apparently ranked above that of growth, but behind that of price stability.[84] The German monetary authorities consistently favored price stability over payments balance by their restrictive credit policy.

This attitude could, however, be interpreted as in fact favoring pay-ments surplus over price stability (Chapter 6). In times of surplus, monetary ease was occasionally provided for the sake of overall ex-ternal balance, but only due to the understanding that liquidity effects of overall payments surplus would in any case have produced the same monetary ease.[85] On the other hand, even such surpluses in the basic payments balance were cited as requiring restrictive credit policy measures to offset the rise in domestic liquidity, despite the slower pace of capital formation and growth which might be entailed.

Several lyric pronouncements on the elegance of the gold stan-dard and its rules notwithstanding,[86] the Bundesbank was convinced that payments-balance problems would not be solved by "the synchroni-zation of creeping inflation," a phrase which justly epitomizes attempts at monetary adjustment by surplus countries with inflation-prone trade partners. German authorities wished to increase pressure on trade-partner nations to reverse their own policies; the Bank held that sur-plus nations need not be "good creditors" while the deficit countries were neglecting their part of the "rules of the game."[87]

Yet international payments deficits, too, according to the Bundes-bank's pronouncements required contractive monetary measures, be-cause the former are symptomatic of lack of export competitiveness and of excessive costs.[88] Again, in 1962, the Bundesbank took the position that payments deficits "facilitate" restrictive policies, while in early 1966 the Bank claimed that its progressive restrictions were merely intended to "follow the market."[89]

It is quite evident from this much study of the German thinking on macroeconomic goals that these goals were not ends in themselves, but were more or less clearly linked to income-distribution, social-order and geopolitical goals. There are indeed explicit indications from the whole ideological spectrum of effective decision-makers that all economic goals are ultimately subordinate to the more tacit national objectives relating to social order and geopolitical position.

NATIONAL OBJECTIVES AND
PAYMENTS-BALANCE POLICY

Social-Order Objectives

In addition to, and indeed behind, the standard macroeconomic goals of economic policy, and in close connection with the more or less predictable interests of various sectors, it is specially neces-sary to take due account of the German concern for an overall

social-political-economic order.[90] The evidence for the strength of
this concern is easy to find. The American reader may note, in
perusing the Table of Contents of a representative German economic
periodical, that economic policy is discussed in rather different terms
than in the United States. Much stress is laid on social order, income-
and wealth-distribution, welfare considerations, and planning. The
Labor Minister's full title, as another example, is "Minister of Labor
and Social Order." An entire school of political economy centering
on social-order problems--the followers of Walther Eucken--has in
fact flourished in postwar Germany, and has seen its ideas adopted
by leading economic policy-makers, such as former Chancellor
Erhard.[91] Considerations of social order have thus occupied a place
in the forefront of all policy discussions.

The emphasis on social order in postwar Germany, however it
may be overlaid with party-political rhetoric and other special plead-
ing, has its origin in fundamental circumstances. The first of these
is that turn of mind called "German thoroughness," which may denote
anything from profundity to logical consistency to extreme judgments.
It has been noted, almost always in a slightly pejorative way, in various
connections by Germans of all social-policy persuasions.[92] German
history has also played a part in order-consciousness. Germany's
primary industralization and its unification were both relatively recent
and relatively hasty. Hence they were more conscious and less pleas-
ant processes, tending to emphasize the variability of social structures.
And social order in Germany has, superficially at least, been in fact
something of a variable throughout the past century. Belated unification and central-European geography have a large responsibility in this.

The turbulence of the past half century has made the old-liberal
era before 1914 into a sort of shadow norm, to which out-of-context
comparisons are made over and over.[93] The result is a highly ideal-
ized and only half conscious picture of a period when Germany was a
great power and a great exporter, and when the world operated under
a stratified social system and an "automatic" monetary system.[94]

According to Walther Eucken, emphatically if less consistently
seconded by thinkers from Lenin to Keynes, price stability is the
most important technical bulwark of the liberal social order.[95] It
may be remarked that this usefulness in the defense of social order
also provides a useful psychological bulwark of the price-stabilization goal, raising the domestic and foreign parity of the currency to
the status of a religious or philosophical tenet.[96] This interplay of
goals also helps the social-order question to prominence.

Considerations of a geopolitical nature, as well, support the
current social-order emphasis. Germany must deal with the East

while staying a part of the West. Leading Germans consider that ad hoc non-principled policy-making is no match for the eastern system, and that Germany's social market economy is therefore the only existing answer to the challenge of the East in this field.[97] In a somewhat different sense, but with the same geopolitical overtones, the social market economy has also been termed a temporary social strategy for easing Middle-European tensions.

In a narrower focus, the strength and soundness of the Federal Republic's postwar social structure have been cherished as a means of ensuring power weight for the western state's social organization in a reunification of the nation.[98] This element of German social-order consciousness has been much weakened in the era of the Brandt Ostpolitik.

The Ordoists of strictest observance are obsolescent today.* Their old-liberal doctrine was more readily applauded in the forties when it seemed directed against regulation by the Allied occupation and in the fifties when it insinuated a self-congratulatory explanation for the "economic miracle" of recovery, than in the sixties when its postulates collided rather obviously with growing concentration of market power,[99] and with the structural concessions associated with European integration. For the Ordo-liberals, on the contrary, the social market economy was itself a construct that was freely exportable, at least to the rest of industrial Europe. Even in 1971, however, the contrasting phrases "free market order" and "planned-economy model" were considered usable political rhetoric by the Opposition.[100]

In terms of content, the still-prevailing German concept of social order is "neo-liberal," envisaging individual freedom modified by collective welfare considerations. The product of the market economy is to be used and guided by the objectives of the greater social whole of which the market is but a part. The details of the system are very largely economic, reflecting the prime interest of German public opinion.[101]

The social market economy is founded on market-directed allocation and distribution. Mises' market-conformity criterion is often applied to economic-policy measures, despite the great discrepancy between the competitive model of the criterion and the modern reality.[102] Now the smooth working of markets requires "first and foremost" stability of prices.[103] It has already been noted that German

---

*"Ordoists" is a term for the circles led or influenced by Walther Eucken, and associated with Freiburg University and the ORDO yearbook.

leaders often fear loss of international competitiveness as leading to
the end of middle-class saving. Given the German hyperconscious-
ness of the value of money, price stability is held to be a means to
social stability,[104] or even the ultimate test and expression of social
stability.[105] The degree to which social order and price stability are
entwined is illustrated by the way in which the Council of Experts takes
it for granted that society will wish to undo the income-distribution
effects of any price inflation it may permit.[106] Again, a class content
informs the very concepts of wages and pensions: German officials
were able to sue in court for a "maintenance" (Gehalt) more commensurate with their rank--and to win.[107]

For many in Germany, the ideal of a liberal social order includes small government, a low overall tax burder, and conservative
fiscal notions.[108] These ideas are often reinforced by fears for price
stability and the balance of payments, which may be endangered by
state inflation.[109] For this reason, the independent postwar German
central banks have had easily as much respect as, and certainly more
publicity and influence than, the German supreme court.

In selecting areas of government activity for elimination, infrastructural investment and defense are less often attacked than social-
welfare expenditures.[110] In former Chancellor Erhard's ideal state,
the "formed society," the citizen must "freely develop his private
initiatives precisely also in self-provision for the vicissitudes of human
life such as sickness, accident, unemployment, incapacity for work in
old age, etc."[111]

Such an influential popular medium as Die Welt expressed the
feeling that investment fell off in late 1970, less as a result of restrictive policies than through fear of the "social experiments" of the
government.[112] The Brandt government's program of "inner reforms,"
with its explicit recognition that the public sector must expand, has
indeed offended directly against many entrenched ideas, causing noticeable insecurity among industrialists.[113]

In a modern industrial democracy, it is probably illogical to expect tax money to be available for significant social reform. Thus
Finance Minister Möller was forced to admit that his 1971 budget was
"procyclic," since borrowed money was needed for the reforms.[114]
This avenue to reforms was in turn criticized by former Defense
Minister Strauss (CDU) as a typical socialist measure, aimed at popularity but leading to inflation--an assessment which, in its most literal
meaning, can hardly be rebutted.[115]

The upshot of this debate may be indicated by the results of a
poll taken for the Taxpayers Association of Hamburg: "ninety-one

percent of the citizens" agreed to the proposition that price stability should be sought at cost of "somewhat slower" reforms.[116]

On the party-political scene, German concern for social order was embodied in the moderate coalition (sometimes nicknamed "The Political Cartel"), which long antedated the formal party coalition of 1965.[117] The objective of the moderates is of course to thwart any radical movements.[118] Such movements are not altogether invisible in Germany, and their appearance on national ballots there has aroused far more concern than analogous situations have done elsewhere. However, even this motive for social-order concern has recently receded with the waning influence of the much-discussed rightist National Democratic Party.

The impact of these goals on balance-of-payments policy has mainly appeared in a reluctance to attempt adjustment through monetary expansion, especially since really effective measures would have to be drastic and perhaps continuous. In the light of the priority accorded price stability, such measures could be extremely dangerous to their authors.[119] By the same token, adjustment through exchange-rate manipulations or other methods of emphasizing domestic demand could be equally dangerous. Such a concession to the difficulties of Germany's trade partners at the expense of well entrenched German heavy industry, could unite nationalist and industrialists.

Although the implied refusal to adjust implies continuous inflationary pressure from the payments balance, the resulting creeping inflation can be plausibly blamed on big government's planning-and-welfare propensities. Yet as guidance by market forces falters and wage-price freezes and incomes policies are heralded as substitutes, it is becoming increasingly difficult, in Germany as well as elsewhere, to find truly system-conformed policy measures to combat inflation.

Particularly in the present era of rapid change, it would be foolish to characterize German social-order concern in a definitive way. The emphasis on objective interests and on payments-balance applications in the above discussion is not meant to deny the subjective goodwill or the beneficial possibilities of the social-order debates.

Geopolitical Objectives

Concern with Germany's geopolitical position appears to incorporate and override all other public goals, to judge by the pronouncements of spokesmen from the whole spectrum of ruling moderate political opinion.[120] This concern has found expression in two

distinct but related phases in the period under review. The objective
during the first phase can be summarized as survival of the West
German system in its politically and geographically exposed position
pending reunification.[121]

The second-phase objective may be described as survival of the
West German system through fostering of, commitment to, and possible
dominance of a broad and deep west European union. This change of
emphasis had two main grounds: the obvious solidification of world-
wide vested interests in the division of Germany, and the need for
small European states to defend themselves from United States financial power. An important intermediate step between the two phases
of policy was the Brandt government's initiation in 1969 of active steps
toward détente with the East. These transitional and second-phase
geopolitical goals will be discussed, along with the most recent events,
in Chapter 7.

The first aim above implies sufficient maneuverability between
the eastern and western camps, based on friendship with a strong
western bloc, to take advantage of openings for an eastern détente,
together with internal preparedness to assimilate the areas to be reunited.[122]

Friendship with a strong western bloc requires sensitivity to
foreign concerns about the German payments balance and avoidance
of any action disruptive of western solidarity and strength.[123] Germany
feels itself particularly dependent on the United States, and has made
repeated concessions to United States demands on the troop-money
issue.[124] Germany is also highly sensitive to world criticism of
its payments surpluses, [125] so long as these do not take the form of
open pressure which would be politically embarassing at home: the one
image perhaps most damaging to a German regime is still that of the
"stab in the back"--of having made unwarranted concessions under
foreign pressure, as (supposedly) at Versailles in 1919.[126] Although
Germany is much concerned to maintain NATO troops within its
boundaries, the Czech crisis of 1968 reduced fears on that score for
the moment, thus freeing Germany for its independent role in the
Bonn conference of that year.[127] There, thinly veiled threats of troop
withdrawals were rebuffed.[128]

To avoid disruptions to the western alliance, Bonn must be prepared to sacrifice its payments surplus whenever this threatens either
to drive its trade partners to protectionism[129] or to weaken the Bretton Woods system which permits the favorable German trade and
financial position.[130]

Throughout the sixties, Germany has been widening its options
in the East.[131] Financial strength supports German maneuverability,

removing the domestic and international stigma of bargaining from weakness. In the words of Economics Minister Schiller, Germany need no longer be an economic giant and a "political dwarf,"[132] especially in those fields, like the monetary field, where domestic policy shades over into foreign policy. Germany, according to the Minister, must use its economic and financial tools for foreign-policy goals, while "classic" foreign policy must be postponed until reunification.[133] Chancellor Kiesinger and Dr. Emminger of the Bundesbank have echoed this line of thought.[134] The Council of Experts saw that foreign-policy uses of economic tools may prevent the execution of a consistent economic policy.[135]

Part of Germany's monetary strength is a matter of the prestige of a "strong" currency.[136] "The respect for a country [is] considerably determined by the quality of its currency; also its economic and political freedom of action is largely dependent on it."[137] According to opinion polls, Germans are quite proud of the DM's present world role.[138] Partly again, German strength stems from the nation's hoard of reserves which can help it to give development aid in the "third world," and inter-central-bank aid to its allies. In general, the great German export success itself is felt to have brought Germany from postwar "insignificance" to world respect.[139]

Germany's surprisingly strong stand against its united allies and its cavalier-seeming style in November 1968 were accompanied by widespread speculation at home and abroad that the "balance of power" had shifted to Bonn.[140] More outspoken journalists wrote that Germany would "never again" be a second-class ally.[141] This again illustrates the reality, at least psychological, of this objective.

Internal preparedness to assimilate reunited territories, finally, requires a healthy social system and sufficient industrial power both to dilute and absorb eastern elements and to provide the reunited country with a per capita industrial production commensurate with "great power" status. (As an indication of the seriousness of this task: in 1967, if industrial production per capita in France is set equal to 100, that in West Germany was 152, while that in East Germany was 131.)[142] The connection of this objective with social-order goals and with export-industry interests is fairly close.

The development of Germany's geopolitical objectives in the past two years will be discussed in Chapter 7.

DOMESTIC INTERESTS AND
PAYMENTS-BALANCE POLICY

Interests in Functional
Income Distribution

A third major class of goals underlying economic-policy formulation, and not entirely separable from the objectives already discussed, comprises the interests of groups. Policy-makers and observers alike claim that interest groups in Germany are unusually
strong, well defined, self-conscious--and cynical.[143] The Council of
Experts has called this class of goal more important in many regards
than the major avowed goals.[144] Certainly, the links of the income-
distribution issue with price stability and with the balance of international payments ought to be fairly clear to policy-makers.[145]

One need, once again, only glance over the Table of Contents of
a German general economics periodical to note the marked emphasis
which income distribution receives in German economic thinking. In
part this emphasis has its explanation in Middle-European events of
the past half century; in part it may reflect an older conception of
political economy in which income distribution perhaps seemed reasonably amenable to study in market-mechanical terms; in part , too, it
is a reflection of the influential conviction that the income-distribution
question is "political dynamite."[146] Fundamentally, indeed, the question has become crucial largely because of the fading of belief in the
market as an automatic and defensibly fair distributor of incomes,
and because of the related international upsurge of inflation.[147] The
consequent recent emphasis on incomes policy, normally carrying a
strong connotation of repressing labor's income share, has already
been discussed.

Many factors account for the political explosiveness of the income distribution question, which has been called the biggest issue of
the 1969 German election.[148] Germany's existing income distribution
is relatively skewed.* Its tax structure on balance probably aggravates
this situation.[149] Germany's factor-endowment proportions are shifting, causing labor-market tensions, while foreign labor from poorer
countries is being actively recruited. Meanwhile the chronic balance-
of-payments surplus appears to be forcing German workers to finance
the higher living standards in richer deficit lands.

---

*Data in this area are only sketchy (JG 1964, Section 114; JG
1965, Section 192; see also Chancellor Brandt's " inaugural" address,
AP 1969, #85, p. 4).

Over against this state of affairs stand the traditions of the Social Democratic Party, which in the period under review moved from opposition, to coalition, to governing.[150] The labor unions, too, while economically and ideologically in transition, have a strong tradition in favor of the "political wage," i.e., wage shifts which alter the distribution of income.[151] After the wildcat strikes of September 1969, union memberships have become more radical, and have pushed their leaders into bolder stances.[152] Yet the controversial "codetermination" of wages by labor and property, which has been debated in Germany for twenty years, has not been achieved even by the "Socialist" Brandt government.

The shadow of eastern Germany falls on this area also. Bundesbank President Blessing complained that the image of the Democratic Republic, which "enjoys" comparative equality of income distribution, "radiates" into the Federal Republic. In much the same vein, the Council of Experts urged changed attitudes toward work and labor discipline, "such as even the socialist countries are developing."[153] The western republic has also been contemplating the day when it might be called upon to assimilate the east socially.

As against these factors of tension and change, the stance of the industrial "work-givers" associations continues to oppose wage rises to "make up for" past income shifts or to "anticipate inflation."*[154] Taken literally, along with "competitive" pricing under the stimulus of foreign demand, these ideas amount to a call for a steady erosion of labor's income share. Former Chancellor Erhard also at one time raised the issue of income shifts in connection with social integration into the Common Market, going so far as to exclaim that German workers couldn't "morally" live better than other European workers.

Any impasse over income distribution could reawaken latent radicalism in Germany and perhaps resuscitate its former alliance with property.

In the light of these sensitive problems, Germany's international payments situation has been specially difficult to meet. "Excess" foreign demand produces price inflation through its liquidity and direct-price-transmission effects. But this excess demand can only be finally eliminated by price inflation. In the early sixties German leaders reached a rather vague consensus that some control over this situation could be had by instituting an "incomes policy"--although "wages policy" was apparently uppermost in many minds.

---

*In German, a "work-giver" (<u>Arbeitgeber</u>) is an employer, a "work-taker" (Arbeitnehmer) is an employee.

When the upvaluation of March 1961 was widely criticized a-
broad as insufficient to stem speculation, the Bundesbank deliberately
permitted an internal price rise to continue the realignment of German
with foreign price levels. This realignment had a noticeable effect on
labor's share of national income, which then rose at its fastest pace
of the period under review.[155] Incomes policy became an especially
acute desideratum at this juncture, and was in fact repeatedly urged
on surplus nations by foreign and international bodies.[156] The ensuing
discussion in Germany culminated in the introduction of the Council-
of-Experts bill in mid-1962.

The Council of Experts has in some ways far transcended the
mandate many of its sponsors intended. (See the following section.)
It has, however, also developed a recognizable income-distribution
outlook. Despite many rather technical-looking reservations, the
basic element in the Council's incomes policy has been the simplified
productivity wage.*[157] As the Council acknowledges, this productivity-
wage guideline assumes a given functional distribution of income as
"developing" in the given state of "competition." Stripping the quoted
words of euphemism, the guideline assumes the functional income-
shares that have developed from a given degree of monopoly, and it
makes little provision for these shares to "develop" any further.
Indeed, the Council elsewhere calls it an "open question" whether a
noticeable long-run reduction of the profit share of national income is
possible. That the degree of monopoly is rather high in Germany may
be confirmed, among much else, by the fact that in many industries
wage changes have not been significantly related to price changes.
The Joint Working Group of the German Economic Research Institutes
affirmed in its 1971 report that the degree of monopoly in the goods
markets had increased in recent years.[158]

The Council seemed to confirm its adherence (at least for policy-
formulation purposes) to its implicit simplified income-distribution
model when it stated that a lower "profit rate" (which in the context
is the Council's diplomatic synonym for "property share of income")
will lower either investment or prices.[159]

In proposing a productivity-wage guideline the Council is agree-
ing with a constantly emphasized thesis of the Bundesbank.[160] President Blessing also understood that crude productivity wages freeze
functional income shares, but felt that this guideline would help

-----

*Stability in payments balance, in capital-costs per unit of out-
put, and in terms of trade was indeed stipulated in the original formulation; but the Council of Experts later (JG 1969, Section 75) modified its formulations to eliminate these unmeasurable elements.

distribute productivity gains to fixed-income receivers.[161] Since such distribution could only take place if prices fell, this line of reasoning seems to ignore the very inflationary structure which makes incomes policy a relevant issue.

Under President Klasen the Bundesbank pleaded for restraint "on both sides" in setting wages. Wage rises above "productivity" would "automatically" produce price rises. In this presentation, wages seem subject to discretion and moderation, while prices are automatic. The implicit technical assumption is competition in goods markets, bilateral monopoly in labor markets. This may be closer to the truth in Germany's open economy than it is, for example, in the United States.

The productivity-wage guideline has also been favored by industry, the OECD ("for simplicity") and the European Economic Community.

The income-distribution model behind much of this thinking can be made explicit rather easily.

(IV. 1) $W = (Y - Y^K)/L$

(IV. 2) $= \dfrac{1/PQ}{1/PQ} \cdot (Y - Y^K)/L$

(IV. 3) $= \dfrac{(Y - Y^K)/Y}{L/PQ}$

(IV. 4) $= (Y - Y^K)/Y \cdot PQ/L$

(IV. 5) $= \lambda \cdot P \cdot \pi$

Where W = average wage rate = Y^L/L
$\quad Y$ = nominal national income = $PQ = Y^L + Y^K$
$\quad L$ = labor units employed
$\quad Y^K$ = property income
$\quad Y^L$ = labor income = WL
$\quad P$ = price level
$\quad Q$ = real output
$\quad \lambda = Y^L/Y$
$\quad \pi = Q/L$

Here a rise in the productivity wage (W/π) must raise either labor's share in national income or the price level.[162]

The productivity-wage guideline is also weak in that it suppresses the completely analogous formulations that can be made based on property-income share, government-income share, or the payments-balance "share." If any of these magnitudes rise relative to productivity, the price level will rise. If in such a case labor is not to "anticipate inflation" in its wage demands, its income share must decline. Productivity wages and imported inflation together, therefore, will tend to lower labor's income share. In response to the repeated shortrun attempts to apply the crude productivity-wage guideline, Minister Schiller had to point out the meaninglessness of such a procedure.[163]

Indeed, inflation of any origin may be expected to favor the property-income share, since prices are freer to move at short-term than are the pace-setting industrial wages.[164] This is because the very nature of collective bargaining, and of the service "labor" has to sell, dictates long-term wage contracts. Escalator clauses based on price-level experience cannot eliminate this lag without retroactive features.

Further, unless a rise in wages, intended to make up for wage lags, also raises labor's average propensity to save, labor's income share will fall further. (See equation III in Chapter 1.) Thus wage lags can most effectively be recovered by increased wages in the form of savings.[165] Such measures have been under discussion and voluntary trial in Germany for years.[166]

In connection with all of the preceding paragraphs, the following caveats must be emphasized. The overall long-run proportions of functional income distribution are set by the "physical" factor endowment; the social power of the classes of income receivers, based on the society's ideology and expectations;[167] and the degree of monopoly, i.e., the legally-based elements of social power concerned with property rights, the openness of the economy, and the like. The merely arithmetic and tautological elements of the income-distribution situation must be looked upon as recitations of possible means of shifting income distribution and so of expressing a shift in social power.

Again, the suggestions about income-distribution mechanisms derived from identities are especially vulnerable to misplaced assumptions of ceteris paribus. This assumption, which is inevitably implicit in any explicit formulation, often excludes from consideration unexpressed mechanisms which are actually at work in reality.

Finally, the underlying measurements of the variables entering into income-distribution formulations are often weak. For example, where "theory" elegantly claims $P \cdot \pi \cdot \lambda = W$, the actual numerical manipulations that are possible are carried out in terms of

$$PQ/Q \cdot \frac{WL/L}{WL/PQ \cdot PQ/Q} \cdot WL/PQ = WL/L^*$$

Here, the measured variables are PQ, WL, L and Q. Thus W is not directly measured, and π itself only <u>seems</u> to be physical. Since Q is derived statistically from PQ, it depends on demand; and since L is actual manhours worked, it too depends on demand.

The continued popularity of productivity-wage guidelines is a revealing commentary on the poverty of the market-based rationale of income distribution under imperfect markets.[168]

The tendency of payments-balance surplus to occasion a redistribution of income up the income scale has already been explained, as has the tendency of the actual German policies to produce an import of labor from countries of lower marginal labor productivity. Under defensible assumptions, this can readily be shown to cheapen labor relative to the situation warranted by factor endowments and technological possibilities. (According to a poll, interestingly, seventy-three percent of Germans would express the opinion that foreign workers should not be imported into Germany at all.)[169] While the alternative to payments surplus, accelerated inflation to adjust international price levels, would itself tend to transfer income to the wealthy, it would at the same time reduce the advantage of the export industries. Finally, correcting the liquidity effects of payments surplus through private capital exports would, by reducing domestic demand and increasing foreigners' liquidity, preserve both the export industries' advantage and the general income-advantage of property. Even governmental capital outflows would have much the same effect, if the funds were borrowed domestically or were raised by the regressive tax system. The strategy least favorable to property (short of a once-for-all adjustment) would be to correct the payments balance by inflation-financed government capital export. Thus under fixed exchange rates all the possible reactions to a continuing surplus-producing payments-balance disturbance favor property, and most of them also favor the export sector.

Sectoral Interests

Obviously, a "key issue" in the examination of postwar German balance-of-payments policy is the extent to which it has been influenced by the interests of export-oriented industry.[170] Since the motivations

---

*Symbols are as in Equations I through IV.

and causes of Germany's surplus are the theme of this entire study,
only the most striking institutional influences will be noted here. The
influential position of the export branches in Germany is explained
by a number of factors, besides the postwar structural processes already noted.

German export industry is generally credited with political
strength at least commensurate with its economic importance. In
addition, heavy industry in Germany has a specially close institutional
connection with the financial community and in particular with the
three "big banks." These big banks have shown a remarkable tenacity
of their power position through all the vicissitudes of the past half-
century, and today maintain close relations with the monetary authorities.

The Bundesbank has called the export sector its "chief ally" in
its price-stabilization campaign.[171] This sector has remained influential in the Bundestag throughout the period under review, leading
the opposition to the revaluation of 1961, opposing the 1964 and 1968
border-tax adjustments, and resisting the 1969 revaluation.[172]

German heavy industry as a whole appears to have reacted
consistently unfavorably to any proposal calculated to require measurable restructuring of that sector. Both flexible exchange rates and
full adjustment through financial policy, for example, would realign
the German domestic price-level with the effective price level abroad,
and so spur a reorientation of German resources, very possibly entailing some losses of capital values in the great industries affected.[173]
Both of these classes of measure have been opposed by German industry throughout the period under study.[174]

To discountenance effective adjustment policies is tacitly to accept
the automatic effects of non-adjustment, notably a more or less gradual
inflation. True, it has been claimed that domestic cost rises through
this inflation are at least as harmful to the export industries as would
be effective price drops abroad through revaluation.[175] However, the
imported inflation affects the export-oriented industries' foreign and
domestic prices before their domestic costs. In the face of a progressive international disparity of price levels, such a lagged inflation
would necessarily remain insufficient to remove the competitive advantage of German exports. It would in fact further the export bias
of industry and the skewness of income distribution, particularly if
it were reinforced in these effects by a tight domestic monetary policy.

German agriculture is protected from imports and subsidized
in exporting according to a Common-Market harmonization scheme
based on the pegged-exchange-rate system. Continued undervaluation
of the DM increases the protection and the subsidy.

The traditional strength of the great German banks has been noted. The popularity of their intermediation and their consequent financial dominance of the capital market have likewise been explained. The banks' influence is further enhanced by the apparently unusual number of interlocking directorates with firms dependent upon them for capital.[176] The largest German banks also habitually vote the shares of stock deposited with them by customers (Depotstimmrecht).[177] Finally, the banks are influential in the state levels of the federated central-banking apparatus.

The institutional connections of the great banks to heavy industry appear to identify the perceived interests of the two sectors.[178] It is notable that the savings banks, less tied to heavy industry, publicly show much more recognition and fear of imported inflation than do the great banks.

Lasting undervaluation also requires restrictive monetary measures to reabsorb inflows of liquidity from the payments balance. The resulting dear money can be shown a priori to benefit bank profits in most normal circumstances.[179] The Council of Experts points out that it did do so in Germany.[180]

The Position of the Financial Managers

Here attention will be directed to another kind of "interest," that of the financial technocracy, which is not altogether different from other interests concerned with power and income, and which is certainly capable of influencing policy.

The well-developed cooperation among national monetary authorities is "the most important characteristic of the present phase of the international monetary system."[181] Bundesbank President Blessing calls this cooperation "the most essential part of the gold-exchange system" and French Finance Minister Giscard d'Estaing points to its "very happy effects."[182] Since World War II there has been a growing technicization of monetary controls, resulting in a behind-the-scenes expertise which is neither the outright political money control of wartime nor the impersonal automatism of gold.[183] "Cooperation" of this kind is made necessary by a system of exchange rates which, while pegged, are rarely permitted to force real adjustment. Although fixed rates are credited with automatism by their advocates, pegged and supported exchange rates require more, rather than less, "cooperation" than would flexible rates. These latter, although accused of requiring or tempting over-much intervention and of fostering market confusion, could probably stave off the market confusion recently experienced with far less than the present level of intervention.[184]

As matters now stand, with vast inter-central-bank support arrangements, with various IMF instruments and international agreements supplying ever larger proportions of the world's international liquidity, with the resplitting of the gold market and with the subsequent arrangements with South Africa, it is no more than the truth that highly technical and routine cooperative management by men deeply involved in the respective national financial communities can move the world monetary system into positions where the political leaders are presented with faits accomplis.[185] A system characterized by abrupt, publicly undiscussed monetary measures such as revaluations is more authoritarian than democratic.[186]

Some clue to the attitudes of the cooperative managers may lie in the thoughts expressed by Vice President Otmar Emminger of the Bundesbank, who holds the "portfolio" for international affairs among the Bundesbank directors and who accordingly is Germany's representative in most important international monetary bodies. Dr. Emminger's remarks on international monetary arrangements have recently shifted their focus from more general world-wide cooperation to more closeknit EEC integration. The first of these two emphases will be discussed here, the second in Chapter 7.

In Dr. Emminger's earlier, more general, formulations, a special (identifiable or responsible) international monetary coordinating organization is not needed.[187] What is required is not more explicit machinery, but rather "harmony" in the "philosophy" of the international monetary managers.[188] As Emminger suggestively points out in a closely related passage, mass democracy and welfarism often conflict with balance-of-payments discipline.

Emminger proceeds from the assumption that the money managers are in a position to present the parliaments with the choice of reducing welfare commitments or facing a balance-of-payments catastrophe.[189] A historian might detect an interesting parallel between this view of Western integration and Hamilton's ideas on American union.

Within such a technocratic system, the German financial authorities see themselves as carrying special weight, partly because of German financial strength, and partly because of the domestic independence of the German monetary authorities themselves.[190] Given their position within the cooperative international system, the German monetary authorities have generally favored the pegged-exchange-rate system and decentralized, cooperative world monetary integration. The peg system, which requires compensating reserve movements, is a necessary element in the financial strength of Germany and thus of its monetary authorities. It is this system also, as opposed to the gold standard, that makes necessary the managerial cooperation. The

Bundesbank long felt that the crises of the pegged system could "force" "philosophical harmony" (and perhaps social-policy harmony) in the Common Market. The Bank has also speculated that a Common-Market bloc, once formed, could possibly force the same "harmony" on the world.[191]

This "philosophical" integration appeared to be worth some risk to the more obvious trade and payments integration, in the eyes of Germany's money managers. Thus, for example, it was hoped that protecting the exchange-rate pegs by a coupon or border tax, though disruptive of integration in the ordinary sense, might eventually force stabilization measures on Germany's trade partners.

Here it appears that both purely bureaucratic interests and considerations of social order and world position may have influenced the German monetary authorities in their attitude toward the adjustment mechanism. The mutual impacts of European monetary integration and the European financial technocracy will be developed in Chapter 7.

CHIEF GERMAN PAYMENTS-BALANCE POLICY INSTITUTIONS

A review of the German balance-of-payments policy environment can be conveniently completed by a discussion of the organization, institutional position and characteristic thinking of the three most prominent and most articulate balance-of-payments policy-making and policy-debating agencies. These are the Council of Experts, the Bundesbank and the economic cabinet of the government.

Each agency's institutional position and personnel help to determine how the goals investigated above bear on that organization's policy. Goals are borne in on the policy agencies through the need to remain effective by ensuring official and public cooperation and support; through the psychological preoccupations of the agencies' decision makers, who are normally imbued with the general social goals, yet tend to assess the general welfare in terms of their own past experience; and through the personal and group interests of the decision makers. These relationships will be noted as necessary in the discussion to follow.

The Council of Experts

The German economic policy-formulating machinery contains an agency of somewhat unusual constitution, the Council of Experts for the Evaluation of Economic Trends.* This was appointed as of February 14, 1964 (law of 14 August, 1963) to research and report annually thereafter on the workings of the German economy. The Council's observations were to be aimed at the goals of price stability, "high" employment, "equilibrium" in international payments, and growth, within the framework of a free market economy.[193] Also to be considered were wealth and income distribution, the "balance" of supply and demand, and any undesirable trends.

It is interesting to remember that the creation of the Council resulted from widespread income-distribution concerns, which have, however, received relatively little attention in its charter.[194] It is also worthwhile to note that the Council has given no special prominence to this article of its mandate.[195] The most obvious ground for this has been a lack of adequate statistics. Every year the Council has called most pointedly for improvement in this area from its legally assigned secretariat, the Federal Statistical Office.[196] However, the statisticians and the Bundesrat, supported by the Finance Minister, have repeatedly rebuffed these requests.[197]

The Council was to be composed of five men appointed by the federal government for five-year terms. The work is essentially of a "part-time" nature. In March 1968 and annually thereafter one member, chosen by lot, was to withdraw. Since Council members must be economic experts, but cannot have been employed in an economic-policy capacity, except as a teacher, during one year prior to appointment, only professors and those retired from other occupations are practically eligible.

The Council's Evaluation is officially addressed to the Bundestag, but is to be retained first by the cabinet, for time periods which were altered in 1967 after the Council complained of delays in almost every year.[198] The new arrangements did not prevent the 1968 report from being more seriously delayed than ever before.

The Council is forbidden by its charter to recommend specific measures. This provision has effectively become a dead letter, inasmuch as the Council's projections and predictions necessarily always examine the pros and cons of alternative policy choices. Over the

---

*Official translations of the Council's title vary. The title pages of English editions of the Evaluations read "Council of Experts on Economic Development;" the Council's secretariat published a letter (JG 1964, p. 144) addressed to the "Council of Experts for the Evaluation of the Country's Economic Trends."

years the Council has become bolder with fully detailed policy pro-
posals.199

Although the Advisors are appointed by the government, few ap-
pointments could be suspected as attempts to "pack" the Council in
favor of the current policy. The Council also needs some minimal
cooperation of government in order to function; yet, as it has in fact
received even less cooperation, on the whole, than the law prescribes,
the Council's obligation to the government is weak even in this regard.
The Council needs a modicum of popular support, and has by and large
achieved it through evident consistency and independence, some catchy
ideas, and apparent full acceptance of the German socioeconomic order
as it stands. The personal background of the Advisors may be expected
to make them tend toward academic formulations of goals, institutionally independent in analysis but well within the socially "safe" degree
of radical criticism.

From February 1964 until March 1968, the Council was composed
of three professors of economic subjects and two retired civil servants
and statesmen. According to its own assessment, the Council was not
chosen with an eye to its possible unanimity, although others expressed
doubts about the choices.200 The Council, in any case, showed a surprising degree of unanimity. During this early period of unanimity,
the Council also displayed great consistency and a certain adroitness
in public relations. It demarcated for itself areas of direct involvement (as in initiating "concerted action" talks), created politically
effective concepts and phrases, and attempted to mobilize a "constituency" among the public.

Almost at once, the Council put before the public the concepts
of domestic and foreign "protection" of German growth policy.201
By this was meant employment of any of various alternative safeguards
against inflation resulting from cyclical policy designed to ensure steady
growth.202 The safeguard measures were to prevent domestic inflation in times of expansionary policy and imported inflation in times
of restrictive policy.

The twin safeguard measures gradually elaborated by the Council
were "incomes policy" and upvaluation or a surrogate. The exact forms
of each of the two measures would necessarily be interdependent.203
In its 1965 Evaluation the Council tried to interest the government in
its incomes-policy concept of "concerted action," a form of indicative
planning of functional national-income shares. This was made necessary,
in the Council's view, by the phenomenon of wage lag, which required
stabilization cooperation among social and economic sectors. Since the
government's budgeting was based on expected revenues, its cooperation was also essential. In the debate on the Evaluation, Chancellor

Erhard refused to take part in concerted action, although he himself had been among the first to suggest incomes cooperation in 1955.[204] The government instead demanded a "simultaneous" halt to all price and wage rises, without previous restructuring of government finances.[205]

Undaunted, the Council undertook to inaugurate regular concerted-action talks with business and labor groups.[206] Response to these initiatives was good, partly because the Council, as opposed to the government, had consistently given both labor and business credit for price restraint, while castigating the disorder in government finances.[207] The phrase "order in government finances," which became the slogan before which the Erhard government fell, received great impetus in the Council's Evaluation.

The new grand-coalition government gave the Council's 1967 Evaluation its first really orderly, reasonable and even friendly response. The Erhard government, by contrast, had ignored the Council's initial warnings of June 1964, questioned the 1964 Evaluation's legality, and raised the same issue in 1965.[208] In this "cold war" the government also avoided meeting or consulting with the Council.[209]

Economics Minister Schiller of the new government associated his Ministry with the concerted-action talks.[210] He had previously defended the Council "passionately" against Chancellor Erhard.[211] Although Minister Schiller studied the Council's latest, more detailed and quantified incomes-policy concept, the "framework pact," the Council found it wise to withdraw the idea after it was rejected by the Christian Democrat leadership, amid general criticism.[212] Minister Schiller was also able to request and receive from the Council its support of his fiscal expansionary program for the slump.[213] Large parts of the Stability Law, as finally passed (Chapter 5) incorporated the Council's ideas.[214]

The more receptive new government was, however, not ready to accept the Council's concept for foreign "protection" of German policy: greater exchange-rate flexibility. Only this, the Council argued, could stop imported inflation, which itself made the framework-pact wage guidelines unfair to labor.[215] Three Council members had signed the international economists' declaration of support for broader flexibility in February 1966.[216]

The appointment made to fill the March 1968 opening on the Council perhaps reflected the Kiesinger government's concern over the Council's exchange-rate stand. The withdrawing retired official was replaced with a fourth professor, Wolfgang Stützel, a former banker and editor of the central-bank Monthly Report, who was known for his view that the Bundesbank should defend the parity in order to force the government and Germany's trade partners to alter their policies, even if this meant importing inflation for long periods.217 Stützel thus articulated within the Council the current views of the cabinet majority and the Bundesbank.

A harmony of the three major policy agencies was not to be thus created, however. As the French and Czech crises shook Europe over the summer of 1968, and mobile money began once again to favor the basic strength of the DM, disagreement appears to have mounted within the Council. In mid-September 1968, Professor Stützel resigned his Council membership, citing, in general terms, this disagreement.218 Not two weeks later the Council asked Chancellor Kiesinger to apply some form of external "protection" before speculation forced his hand. This warning was repeated twice more in October.219

There was a great deal of apparent confusion over the annual Evaluation, which was received at the Chancellery on November 18, 1968 with a plea for immediate publication. On November 19 the border-tax adjustment was decided by the cabinet (Chapter 3). Despite wide criticism, the Bundestag debated this measure without having seen the Evaluation. Again in 1969, the Council's Special Evaluation, submitted during the May crisis, was not published for weeks.220 On both these occasions, the Council, unable to mobilize its public constituency, personally and dramatically intervened in the government's deliberations.*

Minister Franz-Josef Strauss publicly labelled the Council's activities "terrorist influencing" of others and "manipulation of opinion." The hysterical tone of this reaction from a leading Minister is eloquent testimony to the growing power of the Council. Strauss' tone also provoked the indignant resignation of one Council member. The other four members remained to participate vigorously in the fall 1969 exchange crisis, releasing two Special Evaluations and a letter to Minister Schiller, all stressing the desirability of revaluation and even of flexible exchange rates.221

Throughout 1970, the Council blamed continuing inflation on the lateness of the 1969 revaluation. However, the Council began urging

---

*In May 1969, Dr. Emminger of the Bundesbank and Hermann Abs of the Bank Association were asked to argue the revaluation question privately before Chancellor Kiesinger. While this debate was still underway, members of the Council appeared to urge the introduction of flexible exchange rates, a démarche which Bundesbank President Blessing, himself then advocating upvaluation, very promptly labeled "disastrous" (AP 1969, #39, p. 4).

restrictive financial-policy measures almost at once, especially upon the reluctant government. Although prepared for a shift of policy since the government's mid-year package of measures, the Council as a whole in fact saw no real grounds for relaxation until after the floating of the DM in mid-1971.[222]

Altogether, the energy, boldness and persistence of the Council has been remarkable, even given its formal independence. Its earlier unanimity and decisiveness has, it is true, to some extent weakened since the complete turnover of the Council after mid-1969, and the advent of frequent legally-required resignations. The Council does not consider itself an advisor to the government, but rather an aid to public judgment.[223] It has developed its own channels of influence and its own constituency, whose "trust" it has on occasion refused to disappoint, and from whom it at one point refused to "ask for more sacrifice."[224] In spite of its claim not to wish to override political opposition, the Council in its first five years did in fact do so, eventually "capturing the government," which slowly absorbed each of the Council's ideas.[225] The combination of independence and strictly technical presentation has aided in this success: the Council's ideas cannot be dismissed as party-political apologia, as is possible in the United States. The government complained bitterly of the 1967 Special Evaluation that it was a "directly effective economic-policy measure" in the form of a self-fulfilling prophecy.[226] The very publishing of the report, it was held, affected the marginal efficiency of capital (i.e., expectations), tying recovery to the government investment program supported by the Council.

By means both public and private, both powerful and subtle, the Council has in some degree "sold" all of its original ideas to German policy-makers. An example of this is the most recent experiment in floating exchange rates (Chapter 3) considered well-nigh unthinkable at the Council's inception. Another example is "concerted action," a form of mild indicative planning adopted by the Economics Ministry, participation in which has at times been regarded by some outsiders as a privilege.[227] It might not be unrealistic to refer some of the Council's fervor and persistence to the memories of interwar economic-policy blunders which are quite vivid in the minds of German economists of the Council's generation.[228]

The Bundesbank

While not quite so constitutionally unique as the Council of Experts, the Bundesbank occupies an unusual position among central banks. Created in 1958, after a long debate, from the less centralized Bank deutscher Länder, the Bundesbank, both de jure and de facto, is able to implement its policy ideas with more independence of the current political administration than perhaps any other central bank.[229] "The organs of management of the Deutsche Bundesbank are on a par with the highest federal authorities and are not subject to instructions from the federal government."[230] The Bank "is a special part of the executive, entrusted as an autonomous body with the responsibility for monetary and credit policy." Its obligation to support general economic policy "consistent with its functions. . .is not to be interpreted as meaning that the Bundesbank's policy must be subordinated to general economic policy." The law provides for mutual consultation, but makes no real provision against prolonged conflict, between Bundesbank and government.[231]

Karl Blessing, a Reichsbank officer and director until 1939, later German chief of Unilever,[232] was the Bundesbank's President throughout the period under review, until the end of 1969.* Beginning with 1970, Hamburg banker Karl Klasen, an old friend of Economics Minister Schiller, assumed the Bundesbank's presidency.[233] Both Presidents are members of the Social Democratic Party. They were assisted by an ex officio Monetary Council, composed of selected members of a wider Board of Directors chosen on a federal basis. These men, who operate all the monetary tools at discretion, must by law be financial experts.[234]

By administrative agreement, the government must consult with the Bundesbank before making parity changes. The Bank is not legally bound to defend any parity.[235]

The Bundesbank's elaborate legal independence of government does not mean that it can always follow the monetary course of its choice. Quite apart from the problems caused by the payments balance, an uncooperative government can make the Bank's policies politically impossible. Despite the traditionally firm public and business support of the Bank, too much leaning against a government policy of expansion, for example, will call forth protests from domestic-oriented firms. In general the Bank has been in agreement with the·ideas of the German financial community, which themselves have been consistently favorable to the kind of "sound," "stable" milieu needed by modern concentrated industry, and especially by export-oriented industry. The Directors of the Bank appear to be personally involved with the announced macroeconomic goals, with the conceptions of the financial community, and with the viewpoints of the cooperative world financial managers.

---

*The only President of the earlier Bank deutscher Länder, during its existence, had a strikingly similar career (Veit, Grundriss, p. 572n).

The Bundesbank has not been hesitant in exercising its powers,
not only claiming autonomy for itself, but also frequently insisting
that government conform to the Bank's policy intentions.[236] In its
pronouncements the Bank has handled traditionally political areas,
warning the government on such matters as "election gifts"and the
"illusions"in its social policy.[237] On the very day of the Kiesinger
government's first policy declaration, the Bank issued a pointed
refusal to cooperate.[238] In the Stability Law debate, Bundesbank
President Blessing was accused of reinforcing his point of view with
threats concerning future monetary policy. Blessing also replied
(in the negative) to the Council of Experts' 1968 Special Evaluation
even before the government could do so, to the chagrin of Economics
Minister Schiller.[239] President Klasen's outspoken criticism of
government policy and of current wage negotiations, on occasion of
refusing to lower rediscount rate in January 1971, was accused of
being a political "demonstration"and of being in effect an attempt to
conduct fiscal policy.[240] Despite this, the Bank and its supporters
react sharply to either control or criticism of the Bank as "bringing
the Bundesbank into politics."[241]

Powerfully influenced in its institutional shape and through its
personnel by memories of Germany's two great inflations, the Bundesbank has consistently seen defense of the DM's domestic value and
international parity as the primary goal, not only of its own, but of
all economic policy.[242] The links seen by Bank spokesmen among
price stability, growth, social policy and the payments balance have
been explored above. In practice, the Bundesbank has had to give way
steadily in its crusade for price stability: injections of new money
were made at a steady pace (Tables L), and elaborately explained in
the Bank's commentary as merely meeting "the needs of trade."[243]

In regard to the external parity and its repercussions, the
Bundesbank was a consistent exponent of the "stability-export"thesis:
it saw Germany as capable of forcing its trade partners to adopt
policies designed to end their ex ante inflation, and minimized the
dangers of growth bias and growth export, liquidity overhang, boomerang, and creeping inflation. Under extreme speculative and political
pressure which threatened the international monetary system, however, the Bundesbank has both in 1961 and in 1968-1969 agreed to
the wisdom of revaluation of the DM.

Under Klasen, the Bank has supported the government's stance
on European monetary integration, calling for harmonization of
social, economic and political structures as a prerequisite for union.

The Bundesbank long complained bitterly that it was being
forced by the government's policies to bear the whole burden of price

stabilization; but at the same time the Bank seemed to feel that it could succeed eventually in forcing government to conform to "the dictatorship of empty coffers."[244] As restrictive monetary measures seemed likely to stop growth before they could stop inflation, the Bundesbank began to emphasize policy-mix considerations. However, the Bank continued to distrust the rounded anticyclical tools favored by Minister Schiller and the Council of Experts. In the event, the Bank under Klasen has had to complain of the government's slowness to use its restrictive anticyclical tools.

Characteristic Bank thinking on income-distribution has been noted above. It may be added here that President Blessing's public observations on social processes were full, but often seemed superficial,[245] while President Klasen has been somewhat more reticent in this field.

The Economic Cabinet

The third important official policy body is the government's "economic cabinet," comprising ten ministers under the chairmanship of the Economics Minister. In most respects its nature, activities and goal-orientation do not differ much from those of other similar parliamentary-based bodies. The policy attitudes of the successive governments cannot be detailed here, but will be made clear wherever desirable for the understanding of given policy discussions.

An unusual and at times important feature of the Federal Republic's Basic Law is the provision (Article 5) that ministers are independent in their respective functions and bear individual responsibility for them, although the Chancellor remains responsible for the government's "general line of policy."[246] This provision is of importance in understanding certain aspects of the public split in the grand-coalition economic cabinet, whose leading ministers were of different parties. The spectacle of intra-cabinet accusations and insults, and of outright refusals of cooperation with the Chancellor over exchange-policy questions, was made possible by this provision.[247]

The cabinet's control powers are widened and streamlined through the governmental financial planning which formulates and guides a five-year financial plan, the monthly meetings of the Public-Authorities' Cyclical Council, quarterly "concerted-action" sessions with the Council of Experts and labor and property groups, and the publication of annual "orientation data." Economics Minister Schiller's close connection with academic and research circles has facilitated fruitful cross-fertilization and an occasional publicistic alliance.

The Bundestag has constitutional authority over monetary and international-payments policy.[248] However, the practical powers of the Bundestag as such and of its committees are in fact quite limited. As might also be expected under the parliamentary system, the German Bundestag has no counterpart of the United States Joint Economic Committee.

Although the viewpoints and interests of sectoral organizations, political parties, foreign and international entities, theoretical publicists, and individual politicians have all influenced German balance-of-payments policy formulation, these influences will be sufficiently developed in the appropriate sections of the present study. They were not given individual space in this chapter, because they displayed few relevant unique features of an organizational nature.

The foregoing chapter has attempted to present in one place the chief strands in the motivational environment of German balance-of-payments policy formulation in the period under review. It is certain that, whether from inability to understand their own problems, or from cynical unwillingness to do so, these influences have occasionally been in error as to "facts."[249] But decision-makers' opinions on the "facts"are themselves facts. Thus these interests and institutions effectively constrain the possible tactical policy responses to the logical and market-mechanical situation presented in Chapter 1. The range of these possible tactical policy responses, with their relations to the causes and effects of disequilibrium and to the goals and interests of policy-makers, will be explored in the following three chapters.

NOTES

1. J. Madison, ("Publius"), The Federalist, #10, (1787); M. Tullus Cicero, De Re Publica, ed. H. Schwamborn (Paderborn, 1969), p. 34 (Section 47); C. Mills, The Power Elite (New York, 1956), Chapter 12; G. Bombach, "Ursachen der Nachkriegsinflation und Probleme der Inflationsbekämpfung,"Stabile Preise in Wachsender Wirtschaft (Tübingen, 1960), p. 193; C. Hudeczek, Geldprobleme der Europäischen Wirtschaft (Düsseldorf, 1961), p. 37; H. Linhardt, Kritik der Währungs- und Bankpolitik (Köln-Opladen, 1963), p. 8.

2. K. Schiller, Der Ökonom und die Gesellschaft (Stuttgart, 1964), p. 36.

3. G. Schmölders, Psychologie des Geldes (Reinbeck, 1966), p. 191 ff.; G. Schmölders, Geldpolitik (Tübingen, 1962), p. 60 ff.

4. K. Blessing, Die Verteidigung des Geldwertes (Frankfurt,

1960), p. 42; Minister Schiller, Federal Republic of Germany, Bundesbank, Auszüge aus Presseartikeln (1967), #13, p. 2; Federal Republic of Germany, Sachverständigenrat zur Begutachtung der gesamtwirtschaftlichen Entwicklung, Jahresgutachten (1970), Sections 206, 213; AP (1970), #35, p. 4.

5. Sincere or not, the demand for growth, interpreted as doing the same things faster, perhaps serves some interests as a handy smokescreen behind which to obscure the need, and deny the possibility, of true change and reform. See Chancellor Brandt, AP (1971) #18, p. 1.

6. AP (1970) #39, p. 5.

7. L. A. Hahn, Ewige Hochkonjunktur und kommandiertes Wachstum (Tübingen, 1967); L. Erhard, The Economics of Success (Princeton, 1963), p. 132; Federal Republic of Germany, Bundesbank, Annual Report (1967), p. 40.

8. JG (1966), Section 213; AR (1966), p. 18-20; AR (1968), p. 26.

9. JG (1967), Section 67.

10. JG (1967), Sections 484-485.

11. AR (1965), p. 12.

12. Deist in Sozialistische Partei Deutschlands, Report of the Proceedings of the Annual Convention (Bonn, 1958), p. 182.

13. Federal Republic of Germany, Bundesbank, Monthly Report (Oct 1962), p. 44; MR (Jan 1963), p. 26; MR (Jan 1966), p. 6; MR (Oct 1966), p. 6; K. Blessing, Im Kampf um Gutes Geld (Frankfurt, 1966), p. 33, 139.

14. MR (Aug 1966), p. 4.

15. MR (Jan 1963), p. 27.

16. AR (1968), p. 26; MR (Jan 1963), p. 30; O. Emminger, Währungspolitische Betrachtungen (Frankfurt, 1956), p. 15.

17. MR (Nov 1966), p. 4; MR (Jan 1967), p. 5; AR (1967), p. 32.

18. MR (Oct 1966), p. 4; MR (Jul 1967), p. 5.

19. AP (1969), #1, p. 10; Erhard, Economics, p. 253, 254.

20. Erhard, Economics, p. 327 ff. and 338.

21. AR (1966), p. 10.

22. AR (1966), p. 10; AP (1966), #87, p. 5; Blessing, Kampf, p. 20.

23. AP (1970), #43, p. 4; AP (1970), #38, p. 7.

24. MR (Nov 1961), p. 3; AP (1967), #91, p. 3; AP (1968), #43, p. 2; AP (1968), #79, p. 1; AR (1968), p. 25; AP (1970), #28, p. 7.

25. JG (1967), Section 76.

26. JG (1967), Section 95.

27. JG (1966), Section 78.

28. JG (1966), Section 81; JG (1967), Section 108.

29. AR (1969), p. 25

30. JG (1965), Section 73.

31. JG (1966), Section 81-82; JG (1967), Section 237 ff., Section 307.

32. Federal Republic of Germany, Sachverständigenrat zur Begutachtung der gesamtwirtschaftlichen Entwicklung, Sondergutachten (1970), I.

33. AP. (1970), #88, p. 6.

34. Federal Republic of Germany, Bundesministerium für Finanz, Finanzbericht (1968), p. 21.

35. AP (1967), #104, p. 4.

36. FR (1969), p. 116.

37. French Finance Minister Giscard D'Estaing in AP (1970), #86, p. 11.

38. FR (1969), p. 116.

39. Minister Schiller, AP (1971), #6, p. 2; Chancellor Brandt, AP (1970), #38, p. 6.

40. AP (1970), #38, p. 7; AP (1970), #39, p. 7.

41. JG (1968), Section 272.

42. JG (1964), Section 238.

43. JG (1967), Section 223,

44. German Economic Review, Quarterly, (1968), #3, p. 261.

45. JG (1968), Section 271, 271n.

46. FR (1969), p. 116.

47. MR (Aug 1966), p. 3; L. Erhard, Wirken und Reden, 1952-1965 (Ludwigsburg, 1966), p. 136, 150, 372; JG (1965), Government Reply, Section 20; JG (1964), Section 252.

48. Erhard, Economics, p. 284.

49. AP (1970), #34, p. 5.

50. The Economist, Quarterly Economic Survey (Germany), Quarterly (1962), II, p. 5; Prof. Kangel, Head of Deutsche Institute für Wirtschaftsforschung, AP (1969), #11, p. 5.

51. L. A. Hahn, Fünfzig Jahre zwischen Inflation und Deflation (Tübingen, 1963), p. v; Blessing, Kampf, p. 289.

52. Blessing, Verteidigung, p. 114, 198, 200.

53. Strauss, AP (1968), #15, p. 7; O. Veit, Grundriss der Währungsoplitik (Frankfurt, 1961), p. 187; Hahn, Jahre, p. 18, 21 and throughout; Erhard, Economics, p. 373; JG (1966), Section 201; JG (1969), Section 246.

54. O. Emminger, Währungspolitik im Wandel der Zeit (Frankfurt, 1966), p. 64.

55. Writing in his eighty-fifth year former central-bank President Wilhelm Vocke recently contributed several newspaper articles which--after recalling that both German upvaluations were followed by inflation , stating that "every inflation" leads to "economic decline and finally collapse," invoking the consequent "frightful moral and material damage to the people," and exclaiming over the plight of "the poor savers"--proposed, as the only practical means for avoiding a

"third inflation," that no further increases in public expenditures be allowed, particularly since the currently proposed increases involved "social planning" (AP [1970] , #80, p. 2ff.). (Needlessly invidious carping at individuals' words is to be deplored. But the psychological factors discussed in the text are crucial, and cannot be allowed to pass without a weighty and representative example. The author would be surprised if any reader of the German press should feel that the article cited here was not typical of a large body of writing, or was unfairly synopsized here.)

56. Federal Republic of Germany, Bundesministerium für Wirtschaft, Wissenschaftliche Beirat, "Report on Prices," Bundesanzeiger # 32 (1968), p. 3; AR (1965), p. 13.

57. AR (1967), p. 24.

58. Erhard, Wirken, p. 97.

59. President of German Wholesale and International Trade Association, AP (1970), #72, p. 5.

60. Schmölders, Geldpolitik, p. 276; Hahn, Jahre, p. 198; Blessing, Kampf, p. 286.

61. Finance Minister Möller (SPD), AP (1970), #32, p. 2.

62. MR (Nov 1970), p. 5.

63. President of German Wholesale and International Trade Association, AP (1970), #38, p. 5; Erhard, Economics, p. 253.

64. MR (Aug 1964), p. 4; MR (Jan 1963), p. 27; President Abs of the Bank Association, AP (1969), #10, p. 2; President of German Wholesale and International Trade Association, AP (1970), #38, p. 5.

65. MR (Oct 1966), p. 4.

66. Bundesbank Director Otto Pfleiderer, AP (1970), #84, p. 7; Swedish Premier, AP (1970), #79, p. 7, Dutch Finance Minister, AP (1970), #86, p. 2; Austrian Central Bank President, AP (1970), #78, p. 4; OECD Secretary-General, AP (1970), #87, p. 8.

67. AP (1970), #73, p. 10, 11, 14; AP (1971), #12, p. 4.

68. AP (1970), #37, p. 6.

69. AP (1970), #73, p. 14; AP (1970), #40, p. 4; AP (1970), #76,

p. 7; AP (1970), #73, p. 10 f.; AP (1970), #94, p. 10; AP (1971), #2, p. 4; AP (1970), #80, p. 11; AP (1971), #1, p. 11; AP (1971), #4. p. 16; AP (1970), #91, p. 13.

70. AP (1970), #76, p. 6 ff. It is interesting to note that the Keynesian doctrine of monetary and fiscal intervention itself was designed around one core feature: the unobtrusive erosion of real wages (D. Patinkin, Money, Interest and Prices [New York, 1965], p. 281-285; R. Ball, Inflation and the Theory of Money [Chicago, 1964], p. 56 ff.).

71. AP (1971), #6, p. 1; AP (1971), #9, p. 3.

72. AP (1971), #3, p. 5. A recent report of the Scientific Advisory Council of the Federal Economic Ministry forms an interesting variation on the same inflationary concern: it suggested the introduction of contractual escalator clauses (AP [1970], #91, p. 5).

73. AR (1969), p. 7.

74. JG (1967), Section 247.

75. K. Arndt, former Parliamentary State Secretary to Minister Schiller, AP (1970), #74, p. 5; SG (15 May 1970).

76. Blessing, Verteidigung, p. 117; Blessing, Kampf, p. 286, 287; MR (Nov 1961), p. 5; MR (Oct 1966), p. 4; AR (1967), p. 23; MR (Jul 1969), p. 4.

77. MR (Feb 1967), p. 3, 4.

78. MR (Jan 1967), p. 46.

79. MR (Feb 1967), p. 4.

80. AP (1969), #66, p. 1.

81. MR (Aug 1966), p. 3; MR (Oct 1966), p. 4; MR (May 1967), p. 5; AR (1967), p. 3.

82. MR (Oct 1966), p. 40; MR (Feb 1967), p. 4.

83. AR (1967), p. 28.

84. MR (Nov 1961), p. 5.

85. MR (May 1961), p. 6.

86. MR (Nov 1961), p. 3; Blessing, Kampf, p. 49-50.

87. MR (Nov 1961), p. 6.

88. MR (Aug 1965), p. 5; MR (Jan 1966), p. 45.

89. MR (Oct 1962), p. 44.

90. Erhard, Wirken, p. 38.

91. The adaptability of Eucken's market-economy notions to the reality of German economic structure resulted from two facts: first, the apparent destruction of the German oligopolies and cartels by the war; and second, Eucken's own psychological approach to the definition of a market economy. Eucken did not proceed from the model of a perfectly competitive market and then derive the technological drive toward monopoly. Writing in 1939, he started with the "ideal type" of a centrally controlled economy, and then distinguished the opposed ideal type, the "intercourse economy," as any arrangement in which two or more entities were organizationally independent and in rivalry (W. Eucken, Die Grundlagen der Nationaleconomie [Berlin, 1950], p. 79). This dichotomy, the location of its dividing line, and the replacement of the word "intercourse" (Verkehr) by the word "market" (Markt), were sufficient to make Eucken's ideas--or at least his words and his prestige--serve many perhaps unintended ends in the subsequent discussions.

92. Schiller, Ökonom, p. 228; Blessing, Verteidigung, p. 6, 230; Emminger, Betrachtungen, p. 8; Hahn, Jahre, p. 80, 83; Schmölders, Politik, p. 36; W. Goethe, Gedichte, Eine Auswahl, ed. L. Kaim (Leipzig, 1949), p. 57.

93. JG (1964) Government Response, Section 5; Blessing, Verteidigung, p. 33.

94. Erhard, AP (1968), #42, p. 1; Blessing, Kampf, p. 213; Blessing, Verteidigung, p. 119-121, 125, 923 ff.

95. W. Eucken, Grundsätze der Wirtschaftspolitik (Hamburg, 1959), p. 183 ff.

●   96. Hahn, Jahre, p. 232.

97. A. Müller-Armack, "The Principles of the Social Market Economy," German Economic Review (June, 1965), p. 100.

98. On 2 August 1958, the State Secretary in the Federal Ministry for All-German Affairs called citizens' attention to the

recommendations of the Research Council for German Reunification Problems on the subject of post-reunification legal action on the organization of production. According to these recommendations, East German productive units "are to be reconstituted after reunification with the goal of the restoration of private property and Rechtsstaatlichkeit" (Federal Republic of Germany, Press and Information Office, The Bulletin #146 [5 August 1958], p. 1468). See also P. Propp, Zur Transformation einer Zentralverwaltungswirtschaft sovjetischen Typs in eine Marktwirtschaft (Berlin, 1964).

99. Der Spiegel (18 January 1971), p. 38 ff.

100. AP (1971), #10, p. 7.

101. JG (1965), Section 271. One variant of the social-market economy was outspokenly political-institutional in its goals. The "formed society," an idea which circulated among Christian Democratic thinkers during the Erhard government, foresaw a state apparatus, manned by "specialists," which would set "general-welfare" goals for an array of institutionalized interest groups. This form of corporatism condemned "democratism" as "the logical transitional step to the total collective in which all human dignity and freedom is absorbed by totalitarian powers." (G. Briefs, "Der Unternehmer in Wirtchaft und Gesellschaft," Gesellschaftspolitische Kommentare (1965), p. 171.) To the extent that this idea can be saved from being merely the contentless, ideological facade of monopolist domination, its salvation is due to the specific meanings, derived from Catholic social thought, which can be attached to such concepts as "general welfare" and "specialists."

102. Schiller, Ökonom.

103. Erhard, Economics, p. 372; Emminger, Betrachtungen, p. 5.

104. Müller-Armack, p. 101.

105. JG (1967), Section 262; Erhard, AP (1968), #44, p. 7.

106. JG (1966), Section 282.

107. JG (1966), Sections 211-213.

108. JG (1967), Sections 134-136; Blessing, Verteidigung, p. 43; Erhard, AP (1968), #44, p. 3, 7.

109. Emminger, Betrachtungen, p. 83.

110. Frankfurter Allgemeine Zeitung (14 Dec 1966), p. 6.

111. Wirtschaftswissenschaftliches Institut der Gewerkschaften, Berichte (1966), Heft 1, p. 16.

112. AP (1970), #85, p. 9; AP (1971), #46, p. 7.

113. Brandt, AP (1970), #74, p. 3; AP (1970), #92, p. 4; Brandt, AP (1971), #18, p. 1 ff.; AP (1971), #35, p. 10.

114. AP (1970), #72, p. 6.

115. AP (1970), #32, p. 2.

116. AP (1970), #76, p. 4.

117. G. Müller, Die Bundestagswahl 1969 (Munchen, 1969), p. 8.

118. Erhard, Economics, p. 122-123; K. Kiesinger, "State of the Nation in Divided Germany" (Address, 17 June 1969), Federal Republic of Germany, Press and Information Service, The Bulletin (Supplement) (24 June 1969), p. 5, 7.

119. Blessing, Kampf, p. 67.

120. Erhard, GER (1963), #4, p. 369; Emminger, Politik, p. 51; Schiller, Ökonom, p. 219, 230; JG (1964) Government Response, Section 10.

121. H. Abs, AP (1969), #1, p. 12; Blessing, Kampf, p. 68-69; Christian Democrat platform in G. Müller, p. 95.

122. AP (1968), #82, p. 7; JG (1964) Government Response, Section 10; Kiesinger in G. Müller, p. 59; Erhard, Economics, p. 347.

123. Social Democrat program in G. Müller, p. 103.

124. Blessing, Verteidigung, p. 202; BRD Bulletin (28 May 1969), p. 145; Erhard, Wirken, p. 129; Director Ponto of the Dresdner Bank, AP (1970),#5, p. 5; JG (1968), Section 5; AP (1968), #57, p. 12.

125. Erhard, Wirken, p. 256; Blessing, AP (1967), #3, p. 1; Erhard, Economics, p. 350; Hahn, Jahre, p. 121; L. A. Hahn, Ein Traktat über Währungsreform (Tübingen, 1964), p. 155; JG (1964), Section 162; AR (1966), p. 26; Organization for Economic Cooperation and Development, Economic and Development Review Committee, Survey (Germany) (1969), p. 8; Kiesinger in BRD Bulletin (7 Jan 1969), p. 3.

126. QES (1966), p. 2; Berliner Handelsgesellschaft, AP (1968), #83, p. 11; Strauss, AP (1969), #81, p. 5; Strauss in G. Müller, p. 46; AP (1968), #81, p. 4; Schiller, AP (1969), #38, p. 9.

127. AR (1968), p. 38; AP (1968), #62, p. 8.

128. AP (1968), #82, p. 11; AP (1969), #41, p. 3.

129. Schiller, AP (1968), #46, p. 3; Arbeitsgemeinschaft Deutscher Wirtschaftswissenschaftlicher Forschungsinstitute, Die Internationalen Währungsprobleme in der Weltwirtschaft der Gegenwart (Supplement to Zeitschrift für Angewandte Konjunkturforschung #14) (Berlin, 1967), p. 11.

130. Bank Association, AP (1967), #27, p. 9; Hahn, Traktat, p. 27.

131. G. Müller, p. 24; BRD Bulletin (28 May 1969), p. 145.

132. Die Welt, AP (1969), #73, p. 9.

133. AP (1968), #36, p. 2; Social Democrat 1969 platform in G. Müller, p. 111.

134. AP (1968), #21, p. 1; AP (1968), #22, p. 3.

135. JG (1964), Section 256.

136. Blessing, Verteidigung, p. 208; Blessing, Kampf, p. 203; AP (1968), #83, p. 17.

137. Blessing, Kampf, p. 231.

138. Schiller, AP (1971), #6, p. 2; AP (1969), #38, p. 9.

139. Emminger, Betrachtungen, p. 18; Blessing, Kampf, p. 302.

140. AP (1968), # 86, p. 12; AP (1968), #82, p. 2.

141. Volkswirt (1968), #41, p. 9.

142. AP (1968), #78, p. 5.

143. Schiller, Ökonom, p. 166; Erhard, GER (1963), #4, p. 376; Hahn, Jahre, p. 107; Hahn, Traktat, p. 184.

144. JG (1967), Section 256.

145. S. I. Katz, Sterling Speculation and European Convertibility: 1955-1958 (Essays in International Finance # 37) (Princeton, 1961), p. 27 ff.

146. Blessing, Verteidigung, p. 91-92.

147. This state of affairs may profitably be contrasted with that reflected in the then Deputy Schiller's comment of 1963: "Precisely the triple combination of dynamic market economy, monetary and fiscal overall guidance and welfare policy has shown itself to be the solution that is abreast of the times" (K. Schiller, Stabilität und Aufstieg [Wirtschaftspolitische Tagung der SPD] [Bonn, 1963], p. 33). Eight years later, as indeed Schiller's formulation would lead one to expect, this assessment is itself no longer abreast of the times.

148. New York Times (28 Sep 1969), p. 3.

149. Blessing, Verteidigung, p. 14; AP (1969), #91, p. 8.

150. G. Müller, p. 15.

151. OECDS (Jan 1963), p. 20.

152. AP (1970), #82, p. 4.

153. JG (1967), Section 257.

154. JG (1966), Sections 192-197.

155. AP (1969), #55, p. 3.

156. OECDS (Jan 1963), p. 20 ff.; Organization for Economic Cooperation and Development, Economic Policy Committee, Working Party Three, The Balance of Payments Adjustment Process (Paris, 1966), Section 49a.

157. JG (1967), Section 322; JG (1964), Section 248.

158. JG (1966), Section 243; Council of Experts Special Evaluation, May 1971, AP (1971), #44, p. 8; Joint Working Group of the German Economic Research Institutes, AP (1971), #35, p. 6.

159. JG (1965), Section 90.

160. Blessing, Verteidigung, p. 266; Emminger, Politik, p. 101; Blessing, AP (1969), #91, p. 5.

161. Blessing, Verteidigung, p. 190; Blessing, Kampf, p. 275.

162. This reasoning can be carried further. Where E = employes, A = economically active population, Y^L/E = e, Y/A = a, E/A = Λ, and others symbols are as in equations (IV), $W/P\pi\Lambda = \lambda/\Lambda = Y^L/Y \cdot A/E = Y^L/E \cdot A/Y$ = e/a. In this case, if W/π is a constant (productivity-wage guideline) and P is a constant (price-stability dogma); and if technological progress and consequent industrial concentration raise π and Λ (employes as a proportion of the German work force rose from sixty-eight percent in 1950 to eighty percent in 1964, mostly as a result of shifts out of agriculture--JG [1965], Section 91); then e/a must fall. If, further, in modern life increases in real income add to discretionary spending power only, i.e., they add little to satisfaction from the use and maintenance of the things bought, then the dominant significance of personal income and expenditure is as a means to and an indicator of relative social position. In this case, the drop in e/a resulting from the application of the Bundesbank-Council incomes policy could well be called, by analogy, a modern form of "immiseration of the proletariat." In fact, Germany's proportion of economically active persons to population has fallen (FR [1969], p. 24), so that e/income-per-capita has risen slightly over the period under review. However, if, as seems most likely, the increase in non-active (dependent) population was proportionately lower among property-income receivers than among workers, the effect suggested in this note is reinforced on a personal basis.

163. AP (1970), #85, p. 4.

164. M. Bronfenbrenner, and F. D. Holzman, "A Survey of Inflation Theory," American Economic Review (September, 1963), p. 646 ff.; JG (1969), Sections 215, 218, 65 ff.; SG (1969), II, p. 3.

165. Schiller, Ökonom, p. 239; JG (1968), Section 287.

166. AP (1970), #75, p. 5; AP (1970), #11, p. 6.

167. B. Külp, "Der Einfluss des Aussenhandels auf die Einkommensverteilung," Weltwirtschaftliches Archiv (1966), p. 135.

168. The whole marginal-productivity theory of factor pricing, when used as a legitimation of market-determined income shares, is open to a similar objection, that of begging the question. Let M stand for marginal revenue product, W for wages, L for labor units, and L-superscript for "of labor." Then the wage bill is said by the theory to approximate LM^L. Yet what is in fact measurable is LW, where L itself is a questionable statistic, due to the lack of an analytically meaningful unit for labor. Thus M^L is never measurable except

ex post, as $M^L = W$. But this is not an observation; it is the doctrine which was to be supported.

169. German Tribune (25 June 1970), p. 5.

170. P. Boarman, Germany's Economic Dilemma (New Haven, 1964), p. 290.

171. JG (1967), p. 229.

172. Hahn, Jahre, p. 180; Council of Experts, Position Paper (1964), JG (1965).

173. Arbeitsgemeinschaft, p. 80.

174. JG (1967), p. 221-229; AP (1968), #54, p. 3; AP (1968), #55, p. 3; AP (1968), #60, p. 4; AP (1968), #60, p. 10; AP (1968), #66, p. 3.

175. Hahn, Jahre, p. 118.

176. E. Brehmer, Struktur und Funktionsweise des Geldmarkts der Bundesrepublik Deutschland seit 1948 (Kieler Studien) (Tübingen, 1964), p. 77.

177. Der Spiegel (18 Jan 1971), p. 38; QES (1964), III, p. 2; QES (1965), II, p. 6. Although "the dominant position of the banks in pre-war Germany had come to a considerable extent from their ability to vote by proxy the shares deposited with them by their customers" (R. Loehr, The West German Banking System [n.d., 1952], p. 57), United States Occupation attempts to end this arrangement were eventually defeated by the opposition of Germany, France and Britain.

178. AP (1968), #55, p. 7.

179. S. N. Sen, Central Banking in Undeveloped Money Markets (Calcutta, 1952), p. 174.

180. JG (1965), Section 200.

181. Organization for Economic Cooperation and Development, Ministerial Conference, Statement (Paris, August 1964), p. 25n; R. Sayers, Modern Central Banking (Oxford, 1958), p. 79; see also OECD3, Sections 64, 65, 74.

182. AP (1970), #86, p. 11; AP (1968), #65, p. 1.

183. Veit, Grundriss, p. 314.

184. G. Haberler, Money in the International Economy (Cambridge, 1965), p. 32-34; Hahn, Jahre, p. 238; G. N. Halm, International Financial Intermediation: Deficits Benign and Malignant (Essays in International Finance #68) (Princeton, 1968), p. 9; E. Sohmen, Flexible Exchange Rates: Theory and Controversy (Chicago, 1961), p. 70; M. Friedman, Dollars and Deficits (Englewood Cliffs, 1969), p. 272.

185. Schmölders, Geldpolitik, p. 275-280; Friedman, Dollars, p. 273.

186. JG (1967), Section 311; R. Sayers, Central Banking since Bagehot (Oxford, 1957), p. 441; H. C. Simons, "Rules vs. Authority in Monetary Policy," Journal of Political Economy (February, 1936), p. 29; also see Unions Association President E. G. Vetter, AP (1969), #83, p. 5.

187. Emminger, Politik, p. 127; Bundesbank President Blessing also expressed this opinion, AP (1969), #15, p. 6; AP (1969), #39, p. 3.

188. Emminger, Politik, p. 122 ff.

189. Emminger, Politik, p. 108.

190. AP (1968), #77, p. 3; JG (1964) Government Response, Section 12.

191. Blessing, Kampf, p. 122, 171-172.

192. F. Machlup, International Payments, Debt and Gold (New York, 1964), p. 493.

193. JG (1964), p. v.

194. Schiller, Ökonom, p, 164; Erhard, Wirken, p. 10; OECDS (1963), p. 21.

195. GER (1967), #2, p. 159n.

196. JG (1964), p. 144; JG (1965), Appendix 3; JG (1966), p. viii.

197. FR (1967), p. 223 ff.

198. JG (1966), p. vi.

199. JG (1966), Section 231.

200. JG (1967), Section 221; Hahn, Jahre, p. 135; Süddeutsche Zeitung, AP (1967), #101, p. 12.

201. JG (1964), p. vii; The "protection" phrases apparently originated in Bergründung züm Regierungsentwurf Bundesbankgesetz (AIII), Bundestag Drucksache 2781, 2. Wahlperiode (1953), p. 4 ff.

202. JG (1966), Section 92.

203. JG (1966), Section 250.

204. JG (1967), Section 228; Erhard, Economics, p. 336.

205. JG (1965) Government Response, Section 17.

206. JG (1965), Section 187; JG (1966), Section 241 ff.

207. JG (1965) Government Response, Section 7; JG (1964), Section 123, 249; JG (1965), Sections 96, 181e; JG (1966), Section 106; JG (1968), Section 285.

208. JG (1964), p. v; JG (1965), Section 192m; JG (1967), Section 221; JG (1965) Government Response, Section 27.

209. Schiller, AP (1968), #89, p. 5; JG (1966), p. viii.

210. GER (1967), #3, p. 187.

211. AP (1967), #101, p. 13.

212. JG (1967), Section 314; JG (1968), Section 184; Volkswirt (1968), #46, p. 11.

213. SG (1967), Section 1.

214. AP (1967), #101, p. 14.

215. JG (1967), Section 98.

216. AP (1966), #16, p. 2; JG (1967), Section 310.

217. W. Stützel, "Ist die schleichende Inflation durch monetäre Massnahmen zu beeinflussen?" Beihefte zur Konjunkturpolitik #7 (Berlin, 1960), p. 10.

218. JG (1968), p. x.

219. JG (1968), p. ix.

220. Volkswirt (1968), #49, p. 20; AP (1969), #51, p. 3. This particular problem has been overcome by the Council in recent years

by releasing the Evaluations within the government before their offical publication date (AP [1971] , #44, p. 14).

221. SG (1969), II, p. 5; SG (1969), III, p. 12.

222. Professor Claus Köhler, who is said to be "close to labor," pleaded for expansion in the May 1970 Special Evaluation and in the 1970 Annual Evaluation. In its May 1971 Special Evaluation, the entire Council asked for financial-policy ease (AP [1971] , #44, p. 9).

223. JG (1965), p. vi; JG (1966), p. vi.

224. JG (1966), Section 244; JG (1965), Section 191b.

225. Erhard, Volkswirt (1968), #46, p. 11; former Economics Minister Schmücker, Volkswirt (1968), #49, p. 20; Volkswirt (1968), #49, p. 2; Volkswirt (1968), #46, p. 11; AP (1966), #93, p. 2.

226. AP (1967), #28, p. 6.

227. AP (1969), #83, p. 4.

228. Hahn, Jahre, p. 81-82.

229. Veit, Grundriss, p. 188; Schmölders, Geldpolitik, p. 148.

230. W. Schmidt, "The German Bundesbank," Bank for International Settlements, Eight European Central Banks (London, 1963), p. 56.

231. G. Gutman, H. J. Hochstrate, and R. Schüter, Die Wirtschaftsverfassung der Bundesrepublik Deutschland (Stuttgart, 1964), p. 39. Drafts of its foundation law calling for its outright subordination, or for a formal conciliation process, were rejected, as was the suggested prescription of employment and payments-balance goals (J. Hein, "The Mainsprings of German Monetary Policy, " Economia Internazionale [August, 1964] , p. 318). Despite existing administrative arrangements for coordination of Bundesbank and government policy, the German monetary authorities seem given to engineering more "impersonal" market pressures on government (Schmölders, Geldpolitik, p. 137, 149).

232. Blessing, Verteidigung, p. i.

233. AP (1969), #92, p. 1.

234. Schmidt, p. 62.

235. Schmölders, Geldpolitik, p. 134, 141.

236. MR (Apr 1967), p. 26; AR (1967), p. 28; MR (Jan 1967), p. 5.

237. Blessing, Kampf, p. 212.

238. AP (1966), #93, p. 6.

239. AP (1968), #51, p. 6; AP (1969), #11, p. 2.

240. AP (1971), #6, p. 4.

241. President Friedrich Dietz of the Wholesale and International Trade Association, AP (1969), #89, p. 7.

242. Emminger, AP (1969), #11, p. 1.

243. The Reports of the Bundesbank are perhaps fuller than those of any other central bank (Chapter 5). If never to apologize, never to explain have been held up by a famous central-bank governor as the ideal twin policy, then the Bank's continual explanation may be suspect as apologia.

244. Blessing, Kampf, p. 286.

245. Blessing, Verteidigung, p. 63 ff.

246. GER (1964), #3, p. 245. Another characteristic feature of the Federal Republic government is the influence of the so-called "subsidiary government" of the Chancellor's Office, manned by specialized experts.

247. Wall Street Journal (26 Sep 1969), p. 1; New York Times (28 Sep 1969), p. 1.

248. Basic Law, Articles 4, 5.

249. Hahn, Traktat, p. 32; J. M. Keynes, A Treatise on Money (New York, 1930), II, p. 405; JG (1966), Section 231; Hahn, Jahre, p. 107.

CHAPTER

3

THE
POLICY
ALTERNATIVES:
ADJUSTING
TACTICS

NON-INTERVENTION AND INTERVENTION
IN REAL ELEMENTS

Germany's overall response to the balance-of-payments situation and aims developed in the preceding chapters can in principle be
either one of adjustment or one of non-adjustment. These alternative
basic responses can be called balance-of-payments strategies. Adjustment measures aim to restore the overall international compatibility
of the elements affecting the payments balance, by directly modifying
these elements as far as possible. Such tactics may at the same time
foster the automatic adjustment mechanisms set in motion by the incompatibilities of basic disequilibrium. Non-adjustment measures,
on the other hand, attempt to perpetuate the overall incompatibility by
retarding the automatic adjustment mechanisms which are its normal
effects.[1] In the present chapter, the potential adjusting policy measures will be investigated from the German point of view, viz., that of
a surplus country. In Chapters 4 and 5, a similar investigation of
feasible non-adjusting policies will be made.

Adjustment Through Non-Intervention

Two approaches to the adjustment of a surplus are conceivable,
which may be called respectively active and passive. A passive approach would rely on the expectable mechanical effects of a surplus
to work toward adjustment in the ways which have been described in
Chapter 1. Such an approach to adjustment by Germany can be expected
to succeed only slowly and with difficulty. The two reasons for this
were introduced in Chapter 1. First, the market-mechanical adjustment tendencies inherent in payments-balance surplus require appreciable time to produce full international adjustment after any initial

one-time disturbance. This is evident from the mere recital of the
workings of the mechanisms. Indeed, if only inconsiderable time were
required for adjustment in this way, no payments imbalance could arise
where its mechanical effects were permitted to operate.

At the same time, however, there exists for Germany a continuous source of disadjustment, which can be fully offset through lagged
adjustment mechanisms only by permitting them a correspondingly
continuous operation. This continuous source of disadjustment lies in
the structurally different tendencies to inflationary monetary expansion in Germany and in Germany's chief trade partners.[2] The German factors involved have already been discussed in detail. The
relevant economic structure of the United States can here be cited
as an example of the situation in Germany's major trade partners.
Concentrated market power in the United States makes even the older
choice between inflation and unemployment less feasible today. "Stag-
flation," in which both these evils are present, is becoming increasingly
difficult to eliminate with conventional macrofinancial tools. Inflation
must be tolerated, to keep unemployment within acceptable bounds in
a socially tense situation where unemployment has differential impacts on various social groups. An expensive foreign policy also reduces the leeway for fighting inflation. At the same time, the economic magnitude of the United States makes it at once the world's
largest foreign trader and the world's most "closed" economy, in
terms of the proportion of international payments to national income.
This situation allows the United States to adopt expansionary financial
policies without corresponding economic fears for the balance of
international payments. The market power of the United States was
also an element promoting the dollar's acceptance as a key currency.
This acceptance has so far ensured that the United States can finance
payments deficits largely through increased dollar liabilities abroad.
The recent steady increase in official dollar holdings has permitted,
and practically forced, even nations with relatively open economies
to respond to internal tensions through inflationary policies. The
discrepancies between such factors as these and the German conditions already described constitute the continuous source of disadjustment felt by Germany.

Under these circumstances, a passive approach to payments-
balance adjustment, relying on market-mechanical effects of surplus,
is logically assimilable to a deliberate, active attempt to adjust
through macrofinancial policy. Further consideration of this class
of policy will therefore be deferred to a later section of the present
chapter.

Direct Intervention in Tastes

The second general approach to payments-balance adjustment
is the active. It seeks to intervene directly in the causes of the

imbalance. It will at the present stage of the discussion be assumed
that nothing can be done directly to counteract either the technological
imperative toward large-scale operations or the implications of Germany's Middle-European geopolitical position and Middle-European
history, although these are among the most basic factors underlying
Germany's payments-balance situation.

If the elements more immediately affecting the payments balance have been correctly enumerated and categorized in Chapter 1,
the possible individual adjustment tactics can be similarly catego-
rized.3 Thus adjusting measures would bear on real, on market-
structural, or on financial elements. In the succeeding pages, each
of the various possible areas of policy intervention in the market-
mechanical balance-of-payments process will be examined in the light
of its expectable impact on German goals and interests and in regard
to the availability or development of tools to implement the tactic.

In Chapter 1, the "real" elements of balance-of-payments compatibility were divided into tastes, factor endowment, and technological methods. Direct alteration of real elements--i.e., not through
long-term financial-policy incentives--is the means of adjustment
furthest removed from the normal economic tools of government.
Tastes and national factor endowments indeed are normally taken to
be givens in a liberal economic system: the system is thought of as
adjusting to them and not the reverse.*4 Since, too, no consistent
theory of their origins is available, it may be argued that movements
in these elements are random, and hence tend to cancel one another.5

However, the German policy discussion has produced certain
suggestions even in this area. In the realm of tastes, for example,
a campaign to encourage foreign travel by Germans is conceivable.
But it is likely that German international travel will grow spontane-
ously so fast as to leave little marginal return to deliberate policy
efforts. In addition, there seems to be a specific "boomerang" effect
of German outpayments for travel: countries favored by German
travellers seem to favor German exports (Tables A32).

It is at least conceivable that German tastes for foreign goods
per se could be stimulated, as a way of offsetting the effect of relative
factor endowments on Germany's balance of payments. But in a land
rich in capital, there is little hope of artificially increasing demand

---

*The opposite proposition may well be true, but it implies re-
strictions on traditional freedoms which are philosophically difficult
to acknowledge and, even worse, it makes the market and electoral
apparatus of our system philosophically pointless.

precisely for goods producible exclusively by foreign factors.

There is no indication that either of the measures suggested above has been taken, or even seriously debated. On the contrary, export-promotion expenditures, even by the government, have grown disproportionately to Gross National Product or to foreign trade over the period here studied (Tables A3411, A3412). In addition, export credits are financed by several government and para-governmental agencies on favorable terms;[6] German foreign aid has also been tied to projects so as to favor German exports (Chapter 4).

Direct Intervention in Factor
Endowment and Methods

Direct measures to alter Germany's technological methods, i.e., the factor proportions in actual use, might alter its trade balance. Essentially, such measures would shift German applications of technology so as to require more imported inputs. Labor-intensivity could be raised, on the one hand, so as to raise remittances abroad by foreign workers. But the German economy appears to be so labor-intensive already, relative to its potential, as to impede growth. This is a concomitant of the real export of capital (implicit in an export surplus), and of the deliberate import of labor. As noted above, there is probably also a political limit on the importation of foreign workers.[7] Finally, foreign workers' remittances seem to have their own specific boomerang effect on German exports.

Raw-materials intensivity in production could be raised to increase outpayments to suppliers. Yet German industry is already quite dependent on imported materials, even when, as in the case of coal, these compete directly with important domestic products. Actual encouragement of these imports would directly contradict the public policy of supporting transitions in agriculture and mining, and would no doubt prove political dynamite.

Raising the capital-goods input-intensity of German industry, so as to require the domestic application of more of the resources presently devoted to exports, is in itself a step with some promise. Such a shift of factor proportions has been suggested on general grounds, and as a means of reducing the outflow of foreign-worker remittances. The latter effect would of course tend to offset the intended reduction of the payments surplus. Tax measures to encourage investment (or to discourage employment of labor) also have such a methods-altering effect, and would ease the balance-of-payments situation, provided the new investment were in domestically oriented industries. However, it is hard to see how, in a liberal economic

system, capital-intensivity can be <u>directly</u> raised, i.e., short of permitting the balance of payments to influence prices sufficiently to
draw in foreign capital goods; for this latter is essentially a monetary,
and not a "real" (or direct), adjustment-policy measure.[8]

Neither capital goods nor raw materials have been encouraged,
or even permitted, to redress Germany's payments balance. Labor is
recruited from labor-abundant lands precisely as the one factor whose
movement still can provide an outlet in the face of non-adjustment in
other directions. Thus it is a more or less mechanical accompaniment
of the overall non-adjustment, and is not a policy measure designed to
relieve it. Political and social forces will doubtless prevent its going
so far as to counteract a general payments disequilibrium importantly.

Direct intervention in the real elements of the balance of payments does not offer a highly practicable, politically feasible, or
system-conformed solution to Germany's problem, and there has
accordingly been little discussion of such intervention.

STRUCTURAL INTERVENTION IN
PRODUCT AND FACTOR MARKETS

A more promising class of measures embraces those directly
affecting the structures of markets. In Chapter 1, structural elements
in product, factor, and foreign-exchange markets were distinguished.

Direct Intervention in
Product-Market Structure

In the international goods market, it is to be expected that relaxation of quantitative controls and lowering of tariffs on German
imports would tend to help balance Germany's international payments.
Indeed, broadening the range of traded goods relative to non-traded
goods (opening the economy) is the only non-temporary and non-lagged
way of hastening the price-realigning effects of payments surplus.
Trade and exchange policy administration was transferred from the
jurisdiction of the monetary authorities (where it had been subject to
Occupation control) to that of the Federal government in September
1961.[9]

Most commercial control tools are also subject to the multilateral dispositions of the Common Market and the General Agreement
on Tariffs and Trade, which have by and large reduced both trade
barriers themselves and the leeway of nations to change them. A
notable exception to this trend was the increase in German turnover-tax

rebates made necessary by the application of GATT rules to the Com-
mon-Market-dictated shift to the "French" turnover-tax system in
1967. This change may have effected a virtual devaluation of two to
four percent.[10] Although German sources usually note the restriction
of the nation's leeway and discretion on trade controls, some tariff
reductions six months ahead of Common-Market schedules were enacted
in mid-1964, over strenuous opposition from industrial interests.[11]
Since the German government itself has pronounced its aversion to the
use of taxation measures to combat fundamental disequilibrium,[12] the
November 1969 border-tax adjustments will be discussed under the
guise of an intended substitute for revaluation on a later page.

Indeed, Germany's position, geopolitical and economic, within
the Common Market, NATO, and the OECD during the period under
review, together with its heavy dependence on exports, would seem
to have made a consistent stand in favor of the freest possible international economic relations the indicated policy for Germany.[13] Yet
the need to retain an international tariff bargaining position, domestic
politics, and public-finance considerations place a lower limit on any
one nation's trade barriers. Indeed, a renewed trend to protectionism,
led by the United States, has resulted from the long-standing world
concern over that country's payments balance. Germany has in fact
over the years agreed to "self-restriction" of some of its exports, to
ward off protectionism abroad.[14] On the whole, however, the leeway
in this area for an effective adjustment policy by Germany has been
limited.

In a related area, it is unlikely that the German authorities will
wish to eliminate NATO troops now stationed in the country, and so as
it were release the United States and British pledges to defend Germany. The recent prominent American discussion of this possibility
has aroused decided official concern in Germany. Even from a financial standpoint, indeed, a troop-repatriation policy has little to recommend it, since standing alone at this time would probably entail staggering defense costs for Germany. Some of the NATO troops were in
fact removed under the 1967 tripartite agreement on troops costs, and
further reductions in strength have been studied at intervals; yet these
moves certainly suited United States needs more than they did German.

Few tools for the restructuring of domestic goods markets for
the benefit of the payments balance are within reach of German authorities. Chancellor Erhard, the Council of Experts and Minister Schiller
have all called for measures toward more competitive domestic market
structures, and have suggested that such increased competition might
help reduce Germany's export bias.[15] It is possible that more competition might make wages in export industries more sensitive to profits,
and make wages in domestically-oriented industries more responsive

to those in foreign-trading industries. This opening of the economy would hasten the working of the direct international price-transmission effect, and so increase the effectiveness of its readjustment action. The Scientific Advisory Council of the Economics Ministry counselled allowing the growth of non-export-oriented firms by giving subsidies for retraining rather than for production.[16] This measure, too, might conceivably have an effect on the direct price-transmission mechanism. But neither measure could without ruthless direct intervention actually reduce the export bias. Most recently, Finance Minister Möller declared that the Brandt government would not intervene to destroy the large export-oriented firms, but might subsidize desirable restructuring.[17] In the case of large diversified firms, however, the fungibility of money makes even the most rigorously administered subsidy into a simple net increase in the firm's resources.

On the other hand, it is quite possible (as noted in Chapter 1) that German industry presently enjoys its export advantage precisely because it is relatively more competitive than foreign producers. It is hardly to be expected, however, that German authorities will express a desire that their antitrust agency allow more concentration of German industry for the avowed purpose of making it less competitive abroad and higher-priced at home. Such a line of policy would find socialists, nationalists, conservatives and industry in opposition. In fact, the 1967 shift to a value-added turnover tax system may be expected to impede vertical integration, and so to slow the pace of any necessary German structural adjustment of this type.[18]

Even a policy of outright credit-policy discrimination, aimed at revolutionizing Germany's industrial structure,[19] would probably be rendered largely ineffective by the self-financing of export industry and its domestic ramifications, as well as by the widespread institutional relationships of German banks with export industry. In a similar connection, Wilhelm Hankel of the Economics Ministry noted that German firms are becoming increasingly "restriction-proof."[20] In fact, it is precisely Germany's export industry that presently enjoys the bulk of government-sponsored credit advantages.[21] In view of the life-and-death national importance imputed to German export industries in the present study, this situation is hardly surprising.[22]

There is no indication that measures to alter domestic goods-market structures have in fact had any impact on the German payments balance.

Direct Intervention in
Factor-Market Structures

The recent worldwide suggestions for an institutionalized incomes policy, and their applicability to the German labor market, were discussed in the preceding chapter. Direct measures to alter the structure of the German capital market offer a possible solution for Germany's international payments problems. A reformed capital market would be more responsive to the market supply of funds, and so would allow a balance-of-trade surplus to stimulate a reduction of interest rates and an outflow of money capital. The expectable impact of this tactic may be illustrated by assuming that the entire balance-of-trade surplus is to be offset by a long-term private capital outflow created by rearrangements of market structure alone. The current-period overall external accounts would then be in balance, relieving Germany of the immediate external odium of an international reserve movement. There would therefore be no net effect on commercial-bank liquidity, no expectable effect on the money stock, and thus, according to the analysis made in Chapter 1, no effect on the further evolution of the external balance. The latter would remain in balance as long as the capital outflow persisted. If foreign and domestic price levels continued to differ, nevertheless, the price-transmission effect would still produce inflation. If the respective price levels progressively diverge, moreover, the export of capital needed for overall balance must grow from period to period. It is hard to see how mere restructuring of the capital market could bring about such a progressive rise in real German saving.

Two types of measures could, however, at least tend toward these general consequences. One type consists of measures to make the capital market broader and more sensitive, so that interest rates would fully reflect the supply and demand conditions in the country as a whole. This would require overcoming the problems referred to in Chapter 1. Thus the market would relatively encourage non-export industries, which at present have less access to capital. The second type of measure consists of price-discriminating interventions in the capital market, aimed at lowering (especially long-term) interest rates without inflating the money stock. The latter type of tactic, being fundamentally an attempt to correct the payments balance rather than adjust it, will be discussed in Chapter 4.

The general strategy of engineering a net private capital outflow as a means of correcting the payments imbalance has been a project close to the thinking of the German monetary authorities throughout the period under review. As early as 1958, Karl Blessing saw the capital market as the answer to Germany's problem (Chapter 4, note 8). In 1961, United States Treasury Secretary Dillon also called for more openness in European capital markets, so as to reduce their attractiveness for United States capital.[23]

The policy of broadening and opening the whole capital-market structure has been given much study by all German authorities. This tactic may be viewed under two aspects: that of positive measures to restructure the market and that of maintaining a reasonably stable atmosphere for the development of the market.

In the former sphere, a pressing need has been to reduce the preponderant influence of large financial institutions, especially banks, on the capital market. This requires encouraging the sale of equity-financing instruments by firms and their purchase by non-financial entities. The Corporations Law of 1966 provides for somewhat more financial disclosure by publicly-owned firms and for more stockholder control. In the face of entrenched aversions to equities on both sides of the market, however, this mild measure must be regarded as ineffective. Of the same order was the abolition of some subsidies on bank savings, especially since the general freeing of intermediary interest rates in 1967--although ending cartel-like agreements among banks--actually tended to reduce the interest advantage of equities.[24] Differential tax treatment of intermediated and non-intermediated saving also still favors bank intermediation. Finally, the recent policy of decapitalizing the social-security institutions has reduced their stabilizing role in the capital market.

At the same time, the German authorities have been unable to provide really calm capital-market development, or to stabilize bank participation in the markets. A brief look at recent capital-market policy will confirm this.

During the entire period under review, the Bundesbank's capital-market policy was constrained by two related major structural problems. The dominant position of the banks in the capital market made the latter very sensitive to money-market interest rates (Chapter 1), while the capital market's integration with international markets made German interest rates largely dependent on world interest rates.[25]

Thus, while the Bundesbank was trying to force governmental and government-subsidized investment demand out of the capital market in 1965-66 in the interests of price stability, interest rates rose steadily as inelastic government-connected capital-market demands resisted reduction.[26] As bank liquidity was squeezed, the banks deserted the capital market, leaving it "destroyed."[27] The Council of Experts heavily criticized both government and central bank for this debacle, but the Bundesbank answered that price stabilization was more important than the health of the capital market.[28]

As a result of this situation, the Economics Ministry stopped all government capital-market emissions from July to September 1965, and after May 1966 government in general shifted into short-term borrowing.[29] Firms meantime borrowed abroad as the international interest differential in Germany's "favor" increased, fostering a great influx of capital and straining the payments balance. Tight money and the confusion on the capital market precipitated the recession of 1966/67. The new Kiesinger government hastily organized an all-government capital-market queue to nurse the weakened market.[30]

In these circumstances, an expansive monetary policy was needed, for both recovery and growth,[31] and for reversing the international capital flow. However, since lowered interest would mean renewed erratic government borrowing, there was much sentiment behind a Stability Law which would formalize the restraints on government capital-market demand.[32] This provision was passed, institutionalizing an artificial situation, and the Bundesbank felt free to reduce capital-market interest rates.

Merely furnishing more liquidity to commercial banks, however, while it noticeably stepped up bank participation in capital-market supply, did not fully accomplish the Bundesbank's objectives. As has been noted, long-term securities are among the first assets eliminated from the portfolios of German commercial banks in need of liquidity, and among the last assets restored in phases of easy money. Among the first assets to be increased in the period in question was foreign lending, to increase which the commercial banks actually began to borrow from the central bank, as the international interest-rate differential in the short-term market was swiftly reversed.[33] The long-term rates, however, started downward only very slowly.

In the light of this experience, the Bundesbank decided in the fall of 1967 to break precedent by buying long-term securities in the open capital market in order to bypass the sluggish channel through the banks.[34] To offset the liquidity effects of this operation, the Bundesbank simultaneously sold its own short-term paper to the commercial banks. These actions succeeded in lowering capital-market interest (average yield of taxed bonds quoted)[35] from over eight percent in mid-1966 to about 6.7 percent at the beginning of 1968.

A basic part of the non-structural program for engineering a net capital export (Chapter 4) was the discouragement of gross capital import. Various measures were adopted, including a retroactive income-tax withholding on interest from German securities. This measure produced a genuine confidence crisis on the capital market.[36]

Finally, the real or manufactured fiscal troubles of the federal government led to a series of measures essentially aimed at the planned decapitalization of the social-securities institutions. This led to a reversal of their traditional securities-demanding role in the capital market, and so to further confusion of capital-market expectations.

As a result of this medley of conflicting policies, as well as to the various capital-accounts-centered balance-of-payments programs of Germany's allies and the disturbing effects of several speculation crises, the atmosphere of the German capital market has been far from serene over the past eight years. The near-chaos and subsequent debility of the market and the institutionalization of certain elements of uncertainty cannot have improved its long-term or "structural" atmosphere.[37]

Despite capital-market policies little calculated, on the face of it, to produce this effect, Germany maintained a net outflow of long-term forms of private capital in 1967, 1968, and 1969. This reversal appears to be attributable to capital-control measures in Germany and abroad, the French and Czech crises, and changed international interest-rate differentials, rather than to any success of Germany's capital-market structural measures.[38] The interest-rate differentials will be discussed repeatedly in later sections, while the various balance-of-payments discriminatory programs will be examined as non-adjustment measures in Chapter 4.

STRUCTURAL INTERVENTION IN EXCHANGE MARKETS

Flexible Exchange Rates

The German debate on the appropriate exchange regime and exchange rate grew steadily more vigorous over the period studied; after the revaluation of 1961, it was effectively reopened by the Council of Experts in its first Evaluation,[39] and culminated in an outright split in the grand-coalition cabinet, in the election issue of 1969, and in the revaluation of October 1969.[40] Thereafter, discussion continued to and through the mid-1971 floating of the DM, as described in Chapter 7.

For the foreseeable future, as explained in the preceding chapters, German psychological, social and political institutions appear likely to aim at noticeably less price inflation, and to actually achieve less expansionary pressures on the payments balance, than those of its major trade partners. Insufficient monetary expansion relative to all other factors affecting the balance of payments will produce basic disequilibrium, and is logically equivalent to exchange undervaluation. The progressive disparity in prices and costs resulting from international social and political differences, and the consequent payments imbalances, can be permanently reconciled only by an exchange-rate regime which permits progressive adjustment of parities.[41]

The regimes which permit this are of three general types: fully-flexible exchange rates, periodic revaluation of pegged rates, and rates of limited flexibility. From the first, the Council of Experts has advocated, in principle, full flexibility for Germany, and others have joined in demanding consideration for this solution.[42] More recently, however, the Council of Experts has contented itself with suggesting a wider band with a self-adjusting parity.

Fully flexible exchange rates would, in principle, end all liquidity effects of the payments balance. A net overall income effect would likewise be excluded, and the direct international price-transmission effect would also be weakened. However, if the (narrowly-defined) trade balance continued skewed, shifts of income on a sectoral or functional level would continue. Under full flexibility, as long as individual classes of goods remain different in price, some direct price-transmission effect can obviously continue.

Whether the fluctuations in the exchange rate would do a better or a worse job than reserve movements in the international adjustment of real economic structures is an academic question at best, in view of the market-structural and macrofinancial distortions which must systematically overlie the elements of comparative advantage in the modern economy.

Despite the expectable advantages of flexible rates in combating the effects of a payments imbalance, the fear has been expressed in Germany that any tampering with the exchange system would disrupt the solidarity either of the Common Market or of the Atlantic community.[43] Three main disruptive possibilities have been seen.

First, any exchange-rate measures by Germany alone have been pictured as "unilateral," and so displeasing to its allies.[44] In the state of opinion which until very recently prevailed, it may be conceded that any unilateral floating of the German currency would have been most unsettling, both to commercial and to political trust. At the present moment, as central bankers themselves are groping toward more flexibility, and periods of floating for the DM and for the Canadian dollar have been tolerated by the IMF, this particular form of the "disruption" thesis has lost some of its force. This class of objection, inconsistently enough, cannot be legitimately applied to revaluations within the Bretton Woods pegged-rate system, which provided for and indeed actively anticipated adjustment through revaluations.[45]

Restructuring of the exchange system can also weaken western solidarity by making international commodity-price supports, such as those for Common Market agriculture, technically more difficult to negotiate.[46] Originally, these supports were tied to fixed exchange rates. Yet this "grossly inefficient" protectionist scheme can at need be otherwise anchored.[47] A more real element in this discussion is the fact that German undervaluation under pegged rates increases the protection and subsidy enjoyed by German farmers under Common-Market-approved schemes.[48] Since the French devaluation, however, which unilaterally cut off the French agricultural market from its biggest supplier,[49] it has been possible in Germany to suggest that agricultural "harmonization" must be secondary to a solution of the chronic international monetary crisis. The 1969 and 1971 actions of floating the DM, with continuing agricultural protection through fiscal offsets, also demonstrated that this form of "disruption" was no longer an overpowering deterrent to exchange-rate manipulations. The EEC Commission's initial opposition to Germany's offset-tax solution to the agrarian problem of revaluation only intensified German doubts about the wisdom of the isolated harmonization of agrarian policy.[50]

The third class of disruption foreseen in a more flexible exchange-rate regime concerns the effects of uncertainty about future exchange rates on traders and investors.[51] In reply to this, it may be said that normal movements of exchange rates in response to market forces should be reasonably gradual under ordinary circumstances. German exporters would in any case usually be unaffected by rate changes, as their billing is normally in DM.[52] German importers would be nearly unaffected to the extent that they would continue to use a broader, improved forward market to acquire exchange;[53] the additional costs and premiums entailed by such a market would be moderate, and not proportional to the social costs of subsidizing foreign trade through the fixed-rate system.[54] However, the Council of Experts in its most recent Evaluation, in arguing against intra-European exchange-rate flexibility, denies that these premiums would be moderate.[55]

Long-term investment would not face greater exchange risks under the new system than under the old. With the costs of repeated forward-cover contracts calculated as part of costs, investors would face even less overall risk than at present. The degree of uncertainty, and indeed chaos, both in the market and among responsible policy-makers, that is possible with politicized and delayed decisions under moveable pegs, is well illustrated by September and October 1969.

The claim just made, that a flexible-exchange-rate system would bring improved conditions for trade and investment, rests on the effective exclusion from exchange markets of government intervention and of destabilizing speculation. The first exclusion is more a matter of definition than of reasoning about the reality of such a situation. "Guided flexibility" in the sense of competitive interventions and man-ipulations would of course be very little, if at all, preferable to the present system. In view of the size of the "non-monetary" international financial operations of modern governments, this problem of creating really free rates might prove insoluble.

The lively, if repetitious, discussion on the crucial question of disequilibrating speculation has gone far beyond the borders of Germany.[56] As a technical--that is, a logical and definitional--matter, academic opinion seems to favor the view that it would not be a great danger.

In the background of the highly involved technical debate over flexible rates stands probably the most powerful German economic-policy interest, export-oriented industry. At least from the short-run viewpoint of this interest, a flexible-exchange-rate regime would be the least welcome solution to world monetary problems. Flexible exchange rates, by at once lowering DM-effective foreign demand, would force an abrupt adjustment on Germany's export-biased industry. But, unlike an adjustment through monetary expansion, for example, it would not simultaneously raise domestic demand in DM. Given the downward inflexibility of factor prices, the reorientation of resources would be enforced but not facilitated. The result would be a tendency to lower prices, profits, and property values, and possibly a period of confusion and unemployment. Since export-oriented firms are Germany's investment leaders, these effects would be spread and multiplied.[57] This picture is not one which German statesmen can face with confidence, given Germany's domestic and foreign political situation. Again, the massive government programs, which might be necessary to avoid the result pictured above, might dangerously exacerbate barely hidden differences in attitudes within Germany on questions of social, economic and political order. In more cynical phraseology, "prosperity" in oligopolistic economies demands mani-pulable final demand, associated with a manipulable value of money. In smaller, more export-dependent countries, this means manipulable foreign demand and exchange rates. Truly flexible rates would destroy the manipulative framework of international monetary "cooperation."

In this connection, the observation has been made that increased exchange-rate uncertainty would exclude marginal firms from the export markets, thus reducing Germany's export supply elasticity.[58] This would be particularly true of manufacturers of investment goods, whose uncertainty is increased by their necessarily longer export contracts. The force of this observation, of course, depends on judgment about uncertainty under various exchange regimes. It should be emphasized in this connection that suboptimal regions of flexible exchanges cannot be expected to solve all adjustment problems.[59] This increasingly important theme will be taken up again in Chapter 7.

A final related objection to flexible exchange rates is that they would eliminate the anticyclical effect of foreign demand.[60] Cyclically

higher and lower DM prices would not have so direct an impact on
foreign markets, because the DM prices of foreign currencies would
also rise and fall cyclically. The appropriate response to this observation was given by the Council of Experts: the flexible-rate system
would free the monetary authorities from the necessity of tailoring
monetary policy to payments-balance needs.[61] The authorities could
thus concentrate on combating domestic cyclical swings. And this
form of anticyclical action can be taken effectively without having to
await actual movements in general price levels.

It is less easy to find reasoned arguments against another, more
politically flavored class of objections to flexible exchange rates, for
these essentially involve speculation about what people would feel and
do in new and as yet untried situations. What, for example, is to be
made of the assertion that the financial community "wouldn't" be able
to accept, and operate under, the new system?[62] In the mouths of the
practitioners themselves, it is a circular argument of the most vicious.
Coming from non-practitioners, it is a mere impertinence, gratuitously
insulting to the intelligence and resilience of men who are supposed to
make their living by coping with daily change.

Perhaps the most often raised objection to flexible exchange
rates is the fear that they would weaken balance-of-payments "dis-
pline."[63] At present, losses of international reserves put pressure on
governments and on international-trade-sensitive employers to maintain relative monetary stability.[64] A pure flexible-exchange-rate
system would require no international reserve movements and hence
would not exert this kind of coordinating pressure. Over against this
is the consideration that exchange-rate-deterioration may exert even
more such pressure, as it is more immediately and personally felt
by the international trading sectors.[65]

Still, it must be conceded that losing units of (any meaningful)
international reserve is a process with a more or less fixed limit,
whereas exchange-rate depreciation is a logically endless process.
The former may thus carry more connotations of crisis than the latter,
especially in a country whose foreign trade may be of secondary quantitative importance.

On the other hand, precisely this threat of crisis has in the fixed-
peg system thus far ensured an international bail-out operation for
any nation losing reserves dangerously. In other words, the same
pressure relied on by the advocates of pegs to rally domestic forces
for monetary discipline has in fact also at the same time served as
a form of international "blackmail" with which to extort balance-of-
payments aid, and this to the extent of eroding or perhaps de facto
abolishing the system. In this light, more exchange-rate flexibility

would weaken both the above effects of "pressure," with no discernible net effects on stability discipline.

Closely allied to the discussion of exchange-regime discipline is the claim that any exchange system will require international co-operation, after all, with the implication that crisis-ridden overmanagement is preferable to the less complex and strained forms of cooperation which would admittedly be needed with more flexibility. The outcry about "cooperation" may in fact be little more than a reflection of routinarian inertia in the ranks of money managers; or it may possibly reflect some unwillingness to see the money managers' esoteric and authoritarian "money power" made obsolete.

From the point of view of specifically German interests, some opposition to more flexibility in exchange rates may stem from the realization that part of Germany's world power and prestige is linked to its balance-of-payments leverage and its large reserves, which are made possible by the fixed-rate system. Besides strengthening Germany's general bargaining position--even, somewhat paradoxically, in negotiations on allied military support and German rearmament (Chapter 6)--the fixed-rate "discipline" gives some spokesmen in Germany, as the world's second trader, the intellectual grounds for opposing the spread of "inflationary welfarism" at home and abroad. Some in Germany would use this as protecting the German social order, both directly and from unwelcome "demonstration effects."

No German law stipulates the exchange regime to be maintained, a declaration by the government to the International Monetary Fund sufficing to alter the parity.[66] In floating the DM in 1969 and 1971, Germany infringed (with general approval of the parties) an international undertaking, but no domestic obligation. By law the government may, and by administrative agreement it must, seek the Bundesbank's advice on these matters. No formal measures leading to a permanent reform of the exchange system had yet been taken in Germany during the period under review.

Indeed, the German monetary authorities throughout most of the period under review consistently refrained from endorsing any change in the international monetary system. In a major speech in November 1961, President Blessing lauded the gold-standard system as "the greatest, and perhaps the best, known to the world," while upholding the Bretton Woods system and the attitudes toward it of the International Monetary Fund as the desirable "code of monetary ethics and discicipline."[67] In the latter sixties the Bundesbank continued to blame United States and British policies, and not the international system, for the repeated crises.[68] Indeed, the Bank expressly welcomed the crises insofar as they might force the deficit countries to obey the code.

The public conversions of both Minister Schiller and Dr. Emminger to more flexibility gave indications that a change in the official stance might be developing. The sudden 1969 floating of the DM for several weeks over a rather wide range represented a sensational turnaround in official rhetoric, which seems to have triggered hitherto suppressed agreements worldwide.[69] The isolated initial Common-Market objections to the move seem to have been a reaction to Germany's five-percent equalization tax on agricultural imports. The further development of this breakthrough in attitudes will be traced both in the present chapter and in Chapter 7.

Since the DM was restabilized at a new parity on October 24, 1969, however, the 1969 turnaround was in fact only rhetorical, as the result was the same as that of a fixed-ped revaluation, except that the exchange-market chaos preceding the move was calculated to provide a ready, though spurious, object-lesson for belated opponents of flexible rates on the dangers of "floating" exchange rates. [70] The 1971 floating of the DM raised several new issues, to be discussed in Chapter 7.

Movably Pegged Exchange Rates

The second method of realigning effective international price relationships is exchange-rate revaluation under the movable-peg system. In this case, a fixed parity is first defended by accepting and absorbing the mechanical effects of payments-balance surplus for as long as seems feasible; thereafter the price of the currency is allowed to rise to a new parity. Since this is the essence of the Bretton Woods system as applied to a surplus country, and since the period under review is bracketed by two upvaluations, this tactic takes on special interest.

The 1961 revaluation was in fact aimed only at alleviating domestic monetary problems within a politically acceptable international arrangement, and was, probably quite calculatedly, too small to affect external economic relations more than temporarily.*[71] This was acknowledged by a participant in the move, President Marius Holtrup of the Netherlands Bank.[72]

---

*The revaluation decision represented a compromise between a majority of the Monetary Council and Economics Minister Erhart, after the latter reportedly had convinced President Blessing that "the boom could not be brought under control by means of credit policy alone" (i.e., without intolerable external surpluses). MR (Mar 1961), p. 3-4; AR (1969), p. 30.

Industrial interests apparently were most influential in the lateness and littleness of the 1961 revaluation.[73] Even the observed
apparent effectiveness of the 1961 revaluation, and of the "adjustment
boom" that was needed to supplement its price-aligning effect, may
have been largely due to the poor crop year of 1961/1962, which raised
agricultural imports,[74] and to the subsidence and backflow of large
speculative holdings in Germany, themselves merely the result of
the delay in implementing the revaluation. To these factors must be
added governmental "special transactions" undertaken for policy purposes.

The chorus of external criticism, and the subsequent flood of
speculative funds, although they tended to confirm the inadequacy of
the move, did not elicit any serious consideration of further revaluation.[75] This position on the part of the monetary authorities remained
constant throughout the mounting external pressure on German policy
after 1964. A public advocacy of revaluation by the savings-bank
association in late 1964 was shrugged off, and a suggestion by the
Council of Experts of a sliding-scale revaluation was rebuffed. In
fact, the evidence of the present study would suggest that the Bundesbank's intensified concern with inflation after 1964, a concern not
proportionate to that of any other similarly placed central bank, was
itself merely a "smokescreen" to avert pressures for further revaluation.[76]

During most of the period under review, while the relationships
of all the major currencies, and even the future of the international
monetary system itself, stood in doubt, Germany remained quite reluctant unilaterally to undertake currency revaluation: the parity remained "sacrosanct" to the Bundesbank.[77] This price-level realignment measure was to be a "last resort" after adjustment inflation
was put out of reach by widened international price-level differentials.[78]

It has been noted that, although in principle Germany has little
leeway within the Common Market and GATT in manipulating its
border taxes, import duties were lowered beyond international requirements in 1964, over strenuous industry opposition. On the other
hand, the introduction of the value-added turnover tax in 1967, with
its repercussions on German border taxes and rebates, made German
imports around two percent dearer relative to domestic products.[79]
Under the former turnover border tax, imports of classes not produced in Germany (which constitute one fourth of the country's imports) were not taxed.[80] Earlier, more subtle adjustments of border
taxes had also been in the direction of virtual devaluation.[81] The
net tendency of all these measures was thus toward devaluation.

By late 1968, the opinion was widespread that Germany's price level was eight to twelve percent out of adjustment with that of its trade partners.[82] Finance Minister Strauss was quoted as weighing the possibility of a minimum eight-percent German upvaluation in conjunction with devaluation moves by other nations.[83] Economics Minister Schiller in the Bundestag suggested the Bundesbank's figure of 6.25 percent upvaluation, if other nations simultaneously devalued.[84]

Many circles in Germany, however, remained opposed to revaluation and felt, in the 1965 words of the government, that ways had repeatedly been found in the past and further ways could be found in the future, to repress imported inflation.[85]

In practice, international price realignments can take place either in the exchange market through revaluations under the pegged exchange-rate system, or in the goods market through manipulations of any of various border taxes and rebates. The taxation alternative is less thorough (i.e., less assimilable in its effects to the flexible-exchange-rate model) than the revaluation method, for three kinds of reason. First, it is partial, indeed discriminatory, affecting only specified classes of international transactions, while revaluation normally affects all such transactions.[86] Second, the effective price rise of German goods abroad is represented by a rise in government tax revenues, which government can decide to respend within the domestic economy (alternatively, the cheapening of imports at home is represented by a loss of government revenue, which government may decide to recover otherwise). Third, tax manipulations have until very recently been looked upon, by markets, financial opinion and policy-makers, as more temporary and reversible than exchange-rate manipulations.

These considerations, the long-standing search for a substitute for revaluation, and the magnitudes involved, all strongly suggest that the four-percent increase in import taxes and decrease in export taxes that was actually voted in November 1968 was in incomplete palliative, designed to lessen immediate price-effect, speculative, and political pressures, and not to produce long-run adjustment.[87] In other words, by making a four-percent realignment in (most) goods prices, in the face of an acknowledged need for an eight-percent minimum alignment in all prices, the German government was attempting simply to disarm pressures for a real adjustment. In still simpler terms, the realignment was a tactic in a strategy precisely of continued non-adjustment.

This conclusion is strengthened by at least two more pieces of evidence. Minister Schiller, in the first place, defended the border-tax measures on the ground that they were more temporary and more

easily reversible than the exchange revaluation proposed by others.[88]
Schiller pointed out the advantage of flexibility in negotiations with
the new United States administration, which (at least in the interna-
tional-economic field) had been "elected without a program." And
this advantage was claimed for these measures, incidentally, despite
the constant complaint of uncertainty raised against more flexible
exchange arrangements: there are times, it would seem, when politically managed uncertainty is preferable to market uncertainty.

In the second place, it was announced that not only would the
proceeds of the new tax be re-expended, but they would be used to
aid the "adjustment" of the very export and import-competing industries it affected.[89] This meant that the measures would have very
little real effect in realigning German cost prices, since the subsidized factor incomes could remain untouched as a whole. Only Germany's foreign-trade prices would be closer aligned internationally,
bringing an at least superficial relief from external pressures for
revaluation. At the same time, the financial-policy effect would be
somewhat like that of a remission of the import taxes, i.e., of an
increased government deficit. Such financial-policy expansion would
itself normally have a real readjusting effect; but where the foreign-
trading industries are being cushioned by subsidies, the real impact
is problematical.

The Council of Experts at one point argued that merely temporary tax measures only hasten imports, but do not really raise their
long-run rate.90 The exact analog is true of exports, which are
merely postponed by such measures, and not really reduced in their
long-run pace. What is more, this effect is probable in Germany
even under price-realignment measures which are not avowedly temporary, for example, under exchange revaluation: the entrenched
position of foreign-trading firms permits them to take a long-run
view in which any tax measure appears temporary in its real impact.
In fact, German export prices in general adjusted almost at once to
cover the November border-tax changes.[91]

All of these considerations taken together--plus perhaps the
fact that the Bundesbank was already internally in favor of revaluation in the summer of 1968, and Minister Schiller's later avowal that
he had "always" favored revaluation--suffice to place the border-tax
manipulation firmly in the category of "dynamic non-adjustment"
tactics, designed to fight speculative and political pressures for full
adjustment by periodically absorbing some of the international price
disparities.[92] It is interesting to note another aspect of these particular measures: the Council of Experts claimed that the new border
taxes had (politically) "killed" the savings-wages the Council had
proposed as a means to more effective income redistribution.[93]
(See Chapter 2, and Equation III in Chapter 1.)

At the same time, the sharp party-politicization of the whole balance-of-payments issue cannot be overlooked as a factor in German decisions. The Christian Democrats, having refused all advice to revalue, became the political victims of their own consistency.[94] Kiesinger's May 1969 "non-upvaluation" decision was followed in August by France's 11.1 percent devaluation. With elections approaching and opinion polls showing no significant public acceptance of revaluation, the CDU apparently tried to avoid admitting the truth of growing Social Democrat criticism.[95] A prominent Christian Democrat could even express publicly the feeling that upvaluation was "economically right, but politically wrong."[96]

However this may be, the border-tax solution was probably also attractive for fiscal reasons: it provided a new source of net revenue, and it avoided the necessity of paying more for the support of agriculture.[97] Minister Strauss also repeatedly emphasized the apparent "heavy loss" he saw in the writing down of the DM value of the official exchange assets, which revaluation would necessitate.[98] In the face of this politicization of the issue, a kind of tacit technicians' "alliance" among Schiller, Blessing, and Giersch of the Council of Experts began working quietly in favor of revaluation during the May 1969 crisis.[99]

The opposition to revaluation in Germany has come partly from industry, which would thereby lose some of its hidden export subsidy and import protection; partly from financial-policy managers, who fear to disturb the "cooperation" of the international financial system; partly from politicians and their constituents who may be unwilling to lose the prop of the stability-export strategy with its implications of social-order rectitude and monetary soundness. The interests of industry form the core of this resistance. No industry wishes to surrender "the apparent advantages of a slightly undervalued currency."[100] German industry, particularly, with its export bias, would be massively affected by any revaluation which really required significant adjustment. Such a situation could have the double effect of at once causing economic unrest and giving Germany the image of second-class ally, a country which must take up the slack of its partners' lax financial policies. Given certain well-known German readings of history and Germany's present world position, this eventuality might be highly undesirable for its present moderate leaders. However this may be, it has been claimed that the reactions of exporters, even to the rather insignificant revaluation of 1961, made a repetition of the tactic a practically unavailable alternative through most of the period under review.[101]

The 1969 upvaluation presented many points of difference to that of 1961, both in methods and in attitudes. Yet the same basic undervaluation dynamics remained operative. The striking innovation in the 1969 procedure was the "floating" of the DM for almost a month.

A prime issue of the general election, scheduled for late September, was revaluation. Speculation mounted as the election day approached, while official German spokesmen began to refuse to discuss revaluation prospects.[102] For the final two business days before the election, exchange markets were closed. On election eve, both major parties declared their intention not to upvalue after the election.[103] The day after the election, while the ability of the parties to form a government was still unclear, speculative inflows were so great, during a short "pre-market" test, that the exchange markets could not be reopened as planned.[104]

That day, therefore, the existing government, following an earlier suggestion of the Council of Experts, agreed to the Bundesbank's request that the Bank be relieved of its obligation to support the DM, whereupon exchange markets were reopened.[105] Although the Economics Ministry admitted publicly that this move could not be reconciled with the Bretton Woods Agreement, the Executive Directors of the International Monetary Fund at once "recognized the exigencies of the situation that have led the German government to take the action."[106] This show of "sensitive understanding" (by the same Monetary Fund which had been irreconcilable to the floating of the Canadian dollar in the fifties and rather cold to its 1970 floating) was not at once imitated by the Common Market Commission.[107] (See the preceding section.)

Thereafter German discussion centered on the size of the eventual definitive revaluation. Immediately prior to the floating of the DM, the Council of Experts had urged a ten-percent upvaluation.[108] As the float period opened, the Council suggested removal of the November 1968 border taxes, so as to let the market set the new parity freely.[109] This was done in two steps, an immediate temporary reduction of the tax rates involved to zero percent, and full repeal of the relevant law after the repegging of the DM.[110] Another technical hint of the Council of Experts was acted upon during the float period: the Bundesbank from time to time announced rates, just above the current market notations, at which it would sell dollars freely.[111] This was done to keep the market rate higher than the massive backflow of speculative funds would otherwise have allowed.

The DM rate, thus freed and guided, rose eight to nine percent in the first two weeks of the float period, despite the outflow of speculative funds to the value of about four billion DM.[112] For about two weeks thereafter, such outflows ceased (in the sense that Bundesbank purchases of DM fell), while the market exchange rate held steady.

In the face of these developments, German opinion was divided between those who favored an immediate pegging of the existing market rate[113] and those who felt that the new peg should be higher than the current market rate.[114] The purpose of the proposed higher peg was to provide a "credible and lasting solution" and to "put the monetary system on a stable basis for some time to come" in the face of structurally differing inflation rates.[115]

This explicit acknowledgment of the dynamics of undervaluation was coupled with the feeling that the existing market exchange rate did not represent an equilibrium of even the existing supply and demand: this latter feeling was surely justified since, without allowing for the aftereffects of the 1968 crisis and for speculative funds in "long-term" forms, the Bundesbank estimated that twenty to twenty-five billion DM in speculative funds had entered Germany up to the closing of the exchanges, while less than four billion had departed after the floating of the DM.[116] Even by January 1970, less than twenty-five billion DM had been removed from Germany, even including some autonomous return of investment income. Therefore, the DM was still laboring under an overhang of supply depressing its current rate below its long-term level. In the event (after the hurried formality of IMF consultations), the DM was repegged slightly above its last market quotation. Although the claim was made that the new rate included a "reserve" for future world inflationary developments, this reserve cannot be regarded as highly significant in the light of the factors discussed above.[117] The arithmetical effect of the new peg was to make German exports 9.3 percent dearer in foreign currency, and to make German imports 8.5 percent cheaper in DM.

Further "cushions" on the ultimate adjusting effect of the revaluation were brought into existence by the very passage from one parity to another. Among these cushions were: the total repeal of the November 1968 border-tax arrangements; the movement of the DM rate to the opposite end of the Bretton Woods band around parity; the fall in forward-rate discounts offered to importers; the tendency to reduced remittances by foreign workers. Still other classes of cushions are the carry-over of contracts made before revaluation; the fact that reparations payments are stipulated in DM; and the compromise nature of the agrarian support measures, which did not bring home to German consumers the whole effect of revaluation on agricultural-import prices. Thus only with the fall in the rediscount rate in March 1970 did the arithmetically expectable results of the revaluation appear in the market exchange rates.

These developments, and continued inflation abroad, coupled with the inevitable general treatment of revaluation as primarily aimed at domestic price stability, left little doubt that, despite

innovative measures and more open attitudes, the dynamics of undervaluation would soon be in evidence once again.118

Since revaluation is essentially a price manipulation, its success
logically depends on the subsequent evolution of effective international
price relationships. The following figure shows the development of
relevant prices in the period surrounding the 1968 border-tax manipulations and the 1969 revaluation.

In the two years from November 1968 to September 1970, German investment-goods exports rose about fifteen percent in their DM
prices, and about twenty percent in their dollar prices. Despite rapid
inflation abroad during the same period, therefore, Germany's competitive position in the world market was somewhat weakened price-
wise. At the same time, Germany's imports as a whole were no more
than two percent dearer in September 1970 than in November 1968,
and thus were somewhat cheapened relative to domestic-produced
goods.

From another point of view, it is noteworthy with what rapidity
both German and foreign exporters were able to offset the effects
of the border-tax and exchange-rate manipulations of the per-unit
net receipts and net outlays on their products respectively. Three
to six months sufficed to obliterate these effects completely through
price rises.

In the event, the German balance of trade almost at once recovered its strong surplus position, and the overall payments balance
also recovered quickly after speculative inflows and dammed-up
capital-account outflows were repatriated, and after the depressive
effects of anticipated export orders in 1968 and 1969 were exhausted.

Despite the theoretical adjustment aim of revaluation as such,
therefore, indications are that Germany's strategic conception of
revaluation was very similar, except in terms of scope and seeming
permanence, to that of border-tax manipulations.

It is thus fairly certain that the revaluation of 1961 was intentionally inadequate even to the international price relations then current,
while that of 1969 was at least open to fairly swift erosion by inflation
differentials. It is certainly clear that under Germany's circumstances revaluation is effectively a temporary expedient: by 1962 or
1963 the restoration of international price-level differentials had
cancelled any effects of the 1961 revaluation.119 By mid-1971 little
remained of the price effect of the 1969 revaluation. Germany's
share of world markets continued to rise both after 1961 and after
1969.120 Under the circumstances facing Germany in the sixties,

FIGURE 1

Development of Foreign-Trade Prices, 1968-1970

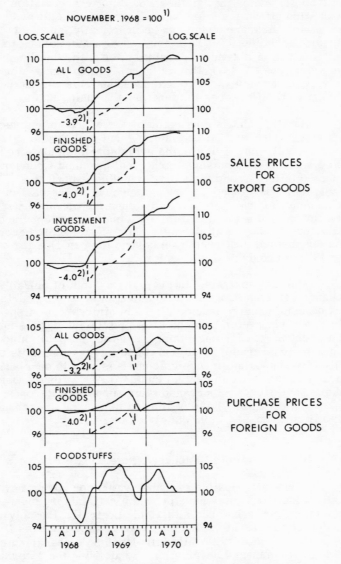

NOVEMBER, 1968 = 100 [1]

LOG. SCALE / LOG. SCALE

ALL GOODS

-3.9 [2]

FINISHED GOODS

-4.0 [2]

INVESTMENT GOODS

-4.0 [2]

SALES PRICES
FOR
EXPORT GOODS

ALL GOODS

-3.2 [2]

FINISHED GOODS

-4.0 [2]

FOODSTUFFS

PURCHASE PRICES
FOR
FOREIGN GOODS

J A J O | J A J O | J A J O
1968   1969   1970

———Net receipts per unit of exports and net outlay
per unit of imports. (1) Original basis for export
goods: 1962 = 100. (2) Average rise or fall in tax burden
due to border-tax changes, based on 1962 trade structure,
as percentage of contractual prices (Council of Experts
estimate). Price indexes calculated free-at-border.
Figure adapted from JG (1970), page 47.

133

revaluation, unless it is to be by truly staggering percentages (which would be self-defeating, as they would make speculation on the next revaluation attractive from an earlier stage), is always necessarily a short-run measure which can be practically ignored by long-run-oriented industries.[121] This point of view has nothing to do with static notions of elasticity-pessimism or with other forms of "loophole theorizing."[122] On the contrary, it is absurdly simple, resting on the planning time-scale of export industries and the deep-rooted international differences in monetary expansion rates.

This viewpoint is confirmed by the chorus of witnesses that the 1969 revaluation was far too late,[123] and probably also too little.[124] Further confirmation lies in the ever more articulate recognition by policy makers of Germany's structural penchant to undervaluation, imported inflation, and virtually invincible export bias.[125] As a result, there developed a growing tendency on the part of German spokesmen to leave quite markedly open the possibility of further revaluation, and even to call for anticipatory, "prophylactic" revaluation before fundamental disequilibrium should again become evident.[126] This discussion, continued even beyond the new floating of the DM in May 1971, is described in Chapter 7.

In the last analysis, however, the system of movably pegged exchange rates can contribute to adjustment only by periodic abrupt revaluations, usually carried out in an atmosphere of speculative crisis, and very often both too little and too late. This method of adjustment makes for uncertainty, and thus probably hinders the growth of international trade, investment, and integration. It is certainly politically unpopular in surplus countries, and is once again being opposed by the German central bank.[127] As a result, German policy makers have steadily increased their support of European monetary integration (Chapter 7) and of limited increases in exchange-rate flexibility (discussed immediately below).

Limited Exchange-Rate Flexibility

Neither fully flexible exchange rates nor abrupt revaluations of otherwise fixed rates have proved a satisfactory answer to the German payments-balance situation. Logically, the only remaining possible restructuring of the exchange regime involves limited exchange-rate flexibility. While fully flexible exchange rates would avoid abrupt managed revaluations by allowing the external prices of currencies to be fixed by market forces, a partially flexible system would have the same aim, but the actual pace of change of the exchange rates would be fixed or limited in advance, either absolutely or as a function of past rates, and could be guided by central-bank support operations.

These possibilities have been reflected in the thinking of German policy-makers. Departing from its early recommendation of upvaluation "or a surrogate" as the alternative to imported inflation, the Council of Experts has recently come to place revaluation itself second to a more smooth and dynamic exchange-rate regime, freed from campaign politics and pressure-group interests.[128] This suggestion found an immediate echo with many experts: ninety-nine economics professors adhered to an open letter of support.[129] And, mirabile dictu, this preachment has in the last few years found a powerful support in the voice of the Bundesbank's leading international monetary expert (and its Vice-President since 1970), Dr. Otmar Emminger.[130] Dr. Emminger, who had already warned against regarding parities as prestige totems, in 1969 advocated guided upward exchange-rate flexibility for surplus countries.[131]

Emminger's original initiative, nicely timed to be at least partly digested before the October 1969 International Monetary Fund annual meeting, seems to have acted as the signal for a quite general reversal of public attitude on the part of the money managers.[132] The official position of the Bundesbank itself remained ambiguous until President Blessing's December 1969 Bundestag testimony, in which he advocated the Council of Experts' wider band and self-adjusting parity for use externally by the European Community as a bloc.[133] By the end of 1969, German public opinion showed some signs of swinging to the new viewpoint.[134]

In addition to numerous more subtle channels, thus, academic and theoretical thinking on this point had, in the independent, articulate and persistent Council of Experts, found an effective institutional channel to policy makers. The idea of limited exchange-rate flexibility had also been making steady headway among various policy groups in the United States.[135]

Even German industry seems to have been educated to the point of contemplating limited flexibility by the border-tax discussion of the fall of 1968: Minister Schiller remarked that he had never heard so many good arguments for upvaluation as he did from industrialists seeking exceptions from the tax.[136] Pragmatists may also have been impressed by the effective upvaluation which had taken place on the forward market.[137]

This section can therefore conveniently be closed with a brief overview of the chief schemes for limited flexibility, with the reasons for the support they have received. Since the theme of exchange-regime reforms obviously cannot be exhausted here, the main emphasis in what follows is on such proposals as bear on German adjustment-oriented policy.

The major suggestions for greater flexibility are wider "bands" of permissible fluctuation around fixed parities, occasional "floating" of parities to gain market indications for a new fixed peg, "crawling" parities guided by authorities in accordance with a formula intended to show the progress of real disequilibrium, and discretionary crawling parities without any obligatory government intervention in exchange markets.

Widened bands would permit differing structurally-determined national credit policies within the EEC to be aimed at price stability without fearing disproportionate capital flows in response to the resulting international interest-rate differentials.138 A system incorporating wider bands of permitted fluctuation around fixed exchange-rate parities is, however, in the long run, open to the same objections as a fixed-peg system in a world of differing national economic structures, since one or the other edge of the band would eventually become the new fixed peg, with unsettling results identical to those of an originally rigid system.139

Germany, while generally favorable to wider bands, is less vitally interested in them than in other, more decisive changes. The new band-width generally contemplated in world financial circles is three percent on either side of parity, whereas the IMF presently permits central banks which intervene in dollars to maintain two percent band-width against all currencies but the dollar.

Exchange rates which on occasion float are only slightly less disruptive than fixed pegs, since they amount to groping for a new peg after having already lost contact with market forces. Germany shows some interest in this possibility, but is not overly concerned with obtaining further sanction for a process already tolerated by the IMF in the German case.

Rates which crawl by formula have found some support in United States circles, on the grounds that the continuous and gradual movement of parities would discourage speculation and make all the mechanical effects of payments imbalance either small or temporary or both. The United States Treasury, wishing to help surplus countries to overcome domestic opposition to upvaluation, supported the objective-formula concept, but (for evident reasons) tried to keep its support unobtrusive.140 The United States Council of Economic Advisors did not reject the idea in principle, but questioned the political feasibility of enforcing a strict formula, or of preventing official manipulation of the formula's indicator inputs. The Federal Reserve System, perhaps with its eye on its conservative banking "constituency," rejected the concept as endangering monetary sovereignty (although this is hardly applicable to the closed United States economy and the key-currency United States dollar).

The actual formula involved in this proposal would have to take into account changes in all the factors discussed in Chapter 1, and would be about as complex or as inaccurate as the fiscal-impact formula under development for use in the EEC's harmonization efforts (Chapter 7). Among the suggested indicators are trends in spot and forward exchange rates combined with trends in official reserve holdings.

Despite some consideration given the idea by the German Council of Experts, German policy rejected the formula crawl, probably precisely because German governments have no wish to be helped to overcome the opposition of their most influential constituents.[141] Britain, too, rejected the concept on the grounds that a forced crawl could prevent concerted action by the EEC.[142] For Britain, a formula devaluation could be self-perpetuating, since import-competing employers would resist wage demands less vigorously if they foresaw automatic increases in protection as the result of higher final prices at home. The same interests which have lamed the IMF code seem to militate against any scheme relying on the acceptance of real adjustment by nations.

Discretionary crawling exchange rates constitute the main German proposal for greater flexibility, especially over against the dollar, but also, at least as a bargaining token, in the EEC integration negotiations (Chapter 7). German Economics Ministry spokesmen have visualized a process not subject to "public" IMF procedures, but limited to a cumulative change of two percent per year.[143]

Although German spokesmen began with suggestions of a one-way flexibility for undervalued currencies only, the general fear of abuse for maintaining "dynamic undervaluation," and Germany's desire to keep the spotlight off surplus countries, has led to some softening of the German position.[144] Governor Olivier Wormser of the Bank of France indicated that any discretionary crawl facility must be two-way "from the principle of symmetry."[145] Yet a two-way discretionary crawl facility holds little promise of a meaningful solution, as governments are domestically far freer to devalue than to upvalue.

None of Germany's exchange-market interventions until May 1971 had been able to eliminate international financial and political pressures on Germany, because none was able to cope with the ongoing international price-level differentiation and transmission. Presently it is indeed doubtful whether Germany could continue to conduct a policy of non-adjustment mitigated by periodic tax and exchange-rate manipulations. In practice, this policy, which has here been called "dynamic undervaluation," had led to increasing economic costs, political pressures, and crises. To continue this policy under pegged exchange rates

would require either more frequent or more drastic discrete manipulations than have hitherto been attempted.[146] Such drastic manipulations would themselves surely be self-defeating and self-aggravating,
invoking ever-increasing uncertainty, speculation and crisis.

Seen from the perspective of this experience, exchange rates
which are free to move indefinitely far, but by indefinitely small
changes, could represent a continuation of "dynamic undervaluation"
by other, more desirable means. Limited flexibility, guided by national
authorities, whether its outside limits are agreed upon internationally
(crawling peg) or merely set by German authorities ("floating"
currency), eliminates what has hitherto been the major drawback of
"dynamic undervaluation" for a nation trying to benefit from such a
policy: the discreteness, and hence measurable size, of the ultimately
needed price-level realignments.[147] This discreteness and measurability of international price-level discrepancies makes speculative
and political pressures for revaluation more probable, and hastens
international price-transmission effects. Guided flexibility would thus
make "dynamic undervaluation" more profitable: to reapply the language
of Halm, it would be "only meant to give the quality of gradualness to
contemplated . . . parity adjustments."[148] All the advantages of undervaluation could in this way be retained while the liquidity effect
and the price-transmission effect were made subject to German control.[149] Acute economic and political crises could thus be avoided.

There is some evidence that guided flexibility has this meaning
for German policy-makers. The first clue is Dr. Emminger's original
double contention: on the one hand, that only surplus countries be
allowed this freedom, and on the other that no internationally guaranteed rate of upvaluation be imposed on the surplus countries.[150] These
two provisions would ensure that a country presently in balance-of-
payments surplus could practice "dynamic undervaluation" without
any competition or control, and would therefore doubtless remain a
surplus country indefinitely.[151] It should be emphasized here that the
crawling peg, as recommended by theorists, is usually to be accompanied by a band,[152] or by a guaranteed uptrend of the parity,[153] or
by an uptrend tied by an agreed formula to ongoing rate experience,[154]
any of which obviates discretionary fine-tuning of exchange rates by
national authorities.

Bundesbank President Blessing long since realized that one-sided
monetary adjustment by surplus countries--in modern conditions,
according to Machlup, the only adjustment mechanism left in operation--
is "a will-of-the-wisp."[155] Can more optimism really be entertained
for the idea of one-sided exchange-rate adjustment by surplus countries? Significantly, this proposal is no longer seriously presented
by Germany.

More clues to influential German thought on guided flexibility may be found in Germany's previous experience with measures for international price-level realignment. Each of these could well be regarded as an instance of guided "flexibility." In 1961 the designedly inadequate price alignment of the upvaluation was eked out with an adjustment boom which was under Bundesbank control, and could be halted before export competitiveness was threatened, i.e., short of full adjustment. In 1964 the tariff reduction was of a scope chosen by Germany, was only six months ahead of the general Common-Market schedule, and may have been largely diluted by concomitant shifts in other taxes. In 1968 one of the most telling arguments advanced for the border-tax adjustments, again of a scope chosen by Germany, was their allegedly temporary and negotiable nature. The 1969 and 1971 floating of the DM had many of the same hallmarks of unilateral manipulation.

The key element in the Emminger-style guided flexibility was the freedom of the surplus country's exchange-rate manipulations from either control or competition from abroad. Such a situation will probably not be accepted internationally. Yet, subjected to control, guided flexibility must pose the same problems for Germany as the pegged-rate system. Additionally, questions could be raised about the technical nature of this control, e.g., can an adjustment formula be found precise enough to permit objective assessment of the correct pace of exchange-rate changes under guided flexibility?[156] Do there exist any indicator inputs for such a formula that would not be subject to manipulation by national authorities? Such general questions must remain outside the direct scope of the present study; however, the German case suggests that the answers here should be "no." In any case, the effective result of the international control, and of the questions with which it must wrestle, would be simply to extend the political problem of exchange-rate changes to the international level.

Subjected to competition, on the other hand, the guided-flexibility proposal is an invitation to subtle forms of competitive devaluation. Movable pegs are more like competitive depreciation than are flexible rates; and the more unilaterally controllable the pegs are, the more they conduce to competitive depreciation. But the latter is essentially destructive of any international monetary system, and thus of any undervaluation advantage to individual nations. Thus, only if subjected to merely formal, but ineffective, international control could guided exchange-rate flexibility subserve a German dynamic-undervaluation strategy. Otherwise it can be at best merely another expedient to gain time.

Does the suggestion of "limited parity adjustment" or guided flexibility represent a fundamentally new departure for German policy thinking?[157] A summary of the position suggests that it does not.

On the adjustment front, the new departure is closely linked to two major facets of current German international economic policy. These are the strategy of adjustment preserving "dynamic undervaluation," and European monetary integration. The revaluation of March 1961, the border-tax manipulations of November 1968, and even the revaluation of 1969 cannot be looked upon as really wholehearted attempts at full long-run adjustment. At the same time, none of these measures was wholly successful in its imputed role as a tactic for diverting the economic and political pressures of undervaluation.

The German position on limited exchange-rate flexibility can thus readily be linked to its longstanding payments-balance strategy. However, limited flexibility would not so obviously harmonize with German visions of European monetary integration. This aspect of the flexibility question will be treated again in Chapter 7. Here the major conclusions of that discussion can be briefly anticipated. In the long view, rigid exchange parities are definitional constituents of a completed monetary union, and only such a union can provide the benefits of independence from the dollar, that all Europeans expect of integration.[158] In the shorter view, it is possible to visualize greater exchange-rate rigidity either traditionally, with France, as tightening payments-balance discipline and making for mutual international adjustment of real structural elements; or, with Germany, as crippling the political power to resist imported inflation, forced lending, and extorted compensatory aid to trade partners.

Externally to the EEC, in a world of inflexible prices and politicized income levels, exchange rates are the only means of, at least accounting-wise, adjusting international differences of structure. Until the latter end, exchange rates must not be frozen. Again, until all remaining barriers to international intercourse are removed, even market-determined parities cannot be long-run equilibrium rates, and so should not be frozen.[159] Thus, German spokesmen claim that the EEC has a natural interest in a sufficiently flexible world monetary system, both internally in the short run and externally in the long.

The flexibility discussion in international bodies has faithfully represented the patterns of national positions. After the 1969 floating of the DM, Working Party Three of the OECD Economic Policy Committee studied all proposals for greater flexibility, referring three possible classes of measures to the IMF for further study: wider bands, temporary floating, and discretionary crawling parities. At the Copenhagen meeting in September 1970, the IMF Executive Director recommended the same three measures for still more study, and specifically rejected exchange rates which would crawl according to a formula. Italy and Germany supported these recommendations, which agreed extremely well with the current German ideas.[160] France and

Belgium made all consideration of increased exchange-rate flexibility
dependent on the outcome of the negotiations for European monetary
integration (Chapter 7).

From the international viewpoint, all merely technical reforms
of the exchange regime seem to be based on assumptions about national
adjustment policies which in effect wish away the basic problems, born
of real interests, facing the international monetary system.

During the period under review, no important long-run effect
on Germany's payments balance was obtained either by market-structural interventions or by direct manipulation of "real" elements. In
the latter area, the prospects of success within a liberal economic
order remain dim. In the product-market structural field, there seems
to be little leeway for restructuring. The institutional problems of
Germany's capital market have rather been aggravated than solved
in recent years. Conflicts of doctrine and interest have throughout
the decade prevented any measures avowedly aimed at restructuring
the exchange regime.

ADJUSTMENT THROUGH FINANCIAL POLICY

The only remaining area of adjustment measures open to Germany
is financial policy. It has been noted that financial policy, embracing
both monetary and fiscal measures, can set up income and liquidity
conditions indirectly forcing a real balance-of-payments adjustment
by replacing foreign with domestic demand and by replacing surplus
savings, represented by the balance-of-payments surplus, with government or private debt.[161] It has likewise been noted that the net effect
of financial policy has in fact been insufficient for basic adjustment in
the period under review.

A fiscal deficit can bring about payments-balance adjustment by
absorbing funds which otherwise would have financed the growth of
central-bank reserves. At the same time, government spending can
add to domestic demand for growth-oriented infrastructural investment
goods, thus presenting export industries with a changed foreign/domes-
tic price relation.

International adjustment through fiscal deficit has been explicitly
advocated in Germany,[162] but the resulting debate has ranged confusedly
over anticyclical, growth and policy-mix questions. This ensemble of
questions will therefore be treated in Chapter 5.

In the credit-policy area, if the central bank purchases assets
net, it incurs debt; and this debt by definition and law constitutes a

high-powered monetary base which can trigger an expansion of effective demand by mechanisms which have already been sketched. The debate about the relative effectiveness of credit-policy measures is neither new nor apparently nearing a final agreement. This debate has seen eminent specialists make seemingly extreme statements of opposite import.[163] Yet the most pessimistic doubts about the efficacity of monetary policy hardly apply to determined expansionary measures, which alone are at issue in the present chapter.

The policy of "adjustment inflation" as such has not been publicly advocated in Germany. Probably it has not even been consciously followed, except during the period immediately after the revaluation of 1961, when it was necessary to drive off the political and speculative pressures for further upvaluation.

Several problems inhibit the use of financial policy for full adjustment in Germany. The most technically telling of these is the probability that, given the structural stickiness of the export industries, really effective injections of domestic demand would have to be very large and thus seriously injure the cherished goal of price stability, with unforeseeable economic and political effects on the German society. As has been noted, heavy industry by definition requires high fixed costs. These costs can only be reduced to competitive per-unit levels by operating at the volume of output made possible by markets beyond Germany's relatively narrow limits.[164] Again, the postwar costs of reconquering Germany's place in the world markets are fairly recent and so appear to be felt as additional fixed costs for longer-run planning purposes.[165] The resulting disproportion of fixed costs, combined with the relative de facto immobility of labor, lengthens the short run for German export industries.[166] That is, they lengthen the time period over which these industries can plan to accept prices below their "normal" full costs without considering permanent reallocation of capital to other production. The ability of German exporting firms to refrain temporarily from absorbing in their prices the full effects of upvaluations and border-tax rises seems to bear this out.[167]

At the same time, these industries have come to expect a progressive divergence of foreign from domestic prices in the postwar era, founded ultimately, as has been illustrated, on such stable elements as (in Germany) the national psychology and history, and (abroad) deep-seated social and structural problems.

In these circumstances, international economic-policy measures entailing an extraordinarily large relative drop in effective foreign prices would be required in order to jolt resources loose from the exporting industries. In view of the leading position of foreign-trading industries in Germany, particularly in the area of investment, such a violent realignment of price levels would disrupt the German economy and society to an unacceptable and even dangerous degree. German industrialists appear certain that the government both realizes this state of affairs, and recognizes the geopolitical advantages of heavy industry-in-being and of the financial surplus itself.168

It is also possible that financial-policy expansion for balance-of-payments adjustment purposes could independently hurt another macro-economic goal, that of growth. Absorption of savings by government borrowing could overload the narrow German capital market and thus cut the outside financing of firms, with undesirable side effects both on interest rates and international capital movements, and on the social-policy and wealth-distribution goals associated with a broad capital market.169 Cutting down firms' access to outside funds may in fact reinforce the export bias in industry, as the export industries would remain relatively independent of outside financing until the adjustment measures had actually succeeded in pumping up domestic demand and costs relative to foreign.

It might be argued in reply that, given the need for government infrastructural investments, non-deficit spending by government would reduce the inside financing of firms through tax revenues. This might indeed be a more appropriate tactic, as the absorption of funds would affect all firms in "normal" proportions, while the disbursement of the funds could by definition only benefit producers for the domestic market. Such a measure of course comes very close to a direct "power-to-destroy" tax intervention in the market system.

Fiscal deficits could in Germany quite conceivably hurt growth also by discouraging savers, who typically mistrust the overall socio-economic effects of large-scale government deficits. This mistrust is greatest and most immediate in the concern over price stability, and, given the intent and the circumstances of financial adjustment tactics in Germany, this mistrust would find itself most justified in precisely that area of concern.

Despite these problems surrounding financial-policy measures toward full payments-balance adjustment, the degree of payments adjustment which Germany has in fact maintained with the outside world, in the absence of effective adjustment measures in the other fields reviewed above, must be ascribed to permitted price inflation. This inflation was the result of various mechanical liquidity and direct price-transmission effects, together with the tacit acquiescence (and vocal protest) of the Bundesbank. Although Germany's imported inflation has thus been considerable, and has had the expectable income-redistributing effects, it must be recalled that the German price level still lagged behind the 1961 parity with Germany's trade partners' to

an estimated weighted average of eight or more percent before the
October 1969 revaluation.

The mass of circumstantial evidence indicates that balance-of-
payments adjustment through financial-policy measures was not a goal
pursued in Germany during the period under review. Not only was
domestic demand not deliberately supported; the monetary authorities
in effect supported foreign demand by inter-central-bank lending.[170]

Pending a full discussion of non-adjusting tactics in Chapters
4 and 5, an interim corroboration of these observations may be found
in a relatively simple, if extremely crude, comparison. Since Germany
entered the sixties with negligible fiscal reserve funds from previous
government surpluses, and with virtually none on deposit with commercial banks, the net effect of all financial-policy measures (monetary and fiscal) must be reflected directly in additions to potential free
commercial-bank reserves (i.e., including those additions due to
changes in legal reserve requirements). Thus, in the light of the tendencies of policy in all the other areas discussed in this chapter,
additions to free commercial-bank reserve money--or monetary base--
can be provisionally accepted as a measure of Germany's effective
financial policy.

At the same time, the balance-of-payments-related variable to
which this financial-policy variable can best be compared is the
"basic" balance (i.e., the balance which does not take into account
capital-export efforts, which are alternatives to adjustment).

Now, while the overall balance-of-payments surplus causes an
equal rise in the monetary base, the reverse is not necessarily true.
In Germany, for example, a rise in the monetary base is in its turn
probably associated with, not an equal, but a larger eventually expectable shift in autonomous payments-balance accounts. Yet, to be
regarded as adjusting, financial policy must be aimed at a future reduction of the surplus at least as large as the existing imbalance.
The marginal deposit-expansion ratio, the marginal income-velocity
of money, the marginal propensity to import, and the "autonomous"
growth of exports together determine, all else equal, by what fraction
of the basic surplus the monetary base must be allowed to rise, if the
former is to be eventually eliminated.

As noted in Chapter 1, all of these ratios (setting aside here the
effects of changes in reserve requirements) have remained within a
reasonably wide range over the period under review. The "expectable"
marginal expansion of effective new monetary base has been about 2.0
(since marginal cash drain has been taken as .33 and the base-period
average legal reserve requirements of March 1961 was around .18).

The marginal income-velocity of "money" was something over 6.5; the marginal propensity to import was about .25. Crudely calculated, therefore: to reflect efforts toward eventual full readjustment of the balance of payments through changes in imports alone, and without any allowance for the growth of exports, new free reserve money (including the effects of changes in reserve requirements) over the period in question should have been about one third as great as the basic balance-of-payments surplus. If this figure is doubled to account for the autonomous growth of exports, new monetary base should have amounted to around two thirds of the surplus, in order to indicate adjustment.

From April 1961 through September 1970, the cumulative net basic balance-of-payments surplus was around seventy billion DM (Tables A); for the same period, the total net additions to free reserve money was around thirty-two billion DM (Tables G). Thus, no matter what the lags in the effectiveness of these financial-policy measures may be,[171] the latter were in any case only about seventy percent as large as they would need to be (under all the above assumptions) in order to show a consistent financial-policy effort for basic payments balance.

Neither fiscal nor monetary policy measures have been used for adjustment purposes in Germany during the period under review. The impression derivable from the discussion thus far is that, while various disequilibrating movements have taken place among the elements influencing Germany's basic payments balance (Chapter 1), no adequate readjustment measures have been taken (Chapter 3), for reasons connected ultimately with Germany's objectives and interests (Chapter 2).

In the following two chapters, the German experience with balance-of-payments tactics not aimed at basic adjustment will be examined.

NOTES

1. H. W. Jenkis, Die Importierte Inflation (Schriften zur Wirtschaftswissenschaftlichen Forschung #15) (Meisenheim, 1966), p. 87n.

2. Federal Republic of Germany, Sachverständigenrat zur Begutachtung der Gesamtwirtschaftlichen Entwicklung, Jahresgutachten (1970), Section 287; JG (1970), Sections 9-13.

3. See also J. E. Meade, The Theory of International Economic Policy, Vol. 1: The Balance of Payments (New York, 1961), Chs. 9, 10, 14, 24.

4. G. Haberler in W. Fellner, F. Machlup, and R. Triffin, eds., Maintaining and Restoring Balance in International Payments (Princeton, 1966), p. 13.

5. F. Machlup, International Payments, Debt and Gold (New York, 1964), p. 358; G. Haberler, Money in the International Economy (Cambridge, 1965), p. 18.

6. Federal Republic of Germany, Bundesbank, Auszüge aus Presseartikeln (1970), #37, p. 8 f.

7. JG (1969), p. 14 n. 3.

8. L. A. Hahn, Fünfzig Jahre zwischen Inflation und Deflation (Tübingen, 1963), p. 206.

9. G. Gutman, H. J. Hochstrate, and R. Schüter, Die Wirtschaftsverfassung der Bundesrepublik Deutschland (Stuttgart, 1964), p. 363; W. Schmidt, "The German Bundesbank," Bank for International Settlements, Eight European Central Banks (London, 1963), p. 87.

10. The Economist, Quarterly Economic Survey (Germany) (1967), IV, p. 5; JG (1967), Section 138.

11. Federal Republic of Germany, Bundesbank, Monthly Report (Jun 1964), p. 34; JG (1968), Section 220 N; JG (1964), Section 117; QES (1964), II, p. 8.

12. Federal Republic of Germany, Sachverständigenrat zur Begutachtung der Gesamtwirtschaftlichen Entwicklung, Sondergutachten (1969), I, Sections 1-5.

13. G. Schmölders, Finanzpolitik (Berlin, 1965), p. 476-477; Free Democrat leader Walter Scheel, AP (1969), #39, p. 30.

14. Federal Republic of Germany, Bundesbank, Annual Report (1968), p. 22.

15. L. Erhard, The Economics of Success (Princeton, 1963), p. 373; JG (1964), Section 246; JG (1967), Section 224; JG (1970), Section 290; AP (1968), #63, p. 7.

16. Federal Republic of Germany, Bundesministerium für Wirtschaft, Wissenschaftliche Beirat, "Report on Prices," Bundesanzeiger #32 (1968), p. 3.

17. AP (1970), #75, p. 3.

18. For a full explanation of this reasoning, see Federal Republic of Germany, Bundesministerium für Finanz, Finanzbericht (1968), p. 188.

19. The United States Treasury suggested in one of its "Progress Reports" on international payments that "the ideal situation" would involve Germany's "putting less stress on producing goods for export" (Wall Street Journal [27 Dec 1968], p. 4).

20. AP (1970), #37, p. 6.

21. See AP (1970), #37, p. 8.

22. AP (1971), #4, p. 7.

23. O. Emminger, Währungspolitik im Wandel der Zeit (Frankfurt, 1966), p. 177.

24. BR, Bundesanzeiger (1966), #126.

25. MR (Jan 1965), p. 4.

26. K. Blessing, Im Kampf um gutes Geld (Frankfurt, 1966), p. 286, 299; MR (Oct 1965), p. 5.

27. MR (Jan 1966), p. 16; MR (Apr 1967), p. 26; MR (Jan 1965), p. 34; MR (Oct 1965), p. 5.

28. SG (1965), Sections 134, 137; Blessing, Kampf, p. 298; AP (1967), #90, p. 2.

29. JG (1966), Section 172; MR (Oct 1967), p. 5; MR (Jun 1967), p. 20.

30. AR (1967), p. 40; MR (Jan 1967), p. 20.

31. AP (1969), #60, p. 5; MR (May 1967), p. 7; AR (1967), p. 40.

32. MR (Aug 1966), p. 5.

33. JG (1967), Section 194.

34. MR (Oct 1967), p. 6.

35. MR (May 1967), p. 20.

36. L. A. Hahn, Ein Traktat über Währungsreform (Tübingen, 1964), p. 189.

37. JG (1965), Section 134a.

38. AP (1970), #84, p. 5.

39. JG (1964), Section 48 and throughout. Revaluation was first authoritatively urged by the Economics Ministry Advisory Council (BR) in 1957.

40. Wall Street Journal (27 Oct 1969), p. 1.

41. J. M. Keynes, A Treatise on Money (New York, 1930), I, p. 356 f.; F. D. Graham, Fundamentals of International Monetary Policy (Essays in International Finance #2) (Princeton, 1943); G. Haberler, and T. D. Willett, The United States Balance of Payments and International Monetary Reform: A Critical Analysis (Washington, 1968), p. 64.

42. JG (1964), Section 240 f.; SG (1969), I, Section 26-28; SG (1969), III; Schiller, German Economic Review (1967), #2, p. 165n; Hahn, Jahre, p. 113.

43. This, and the other objections below, have often been formulated by Emminger (e.g., AP [1968], #15, p. 5), and more recently by the Council of Experts (JG [1970], Sections 302-321).

44. JG (1964), Section 8.

45. Keynes anticipated such adjustments at least as early as A Tract on Monetary Reform (London, 1923), p. 182 ff.

46. JG (1964), Government Response, Section 10.

47. G. Haberler, and others, "Round Table on Exchange Rate Policy," American Economic Review (May 1969) (Papers and Proceedings of the 81st Annual Meeting of the American Economic Association), p. 358.

48. France had insisted on this feature, and almost broke the Common Market over it in 1965 (FR [1967], p. 63-64).

49. AP (1969), #60, p. 2.

50. AP (1969), #85, p. 6; AP (1969), #69, p. 11; AP (1969), #85, p. 3; AP (1969), #95, p. 8; JG (1969), Section 298 ff.; JG (1969), Section 305; SG (1969), III, Section 18.

51. Blessing, Kampf, p. 45.

52. JG (1964), Section 240g; JG (1969), Section 292.

53. Paul Einzig, A Dynamic Theory of Forward Exchanges (London, 1962), p. 500-502.

54. A. Lanyi, The Case for Floating Exchange Rates Reconsidered (Essays in International Finance #72) (Princeton, 1969), p. 6.

55. JG (1970), Section 312.

56. M. Friedman, "The Case for Flexible Exchange Rates," Essays in Positive Economics (Chicago, 1953); E. Sohmen, Flexible Exchange Rates: Theory and Controversy (Chicago, 1961), Chapter 1; S. Arndt, "International Short-Term Capital Movements: A Distributed Lag Model of Speculation in Foreign Exchange," Econometrica (January 1968); G. N. Halm, International Financial Intermediation: Deficits Benign and Malignant (Essays in International Finance #68) (Princeton, 1968), p. 9; M. J. Farrell, "Profitable Speculation," Economica (May 1966), p. 192; JG (1970), Section 305.

57. JG (1964), Sections 8, 10, 33.

58. JG (1967), p. 228.

59. R. A. Mundell, "A Theory of Optimum Currency Areas," American Economic Review (September 1961).

60. Bundesbank Vice President Emminger, AP (1967), #44, p. 3.

61. JG (1967), Section 308.

62. Roosa in M. Friedman, and R. V. Roosa, The Balance of Payments: Free vs. Fixed Exchange Rates (Washington, 1967), p. 52; F. Machlup, and B. G. Malkiel, eds., International Monetary Arrangements: The Problem of Choice (Princeton, 1964), p. 90.

63. J. Viner, International Economics (Glencoe, 1951), p. 205.

64. AP (1970), #72, p. 9.

65. Machlup, Payments, p. 359; JG (1969), Section 282.

66. Schmidt, p. 60; MR (Mar 1961), p. 3.

67. MR (Nov 1961), p. 3 ff.

68. AR (1967), p. 33.

69. IMF, US, UK spokesmen in Wall Street Journal (30 Sep 1969), p. 3 and (1 Oct 1969), p. 3.

70. Wall Street Journal (2 Oct 1969), p. 3.

71. MR (Mar 1961), p. 3; J. Hein, "Monetary Policy and External Convertibility: the German Experience, 1959-1961," Economia Internazionale (August 1964), p. 537; T. Scitovsky, Money and the Balance of Payments (Chicago, 1969), p. 175n; QES (1961), I, Mar.

72. W. Fellner, F. Machlup, and R. Triffin, eds., Maintaining and Restoring Balance in International Payments (Princeton, 1966), p. 135.

73. JG (1964), Section 13; Hahn, Jahre, p. 120; W. Röpke, Geld und Kapital in unserer Zeit (Baden-Baden, 1964), p. 39; W. Gatz, "Gründe und volkswirtschaftliche Wirkungen der D-Mark-Aufwertung," Weltwirtschaftliches Archiv (1963), p. 388.

74. JG (1964), Section 16.

75. AR (1967), p. 30.

76. QES (1965), II, p. 5; Arbeitsgemeinschaft Deutscher Wirtschaftswissenschaftlicher Forschungsinstitute, Die Internationalen Währungsprobleme in der Weltwirtschaft der Gegenwart (Supplement to Zeitschrift für Angewandte Konjunkturforschung #14) (Berlin, 1967), p. 80.

77. MR (Mar 1961), p. 3; Hein, "Policy," p. 537.

78. AP (1969), #56, p. 2.

79. JG (1968), Section 117; JG (1967), Section 470; JG (1966), Section 117; JG (1968), p. 4. Also see QES (1967), IV, p. 1-2.

80. JG (1967), Section 468.

81. FR (1968), p. 206.

82. AR (1968), p. 18-19; AR (1969), p. 15.

83. AP (1969), #38, p. 4.

84. AP (1969), #55, p. 8; AR (1968), p. 23. Later, Schiller was to "remember" that the Bundesbank had estimated the necessary upvaluation at "four to five percent, no more" (AP [1970], #85, p. 2).

85. JG (1965), Government Response.

86. JG (1964), Section 240.

87. SG (1969), Section 10; JG (1968), Section 226. Minister Schiller estimated that the net effect was equivalent to a three-percent upvaluation (AP [1970], #27, p. 4).

88. AP (1969), #11, p. 5; AP (1969), #84, p. 7.

89. JG (1969), p. 39.

90. JG (1968), Section 226.

91. MR (Nov 1969), p. 32; SG (1969), I, Section 10-11. See below, Figure 1.

92. AP (1970), #28, p. 7. Schiller was a leading member of the Economics Ministry Advisory Council when it proposed revaluation in 1957 (JG [1964], Section 12).

93. AP (1968), #86, p. 6.

94. SG (1968), May 1968; Bundesbank President Blessing, AP (1969), #98, p. 4, Nov 1968; Free Democrat President Scheel, AP (1969), #36, p. 10, Feb 1969; Economics Ministry Advisory Council, AP (1969), #36, p. 10, Feb 1969; Minister Schiller, AP (1969), #36, p. 3, May 1969; Savers Association President L. Poullain, AP (1969), #81, p. 6, Aug 1969; forty-six experts, AP (1969), #83, p. 5, Sep 1969.

95. AP (1969), #36, p. 6.

96. Bavarian Economics Minister, AP (1969), #36, p. 9.

97. AR (1968), p. 19.

98. AP (1969), #84, p. 3.

99. Minister Schiller, AP (1970), #4, p. 2; AP (1970), #4, p. 4.

100. Roosa in Friedman and Roosa, p. 50.

101. Bernstein in American Enterprise Institute, International Payments Problems (Washington, 1966), p. 86.

102. AP (1969), #72, p. 4.

103. AP (1971), #15, p. 4.

104. MR (Nov 1969), p. 34.

105. SG (1969), I, Section 36; AP (1969), #73, p. 2.

106. AP (1969), #73, p. 3; AP (1969), #74, p. 1.

107. AP (1969), #4; AP (1970), #38, p. 15.

108. SG (1969), II.

109. SG (1969), III.

110. AP (1969), #83, p. 1.

111. JG (1969), Section 105; MR (Nov 1969), p. 35; SG (1969), III, Section 7.

112. AR (1969), p. 13; MR (Nov 1969), p. 35.

113. AP (1969), #99, p. 3; Popular Bank Association President Horst Baumann, AP (1969), #83, p. 5; Bank Association President Münchmeyer, AP (1969), #83, p. 4.

114. SG (1969), I, Section 25; Emminger, AP (1969), #87, p. 7; Schiller, AP (1969), #84, p. 2, 10; Savers Association President Poullain, AP (1969), #84, p. 10; AR (1969), p. 15.

115. Emminger, AP (1969), #87, p. 2.

116. AP (1970), #8, p. 3; MR (Nov 1969), p. 35.

117. MR (Nov 1969), p. 7; AP (1969), #84, p. 2; AP (1969), #87, p. 2.

118. Bundesbank President Blessing, AP (1969), #91, p. 2; Minister Schiller, AP (1969), #92, p. 4; Bundesbank Vice President Emminger, AP (1969), #92, p. 2.

119. JG (1964), Sections 16, 25.

120. JG (1965), Sections 56-57.

121. AP (1969), #85, p. 11; Bayer, AG, AP (1969), #85, p. 9; Hoesch,AG, AP (1969), #85, p. 110.

122. Machlup, Payments, p. 52; Hahn, Jahre, p. 135.

123. Bundesbank Director Pfleiderer, AP (1970), #84, p. 7; Minister Schiller, AP (1970), #85, p. 1; Bundesbank, AR (1969); Economics Ministry, AP (1971), #8, p. 5.

124. JG (1970), Section 122 ff.; JG (1969), Section 92; SG (1970), I; Organization for Economic Cooperation and Development, Economic and Development Review Committee, Survey (Germany) (1970); Chancellor Brandt, AP (1971), #6, p. 8.

125. Bundesbank Vice President Emminger, AP (1970), #29, p. 3; Chancellor Brandt, AP (1970), #38, p. 3; Bundesbank Vice President Emminger, AP (1970), #6, p. 2.

126. Kieler Konjunkturforschungsinstitut, AP (1970), #76, p. 2; Bundesbank Vice President Emminger and Minister Schiller, AP (1970), #6, p. 3.

127. AP (1970), #72, p. 3; AP (1970), #75, p. 2.

128. JG (1964), Section 6; JG (1966), Section 254; AP (1969), #38, p. 13; AP (1969), #39, p. 2; AP (1969), #52, p. 3, 4; JG (1969), Sections 260, 281.

129. AP (1969), #55, p. 3.

130. AP (1969), #46, p. 16; AP (1969), #63, p. 7.

131. AP (1968), #86, p. 3.

132. International Monetary Fund, Summary Proceedings, Annual Meeting (1969).

133. AP (1969), #98, p. 4; AP (1969), #62, p. 2.

134. Social Market Economy Action Group, AP (1969), #95, p. 8.

135. G. N. Halm, Toward Limited Exchange-Rate Flexibility (Essays in International Finance #73) (Princeton, 1969), p. 3.

136. AP (1968), #84, p. 7.

137. AP (1969), #56, p. 2; AP (1969), #46, p. 9.

138. Bundesbank Vice President Emminger, AP (1970), #84, p. 5.

139. JG (1964), Section 240e; JG (1969), Section 284; G. N. Halm, The "Band" Proposal: The Limits of Permissible Exchange Rate Variations (Special Papers in International Economics #6) (Princeton, 1965), p. 16.

140. AP (1970), #79, p. 11.

141. SG (1969), I, Section 28; Economics Ministry, AP (1970), #39, p. 14.

142. AP (1970), #72, p. 8.

143. Economics Ministry, AP (1970), #39, p. 4; Economics Ministry, AP (1970), #3, p. 6; Bundesbank Vice President Emminger and Minister Schiller, AP (1970), #6, p. 3; JG (1970), Section 287; AP (1970), #80, p. 1.

144. UK Chancellor of Exchequer Barber, AP (1970), #72, p. 9; AP (1970), #79, p. 11; Müller-Enders, AP (1970), #39, p. 14.

145. AP (1970), #39, p. 3.

146. JG (1964), Section 240d.

147. See Halm, Flexibility, p. 16.

148. Halm, Flexibility, p. 26.

149. F. Clauss, "Wirtschaftswachstum und Konjunkturpolitik in der bestehenden Währungsordnung" in Arbeitsgemeinschaft, etc. p. 84-85.

150. AP (1969), #63, p. 1.

151. JG (1969), Section 291.

152. Machlup in Haberler, "Table," p. 369; F. M. Bator, "The Political Economics of International Money," Foreign Affairs (October 1968), p. 51.

153. JG (1967), Section 308n.

154. JG (1969), Section 260.

155. Blessing, Kampf, p. 116; Machlup, Payments, p. 83; also see Fellner, p. 57.

156. See Halm, Flexibility, p. 20, 26.

157. JG (1969), Section 287 f.; Emminger, AP (1969), #46, p. 16; Emminger, AP (1969), #63, p. 7.

158. AP (1970), #80, p. 11.

159. AP (1970), #84, p. 9.

160. Economics Ministry, AP (1970), #36, p. 13.

161. JG (1968), Section 136.

162. Minister Schiller, AP (1967), #31, p. 2.

163. Contrast the statements of H. G. Johnson (Alternative Guiding Principles for the Use of Monetary Policy [Essays in International Finance #44] [Princeton, 1963], p. 7) and the Radcliffe Committee (United Kingdom, Committee on the Working of the Monetary System, Report [U. K. Command 827] [London, 1959]) with those of the Chicago (M. Friedman, "The Quantity Theory of Money--A Restatement," Milton Friedman, ed., Studies in the Quantity Theory of Money [Chicago, 1963]) and "St. Louis" (D. Fand, "Some Issues in Monetary Economics," Federal Reserve Bank of St. Louis, Review [January 1970]) schools.

164. Bundesbank Director L. Gleske, AP (1969), #15, p. 5.

165. President Abs of the Bank Association, AP (1969), #1, p. 10.

166. Labor is less mobile occupation-wise, for lack of sufficient retraining facilities; firm-wise, by reason of many financial and sentimental ties; and location-wise, because of region--(Stamm-) consciousness (JG [1965], Sections 213, 235, 242; JG [1966], Sections 95-98, 195; Hahn, Jahre, p. 185).

167. Wall Street Journal (1 Oct 1969), p. 3.

168. Bundesbank President Blessing, AP (1968), #60, p. 3; President Abs of the Bank Association, AP (1969), #1, p. 10.

169. JG (1968), Section 133.

170. SG (1968), Section 3.

171. JG (1969), Sections 236-239.

4

THE
POLICY
ALTERNATIVES:
NON-ADJUSTING TACTICS
AT THE EXCHANGE LEVEL

NATURE OF THE TACTIC

All the potential policy measures tending to perpetuate non-adjustment must operate by eliminating or retarding the mechanical effects of the original autonomous imbalance, while leaving the causal elements of the situation more or less untouched. If the various effects to be expected from basic international disequilibrium have been adequately catalogued in Chapter 1, the non-adjustment measures open to Germany can here be similarly classified according to their aims of counteracting the income, price, or liquidity effects of fundamental balance-of-payments surplus.

Retarding the Price and Income Effects

Retarding the International Price-Transmission Effect

While, as noted in Chapter 1, the direct international price-transmission effect of basic international imbalance tends to restore equilibrium in an evident way, its working is slow and lagged, depending on the degree of openness of the economy. In an inflationary world environment, the direct price-transmission effect therefore cannot restore full equilibrium as long as national markets are measurably sheltered, as is by definition the case. On the other hand, neither can this effect be directly suppressed by liberal economic-policy measures so long as there is to be any international integration of the economy: only by completely cutting the economy's ties with the world could the price seepage be eliminated. Reducing competition among domestic industries and factors, and particularly between the export-oriented and the domestic-oriented sectors, could reduce the speed of price-level transmission. But this is obviously not an economically or politically feasible procedure.

Thus no measures directly aimed at stifling the price-transmission effect have been taken or discussed in Germany in the period under study.

Retarding the Income Effect

The income effect of balance-of-payments surplus tends to re-establish equilibrium, since the relatively high incomes of those engaged in export industries will stimulate them, all else being equal, to demand more consumption or investment goods. This new demand, increased relative to its analogs abroad, will tend to raise domestic prices and to spill over into imports. Evidently, since this income effect operates through (normally fractional) marginal propensities to spend (as well as through price-elasticities, at another analytical level), and since its first impact is likely to be on profit-receivers with relatively low spending propensities, it will be rather weak and slow in restoring international balance. This can be particularly true where the overall national spending propensities of the trade partners are of unequal force.

By the same token, the income effect works through changes in sectoral and functional incomes and spending, and for this reason is extremely difficult to combat by the general economic measures conformable to a liberal economic system. In Germany, with a large export sector and a relatively recently rehabilitated social-political order, overall income and price levels would have to be held down to crisis levels to repress the income effects in the export sectors.

But such tactics would reinforce the income-distribution biases that made them necessary originally; and the resulting low price level would continually increase the attractiveness of German exports and so continually fuel the income effect itself. This result would only be reinforced by progressive inflation abroad. In terms of techniques, only highly discriminatory measures, such as "power-to-destroy" tax intervention in the nation's key employment and investment sector, could hope to reach and suppress the balance-of-payments income effect in Germany. In political terms, however, such measures would be impossible. In practice, therefore, nothing has been done in Germany in the period under review which could be interpreted as counteracting the income effect of the balance of payments.

Retarding the Liquidity Effect

A much more immediate result of balance-of-payments disequilibrium is the liquidity effect. German nationals receive net short-term foreign claims as a concomitant of the imbalance on other international accounts. If retained in private hands, this liquidity constitutes a demand-stimulating increase in wealth. In the hands of banks, these funds are a virtual increase in free reserves, since, under the pegged-exchange-rate system, they are always immediately redeemable in monetary authorities' credit. If these net new foreign claims are in fact sold to the monetary authorities, they become the counterpart of the new emissions of central-bank credit with which the monetary authorities buy them. Either of the latter cases also tends to restore payments equilibrium through higher lending, demand, and prices. Again, Germany's relatively increased liquidity tends to lower German interest rates internationally, and so to initiate an export of capital.

Once transmuted in this way into official international reserves, finally, these funds are subject to constant international scrutiny as the most visible evidence that non-adjusting policies have been pursued. This aspect of the liquidity effect is especially embarrassing to Germany, with its vital interests in a friendly and harmonious West and in an untrammeled international commercial system.

German policy toward such shifts of liquidity seems to have been dominated by fear of inflation and its consequences. This fear forbade that net inflows of funds be allowed to raise the money supply, raise prices, and so attract net new imports into the domestic market.[1] Because of the danger of permanent loss of international competitiveness, this process represented for the Bundesbank "a make-believe solution."[2] Viewed a priori as being thus prevented from transforming itself into an increase in real capital in Germany, any monetary inflow can be rejected as simply "inflationary liquidity."[3] Since, too, a large percentage of the foreign investment in Germany has been in government securities, any liquidity inflow tended to be seen as inflationary finance of an expanding government sector.[4] But the Bundesbank has consistently resisted the growth of the public sector, even when financed by taxation, and particularly any expansion of "social" expenditures.[5]

The general strategies for combating the liquidity effect of international disequilibrium can for the purpose at hand perhaps best be classified according to the types (or stages) of liquidity affected, viz., official international reserves and domestic monetary base.*

---

*Classification of these measures merely according to the technical tools used is not in this case analytically fruitful. High reserve requirements on foreign accounts and tax advantages to investment abroad, for example, have much the same aim--net capital export. To separate such measures into such categories as "monetary" or

In order to retard the liquidity effect at the "reserves level" ("balance-of-payments correction"), the authorities must divert the short-term foreign claims earned by nationals away from the windows of the central bank where they would be exchanged for high-powered domestic money and would also constitute internationally embarrassing riches on the central bank's books. This diversion implies essentially discriminatory measures (equivalent to "partial upvaluation")--using this term to include also the market-sheltered actions of government-- to set up non-market-determined international financial flows, trans- forming the unwanted monetary claims on foreigners into less liquid long- or short-term capital claims abroad.[6] In other words, the basic payments imbalance (Tables A) is accepted, but overall in- and out- payments (Tables C) are redressed by engineering counterflows in those capital accounts which are responsive to official manipulation (Tables B). This tactic differs entirely from the non-discriminatory policy of allowing the payments-balance liquidity effect to lower in- terest rates and thereby stimulate a capital outflow. The latter policy, as has just been noted, was expressly repudiated by the Bundesbank on many occasions.[7]

On the other hand, to the extent that this "reserve-level" counter- action to the liquidity effect is not possible, the central bank must, under the pegged-rate system, acquire the surplus international reserves as the residual buyer. The authorities may still combat the liquidity ef- fect, however, at the "monetary level," by reabsorbing the credit created by the central bank in paying for these international reserves. This implies restrictive domestic financial-policy measures. This class of measure is discussed in Chapter 5.

Non-adjustment measures involving retardation of the liquidity effect at the "exchange level" amount to discriminatory encouragements to capital export. The pronouncements of all authorities prove that discriminatory engineering of artificial capital outflows as a means of living with a basic disequilibrium without curing it has been a de- liberate and conscious policy in Germany throughout the period under review.[8] This tactic differs fundamentally from still another policy option, that of improving capital markets structurally, so as to permit a "natural" capital outflow. The capital exports discussed here were designed to be, not the result of, but a substitute for, structural

---

"fiscal" would in this context be arbitrary and misleading. The Coun- cil of Experts itself has used an analytical classification of non-ad- justing measures quite similar to that presented here (Federal Re- public of Germany, Sachverständigenrat zur Begutachtung der Gesam- twirtschaftlichen Entwicklung, Jahresgutachten [1970], Section 318 ff.).

improvements or monetary ease. Indeed, they were regarded as a prerequisite to monetary tightness.[9]

The capital-export tactic has been both the subject of much theoretical discussion and the object of many specific measures. In what follows, the general debate on capital exports is first evaluated, after which the specific measures and their repercussions are discussed.

GENERAL PROBLEMS OF THE TACTIC

Direct Impact on Germany's Political Position

In terms of international politics, the encouragement of net capital exports is today acceptable if labelled "temporary." In recent years most nations experiencing payments-balance difficulties have sought a solution in capital-account manipulations, either attempting to engineer discriminatory conditions in capital markets (e.g., the United States "Operation Twist") or instituting capital-account exchange controls (e.g., the United States balance-of-payments programs). Germany, several of whose domestic and international goals are served by a large heavy industry, has reason to give freedom of goods markets priority over freedom of capital markets.[10] "Twist"-like discriminatory schemes to lower domestic interest rates relative to foreign are also a feature of the "policy-mix" schemes which have received much academic, expert, and political support.[11] Technical aspects of policy-mix ideas will be discussed on a later page; here it is necessary only to note their widespread international acceptance. Thus, a successful capital-export effort could avert the odium of payments surplus from Germany without being inacceptable to the world community whose support Germany values.

Even in this case, however, Germany's international position could be weakened by the continuous capital outflow made necessary by the impliedly uncured basic imbalance. Especially if the outflow is in the form of portfolio investment in government securities, Germany could find itself in the geopolitical position of a helpless creditor.[12]

Direct Impact on the Autonomous Payments Balance: the "Boomerang Effect"

Discussion in Germany has been continuous on the efficacity of capital exports in achieving overall payments balance. The most fundamental problem here is the so-called "boomerang effect."[13] The re-export of earned liquidity will stimulate and permit further foreign imports from Germany. These imports are likely to take place almost at once, as long as the fundamental competitive position of Germany (which caused the original surplus) is unchanged.[14] This self-defeating aspect is present even in formally short-term capital exports, if they are likely to remain abroad de facto for long periods.[15]

Many observers have agreed with this reasoning; and no convincing counterarguments have been advanced. The failure of United States postwar capital exports to boomerang noticeably can be simply explained by the fact that this liquidity was sterilized as much as possible by recipient countries. Otmar Emminger, again, claimed that the boomerang would not necessarily be operative, since the price/ specie-flow mechanism involved would not work where there is no price-deflation in the lending country.[16] Yet not absolute deflation, but relative absence of inflation is the relevant condition. Emminger further suggested that capital exports could be in practice guided to the uses least likely to generate a boomerang. Given the fungibility of money, it is difficult to specify what uses these might be. In this respect, the experience with German official capital movements has not been encouraging. Considering even the least subtle relations, development loans lead immediately to reimports of capital on services account, and reparations in kind have led directly to repair and replacement exports. In addition, German aid has been in fact placed so as to stimulate German exports. (See below.)

Even Karl Blessing, who always advocated the capital-export tactic, saw that, for example, a rise in Germany's International Monetary Fund quota would lead to a rise in German exports.[17] Jenkis estimated that the boomerang on German foreign aid was over eighty percent, while that on credit positions with international entities was over one hundred percent.[18]

If the boomerang concept is applicable to capital exports, it is also relevant to any other artificially engineered outpayments; this view reinforces the conclusion that only price effects are ultimately adjusting, and all other mechanisms have adjustment tendencies only through price effects.[19]

Direct Impact on Money-Market Conditions: Liquidity Overhang

Very short-term and volatile exports of capital are probably not subject to the boomerang effect, since they would not in any case provide liquidity sufficient to stimulate imports by the borrowers. By the same token, however, those short-term capital outflows constitute "overhangs" of liquidity over the domestic money and goods markets, ever ready to return to those markets almost at once in response to changed market conditions.[20] Even formally long-term portfolio outflows are interest-sensitive assets to any given current holder, and thus form a species of overhang, especially if the normal market for the securities is abroad.

Such overhanging funds are for most purposes still "in" the lender nation's domestic markets, and thus still represent virtual domestic reserve money and virtual official international reserves. Therefore, domestic monetary policy is constrained to take account of these funds. The one clear advantage of such artificially generated short-term capital exports is that they relieve the central bank of embarrassing official international reserves-in-being.

Direct Impact on Capital-Market Conditions

Engineered capital exports may be damaging to the German capital market, precisely because of their engineered, discriminatory, and hence arbitrary and disruptive nature. The payments-balance-oriented measures which most upset confidence in the German capital market have already been discussed (Chapter 3), and others will be mentioned in the present chapter. To the extent that the capital market was damaged, monetary policy was further restricted and a vehicle of sound economic growth and modern wealth distribution was weakened.

Direct Impact on Growth: "Export of Growth"

The Issue

A more obvious way in which the capital-export tactic can retard economic growth has often been cited. This is the "export of growth,"[21] the sending abroad of German savings and German material resources in the form of an export surplus offset by capital outflows.[22] Here, obviously, the implied alternative situation is not a payments surplus compensated by additions to official international reserves, but rather no payments surplus at all. To the extent that a modern society depends on steady growth to ensure price stability, the capital-export tactic also poses some threat to Germany's anti-inflationary goals.[23]

This objection to the capital-export tactic loses much of its force if Germany is to be regarded as capital-rich.[24] In this case, capital outflows are natural responses to real conditions, and beneficial to world efficiency, in which German investors abroad directly share.

To the extent that market conditions did not stimulate a German net capital export, in this view, the fault lay, not in the actual relative factor endowments, but rather in essentially temporary distortions in the markets themselves, distortions which it would be salutary to override.[25]

International comparisons of factor endowments are problematical. A test of physical capital-richness cannot be applied, because there is no standard measuring unit for capital or labor, nor is there even any practically applicable definition distinguishing labor and capital. Without the latter, international factor-endowment comparisons risk the stultifications associated with discussions of the Leontief paradox.[26] However, it may be stated at once that Germany is capital-rich, in any acceptation of the term, on the world scale.

The relevant issue, however, concerns Germany's relation to countries which are structurally "in the market" for German capital movements. In this connection, it may be noted that only eleven countries absorbed seventy percent of the value of Germany's exports in 1963 (Tables A112, A122, A512, A522).[27] It should be added that the entire question is less pressing in the case of underdeveloped countries with inelastic supply, which will "adjust" quickly to any import of capital and so show a large boomerang in any case. Again, the question at issue here concerns, not (as in Chapters 1 and 2) the postwar changes within Germany's own factor endowment, but rather the relation of that endowment to those of other lands.

Trade-Balance and Related Criteria of Capital-Richness

As noted above, Bundesbank President Karl Blessing at one time advanced a trade-balance test of capital-richness.[28] (At other times-- when capital-richness has been treated as a criterion of the due volume of international aid--Blessing has attributed the trade surplus itself merely to Germany's better monetary discipline, and not to such fundamental factors as capital-richness.[29]) Under free trade, with no non-market transactions and with the exchange rates at equilibrium levels, a current-account payments surplus necessarily implies capital-account exports. But when there is official intervention in the exchange markets, this statement is not applicable. If the exchange rate is pegged to a disequilibrium level, then a current-account surplus is covered either by a capital export or by nonmarket or exchange-rate-support transactions.

Net capital imports or exports depend primarily on international interest-rate differentials. These in turn reflect monetary policy and engineered discriminations in capital markets. These differentials do not depend on the rates of exchange, as long as they are stable, or on relative price-inflation rates. Thus the state of the capital accounts need reflect the state of the payments-balance only through the "rules of the game" (i.e., the willingness of national authorities to permit adjusting changes in incomes and prices), when these are obeyed.

Thus, if interest rates are artificially high, a current-account surplus and capital imports can coexist, and can both be financed by increases in international reserves. Neither would, however, exist at an equilibrium exchange rate. This coexistence can prove only that the currency is undervalued and that a non-adjusting monetary policy is being implemented. Alternatively, if interest rates are artificially low, a current-account surplus may be financed by both an increase in international reserves and an engineered capital outflow.

Capital movements automatically responding to international interest-rate differentials (themselves the result of permitting the liquidity effect to work) must be distinguished from capital movements engineered to substitute for international interest-rate differentials (which have not been permitted to arise), and so to forestall the basic adjustment mechanism. In the face of exchange undervaluation, it is circular to argue from current-account surplus to the propriety of capital exports.30

Former Reichsbank President Hjalmar Schacht, and various United States spokesmen, on the other hand, have virtually equated Germany's hoard of international reserves with capital-richness, by calling for capital outflows as a natural solution to the problem of Germany's growing international reserves. Since the size of the reserve hoard depends directly on the factors discussed immediately above, this "test" of German capital-richness is worthless.31 (Schacht's ideas had technical as well as theoretical problems, as will be seen in Chapter 5.)

Factor-Price Criteria of Capital-Richness

Relative factor prices can be considered a test of capital-richness. By well-known reasoning, if country A's pretrade price-of-capital/price-of-labor ratio is smaller than country B's, country A may be considered relatively capital-rich. But, because of the factor-price-equalizing tendency of all kinds of trade, the ratio examined must be the pretrade one.32 Yet Germany carries on a very lively international intercourse in goods, capital and labor. The hypothetical pretrade price ratios are impossible to reconstruct. Since the country with the export surplus is subject to the direct-price-transmission effect, it may indeed be assumed that the whole range of these hypothetical prices is lower than those abroad and than those observed in international markets. But this says nothing of the ratios.

Röpke and Blessing advanced the notion that Germany's internationally high interest rates proved Germany capital-poor.[33] But interest rates reflect only supply and demand of financial capital and the structural state of the capital markets. Interest rates alone cannot pronounce on Germany's proportional factor endowment. Even if the opposite were the case, capital-market imperfections, government distortion of supply and demand, and the impact of monetary policy would all vitiate the German interest-rate pattern as an indicator.

Factor-Movement and Related Criteria of Capital-Richness

No conclusions regarding Germany's factor endowment can be drawn from its international factor movements. Germany indeed recruits much labor from regions where this factor evidently has a lower marginal productivity than in Germany. Net additions of physical capital, however, from countries with a lower nominal marginal capital productivity, have never been permitted. Even when the nominal interest-rate differential was stimulating a net pecuniary capital inflow, German monetary policy prevented the theoretically expectable results on the balance of trade. With net labor always importable and net capital never importable, Germany's one-sided international factor flow cannot be used to prove anything about its endowment.[34]

Under these circumstances, indeed, a quite artificial apparent "degree of monopoly," or ratio of factor marginal productivities, can be maintained. The inflow of labor would thus represent not a natural response to, and so an indicator of, capital-richness, but rather a factor-movement substitute for the normally expectable net inflow of goods.[35]

Finally, this alleged indicator of capital richness is hard to reconcile with the very capital-export tactic which it is invoked to support. For it would make a financial capital export the cure for a condition caused by the prevention of a real capital import. Once again, it is important to distinguish the normal results of a situation from its artificial substitutes.

The Bundesbank has often at least implicitly advanced the notion that, since labor is "overemployed" or a bottleneck, it must be the relatively scarce element in Germany's factor endowment. But absolute scarcity domestically is not relative scarcity internationally. Again, the market scarcity of a factor reflects the factor proportions embodied in the chosen technological methods as well as the proportions given by the factor endowment. Yet the Bundesbank itself has often complained that German methods are too labor-intensive.[36] What is abundant capital under one production function may be scarce capital

under another. If Germany is using a labor-intensive technology and
only for that reason has a scarcity of labor, then its labor productivity
should be relatively low internationally. This, however, does not seem
to be the case. Perhaps the use of imported labor in one way or another
maintains labor productivity.[37]

Trade-Composition Criterion of Capital-Richness

Another possible indicator of factor endowment is the composition
of trade. All else equal, a physically capital-rich nation will export
predominantly capital-intensive goods and import less capital-intensive
goods. Exchange undervaluation need not affect this inference. The
conclusion seems justified that Germany's exports, with their large
proportion of investment goods and heavy-industrial products (Tables
A111), are more capital-intensive than its imports (Tables A112).

On this ground, the conclusion is warranted that Germany is
relatively capital-rich internationally, provided that technological
possibilities are common to all the relevant countries (including constant returns to scale). This assumption may be made for simplicity,
as no very convincing case can be made against it. It is also necessary
that there be perfect intersectoral factor markets in all countries, or
else the same proportional sectoral wage differentials in all countries.
Some approximation to the latter assumption may perhaps be admitted.

The capital-richness conclusion by this criterion also requires
the same consumption pattern (or, more exactly, the same collective
taste map--or, still more precisely, the same commodity-consumption
proportions under the same commodity-price ratios, regardless of
income level and distribution), plus the same commodity-price ratios,
in all countries. These requirements do not seem to be fulfilled over
the relevant international market, precisely because of great international disparities of income levels and distribution. The entire trade-
composition indicator of capital-richness is much weakened by these
discrepancies.

Conclusions

Germany probably is capital-rich on the world scale. Domestically, labor may be scarce, at least given Germany's technological
methods. Germany's exports appear more capital-intensive than its
imports. These indications warrant a tentative presumption that Germany (always given its methods) is relatively capital-rich internationally, and that therefore it should normally export capital net. The
tests of capital-richness based on international interest-rate differentials, domestic factor-price ratios, international factor movements,
trade balance and stock of international reserves are all quite

inconclusive, either on a priori logical grounds, or because of vague measures or lack of statistics, or because of distorting policy interventions.

If this general conclusion is correct, the market forces that stimulated capital imports in the first half of the decade were distorted and should have been overridden. The nature of the market imperfections involved has already been discussed.

It is also possible to maintain that any capital poverty of Germany is a structural result of war (Germany's postwar long-term gross capital outflow began only in 1957), and must simply be waited out, without sacrificing needed overseas markets in an abortive attempt to "adjust" to it. This idea is borne out by the shifts that are taking place in Germany's factor endowment. Even more plausible is the thought that Germany's current-account surplus itself is very largely tied to world politics (e.g., troop-stationing costs, or the influx of direct investment into the Common Market [Tables A5113]), and that being prepared to sacrifice this adventitious boost in order to protect export markets is the cost of relative political freedom for Germany in its delicate eastern relations.

It is useful to override "incorrect" market indicators by policy measures which generate corrective but discriminatory price signals only if the "incorrect" indicators, and hence the correctives, promise to be merely temporary. Otherwise both the artificial correctives and the supposedly "incorrect" market conditions will continue to coexist and initiate multiple distortions in the economy.

Yet it is not clear how any incorrectness in German capital-market interest rates has been or can be eliminated, either by a discriminatory capital-export policy, or even by any of the other, more structure-oriented measures discussed in Chapter 3. The ways in which the capital-export policy itself has in fact damaged German capital-market conditions have been discussed, and will be adduced again briefly in the following discussions.

In these circumstances, the recent German net capital exports must be attributed very largely to the measures taken abroad, rather than to German capital-export or capital-market-structure measures.[38] This issue will be raised in the next section in connection with the specific measures taken. If the conclusion above is valid, the pre-1967 conditions of simultaneous capital-account and current-account surplus have by no means been permanently exorcized.

The general problems of the non-adjusting capital-export tactic thus are the choice between boomerang of the long-term funds and liquidity-overhang of the short; the possible harm to growth from the export of needed capital and from disruption of the domestic capital market itself; and the possibility of becoming a passive creditor on the world scene.

SPECIFIC MEASURES OF THE TACTIC:
LONG-TERM

Discouraging Gross Capital Imports

Since efforts to engineer net short-term capital outflows are closely related to monetary-policy measures, the long-term and short-term fields will here be discussed separately. Operationally, a net capital outflow can be engineered either by discouraging gross capital imports or by encouraging gross capital outflows. Therefore Germany's discouragement of long-term gross capital inflows will first be discussed.

An attempt was made in 1964 to give the domestic market for long-term government securities an advance opportunity to purchase them; this tactic was, however, a failure, as the foreign demand for the issue was in any case fully met.[39] During 1965 and 1966 the Bundesbank vigorously advocated the twenty-five-percent withholding tax on foreigners' income from German fixed-interest securities, claiming that this measure merely eliminated the German tax haven for such investment. In 1967 the Bundesbank advocated fiscal pump-priming as the chief anticyclical tool, in order to free interest-rate policy to maintain international capital flows in check.[40] In 1968 and 1969, and again in 1970, the same mix of tools was operated in reverse for the same reasons.

The withholding tax on foreign investors was of special significance. This long-delayed, much-discussed, and retroactive measure shook market confidence, and has been blamed for massive foreign sales of securities in 1964, which contributed to the sharp securities-price break of 1965.[41] United States firms especially accelerated the repatriation of profits, spurred by United States balance-of-payments worries.

Dr. Emminger of the Bundesbank claimed that the German capital market was not weakened as a result of the withholding tax, pointing out that DM securities in foreign hands rose 6.3 billion DM over 1964 and 1965.[42] Two answers to this are possible. One concerns the time period chosen, which begins at the low point after the initial shock to confidence. The second observation concerns the exact nature of the

DM securities held by foreigners. Under the coupon tax, foreigners wishing DM securities began to buy non-German DM issues: in 1965 nearly all long-term foreign-issued DM securities were probably bought by foreigners.[43] German firms formed foreign subsidiaries in order to be in a position to issue securities on this market. However, these shifted transactions cannot be credited to the supply of funds in the German capital market; they represented in fact a split in and narrowing of that market.[44]

Encouraging Gross Capital Exports

Private

The encouragement of gross long-term capital outflows requires either fiscal measures to raise and export capital or discriminatory manipulation of capital markets to induce domestic savers to buy foreign assets. The practically constant net inflow of private long-term capital (Tables A5) over the first six years of the period under review was a source of profound unhappiness to the German monetary authorities; even on a gross basis, private capital outflows to counteract this had begun only in 1957, and these were dominated by interest-sensitive portfolio investment (Tables A5211).

The monetary authorities' measures to reverse this situation were necessarily somewhat confusing to the market, for the authorities had set themselves the task of keeping both prices and capital-market interest rates low, although the banks' dominant structural role in the capital market multiplied the impact of money-market conditions on long-term interest rates, and despite the disturbing capital-market activities of the governments. This impossible task produced the contradictory interventions already described (Chapter 3), with their demoralizing effects on the market.

The marked failure of the more general measures to thread this tactical labyrinth made more specifically discriminatory measures desirable. However, fully adequate discriminatory tools for engineering a long-term private capital outflow from Germany were not forged in the period under review. Indeed, the Council of Experts doubts that this is possible, except when parities are "ripe" for change.[45] Given the structure of the German capital market, it was found impossible to separate its rates' behavior from money-market conditions. The techniques of interest subsidies, discriminatory central-bank credit and the like, long denounced by the Bundesbank where government borrowing was concerned, were ignored. An outright bounty on simply getting capital out of the country (similar to that suggested by the Council of Experts) would be disastrously inefficient economically and probably rather scandalous from the nationalistic standpoint.[46] One government attempt to sponsor a loan for development from industry ran into (largely extraneous) political storms raised by the 1961 revaluation, and the experiment was not repeated. Instead, in the Development Aid Tax Law of December 1963 (which lapsed in December 1967, but was renewed in March 1968), tax benefits were conceded for certain direct investment in developing countries.[47]

This measure was the harbinger of a new line of thinking among Germany's capital-export proponents. As rising interest rates world-wide, capital-control programs in major trading countries, and polit-ical and monetary crises combined to reinforce whatever effect German capital-export measures were having, Germany, and especially German banks, began to export a stream of net portfolio investment, especially to governments.[48] This movement was based on a sudden increase in deposits of firms, and ultimately on trade-balance and speculative liquidity.[49]

Since portfolio investment abroad is quite volatile and will be readily repatriated in response to changes in interest-rate differentials or to exchange crises, the German authorities became especially anx-ious to foster direct investment abroad by German firms.*[50] It was also felt that such direct investment could help bolster Germany's international influence and widen its resource base. In fact, Germany's "direct-international-investment account" went from balance in 1968 to growing surpluses in 1969 and 1970.

German consciousness of international financial flows as direct and concrete geopolitical weapons seems to have surfaced in 1965 and 1966, when high spokesmen of industry voiced a "Gaullist" concern over the possibility that the German international-reserve hoard was financing a "dollar invasion" of Germany's industry (Tables A5113). "What has been called the strength of the German economy" (to use the bittersweet phrasing of Chancellor Kiesinger) seemed to some to consist of the unwelcome choice between involuntary and voluntary lending to foreigners. Faced with this choice, many influential Germans proposed schemes for turning the questionable situation into a source of benefit to Germany.

---

*On the other hand, as German interest rates are lowered, DM-securities price-expectations are also lowered, causing foreigners to sell German securities, and thus effecting a paradoxical gross import of capital. Such considerations also reduce the attractiveness of monetary measures as part of a payments-balance-oriented policy mix. (See Chapter 5.)

Hjalmar Schacht's suggestion, echoed by a leading industry spokesman,[51] that the Bundesbank rid itself of excess reserves by making loans in the form of foreign exchange to industry and by using foreign exchange directly to buy up sources of raw materials, was widely discussed.[52] In essence and in the long run, it may be claimed that such is exactly what Germany is doing by its overall policy, but without so obvious a boomerang as the Schacht scheme would have. In any case, domestic inflation will not be alleviated by any disposition of reserves already bought by the central bank that does not involve reabsorbing domestic money.

Fiscal

The second method of engineering long-term capital outflows, fiscal capital export, has been practiced in Germany throughout the period under review (Tables B2-B4). Occasions for such outflows have not been hard to find. Reparations for war damage, repayment of postwar economic aid, and development grants and loans are the chief categories. The Israeli reparations agreement expired in 1965, and Bundesbank prepayments nearly extinguished Germany's London-Agreement debts soon thereafter.

This technique, Bundesbank prepayment of government foreign debt, was employed several times. It not only tended to balance overall external accounts, but also served as an occasion for a speed-up of the repayment schedule for the DM counterpart which the government continued to owe to the Bundesbank. This feature was intended to aid the Bundesbank's anti-inflationary efforts.

In the latter part of the period under review, accordingly, development capital came to dominate government long-term capital exports. Due partly to overt legal tying arrangements on about half of the German aid, the "boomerang" effect of this form of capital export has been very high.[53] This boomerang tendency has indeed been a source of pride to those involved in German aid operations.[54]

The aggregate of these flows is under a fair degree of medium-term control, and is not likely to fall (while Germany has persistent embarrassing surpluses) unless the authorities find good reason for it to do so. In other words, when a period of a decade is under consideration, the general balance-of-payments strategy of a nation heavily involved in exports is at least as long-term and basic a policy line as is its foreign-aid commitment. When large percentages of such a nation's foreign aid are so tied as to effect a demand for further exports almost automatically, the suspicion grows that the aid is not wholly autonomous, but rather payments-balance-induced at the margin. When, as with Germany, a calculated intent to balance international payments by engineering capital exports is thoroughly documented, the case becomes strong for considering all changes in government capital flows as reflecting payments-balance policy.

Some striking examples may serve to clinch this reasoning: in November 1960 Germany increased debt repayments, NATO contributions, "troop money" imports (discussed below) and development aid, but in 1964 the aggregate of these was below the 1959 level.[55] Again, Germany cut troop money and International Monetary Fund contributions during the 1965 period of dwindling surplus and recalled inter-central-bank loans as speculative funds ebbed away in late 1969.[56] By mid-1970, finally, the German government's capital-exports were far smaller than they had been in preceeding months of extraordinary surpluses.[57]

The German authorities, including especially the central bank, and German business spokesmen favored government capital export throughout the period under review.[58] For many of the reasons discussed above, the Bundesbank has treated these outflows as "normal," "desirable," and "harmless," and hence has facilitated them to the extent possible. Again, the inter-governmental central capital-market committee has also tried to foster loans abroad.[59]

At the same time, the insistence of the Bundesbank that government capital exports be financed without recourse to the money- or even capital-market, contributed to the increasing difficulties experienced by the fiscal authorities. The very concatenation of external pressures for German official capital exports and internal pressures for fiscal balance and price stability seems to have given the final push in October 1966 to the debile Erhard government.

Official capital exports were excluded from the Bundesbank's statistics on factors of bank liquidity until 1965.[60] This had the effect of statistically denying the boomerang effect of these operations. Until that date the tradition persisted of regarding these exports as financed out of fiscal funds accumulated some time previously, which had thus reduced liquidity in a previous period. While this remained true in a technical sense throughout the period under study, the elapsed time between the accumulation of government DM deposits and their drawing down for export has not at any time in the sixties been excessive. When tied aid and other highly boomerang-prone outlays are taken into account, the older statistical method becomes "highly questionable."[61] Since this is so, and since the actual rate of flow of the exports is subject to adequate official control, there seems to be no better time period to which to assign them as factors in bank liquidity than the quarter in which they were made. This is the rationale of the Bundesbank figures after 1964; in the present study, this rationale is applied to all such figures.

Recent Experience

In 1968 and 1969 Germany suddenly became the world's largest exporter of long-term capital.[62] In 1967 gross inflow fell more than gross outflow rose, while in 1968 the gross outflow jumped by almost sixty percent (Tables A5, A51, A52, A5211). About half of this outflow was in portfolio form. Much of this change can be ascribed to the worldwide rise in interest rates, to which central bankers had been mutually exhorting themselves for years; to the capital-control measures of the United States, Britain, and France; to the decline of the wave of United States direct investments in Common-Market-based subsidiaries; to an unprecedented volume of offshore (i.e., Eurodollar) financing of United States direct investment; to the shaken condition of the German capital market; and to the aftermath of the French, Czech and Near Eastern crises. Part of the outflows moreover can be attributed to the Bundesbank's crash program to depress German long-term interest rates in 1967, and to the general atmosphere of monetary ease during the period of recovery from the 1966/1967 recession. In 1969, some effect may be ascribed to the peculiarities of the Bundesbank's forward-market operations (discussed below). The 1969 outflow was largely financed by short-term imports of capital as German banks drew down previous exports of money (discussed below), and speculative funds were lodged in long-term German bank accounts.[63] Thus the speculative inflow kept international interest rates from being equalized internationally by the long-term capital outflow.

None of these factors could be counted upon to last.[64] The precariousness of the new situation was underlined by the sharp reversal of Bundesbank thinking on the capital-export panacea. In early 1969 the Bundesbank was warning against excessive capital outflows, especially in portfolio form, as endangering domestic investment and growth.[65] By year's end Germany had registered a sixteen billion DM drop in international reserves and a twenty-three billion DM net long-term capital export. Yet only about ten percent of all long-term capital outflows from Germany in both 1968 and 1969 represented direct investments.

Immediately after the 1969 revaluation, German authorities became concerned over the continuation of record-high long-term capital outflows. "We no longer need the extremely high capital export rate of 1969, to place at the rest of the world's disposal what was withdrawn from it by an extremely high trade surplus." It was thus expressly desired to tailor the capital export to the longer-term probabilities for the current-account surplus.[66]

Considering the sharpness of this hortatory turnaround, Minister Schiller was only prudent in emphasizing that this tailoring was to be carried out "under market conditions," with "no dirigisme," and without "subordinating Germany's capital export to short-term cyclical goals."[67] One market-conformed way to help was the elimination of the coupon tax. "This relic of a special situation must finally go."*[68] At the same time, the Central Capital Market Committee of the German banking community moved to cut back foreign DM issues in the German market.[69] By mid-1970, the Bundesbank's fight against the continuing adjustment inflation and its aftermath of price-wage inflation, plus the easing of credit conditions elsewhere in the world, had reversed Germany's international interest-rate situation. Massive repayments of Euro-loans by the United States were translated directly into equally massive refluxes of Germany's "long-term" capital investment abroad.

In August 1970 Germany experienced the first net inflow of capital in several years. Banks raised almost a billion DM abroad in long-term funds, but reexported about two-thirds of this in short-term funds (as discussed below). Private capital export fell to zero, but almost three fourths of the trade surplus continued to be offset, this time by temporarily rising repatriations of foreign funds and remittances by foreign workers. As the latter also threatened to subside, the German payments balance gave clear evidence of "official long-term capital transactions which depend on political decisions."[70] Official capital exports tripled in May through July 1970 as compared with February through April, amounting to over 2.5 billion DM more than even in the hectic corresponding period of 1969.[71] These transactions certainly bear out the Bundesbank's clear statement that official long-term capital export is autonomous with respect to international interest-rate differentials.[72] Germany's capital-account transactions of early 1971 are traced in Chapter 7.

SPECIFIC MEASURES OF THE TACTIC:
SHORT-TERM

Discouraging Gross Capital Imports

In the short-term field, measures to reverse autonomous capital inflows overlap with efforts to encourage the "export of money" and to combat waves of speculation. Under the government's power to issue and amend Foreign Trade and Payments Orders, and under

---

*But contrast this with the Bundesbank's previous insistence that the tax did no more than eliminate an unnatural tax-haven in Germany (alluded to at the opening of the discussion of long-term capital-export tactics).

special legislation, permits issued by the Bundesbank have been required for the payment of interest on foreign-held sight, time and
corporate deposits, and for the sale of new bank bonds or money-market
paper to foreigners. Sales of money-market paper were forbidden under
this authority throughout the period under review, and loans to Germany
of under five years' term were forbidden until April 1964. In the 1968
crisis, the government invoked its power to require licenses for short-
term capital inflows of all sorts.[73] After August 1964, additional foreign credits received by banks reduced their rediscount quotas (Chapter 5).[74]

During the 1969 crisis a hundred-percent minimum reserve on
banks' foreign liabilities reduced speculative inflows of funds directly
to banks, which thereupon arranged a great increase in direct international "financial loans" among firms and subsidiaries. Altogether
non-banks received around fifteen billion DM from abroad during the
first nine months of 1969. Over half of these funds were then placed
with German banks as time deposits of formally domestic origin.
Similar efforts were made during the crisis of 1971, as described in
Chapter 7. Further details of Germany's attempts to reverse such
inflows will be treated below.

Encouraging Gross Capital Exports

Private

Measures aimed at fostering short-term capital outflows, as
already noted, are liable to the objection that they are merely building
up an "overhang" of virtual official reserves and correspondingly of
virtual high-powered money. And indeed, certain forms of short-term
capital export differ only by a definition's breadth from actual international reserves.[75]

One important channel of short-term capital movements, trade
credit, is not under the authorities' control. The amount of net trade
credit outstanding among nations depends to some degree on interest-
rate differentials and more importantly on the state and prospects of
the autonomous balance as a whole. German experts regard trade
credit as a specially volatile item in Germany's balance-of-payments.

Commercial banks' foreign liquid assets (or "exported money")
are another important form of short-term capital movement. Equally
liquid commercial-bank foreign liabilities are not netted out in the
Bundesbank's "money-export" figures, on the ground that a commercial
bank tends to be passive about the formation and repayment of its liabilities: they are its stock-in-trade and so not subject to frequent manipulation.[76] So long as banks can be persuaded to hold such assets

abroad, corresponding official international reserves and high-powered money need not be created. Encouragement to commercial-bank acquisition of foreign liquid assets is quite similar in its workings and effects to the open-market operations conducted by central banks in domestic assets.[77] However, the Bundesbank discusses and records the two classes of operation separately.

The foreign assets thus held constitute an overhang of liquidity just as does bank-held open-market-eligible paper or unused rediscount lines.[78] Hence the money-export tactic is limited by the Bundesbank's fear of creating obstacles to its own future freedom of maneuver. Aware of this constraint, the bank consistently made allowances for this item in discussing the overall payments-balance position.[79]

In the present study, money exports are not considered part of the basic balance of payments, although they obey the same kind of stimuli as do short-term capital movements by enterprises and a large part of the unrecorded items, because the specific stimuli applied to encourage or discourage money exports are not market-determined or even speculatively determined, but rather policy-determined and discriminatory (Tables B1).

The Bundesbank can encourage money exports in two ways. The first of these is to allow banks to offset foreign liabilities, on which reserves are required, by the amount of their foreign assets. Acquisition of a foreign asset can in this way reduce the overall required-reserve ratio. The reduction, which is effectively increased when discriminatory maximum reserve requirements are applied to foreign liabilities, makes the net rate of return on the foreign asset more attractive. From May 1961 to December 1966 this offset was allowed, and from April 1964 to February 1967 (and also from May 1961 to February 1962) discriminatory and maximum reserves were required against foreign liabilities. In mid-1969 one-hundred-percent average reserve requirements against foreign deposits were applied with, however, small effect, since (as noted above) an estimated two-thirds of the speculative inflow was not directly received by banks.[80] In 1970 discriminatory reserve requirements were once again applied to foreign liabilities of banks (as discussed below).

The second and more finely tuned Bundesbank influence on commercial banks' money exports is the "swap" tool. (The word "swap" is here used to refer to central-bank forward-market dealings.)[81] Since the interest differential in favor of foreign assets is reduced by the costs of the forward-exchange cover involved in purchasing them (and necessarily involved if the assets are to be classed as

liquid, i.e., as relatively risk-free),* the Bundesbank can reduce or
enhance this differential by offering to sell to banks exchange from
its own international-reserve stock, with a commitment to repurchase
the exchange in the future at a more favorable exchange rate.[82]

Indeed, since the Bundesbank is not restricted by law as to the
nature of its international business, it can also create a positive dis-
incentive to money exports by upvaluing the forward DM above its
international Monetary Fund parity (which applies only to spot rates).[83]
This was actually the outcome during the crises of 1960 and 1969,
when much of the foreign-exchange supply of DM shifted to the forward
market.[84] Since foreign assets form an important part of German
banks' liquidity reserves, they are a volatile item responsive to these
changes in interest differentials.[85]

Not only can the Bundesbank adjust its swap premium to circumstances, but it can also restrict swap offers to specific purposes and
indeed refuse to grant swap arrangements at all. Earmarked swaps
were employed during most of the period under review, beginning
with the introduction of the operation in 1959.[86] From March 1964
until November 1967, Bundesbank swaps were available only for the
purchase of United States dollar-denominated treasury bills. After
November 1967, the Bank offered its swap facilities to non-banks.[87]

The swap discount was manipulated to one percent in 1962 and
early 1963 (at other times it was one half to three quarters of one
percent). These less favorable terms were intended to encourage
repatriation of banks' liquid assets. It was hoped thus to reduce
seasonal and policy-thwarting shifts in international payments. In
late 1967 the discount was raised to two percent and more, and by
1968 even exceeded three percent.[88] Since this period was one of
falling interest rates in Germany and rising rates abroad, the swaps-
policy shift was evidently intended to damp "natural" money exports
and thus to keep the effects of the reflation effort at home. In this
way less reflation would be needed, and less liquidity overhang would
be built up. In the speculative crisis of 1968, the Bundesbank managed,
by "remarkable virtuosity" in the rapid reduction of the swap discount,
to reverse the official reserve flow from France, diverting much of
it to the United States.[89] The large commitments generated in 1968
were further increased in early 1969 to encourage return of speculative
moneys. However, as swap commitments fell through April 1969,

---

*In fact, logic seems to demand that, in full equilibrium of all
parties, the forward-exchange costs be based on, and thus virtually
eliminate, the interest differential.

banks' short external assets fell only half as fast. In mid-1969, the swap discount reached 7.5 percent, effectively upvaluing the DM on the forward market. Swap commitments rose rapidly, but banks' external assets rose only one-third as fast. The remainder was able to return to Germany through roundabout (carousel) operations. In the fall 1969 crisis, swaps again statistically offset part of the speculative inflows, due partly to high Euro-dollar interest rates resulting from United States exchange-control measures.[90] No new swap commitments were undertaken after the floating of the Mark. As existing commitments fell to zero by year's end, banks' short foreign assets fell not at all.

In the early part of the period under study, German commercial-bank foreign assets were mostly United States dollar-denominated. Later a general retreat from United States money markets developed, despite interest-rate differentials, as London banks and bank branches took up the role of intermediaries to the United States markets. At the same time a shift to predominantly DM-denominated external assets took place.

As German banks held no required reserves on debt to foreigners whose value at maturity was to be paid out to foreigners, banks could borrow dollars abroad, sell them in the spot market, and re-buy them forward. The resulting DM could then be "money-exported" with the Bundesbank's forward-rate subsidy.[91] When the Bundesbank lowered the forward-rate discount to divert the speculative inflows of late 1968, these "carousel operations" put considerable pressure on the forward rate. In the May 1969 crisis, the Bundesbank was forced to cease its forward operations altogether.[92] Thereafter the Bank reversed itself and held the forward discount very high. Since in the turmoil of the market nearly all transactions were going over the forward market, this practically upvalued the DM. The result was a stream of essentially short-term non-autonomous portfolio outflows.[93] To combat this effect, adjustments were made in August 1969 in the coverage of reserve requirements.[94]

The chief advantage to the German authorities of the money-export tool was that it altered the official overall balance of payments directly and so in effect "disguised" some of Germany's external reserves.[95] This is one of the very few direct impacts on the current balance of payments that can be made by a central bank whose overall interest-rate policy is hampered by the openness of the economy. It has been especially useful and effective in times of acute speculative crisis. The chief drawback of this tool is exactly symmetrical. The operations build up an overhang of commercial-bank liquidity which further hampers the future interest-rate policy of the Bundesbank.[96]

Bundesbank reasoning as to the effect of these manipulations on domestic commercial-bank liquidity has been quite ambiguous, and hence was perhaps intended only for effect, i.e., for a showing of "international monetary cooperation."[97] The hard choice between boomerang and overhang is at least as applicable here as with all other artificial capital export. The growing importance and integration of the Euro-currency market makes this more apparent.[98] In the 1969 exchange crisis, the boomerang on "swaps" appears to have been considerable.[99] Hence many observers feel that "money exports" are "uninteresting," if not harmful, from the long-run payments-balance viewpoint.[100] Money export would be deflationary only if it were paid for by commercial banks with existing reserve money, i.e., when no further reserve money was in prospect; but, when the latter is the case, the banks in fact import money.[101]

Fiscal

A notable area of short-term capital export in Germany is pre-payment of arms imports. The German government has bound itself over the period under review to import stated values of arms and civilian-government needs from the United States and Britain. By prepaying the agreed amounts into special funds in either country, Germany effectively exports capital. At the same time, since the agreed deadlines for ordering and delivering actual imports are seldom many months away, the capital export must be called short-term. (In the present study, these sums are shown in Tables B421 only as long as they are "outstanding.")

These arrangements represent a curious form of interplay between Germany's international objectives and its payments balance. Germany's allies have since 1960 insisted that Germany return some proportion of the exchange it earns from support of NATO troops stationed on its soil, in the form of import orders from the allies.[102] Unlike United States offshore procurement in the past, Germany's offsetting imports are not usually per se advantageous bargains for it, either in price or in quality.[103] Hence the negotiation of these agreements every several years has been delicate, and certain embarrassments have arisen over the administration of the agreements. Perhaps the worst difficulty for all parties has been the United-States-made F104G military aircraft, of which one hundred had crashed in Germany by October 1969.[104]

NATO troop money rose precipitously in the early part of the decade: arms purchases rose from nil to 7.4 percent of government consumption, while government consumption imports rose from 1.1 billion DM in 1957 to 43.2 billion DM in 1963.[105] In recent years this item has remained remarkably steady, despite the many geopolitical and cost-price vicissitudes in Europe (Tables B421). In the last three years of the period studied, Germany made around two fifths of its troop-money offsets in the form of purchases of DM-denominated ten-year 3.5-percent treasury bonds (Tables C21).[106] In 1969, a further two-year tripartite agreement on troop money earmarked 6.08 billion DM for the United States and 1.52 billion DM for Britain. In the 1969 speculative crisis, Germany made a half-billion-DM arms prepayment to Britain.[107] In the 1971 rounds of negotiation, both Britain and the United States demanded real budgetary offsets, as well as the former exchange offsets.

The need to make these large payments abroad has put pressure, not indeed on Germany's external reserve position, but rather on its government budget.[108] Troop money, for example, played no little part in the embarrassments of the Erhard government: fully one half of the unpopular supplementary budget of December 1966 represented troop money.[109]

The United States and the United Kingdom, however, are Germany's chief military allies and chief trade partners, and they provide the key currencies for the international exchange system which provides many specific advantages for Germany.

A final category of short-term capital exports subject to German control may be qualified as "international window-dressing operations" or a "game of hide the reserves."[110] In these operations international reserves are passed between the Bundesbank and other holders of official international reserves. Although some of the recipients of these funds, viz., France and the United Kingdom, stood in very real need of the additional reserves, the term "window dressing" seems highly appropriate from the German standpoint.[111] As an example, Bundesbank loans to central banks (excluding international organizations) peaked at 4.9 billion DM in the midst of the speculative inflows of July 1969; but in March 1970, in a speculative "trough" for Germany, such loans stood at less than .6 billion DM.

From Germany's point of view, these transactions change merely the form, and hardly the substance, of available international reserves (the usual gold- or DM-guarantee does, however, reduce their exchange risk). This is because credit positions of all kinds with international entities are always available to the creditor governments without real impediments, and inter-central-bank lending operations normally make the funds involved repayable within three to six months.[112] The same is also true, in the ultimate analysis, of such arrangements as Roosa-type bond purchases and World Bank loans. German financial circles did take international credit for these loan operations, and at the same time congratulated themselves on these operations as an answer to Germany's "structural" trade-balance surplus.[113] Recently Minister Schiller suggested that deficit countries do their own reserve "recycling" by borrowing on surplus countries' capital markets.[114]

In order to reflect adequately both the non-adjustment "window-dressing" aim of hiding reserves and the substantive near-nullity of such transactions, they are in the present study statistically treated as distinctive parts of the total central international-reserve position (Tables Section C). This conforms to the Bundesbank's presentation after 1 January 1971.[115]

Recent Experience

Recently the growth of the Euro-financial markets and the increasing international-financial sensitivity of multinational corporations have added to the responsiveness of international capital flows to any given stimulus.[116] In effect, this mobile mass of sensitive money represents a colossus of liquidity prepared to overrun in turn each nation that exhibits a high interest-rate pattern on the world scale. Both Britain and Canada accordingly took steps early in 1971 to insulate their domestic credit policies in some measure from the inroads of the Euro-hoards.[117] After the mid-1970 floating of the Canadian dollar, the DM came under another wave of outspokenly speculative pressure.[118] Short-term capital imports by firms also stepped up sharply as international interest-rate differentials widened and massive United States Euro-borrowings were repaid. Even before German monetary restriction had been able to cut profits, firms were borrowing heavily to finance a "forward flight," i.e., an expansion of capacity to outrun rising labor costs through scale efficiencies and labor-saving innovation. At once the Bundesbank countered with the lowering of its three-month dollar swap price.[119] Already on the first of April a thirty-percent marginal reserve requirement on banks' foreign liabilities had been introduced. Once again, banks arranged direct inter-firm international borrowing, which increased bank liquidity while evading the new reserve requirement. These Euro-market flows, like their predecessors, primarily benefitted large firms.[120] In September, accordingly, the Bundesbank was forced to extend the thirty-percent marginal reserve requirement to all new bank liabilities. Very soon, however, even the official spot rate fell to the lower intervention point. Direct central-bank purchases of forward dollars were next contemplated.[121] This would defend the exchange rate while withholding the corresponding new bank liquidity from the German market for the period of the forward contracts. At the same time, a stimulus to money export could still be hoped for. In December 1970, the Bundesbank was forced, on purely payments-balance considerations, to lower the rediscount rate for the second and third times in the year.

Much of the German authorities' effort has been devoted to retarding the liquidity effect of the payments balance at the "exchange level."[122] These efforts have in normal periods been quite successful: in the long run, German official reserves did not change drastically over the period under review, until the most recent quarters. Thus the growth of the unproductive reserve hoard, representing involuntary lending, was largely replaced by voluntary lending abroad, at least some of which represented a more strategic and more economic investment than additional international reserves.[123]

The capital-export tactic also seemed to have been successful in "tiding over"[124] a period of "unnatural"[125] capital inflows, until circumstances, largely (or "only")[126] outside Germany's direct control, reversed the flow. Yet even these circumstances did not appear wholly exogenous from one German point of view. For they represented the long-awaited effects of the "export-of-stability" strategy, by which Germany hoped to pressure its trade partners more or less delicately into balance-of-payments "discipline." A more realistic view, however, would assign the successful export of capital in 1968 and 1969 to foreign exchange controls, to international interest differentials generated by payments disequilibrium and speculation, and to central-bank reactions to these conditions.[127] The resumption of capital imports in 1970 and 1971 appears to confirm this view.

The capital-export policy, viewed as a way of gaining time for the stability-export strategy to be effective, may also be assessed more dynamically, as an attempt not only to offset, but also to eliminate, a basic disequilibrium. In the last analysis, however, since neither the German discriminatory nor the foreign restrictive measures, nor any of the other fortuitous circumstances, truly corrected the original international incompatibilities, a recurrence of the surplus tendency was not prevented.

Thus, engineered exports of capital were long successful in meeting the needs of the German industrial structure for effective currency under-valuation without overwhelming financial and political pressures for revaluation. As a very-long-run strategy, however, discriminatory capital export has lost support as it continued to subsidize the export of growth and to finance United States "dollar imperialism." The macrofinancial-policy problems associated with engineering capital exports are treated in Chapter 5. The overall success of the "stability-export" strategy will be assessed in Chapter 6.

NOTES

1. L. A. Hahn, Fünfzig Jahre zwischen Inflation und Deflation (Tübingen, 1963), p. 33, 47-50.

2. Federal Republic of Germany, Bundesbank, Monthly Report (Aug 1966), p. 5.

3. MR (Jun 1965), p. 4.

4. MR (Mar 1964), p. 10; MR (Apr 1967), p. 29.

5. MR (May 1957), p. 3; MR (Oct 1966), p. 66; MR (Nov 1961), p. 4; MR (Oct 1966), p. 3; MR (Jan 1967), p. 5; Federal Republic of Germany, Bundesbank, Annual Report (1967), p. 32.

6. Federal Republic of Germany, Sachverständigenrat zur Begutachtung der Gesamtwirtschaftlichen Entwicklung, Jahresgutachten (1968), Section 279.

7. K. Blessing, Die Verteidigung des Geldwertes (Frankfurt, 1960), p. 108; MR (Nov 1966), p. 3; MR (Jun 1963), p. 4.

8. President Blessing often called net capital export the solution to Germany's problem (K. Blessing, Im Kampf um Gutes Geld [Frankfurt, 1966], p. 176; Verteidigung, p. 151, 244); he at one time characterized a long list of fiscal capital exports as "an ingenious performance" (Verteidigung, p. 214). Many other spokesmen (H. Irmler, Discussion contribution in Arbeitsgemeinschaft, etc., p. 104; L. Gleske, "Die Finanzierung des wachsenden Internationalen Handels," in Arbeitsgemeinschaft, etc., p. 163; L. Erhard, The Economics of Success [Princeton, 1963], p. 369; O. Emminger, Währungspolitische Betrachtungen [Frankfurt, 1956], p. 17) and observes (W. Gatz, "Gründe und volkswirtschaftliche Wirkungen der D-Mark-Aufwertung," Weltwirtschaftliches Archiv [1963], p. 383; G. Schmölders, Finanzpolitik [Berlin, 1965], p. 478; Hahn, Jahre, p. 118, 146, 208 ff.; L. A Hahn, Ein Traktat über Währungsreform [Tübingen, 1964], p. 2, 94) confirm that precisely the discriminatory or fiscal outflows were an object of policy; these sources are not here speculating on the desirable or allegedly "natural" non-discriminatory capital-export rate. The Council of Experts confirms that forced capital export was a strategy designed to ward off foreign complaints (JG [1968], Section 276). There was even some responsible argument that such tactics would be sufficient for their objective (O. Emminger, "Kapitalexport als Mittel zum Ausgleich der Zahlungsbilanz," Zeitschrift für das gesamte Kreditwesen [1959], p. 814; Organization for Economic

Cooperation and Development, Economic Policy Committee, Working Party Three, The Balance of Payments Adjustment Process [Paris, 1966], Section 47; AR [1963], p. 5, 19; Federal Republic of Germany, Bundesbank, Auszüge aus Presseartikeln [1969], #58, p. 1).

9. JG (1964), Government Response, Section 25.

10. AR (1965), p. 35-36.

11. R. A. Mundell, "The Appropriate Use of Monetary and Fiscal Policy for Internal and External Stability," International Monetary Fund Staff Papers (March 1962); J. M. Fleming, "Domestic Financial Policies under Fixed and Floating Exchange Rates," International Monetary Fund Staff Papers (November 1962), p. 19-20; OECD3, p. 3, 5.

12. JG (1968), Section 203.

13. L. A. Hahn, Geld und Kredit (Frankfurt, 1960), p. 137 ff., 269 ff.; Hahn, Traktat, p. 39 ff.

14. JG (1965), Sections 191a, 150; JG (1968), Section 202; O. Veit, Reale Theorie des Geldes (Frankfurt, 1966), p. 246 ff.; Stützel in G. Schmölders, Geldpolitik (Tübingen, 1962), p. 30; JG (1966), Section 139; AR (1968), p. 18.

15. Hahn, Jahre, p. 136; Hahn, Traktat, p. 44. Also see B. Ohlin, Interregional and International Trade (Cambridge, 1933), p. 429 ff., with references there to Keynes, Böhm-Bawerk and Ricardo; JG (1964), Section 198.

16. O. Emminger, "Zahlungsbilanz und Kapitalexport," Neue Zürcher Zeitung (3 August 1963).

17. Blessing, Verteidigung, p. 166.

18. H. W. Jenkis, Die Importierte Inflation (Schriften zur Wirtschaftswissenschaftlichen Forschung #15) (Meisenheim, 1966), p. 133.

19. Federal Republic of Germany, Bundesministerium für Wirtschaft, Wissenschaftliche Beirat, Wirtschaftspolitische Problematik der deutschen Exportüberschüsse (Göttingen, 1961), p. 25; JG (1968), Section 202.

20. MR (Jan 1965), p. 4; MR (Jun 1964), p. 4, 5; W. Schmidt, "The German Bundesbank," Bank for International Settlements, Eight European Central Banks (London, 1963), p. 82.

21. Hahn, Traktat, p. 94, 195.

22. AP (1968), #76, p. 4; AP (1968), #82, p. 3.

23. JG (1966), Section 213; JG (1965), Section 194.

24. Emminger, "Kapitalexport," p. 814.

25. M. Gilbert, "Reconciliation of Domestic and International Objectives of Financial Policy in European Countries," Journal of Finance (May 1963), p. 176; AR (1967), p. 25, 83; MR (Oct 1962), p. 44.

26. V. Leontief, Input-Output Economics (New York, 1966), p. 100; P. T. Ellsworth, The International Economy (London, 1969), p. 127 ff.

27. JG (1964), Section 147.

28. MR (May 1961), p. 5.

29. Blessing, Kampf, p. 14.

30. Hahn, Traktat, p. 190.

31. Hahn, Jahre, p. 209.

32. P. Samuelson, "International Factor Price Equalization Once Again," Economic Journal (1949), p. 181.

33. W. Röpke, Geld und Kapital in unserer Zeit (Baden-Baden, 1964), p. 30-31; Blessing, Verteidigung, p. 115.

34. Hahn, Traktat, p. 29.

35. Hahn, Traktat, p. 182.

36. MR (Aug 1966), p. 3.

37. W. Fellner, F. Machlup, and R. Triffin, eds., Maintaining and Restoring Balance in International Payments (Princeton, 1966), p. 131.

38. JG (1968), Section 195.

39. MR (Jan 1964), p. 16.

40. MR (May 1967), p. 7.

41. Blessing, Kampf, p. 220, 283.

42. O. Emminger, Währungspolitik im Wandel der Zeit (Frankfurt, 1966), p. 105.

43. AR (1965), p. 4.

44. Blessing, Kampf, p. 222.

45. JG (1969), Section 142.

46. JG (1965), Section 200; Hahn, Traktat, p. 190.

47. Federal Republic of Germany, Bundesministerium für Finanz, Finanzbericht (1969), p. 222.

48. AP (1969), #98, p. 4; AP (1968), #66, p. 3.

49. AR (1968), p. 15; AP (1969), #97, p. 2.

50. AP (1968), #83, p. 9; AP (1968), #75, p. 6; AP (1968), #16, p. 4; MR (Nov 1969), p. 33; AR (1968), p. 92; JG (1969), Section 202.

51. H. Schacht, Schluss mit der Inflation! (Berlin, 1960); E. Schneider, (President of the German Industrial and Commercial Congress), Vorschläge zur Überwindung unserer Zahlungsbilanzkrise (Düsseldorf, 1957).

52. Jenkins, p. 146n.

53. AR (1968), p. 90-92.

54. Hans Joachim v. Stein, "Keine Deutsche Mark in Bar," Entwicklungspolitik (1965), p. 11.

55. Organization for Economic Cooperation and Development, Economic and Development Review Committee, Survey (Germany) (1964), p. 11.

56. AP (1969), #92, p. 1; also see Blessing, Verteidigung, p. 112-113; FR (1967), p. 39; OECDS (1965), p. 15.

57. AP (1970), #80, p. 1.

58. Blessing, Verteidigung, p. 151.

59. AP (1968), #55, p. 6.

60. MR (Apr 1965), p. 34.

61. JG (1965), Section 150.

62. AR (1968), p. 16.

63. AR (1969), p. 4.

64. JG (1968), Sections 86, 97; AR (1967), p. 33; Federal Reserve Bank of New York, Monthly Review (December 1968), p. 243; OECDS (1968), p. 25.

65. Wall Street Journal (18 Apr 1969), p. 2.

66. Bundesbank Vice President Emminger, AP (1970), #8, p. 4; Minister Schiller, AP (1970), #27, p. 4.

67. Minister Schiller, AP (1970), #27. p. 4.

68. Minister Schiller, AP (1970), #27, p. 4.

69. AR (1969), p. 63-64.

70. MR (Sep 1970), p. 40.

71. This included eight hundred million DM under the August 1969 exchange-support (troop-money) agreement with the United States; 275 million DM as the second installment of a ten-year loan; a 200-million-DM acquisition of United States government paper by the Reconstruction Loan Corporation (which functions much like the United States Export-Import Bank); and a 320-million-DM acquisition of Export-Import Bank liabilities. By United States-German agreement, the Reconstruction Loan Corporation will hold up to 600 million DM worth of United States government securities, ostensibly as a means of helping smaller firms make direct investments in the United States (MR [Sep 1970], p. 41n.).

72. AR (1969), p. 87; AP (1970), #84, p. 3; AR (1970), p. 95.

73. Under the 1961 Foreign Economic Law, imports (only) of capital can be controlled for payments-balance reasons for up to three months without Bundestag approval (G. Gutman, H. J. Hochstrate, and R. Schüter, Die Wirtschaftsverfassung der Bundesrepublik Deutschland [Stuttgart, 1964], p. 291).

74. JG (1964), Section 171.

75. Hahn, Traktat, p. 198.

76. For more reasoning on these items, see MR (Apr 1966), p. 37.

77. European Economic Community, Commission, Directorate General for Monetary and Financial Problems, The Instruments of Monetary Policy in the Countries of the European Economic Community (Brussels, 1962), p. 94; JG (1966), Section 281.

78. MR (Apr 1965), p. 29.

79. MR (Sep 1965), p. 13; MR (Aug 1962), p. 13 and throughout. With this contrast the viewpoint of M. Michaely, Balance-of-Payments Adjustment Policies (New York, 1968), p. 27: "Holdings of foreign exchange by commercial banks, on the other hand, are probably not usually counted by the government as part of the reserve for the purpose on hand [i.e., as a target variable]. . . . Commercial banks have presumably been guided by their own initiative in determing the amount of their foreign exchange holdings."

80. AP (1969), #38, p. 2.

81. J. M. Keynes, A Treatise on Money (New York, 1930), p. 124 ff., 132-139; R. G. Hawtrey, The Gold Standard in Theory and Practice (London, 1939), p. 212 ff.; Paul Einzig, A Dynamic Theory of Forward Exchanges (London, 1962), p. 396, 405 ff.

82. G. S. Dorrance, and E. Brehmer, "Control of Capital Inflows: Recent Experience of Germany and Switzerland," International Monetary Fund Staff Papers (December 1961), p. 428; H. Rittershausen, "Swap als Steuerungsinstrument," Zeitschrift für das gesamte Kreditwesen (1960), p. 954; H. Rittershausen, "Das Swap-Geschäft als kreditpolitisches Instrument," Zeitschrift für das gesamte Kreditwesen (1960), p. 813; S. I. Katz, External Surpluses, Capital Flows, and Credit Policy in the European Economic Community (Studies in International Finance #22) (Princeton, 1969), p. 16; E. Brehmer, "Official Forward Exchange Operations: The German Experience," International Monetary Fund Staff Papers (November 1964).

83. Schmidt, p. 83-84.

84, Jenkis, p. 97.

85. MR (Jan 1963), p. 8; Schmidt, p. 77.

86. Jenkis, p. 91.

87. AP (1968), #3, p. 3.

88. AR (1968), p. 25.

89. AP (1968), #61, p. 1; JG (1968), Sections 94, 138.

90. JG (1969), Section 16; AP (1969), #78, p. 1; AP (1970), #40, p. 6.

91. AP (1969), #65, p. 11; JG (1969), Section 132.

92. AP (1969), #38, p. 7.

93. AP (1969), #61, p. 9; W. G. Hoffman, Volkswirt (15 Aug 1969).

94. MR (Nov 1969), p. 36. These exempted banks' liabilities on interest-arbitrage operations from minimum-reserve require- ments only if the liabilities were in foreign currencies and not "asso- ciated" with Bundesbank swaps (AR [1969], p. 91). The efficiency of such pidgeonholing of transactions is doubtful.

95. AP (1970), #86, p. 2.

96. MR (Jan 1965), p. 4; MR (Jun 1964), p. 4, 5; Schmidt, p. 82.

97. AR (1968), p. 22-23; Blessing, Verteidigung, p. 278, 288.

98. Paul Einzig, The Euro-Dollar System (New York, 1964); G. W. McKenzie, "International Monetary Reform and the 'Crawling Peg'," Federal Reserve Bank of St. Louis, Review (February 1969), p. 27.

99. Minister Schiller, AP (1969), #96, p. 10.

100. Hahn, Traktat, p. 98, 102-103; J. Lübbert, "Internationale Kapitalbewegungen als Problem und Instrument der Zahlungsbilanz- politik," Weltwirtschaftliches Archiv (1963), p. 69; Jenkis, p. 99n; AP (1971), #35, p. 16; AR (1970), p. 18.

101. Hahn, Traktat, p. 198.

102. Hahn, Traktat, p. 166; Schmölders, Finanzpolitik, p. 493.

103. Gilbert, p. 182.

104. G. Müller, Die Bundestagswahl 1969 (München, 1969), p. 26, 36-37.

105. For a review of troop-money arrangements, see The Economist, Quarterly Economic Survey (Germany) (1962, January); AP (1967), #34, p. 1; AR (1970), p. 95.

106. Federal Republic of Germany, Bundesbank, Supplements to Monthly Report, Series 3 (Feb 1971), Table 18a, n. 2; AP (1968), #53, p. 3.

107. MR (Nov 1969), p. 34.

108. FR (1967), p. 32.

109. FR (1968), p. 249.

110. Hahn, Traktat, p. 51.

111. For a survey of Germany's participation in international financial help see AR (1966), p. 30; JG (1968), Section 97 and especially AR (1968), p. 40-45.

112. AR (1968), p. 44.

113. AP (1970), #86, p. 14.

114. AP (1969), #96, p. 10.

115. AR (1969), p. 37; MR (Jan 1971), p. 39-40.

116. AP (1970), #40, p. 6; Bundesbank Vice President Emminger, AP (1970), #88, p. 12; Bank of England Governor O'Brien, AP (1970), #92, p. 9.

117. AP (1971), #3, p. 11; AP (1970), #84, p. 5.

118. AP (1970), #41, p. 5.

119. It is true that a Bundesbank spokesman explained the move as demonstrating the flexibility of the central bank, in that downward corrections could also be undertaken (AP [1970], #43, p. 3). Another bland explanation had it that "the object of this forward intervention was gradually to reduce the supply of foreign exchange in the spot market" (MR [1970], p. 42).

120. Bundesbank Vice President Emminger, AP (1970), #84, p. 5; AP (1971), #6, p. 11; AP (1970), #86, p. 13.

121. AP (1970), #43, p. 2.

122. FR (1969), p. 25; Emminger, Politik, p. 73.

123. JG (1964), Section 42.

124. Blessing, Verteidigung, p. 151.

125. Hahn, Traktat, p. 45.

126. JG (1968), Section 195; JG (1965), Section 66.

127. JG (1969), Sections 11, 20, 98.

CHAPTER

5

THE

POLICY ALTERNATIVES:

NON-ADJUSTING TACTICS

AT THE

MONETARY-BASE LEVEL

German policy options aimed at payments-balance adjustment were neglected or otherwise inadequate in the period under review. An autonomous payments surplus in all but two quarters of the entire period was the result (Tables A). In seven of the earlier quarters, however, only gross troop-money receipts (Tables A2) prevented deficit. "Correction" of the payments balance by capital exports (i.e., by combating the liquidity effect at the "exchange level" as discussed in the preceding chapter) was able to reduce the overall surplus in every quarter but two, and in a number of cases even to reverse it (Tables B, EE). In the two cases in which the overall surplus exceeded the autonomous surplus, the increases involved were extremely slight.

However, to the extent that a net increase in official international reserves did in fact take place, net new central-bank credit (Tables EE), constituting a high-powered monetary base, had to be issued. All else equal, if price inflation was to be avoided, in keeping with a policy of non-adjustment and "stability-export," most of this net addition to the monetary base had to be reabsorbed by the authorities. This possibility, too, was consciously treated by the authorities as "a substitute for upvaluation," i.e., as a non-adjustment tool.[1]

FISCAL REDUCTION OF THE MONETARY BASE

Both fiscal and monetary tools can combat the liquidity effect on the "monetary-base level." Fiscal tools in this context are those which affect government liquid savings. Such liquid savings can withdraw from economic circulation, and so redeposit with the central bank, the money released by the central bank in acquiring international reserves.

The German discussion of fiscal payments-balance-oriented measures has been inextricably entwined with the debate on anticyclical and growth-fostering fiscal policy. In this chapter, the framework of German fiscal institutions will first be discussed, after which the developments since the enactment of the "Stability Law" will be reviewed.

Framework for Reduction of Expenditures

Schematically, government liquid saving can be created by lowering government expenditures, by raising tax revenues, or by government borrowing and "sterilizing" of real private saving.[2] The Bundesbank insisted that government operations be financed without recourse to the money market. Until 1967, moreover, the Bank looked with great uneasiness on government borrowing on the capital market. Much of the Bundesbank's effort, as has been noted, was devoted to convincing the government to withdraw its demand from the capital market. In these circumstances, a policy of government liquid saving based on sterilizing private real saving was not feasible. (This tactic was, however, employed as a payments-balance offset by Britain in February 1971.)

Cuts in government expenditures are normally felt to be undesirable inasmuch as they interfere with national goals.[3] Cuts in infrastructural investment and defense outlays are thus seldom proposed.[4] (In 1967, sixty-four percent of Germans polled felt that defense expenditures would be easiest to reduce; Chancellor Kiesinger expressed himself as "quite concerned over this;" over one half of Bonn's "civilian" employees, meanwhile, work for the military.[5]) In the fifties, however, large government surpluses were achieved by not using defense appropriations. Although this policy was calculated to reduce the pressure of liquidity stemming from the payments balance, it was subjected to continuous criticism either as unnecessary taxation contrary to the social order, or as too obvious a reduction of German living standards in favor of those abroad.

On the other hand, expenditures on the extensive welfare and subsidy programs have often been attacked, either as counterproductive, or as incompatible with a liberal social order.[6] Transfer payments, which represent around one fifth of disposable income, not only resist these attacks, but also tend to make short-term price stabilization more difficult, since many are adjusted to cost-of-living changes with a statutory lag.[7]

The defense of various government expenditures by the respective interests has been made easier by the inflexibility of the German budgetary process. Thus, until 1967 overall budgetary balance was a legal requirement.[8] Correspondingly, Teutonic exactitude necessitates a specific legal authorization for nearly every expenditure. Eighty to ninety percent of federal government expenses are thus stipulated by law, and so are not in the discretion of administrators.[9] The Basic Law (Article 113) provides that the cabinet can disapprove any voted outlay. However, in practice this has been interpreted to mean that only whole laws can be rejected as units. Thus no use has been made of this power.[10] In addition, in both the Kiesinger and the Brandt governments, the two Ministers for Economics and for Finance repeatedly gave different emphases to anticyclical fiscal policy.[11]

Yet the parliament is itself weak in financial initiative. Until 1967 the Bundestag Ways and Means Committee approved bills only in terms of their effect on the annual budget balance. Not all money bills were so much as submitted to this Committee. The deadlock of interests in this area (as well perhaps as some well-aimed dramatics) may be reflected in the 1970 suggestion of the CDU Chairman of the Bundestag Ways and Means Committee that all expenditures not legally bound be cut by ten percent.[12] Minister Schiller took a somewhat more discriminating line in suggesting that the 1971 budget be divided into a core and a contingent element.[13]

Essentially, in these circumstances, only government investment was more or less free to change.[14] The "building pause" of 1963-1965 was an example of this, as was the inter-governmental capital-market queuing after 1967.[15] Both measures severely curtailed infrastructural expenditures. Since communal civil-service tenure and pay are set at the state level, these entities have little expenditure leeway except in the infrastructural area, in which they are the most important level of government. The resulting problems of infrastructural investment in roads are probably reflected in the Leber Plan for re-emphasizing railroads.

Changes in government spending not based directly on changes in the objectives of the spending itself are foreign to the traditional thinking of the German voter, whose ideas are based, perhaps more than elsewhere, on older, "public-finance" views rather than on Keynesian, "fiscal-policy" notions. This prejudice against fiscal policy is referred by most observers to the great German inflations of the twenties and the forties, both of which were "state inflations." This attitude, by inhibiting anticyclical fiscal-policy action, is considered to have aggravated the 1966 recession and hindered recovery from it.[16] In this way, earlier Ordoliberals, such as Erhard, who had heavily criticized the Keynesian emphasis on spending and consumption, as leading to stagnation of investment and to centralized economic control, could not be brought to act anticyclically in either direction.[17] The freedom with which the Bundesbank criticizes or approves specific budgetary measures may also be an inhibiting influence on fiscal planning.[18]

The Council of Experts called consistently for steady government expenditures on welfare and infrastructure, and for the implementation of fiscal policy through changes in the revenues side of the budget.[19]

Framework for Increase of Revenues

Changes in taxes for fiscal-policy purposes have been hindered by the general problems referred to above, and by more specifically tax-oriented problems.

Business income taxes have been a stumbling block to a flexible fiscal policy in Germany.[20] These taxes are not administered on a self-assessment basis similar to that of the United States. Instead, official assessments are made before final settlement. This often causes over a year's delay between the receipt of income and the payment of the corresponding income taxes. As a result, tax receipts fall fast with corporate income, but rise only eighteen months to two years after a rise in income.[21] Thus these arrangements have often had procyclical effects on corporate net earnings.[22] For the same reason, on the other hand, government budgets per se have been more nearly anticyclical.[23] The same features of the business income tax make the system cumbrous and difficult to reform.

Variations in depreciation allowances were first proposed in the government's economic report of June 1964 and were then endorsed by the Council of Experts.[24] They were introduced by the 1967 Stability Law.[25] The specific relations of this tool to payments-balance policy will be developed below.

Individual income taxes became steadily more regressive over the period under review, due to inflation's effect on fixed income-tax brackets. A reduction of income-tax rates in 1965 was designed to combat this tendency, and thus had little effect on the trend of revenues collected.[26] In 1968 various tax measures were aimed at raising revenues for anticyclical purposes.

In the tariff field, rate reductions were enforced by Common-Market agreements. The six-month acceleration of the Common Market reduction schedule in July 1964 was a response to payments-balance problems, but not a response in terms of fiscal policy or government saving. A further reduction occurred in July 1968.[27] The turnover tax was adjusted in 1967 to conform to the Common-

Market system. Although some redistribution of the burden resulted, not much change in revenues occurred. The previously discussed border-tax manipulations of 1968 were not fiscal-policy measures in any sense.

In general, German statesmen have been committed, for reasons of social order, to permitting no rise in the overall percentage tax burden on the economy.[28]

Effects of Federalism on Fiscal Framework

The institutional problems of fiscal policy went far beyond the scope of the federal government. The third, or communal, level of government itself accounts for twenty-five percent of government expenditures and two thirds of all government investment.[29] Communal infrastructural investment is a key growth factor, as noted above, yet, since the communes' non-investment expenditures are prescribed at the state level, these investment expenditures must act as buffers.

The microeconomic outlook of the communes further complicates fiscal policy, as it encourages procyclical borrowing and spending.[30] A technical difficulty in coordinating government financial policy is the fact that communal financial statistics are up to two years late in being assembled.[31]

Throughout the period under review, moreover, the federal and state governments have alternatively disputed over and reached temporary truces on the constitutionally instituted split of income-tax revenues between these two governmental levels. This dispute has led to confusion and even mutual contradiction in official budget revenue estimates. Beginning with 1970 the controversy was settled, more or less in favor of the state and local government units.[32] As a result of the differing proportional splits of revenues from various types of tax, the federal government's share of revenues is increased by a shift in the distribution of national income toward profits (as in 1969), and vice versa (as in 1970).

ANTICYCLICAL POLICY AND DEBATE, 1965-1971

Experience

Until 1967, thus, Germany was neither psychologically nor institutionally equipped to operate a fiscal policy.[33] In the light of the acute difficulties of 1965, associated with lowered income-tax and tariff rates and the end of social payroll contributions by employers, the need for longer-range financial planning had been pointed out on all sides.[34] The Council of Experts, for example, summarized the disorder in government finances in 1965/1966 as follows: the budget was out of balance; the federation and states disagreed on the income-tax revenue split, and the federal budget relied upon an illegally large share; the passage of an unpassable tax-raising bill was assumed in the federal budget; the passage of an unpassed law reducing outlays was likewise assumed; "supplementary" and "complementary" budgets were created to disguise clearly foreseen outlays; the budget assumed that some burdens would be taken up by clearly inappropriate public corporations; federal subsidies to the social-security institutions were to be written up in a "debt book" in lieu of payment; and such reliance was placed on revenue rises from rises in the nominal national income, that the excuse given for the 1966 deficit was that prices had not risen as fast as expected.[35]

In response to all these problems, and to the demoralized condition of the overloaded and confused capital market, the Bundesbank pressed the twin goals of intergovernmental financial coordination and medium-range governmental financial planning, as providing more permanent hobbles to largescale and uncoordinated government borrowing.[36] According to Bundesbank President Blessing, these goals were "the core of the Stability Law."

Parliamentary discussion of the bill, however, was accompanied with strengthening indications of recession. The Bank had not relaxed its pressure on government borrowing; the government, faced with the collapse of the capital market, was cutting its expenditure rate as its foreseeable revenues shrank, with the approval of the Bank.[37] The original, restrictive version of the bill came up for debate as the recession was reaching its low point.[38]

At this stage, numerous amendments to the bill were introduced, creating a relatively effective and flexible anticyclical fiscal apparatus for the first time in German history. The government, however, clearly did not much want the new expansionary powers.[39] The Bundesbank was accused of trying to stifle the new amendments with a threat of withholding an expected further lowering of the rediscount rate. In a speech which as it were replied to the new Kiesinger government's policy declaration of the same day, President Blessing reiterated the Bank's views. President Fritz Berg of the Industry Association spoke against the administrative flexibility of border taxes provided by the bill.[40]

The final version of the Stability Law incorporated the original desiderata of formalized intergovernmental coordination, especially in capital-market operations, and a five-year financial planning, with projections every January.[41] In times of boom, liquidity was to be reabsorbed into a cyclical-adjustment fund at the Bundesbank. If this failed, the government was to raise funds to repay its outstanding short-term debt. The new law also incorporated the more flexible tools of administratively adjustable depreciation allowances and administrative deferrals of certain tax obligations. Possible mobilization of fiscal tools against payments-balance surplus (as opposed to deficit), urged by the Council of Experts and worked into a footnote of the draft bill by Minister Schiller, was excised from the final law by the Bundestag.[42]

The First Federal Financial Plan under the Stability Law, covering the years 1967-1971, was the result of sharp negotiations within the governing Grand Coalition.[43] Finance Minister Strauss, who had previously refused to take office unless social outlays were reduced,[44] declared that the Plan was "aimed at restoring order in federal finances and restoring confidence in the financial administration of the government."[45]

On the other hand, the ratio of government investment to consumption was to be raised and private investment was to be fiscally encouraged. Tax write-offs were liberalized from January 1967 and investment taxes were reduced from January 1968.[46] Some taxes were raised, some expenditures, such as welfare and agricultural and commercial subsidies, were cut. The entire federal support of the social-security institutions was abandoned. The large industrial subsidies were untouched or, as with coal, raised.[47] In addition, much borrowing was foreseen to finance pump-priming expenditures during the recession. This action at least reversed the downward race between revenues and expenditures.[48]

With the new acceptability of anticyclical policy as a phrase came discussion of the definition and content of the concept. The Council of Experts argued that a cycle-neutral fiscal policy should increase government expenditures proportionately to the increase in productive capacity, and not to that of nominal Gross National Product.[49] The Council had already rejected as procyclical the Common-Market Council of Ministers recommendation that government expenditures be held to an increase of five percent per year.[50] The projection and indicative-planning features which had been substantially excluded from the Stability Law were introduced by the Council and Economics Minister into their "concerted action" activities.

In accordance with the Stability Law two "extraordinary investment budgets" financed by short-term borrowing were executed in 1967. Under Finance Minister Strauss these pump-priming

expenditures were carried out with great deliberation,[51] and were to
some extent offset by cuts made in the regular budget.[52] The program's
maximum impact was thus delayed until the fourth quarter of 1967,
and Strauss did not escape criticism on this score.[53] In December
1967 income- and social-tax rates were actually raised, and some
deductions were eliminated, with the result that wage-tax revenues
rose while the wage bill fell.[54] At the same time, state governments
by and large failed to indulge in recession deficit spending.[55]

A third investment budget proposed by Economics Minister
Schiller was rejected by a majority of the cabinet led by Finance
Minister Strauss. Between February and April 1968, Schiller's defi-
cit-spending policy was halted, after Strauss, Blessing, and President
Fritz Berg of the Industrial Association had spoken clearly and as it
were concertedly against it. Although the debate briefly waxed acri-
monious thereafter, the French crisis of the following summer, which
itself helped precipitate the fall speculative crisis, suspended the
debate on reflation in Germany. The total cash deficit of all governments in 1967 had been nine billion DM.[56]

The cabinet majority shortly passed from a transitional stage
of advocating "cycle-neutral" action to a restrictive attitude.[57] In
this connection, medium-range financial planning proved the strait-
jacket it was originally intended to be.[58] Alleging a continued need
to restore public confidence in government finances, the cabinet
majority again raised taxes[59] to create a fiscal surplus for 1969 in
order to offset the deficits incurred in 1967.[60] Accordingly the federal
government began retiring the short-term paper emitted in 1967, and
continued to do so in 1969, contracting long-term debt for the purpose.
pose.[61] As the year progressed, however, government borrowing
shifted systematically from the capital market, where the government
had been exposed to much criticism, into the money market.[62]

Minister Strauss held that past deficits cannot be recovered
within the medium-range period by increased incomes working through
unchanged tax rates.[63] He was also anxious to regularize the financial
status of the social-security institutions, which had been the object
of a succession of makeshifts designed to free the federal budget of
its social-security contributions. This financial anomaly precisely
in the social sector no doubt loomed as an ill omen to the Minister.

From December 1968 to March 1969, some fiscal ease was
permitted, with the intention of counteracting the depressive effect of
the new payments-balance-inspired border taxes.[64] By mid-1969
all policy makers were agreed on the danger of an inflationary boom.[65]
The Christian Democrat government majority could boast of having
refused Schiller's third investment plan.[66] Fiscal measures included

delaying of sizable outlays, redemption of debt and the reversal of investment-tax benefits. Since monetary tools were occupied in maintaining a net capital outflow to offset the stubborn trade surplus (not eliminated by the 1969 prosperity), fiscal policy was suddenly thrust into the role of bearing the full price-stabilization burden. This was the easier in that the continuing boom raised fiscal revenues, producing a cash surplus.

On the whole, the Bundesbank fully approved of the government's 1969 fiscal management.[67] Almost immediately after the change of governments and the revaluation, however, concern was expressed over the continuance of inflation. As early as January of 1970, the government announced the establishment of an obligatory anticyclical fiscal reserve fund at the Bundesbank, which by the end of 1970 was to exceed three billion DM. In February the government's newly-passed income-tax reduction was postponed, and interest-subsidies on small-scale saving were increased.

This package of measures apparently did not satisfy the Bundesbank or the Council of Experts. As exchange-rate speculation again increased after the 1969 revaluation, while the "adjustment inflation" was continuing, the Bundesbank, unable to raise interest rates higher, in May urged the government to use its powers under the Stability Law to levy an income-tax surcharge, to be placed in a trust account at the Bundesbank.[68] Also, in early 1970, Minister Schiller himself proposed voluntary prepayment of taxes with interest or bonus features. He was, however, unable to persuade the cabinet to accept this measure.[69] In April, the Council of Experts addressed a six-page letter to Chancellor Brandt, warning that if fiscal policy did not provide more support for the Bundesbank's restriction, a repetition of 1966 with its one-sided credit restriction and consequent recession could occur.[70]

In May the Bundesbank Annual Report called for fiscal support for restriction, including a ten-percent income-tax surcharge and an end to investment-fostering declining-balance depreciation allowances. At the same time, the Council of Experts issued a Special Evaluation calling for higher taxes, with exchange-rate measures to ward off payments-balance problems. In June the OECD secretariat had renewed its criticism of Germany's one-sided monetary-policy emphasis in the fight against inflation. Brandt and Schiller both declined to act, pointing to continued price rises abroad and consequent fear of speculation on the DM. Schiller, however, was not entirely happy with the government's position, and particularly with the cabinet's apparent political decision to emphasize the relatively easy goal of employment security, even at the expense of the less attainable goal of price stability.[71] This decision was made easier by the generally acknowledged blunder of the former government in delaying upvaluation, and thus making short-term price stabilization impossible.[72] The Brandt government was thus in a position both to claim credit for full employment and to refuse blame for inflation.

In June the Bundestag postponed the planned tax reductions indefinitely, and in July and August the Brandt government produced a new package of measures. The declining-balance depreciation allowance was suspended through January 1971, and a lower legal depreciation rate was introduced. A prepayment of income taxes, to be immobilized in the central bank, was also voted. By January 1971, the fund thus created amounted to around one billion DM.

Although Minister Schiller publicly continued to defend the government's policies as correctly timed, he had also begun in mid-1970 to call for a reduction in interest rates.[73] In this Schiller agreed with the Council of Experts and with several economic research institutions, as well as with numerous industry groups.[74] Only at the end of 1970 did the Bundesbank relent and begin to lower rediscount rate and so at least nominally to ease credit. (See discussion below.) At the same time, the Council of Experts was tentatively suggesting the release of the prepaid taxes at the expiry of the stipulated period for collecting them in July 1971.[75]

Conclusions

Regarded as a balance-of-payments equilibrating measure, fiscal absorption of the net new central-bank credit associated with an influx of international reserves must be self-defeating in Germany.[76] It tends to perpetuate or even raise the trade-balance surplus by holding domestic prices and costs down amid rising world price levels. It also tends to favor capital imports by maintaining internationally high interest rates. Even regarded as a non-adjustment measure, fiscal absorption is unsatisfactory, since the politically tolerable limits of government saving are reached far too quickly, as the "Juliusturm"* uproar of the fifties and the anticyclical debate of the sixties demonstrated. Cuts in expenditures alone are politically difficult and economically dangerous in a densely urbanized and highly industrialized society. Raising of revenues alone is in the longer run incompatible with a liberal economic system.

---

*"Juliusturm" is a historical term used, in this instance, to allude to large case balances accumulated in the fifties by the federal government through non-expenditure of tax receipts appropriated for the military.

Fiscal absorption of liquidity is not capable of combating the income-redistribution effect of a balance-of- payments surplus. Hence, when monetary-policy measures are largely paralyzed by the pegged-exchange-rate system, a really "anticyclical" fiscal policy is "hardly democratic."[77] It must reinforce the income-skewing tendencies of the payments surplus itself. Neither can fiscal absorption fully prevent the direct international price-transmission effect of the surplus without similar untoward results.

In the light of these weaknesses, the Council of Experts early suggested that fiscal policy be concentrated on manipulating the investment of firms through measures aimed at corporate profits. Since raising interest rates does not necessarily cut investment, least of all in Germany,[78] the Council suggested that fiscal policy not be used as a liquidity-absorbing tool.[79]

Thus, Germany's fiscal policy in the period under review was weakened and confused by the intertwining of its public-finance (social-order-conformity), payments-balance, and anticyclical goals. And indeed only "closed-system thinking" is capable of disentangling these aspects of fiscal measures.[80] In addition, the policy debate was heavily politicized, and positions thereby frozen.[81] Even if it had been single-mindedly bent on combating the balance-of-payments liquidity effect, fiscal policy would ultimately have been self-defeating and would have reached its political limits without solving the basic problem. The actual impact of fiscal policy on liquidity variables will be made more clear in connection with the discussion of monetary policy tools below.

CENTRAL-BANK REDUCTION OF THE MONETARY BASE

Operation of monetary-policy tools so as to reabsorb the potential free bank reserves generated by an overall balance-of-payments surplus can take three main forms: repayment of government or commercial-bank debt to the central bank, raising of banks' legally required reserves, or sale of assets by the central bank. The first of these can be carried on only to the extent that debt to the central bank exists; the second can be implemented only as long as the commercial banking system is not harmed significantly by the reduction of its profitability; and the third can be prolonged only until a dangerous overhang of bank near-money liquidity has been built up. This much analysis suggests that sooner or later a nation in basis external surplus will have to abandon any non-adjusting payments-balance strategy it undertakes on the monetary-base level.

In a less static context, the only contribution made by monetary

off-setting to the cure of the surplus itself is through the time gained
for the pressure of exchange losses to bear on the macrofinancial
policies of trade partners. For Germany vis-à-vis the United States
and Britain in the period under review, the effectiveness of this contribution was a priori most uncertain. In fact, the "stability-export"
strategy was "successful" in driving both these trade partners into
restrictive measures grossly assimilable to partial "competitive
devaluations." This was in itself hardly the outcome most favorable
to Germany. Neither did any of these results attack the roots of the
underlying international incompatibilities.

The German monetary authorities have been granted all the
powers that "in the light of modern monetary theory and practice, are
appropriate and necessary for controlling the money supply."[82] In
what follows, individual potential tools of the Bundesbank--operation
of central-bank accounts of non-banks, variable reserve requirements,
rediscount, open-market opperations, and moral suasion--will be
discussed in order. Within each discussion, the monetary authorities'
attitudes and the operation of the tool will be treated together, since
the possibilities and constraints on the monetary authorities' own
tools are intimately linked with the authorities' attitudes toward, and
actual exercise of, the powers. This is especially true of so independent and powerful a central bank as the Bundesbank. Fiscal absorption of liquidity will again be touched upon insofar as it was
operative through or otherwise affected the monetary tools. Merely
technical information about the shape of the tools has been put into
the notes.

Accounts of Non-Banks in the Central Bank

The central bank can reduce commercial-bank liquidity by
engineering net repayments of its outstanding loans to non-banks and
by forcing net transfers of existing non-bank deposits to itself.[83]
The Bundesbank may legally accept interest-free deposits from any
source.[84] In practice, the bulk of the Bank's deposits (ranging, over
the period, from three fourths to seven eights) represented the required reserves of credit institutions (on a year-end basis). As
noted in Chapter 1, excess reserves of commercial banks were
normally negligible.[85] Some German firms and foreign entities
accounted for a small (two to four percent) and generally shrinking
percentage of Bundesbank deposits, held mainly for recurring wage
payments (Tables E11).

Public authorities' deposits shrank over the period studied from
about twenty-five to about twelve percent of total Bundesbank deposits.
Almost all of these public deposits were owned by the Federal

Railroads, the Federal Post Office, the Federal Equalization of Burdens Fund, and the state governments. The former three accounts were of technically determined magnitude. The states accounted for about seventy percent of the public deposits in 1961, and steadily reduced their share through 1966, recovering somewhat in 1967, and accounting for only seven or eight percent of all Bundesbank deposits by the seventies. This steady reduction of state non-bank deposits accounted for the bulk of the change in all central-bank deposits over the period under scrutiny. By the end of the period, only a minor fraction of all government deposits were on the Bundesbank's books, the remainder being state and commune deposits in other institutions.

Although the federal and state governments must obtain the Bundesbank's permission to hold commercial-bank deposits, as a matter of comity to both governments and banks the Bank readily grants this permission to the state governments, which have long-standing relationships with local banks.

Thus, whereas in the fifties deposit policy was able to affect commercial-bank liquidity significantly, the end of federal surpluses and the increasingly unfavorable fiscal position of the states combined in the sixties to reduce the Bundesbank's really discretionary power over its government deposits to near-insignificance.[86] Without the authority to pay interest, the Bundesbank has no real upward control over its non-government deposits. It must be concluded that this once-influential instrument was unable to make any contribution to a tactic of combating payments-balance-generated liquidity.*

Central-bank credit to government did not play an especially great role in the operation of overall credit policy.[87] The overwhelming bulk of Bundesbank credit for government purposes was accounted for, on the one hand by the German credit positions with the International Monetary Fund and World Bank, and on account of the liquidated European Payments Union; and on the other by direct claims on the federal government on account of the Bundesbank's book loss on its international assets due to revaluation of the currency (reduced in biennial installments over the period and extinguished in early 1965),** and on account of international claims on the federal

---

*This discussion leaves entirely out of account the anticyclical deposits placed with the Bundesbank in 1970-1971, since these were entirely a matter of fiscal policy, as discussed above.

**In 1969 the analogous loss was absorbed from the Bank's

government acquired by the Bank through prepayment. Manipulation of these accounts for internal credit-policy purposes was easy only in the case of the prepayments of foreign debt, which were intended to accelerate the government's DM repayment schedule.88 On January 1, 1971, the Bundesbank took over direct responsibility for Germany's contributions to international organizations, and these credit items were extinguished.

Short-term credits to government, on the other hand, remained quite small, temporary, and technically-seasonally determined, and hence allowed little leeway for management (Tables E12, E1211). The special investment programs of the federal government, designed to aid recovery from the 1966/1967 slump, have been discussed above. Their monetary impact was chiefly on the Bundesbank's open-market operations, which were mobilized to support the necessary borrowing. By 1968, the Bundesbank had already returned to a policy of non-support for further government debt, which was considerably reduced thereafter.

Bundesbank policy was thus generally passive to the operation of all of its non-bank accounts. Where the Bundesbank occasionally took an active role, this was not motivated by payments-balance goals and was not in the direction of liquidity absorption.*

The monetary authorities were also generally passive to such technical items as float and the Bundesbank's own capital accounts. The present study therefore statistically treats all these accounts,

---

reserves. The Bundesbank restored this reduction of reserves by withholding payments of central-bank profits due to the government. The revaluation loss, less repayments, was carried in a special column of the Bundesbank condition statistics as an accounting convenience.

*The government's demands for credit are themselves, of course, not wholly unrelated to other payments-balance management devices. Government capital exports, for example, generate pressures to fiscal deficit, which may demand that the monetary authorities either support the capital market or directly finance the government. In Germany, direct short-term finance of government capital exports was avoided during periods of high economic activity only at the expense of heavy pressure on the capital market. Later, direct support of that market became necessary, impinging on the Bundesbank's open-market operations. Finally, in the 1966/1967 slump direct short-term credit to government by the banks was considered harmless, and indeed necessary for reflation.

as well as non-bank accounts with the Bundesbank, in such a way as to indicate clearly that they formed a given, to be reckoned with by the monetary authorities in operating their balance-of-payments policy, rather than a tool to be operated by them (Tables Section E).

Variable Reserve Requirements

In the fifties, before significant open-market paper was available, the Bundesbank made variations in the legally required reserve ratio against commercial-bank deposits rather frequently, to tie up bank liquidity and so inhibit its impact on the money stock.* Thereafter until 1969, however, reserve-requirement variations were used rather sparingly, and (with almost no significant exception) only in a downward direction (Tables F1, G1). The Bundesbank was somewhat reluctant, in word and deed, to use increased reserve requirements for a payments-balance offsetting tactics. This was the more remarkable in the light of the weaknesses in the Bundesbank's open-market tool (discussed below).

According to the Bundesbank, reserve-requirement changes were to be used only to adjust to long-term, structural changes in

---

*Throughout the period reviewed, the numerator of the required ratio was the average each month of central-bank deposits (alone) held on four weekly reporting days (hence the special ratios required outside of towns with Bundesbank branches). The denominator was a similar average of all credit-institution liabilities of under four years' term (net of current-account loans). One month's interest at three percent p.a. above the rediscount rate was charged for each reserve deficiency. The maximum legal reserve ratios were thirty percent for sight deposits, twenty percent for time deposits, and ten percent for saving deposits. The Bundesbank was empowered to differentiate required ratios as between average and marginal deposits, large and small banks, nationalities of deposit-holders, and bank locations (MR April 1965, p. 30, 33; Schmidt, p. 76; C. Fousek, Foreign Central Banking [New York, 1957], p. 54). Although the averaging of reserves and deposits for ratio calculations, together with the strong intra-monthly and seasonal fluctuations in depostis, caused some apparent fluctuations in the quarterly ratios, excess reserves rose above one percent of deposits only in a dozen crisis weeks, and reached one percent only at isolated quarter-ends. Therefore it was the Bundesbank's practice, followed in the present study, to take the actually held central-bank deposits of banks to the statistically equalivent to their legally required reserve deposits.

bank liquidity.[89] Partly, this caution was due to the uneven distribution of liquidity among German banks, which makes the impact of reserve-requirement variations especially crude and arbitrary.[90] The Bundesbank's unique array of reserve-requirement categories may also be designed partially to compensate for this.[91] The Bundesbank Council, composed as it is almost exclusively of individuals close to or representative of the financial community, may also have been unwilling to encroach overmuch upon commercial-bank profits by tying up bank's costly reserve money in non-earning required deposits (as not even vault cash is countable toward the requirements, and the Bank is not empowered to pay interest).[92] This view may find some substantiation in the seeming inconsistency between the Bank's apparent judgment that structural developments in bank liquidity required the release of reserve deposits over most of the period reviewed, and the Bank's other pronouncements on the dangers of monetary expansion.

Over the entire period under review, commercial banks' required reserve ratios were lowered by about thirty percent during the months from February to December 1961, were raised by ten percent in mid-1964, were lowered again by about thirty percent over the year 1967, were raised in two steps by over twenty-five percent in mid-1969 (only to be lowered again), and were raised in two steps by over ten percent in January 1970, and by over thirty percent in the second and third quarters of 1970. This record, extending over expansive and contractive, normal and crisis periods, makes it fairly plain that the Bundesbank was, at least through 1969, reluctant to use the reserve-requirements tool for offsetting a basic balance-of-payments surplus. The brief rises in the requirement in 1969 indeed had some effect in absorbing payments-balance-generated liquidity, but could also be seen as merely restoring the very deep cuts in the requirements made during the recovery from recession. The Bundesbank protested that it had finally been driven to this measure by exchange-rate speculation and an unwillingness to raise rediscount-rate-sensitive German interest rates any further.[93] The reversal of this increase after revaluation bears out such an assessment.

The same motives prompted the 1970 increases in reserve requirements, whose whole form reflected the desire to absorb inflowing liquidity without raising the German interest-rate structure. This interpretation applies particularly to the introduction in April of high marginal reserve requirements on growth of non-residents' deposits in German banks. Banks evaded this regulation by arranging inter-firm short-term international loans, which, upon the deposit of the proceeds, raised German bank liquidity without incurring the discriminatory marginal reserve requirements. All reserve requirements were raised by fifteen percent in July, while the discriminatory requirement remained applicable to foreign liabilities of banks.* This renewed attempt to absorb the payments-balance inflows did not discourage the evasive maneuvers of the banks. In September, therefore, all new deposit liabilities of banks were subjected to marginal reserve requirements, ending the discriminatory feature. Technical loopholes in the ruling were closed over the succeeding month. Finally, in December 1970 the marginal requirements were consolidated in a fifteen-percent increase in average reserve ratios, while the discriminatory marginal rate on foreign liabilities was reinstated, perhaps for its leverage in encouraging money exports (discussed in Chapter 4). No further action in this field was possible until after the floating of the DM in May 1971, after which a further fifteen-percent increase in domestic reserve requirements became feasible.

There were two interesting responses of the reserve-requirement tool directly to the external balance. The less significant was the slight lowering of reserve requirements for the month of December only in 1965 and 1969. In 1965 this represented an attempt to forestall repatriation of commercial banks' foreign short-term assets in order to finance the seasonal year-end demand for credit. By making funds available for one month only, the Bundesbank hoped to obviate the temporary balance-of-payments surplus consequent on repatriation.[94] In 1969, the one-month reduction of required reserves was in response to the same seasonal credit decline, this time during a period of post-revaluation reflux of speculative liquidity.

The more significant use of reserve requirements to respond to the external balance was the discriminatory requirement of the highest legal reserve ratio against deposits of foreigners from early 1964 to early 1967, in 1968-1969 and again in 1970, and the facility granted banks at times to offset their foreign assets against their foreign liabilities, for reserve-ratio calculations. These measures, forming part of the manipulation of foreign short-term commercial-bank assets, have been analyzed above.

Rediscount and Other Credit to Banks

The effectiveness of rediscount rate as a payments-balance offsetting tool was reduced in the period under review by the

---

*It is interesting to note that this measure was announced by the Bundesbank two weeks in advance, with the provision that its severity was to depend on the restrictive action taken by the government.

Bundesbank's desire to remain a major supplier of credit.[95] Thus total central-bank credit to banks on a year-end basis (Tables F2) grew fairly steadily, corresponding to the growth of commercial-bank liabilities, over the entire period reviewed, faltering noticeably only in 1963 when the basic external surplus position was recovered after the 1961 revaluation (thus providing another source of liquidity), and during the speculative crises of 1968 and 1969.

The Bundesbank's desire to keep the market "in the bank" is a natural reaction to the weakness of its open-market tool and to the (apparently partly deliberate) stiffness of its reserve-requirement tool.* It is also desirable, in view of the uneven distribution of liquidity in the banking system, to have a more direct means of influencing the liquidity of individual banks. Until 1967, moreover, several "market" rates of interest were virtually tied to the rediscount rate. Keeping the market in the bank, however, means competing with money-market interest rates influenced by the basic balance of payments and by interest rates abroad. Under these circumstances it is precisely basic surplus (tending to be associated with relatively low interest rates abroad and so with automatic influxes of bank liquidity) which will be least tractable by this tool.

Thus after a brief rise to five percent in 1960 during the attempt to suppress the export-fed boom, the Bundesbank lowered its rediscount interest rate to three percent over the year 1961 to reinforce the effect of the revaluation and so fight off continued speculative inflows.[96] This

---

*Since this attitude of the monetary authorities requires that the Bundesbank treat rediscounting less as a privilege than as in effect a right (MR [Apr 1965], p. 30), a more flexible supplementary rationing arrangement is provided by a system of changeable standard quotas based on bank liabilities (AR [1967], p. 94), plus an advance-against-securities facility at a one-percent-higher interest rate. The existence of the unused quota thus "liquifies" the banks' eligible assets to that extent (Schmidt, p. 71). In the period under review, quota standards were raised in early 1961 as part of the post-revaluation credit relaxation, cut ten percent in two installments in late 1965 and early 1966, and cut again in mid-1969. The motivation of each of these moves is fairly obvious from its timing. While evidently connected with payments-balance policy, they had no real effect on the key monetary-policy variables as developed in this study (but see S. I. Katz, External Surpluses, Capital Flows, and Credit Policy in the European Economic Community [Studies in International Finance #22], [Princeton, 1969]; G. Garvy, The Discount Mechanism in Leading Industrial Countries Since World War II [Washington, 1968], p. 125).

three-percent rate was maintained throughout 1962, 1963 and 1964.
The large basic surplus in 1963 eased credit and forced the Bundesbank
to keep a low rate in order to be in touch with the market. Low short-
term rates abroad had lowered the Bundesbank's "external margin,"
i.e., its leeway to raise rates without precipitating a counterproductive
repatriation of commercial-bank short-term assets. Even so, the call
rate fell below the rediscount rate late in 1963, and there was very
little net use by commercial banks of rediscount facilities in 1962 and
1963.[97]

It was apparently the basic deficit of 1965 which stirred the
Bundesbank to raise its rate to four percent, to help restore "competitive" cost levels, and to get its rate above a market rate which the
deficit was raising. The Bundesbank may also have been trying to
falsify the Council of Experts' prediction in early 1965 of a three-
percent annual price rise, due to the international price-transmission
effect.

The further rise in rediscount rate in June 1966, to five percent,
when the basic balance-of-payments situation was improving and all
domestic indicators had already peaked, was also explained as needed
in order to get above the market, since commercial banks were finding
the Bundesbank their cheapest source of funds, and had accepted
central-bank credit to a record total, approaching their quotas.[98]
Indeed, a form of "federal-funds" market in unused rediscount quotas
had grown up. The rise in interest rates abroad was also considered
opportune, as it increased the "external margin."[99] The "stagnation"
of the external balance due to rises in the productivity wage and an
"ominous" decline in the private savings rate were also cited by the
Bundesbank.[100]

In the background of these explanations stood the Bank's concern
over the fiscal outlook. The coming year's budget appeared not much
improved since the "disorderly" election-year budget of 1965, in which
the government had approached the capital market against the Bank's
pleas, thus posing a threat to the capital outflows desired by the
Bank.[101] The 1966 prospects were further darkened in the Bundesbank's
eyes by the increasing pressures of the United States and Britain for
a new settlement on troop costs, and of Israel for renewals of aid and
reparations, both of which would further unbalance the fiscal budget.
In the light of these elements, the mid-1966 rediscount rise may have
been in part designed to warn the weakening Erhard regime (now
notably lacking in support from German industry) away from the
capital market.[102]

The precipitous drop of the rediscount rate from five to three
percent in early 1967 was a reflationary response to the slump, the

concomitant large balance-of-payments surplus, and the consequent complaints of trade partners. It was also some further evidence of the Bundesbank's attempt to keep the market in the bank in spite of the externally induced fall in market rates. However, the reductions of the rate seem to have been undertaken with great reluctance. In late 1966, when the new Kiesinger government publicly called for lower interest rates, Bundesbank President Blessing answered, equally publicly, with a refusal. After the Council of Experts had also called for monetary ease, the Bank conceded a lowering of the rediscount rate, which, however, Economics Minister Schiller still regarded as too small. Thereupon a second rate reduction was approved.

Despite the fall in the rate, however, the rediscount window absorbed commercial-bank liquidity heavily in 1967, and contributed little to bank liquidity in 1968. Funds for banks remained cheaper elsewhere as the external surplus continued while the Bundesbank was supporting fiscal borrowing for pump priming.[103] The turnaround in official anticyclical thinking in 1969 was reflected in the two increases in the rediscount rate, to four percent in April and to five percent in June. A last-minute rise in the rate to six percent in September may have been intended to anticipate the back-flow of speculative funds during the period of floating the DM.

The continuance of the adjustment boom stemming from the delay in revaluation, together with the briefly massive outflow of speculative funds after the actual revaluation, and the surprising momentum of German long-term capital exports beyond the revaluation, provoked a further rise in the rate to 7.5 percent in March 1970. The Brandt cabinet questioned the "lateness in the cycle" of this move.[104]

The reluctant moves toward fiscal restriction over 1970 were met by equally reluctant moves toward monetary ease by the Bundesbank. In July the rediscount rate was reduced to seven percent in response to international payments pressures generated by the floating of the Canadian dollar and by the lira crisis. As interest rates abroad continued to ease and Germany's payments-balance surplus again caused concern, the Bundesbank in December 1970 lowered the rediscount rate in two steps of a half percent each, bringing German interest rates closer to parity with those abroad. Both Minister Schiller and Bundesbank President Klasen were anxious to prevent the domestic economy from interpreting these reductions of the rate as signals that internal stimulus was desired.[105] The payments-balance orientation of these moves was thus repeatedly stressed. Minister Schiller, however, conducted a mild propaganda for more macrofinancial ease, remarking through his Ministry's status report for the fourth quarter of 1970 that the rediscount moves were "also appropriate on domestic economic considerations."[106]

In January 1971, however, President Klasen took the occasion of the Bank Council's refusal to make a much-discussed further rediscount-rate reduction, to read the government and the collective wage bargainers a lesson on wage and price moderation. With this Blessing-like incursion into highly politicized territory, Klasen seemed to return to the Bank's pre-1967 tactic of making specific recommendations sanctioned by the threat of the monetary authorities' general power to restrict credit. The final lowering of the rediscount rate before the 1971 floating of the DM is discussed in Chapter 7.

Through most of the period reviewed here the rediscount tool was not vigorously operated toward the specific goal of neutralizing external surpluses, due primarily to the limits imposed by foreign interest rates in Germany's open economy and to the Bundesbank's desire, given the state of its other tools, to remain a normal supplier of liquidity. On the contrary, the rediscount tool did reinforce the effects of external deficit in 1965/1966 and of surplus in 1967. As the open-market tool became somewhat more flexible, the Bundesbank began to use its rediscount leeway to absorb liquidity, as in 1967. The swift rises in rediscount rate in 1969 and 1970 responded more to the crisis atmosphere generated by the payments balance and the revaluation than to any underlying long-term conditions. The December 1970 reduction of the rate, however, again explicitly showed the payments-balance limitation on interest-rate policy in Germany.

A characteristic use of the rediscount tool for balance-of-payments purposes entered into the Bundesbank's campaign against capital imports and money imports by banks. This was the disposition, discussed above, that rediscount quotas be reduced by the amount of any bank borrowing abroad (other than to finance imports). Given the secondary character of rediscount quotas in the period under study, and the import-finance loophole, it is doubtful whether this arrangement had more than psychological effect.

Open-Market Operations

German open-market policy has been hampered by several factors. The most fundamental of these is the relative narrowness of the money-market itself, which consists almost entirely of banks and insurance institutions. Pre-war antidisintermediation agreements limiting money-market participation are still in force, and are supported by the Bundesbank to prevent "structural change" in banking.[107] Banks thus commonly hold open-market paper to maturity or resell it to the Bundesbank, limiting the impact of credit-market policy on non-bank liquidity.[108]

For the same reason, the Bundesbank is more passive in its

open-market operations--more dependent on positive action by the commercial banks--than would be the case in a wider money market.[109] Bundesbank President Blessing was always well aware of this weakness. His first significant open-market measure was the placement in mid-1960 of a billion DM in open-market paper with the ad hoc Federal Loan Consortium of banks. This consortium undertook not to resell the paper (which would at once have returned to the Bundesbank's portfolio) within two years.[110] In mid-1961, after the modest revaluation and the supplementary initiation of the "adjustment boom," "Blessing's billion" was released from this pledge.

The lack of "ammunition" was another limitation on German open-market operations. As the period under review opened, state and federal treasury securities and those of the Federal Post Office and Federal Railways, as well as prime bankers acceptances, were considered subject to the Bundesbank's "money-market regulation." (The Bank's open-market operations are supposed to be aimed "only" at regulation of the money market.)[111] These items were relatively scarce in 1961, and, for the purposes of open-market ammunition, they were eked out with mobilization paper.

Mobilization paper is a unique German arrangement. In addition to the more or less variable book and special credits discussed above, the federal government is also responsible to the Bundesbank for a stable sum of just over eight billion DM in "equalization claims." These are three-percent bonds, salable only at face value, issued to credit institutions of all sorts (including the central bank) in connection with the currency reform of 1951. Since 1955, the Bundesbank has been entitled to exchange these now effectively unmarketable claims at will for so-called mobilization paper, consisting of non-interest-bearing treasury notes of any maturity and denomination requested by the Bundesbank.[112] This mobilization paper can in turn be sold by the Bundesbank to commercial banks at varying discounts.

Potential open-market ammunition was further increased by the Stabilization Law of mid-1967, which provided that the government can issue to the Bundesbank up to a further eight billion DM in "liquidity paper," similar in all respects to mobilization paper, except without the necessity of exchange against equalization claims. The deficit tendency of governments at all levels in the sixties (discussed above) and the inclusion, during the recovery effort of 1967, of federal and state medium-term notes in the Bundesbank's "money-market regulation," also added to the potential range of open-market operations.[113] Direct support of the ailing capital market, first undertaken late in the period under review, again added to the potential magnitude and impact of open-market operations. Thus strengthened, the open-market tool in Germany assumed greater significance.

The Bundesbank considers itself technically "passive" as to the volume of its open-market transactions. In principle, the Bank is willing to buy and sell with all comers at the buying and selling interest rates it announces.114 The Bank has, however, in the past requested the social-insurance institutions, which normally hold a goodly proportion of their assets in bank deposits, to purchase mobilization paper. The Stabilization Law of 1967 gives the Bundesbank the power to require such purchases in amounts tied to the institutions' financial position.115

The Bundesbank made fairly full use of the mobilization-paper facility to acquire open-market ammunition in its effort to damp the 1960 boom (Tables F32). Thereafter, both the post-revaluation easing of credit and the increased issue of government securities to finance the budget allowed a progressive reduction of mobilization paper through 1966. (Mobilization paper exists only in "outstanding" form: upon its return to the Bundesbank it is automatically reconverted to equalization claims. Similarly, "liquidity paper" is extinguished altogether upon repurchase.) Indeed, the money-market issues of the government in 1966 (made necessary as an alternative source of funds by the "nursing" of the capital market) required that the Bundesbank absorb as little funds as possible from the banks.

During the reflation effort of 1967, the Bundesbank slightly increased the outstanding mobilization paper to absorb liquidity while buying securities on the open market to drive down long-term interest rates, when the banks had failed to use their restored liquidity in the capital market.116 On the whole, the Bundesbank remained a permanent net buyer of government securities until mid-1968. Thereafter the Bank was forced to intervene with "massive sales" of open-market paper.117 After the revaluation of 1969, some repurchase of open-market paper took place, to be followed in the latter part of 1970 with record-breaking sales. By January 1971 the Bundesbank was forced to make its first sales of "liquidity paper," because it had sold all eight billion DM worth of authorized mobilization paper.118

A most remarkable phase of open-market policy in the period under review was the consistent series of net open-market phases during the balance-of-payments deficit year 1965. These purchases represented an unsuccessful effort to drive down long-term interest rates, and to ward off a capital-account payments surplus. They also were aimed at continuing the 1962-1963 policy of stabilizing banks' holdings of liquidity reserves in the form of domestic, rather than foreign, assets.

Since the great increase in circulation of treasury securities, especially medium-term securities, in 1967, an element of debt management has entered into the Bundesbank's open-market operations

for the first time.[119] The Bank therefore acted to fund the government's medium-term debt during the boom which developed in 1968-
1969, when it was hoped such action would be deflationary.[120]

Despite the great recent activity of this tool, the fatal flaw of
Germany's open-market policy has remained the fact that, due to its
legal form and to the narrowness of the money market, mobilization
and liquidity paper is in fact as liquid as reserve money.[121] Its very
existence, as a virtually invented "asset" for the central bank to sell,
indicates how heavily strained the German open-market tool is, to
achieve even a seeming absorption of bank liquidity.

Moral Suasion

Moral suasion is an important component of the Bundesbank's
repertory of policy means. For example, during the 1961 "adjustment
boom" the Bank continued to try to "talk prices down," in hopes that
the boom would thus affect only the foreign-trade multipliers of income,
and not prices.[122] This form of merely verbal discriminatory measure
occasions some mistrust of the central bank's reporting service;[123]
indeed, Bundesbank President Blessing has stated that the Bank's
very extensive reporting service is one of its policy tools.*[124]

In public, the Bundesbank's appeal seems to be mainly to the
preoccupations and technical knowledge of the typical business manager.
Accordingly, its style has often had a didactic, authoritarian, even
Olympian ring. Its analytical content is often decidedly repetitive.
The frequent appearance of Bundesbank directors on radio and tele-
vision corroborates the impression that the Bank's audience is not
primarily technical.[125] This form of "moral suasion," not aimed at
banks, contrasts strongly with the frequent appeals from industry and
banking quarters not to "politicize" the "technical task" of the Bank.

Credit Ceilings

In 1965 directly imposed ceilings on commercial-bank lending
(or on its rate of expansion) were seriously considered for a short

---

*The present writer, however, would be extremely ill-advised
to attempt to deny the enormous usefulness of the Bundesbank's
incomparable reporting service. A glance through the notes of the
present study would, in any case, be sufficient to make ridiculous any
such attempted denial.

time. Suggested by the Council of Experts as a possible alternative, and endorsed by the governmental Financial Reform round table, they were briefly approved also by the Bundesbank as a means of shortening the "braking time" of credit policy measures.[126] Before the ceilings could be written into the Stability Law drafts, however, banking and industry circles had opposed them as having differential impacts on banks and so reducing Germany's already somewhat problematical banking competition. Minister Schiller also opposed the ceilings on this ground.

During the discussion, the Bundesbank reserved its stand, perhaps fearing the added responsibility the new powers would bring.[127] By apparently cutting through the technical dilemma of credit policy vis-à-vis the balance of payments, such a move could more than ever thrust the Bundesbank into the position of bearing the whole burden of stabilization. Real power to override the merely technical credit-policy dilemma (discussed below) could also expose the underlying non-technical nature of that dilemma to public scrutiny. It will be suggested below that this may be contrary to many German interests. However, President Klasen in 1971 seemed to attempt to revive consideration of portfolio controls, as well as other administrative-control measures, as described in Chapter 7.

Summary and Conclusions

In 1961 and 1962, German credit policy was aimed at stimulating a boom to supplement the inadequate price-level alignment of the 1961 revaluation. In 1964, German exports slowed as a result of the Italian and French stabilization efforts and the British imposition of a border tax.[128] Credit authorities promptly announced a tightening.

Since this policy coincided with boom conditions abroad, the export suplus rebounded in textbook fashion to offset the Bundesbank's braking effort.[129] Therefore, bank credit continued to accelerate through 1965--despite the Bundesbank's restrictive policy--based on repatriation of banks' foreign liquid assets, the trade surplus, and the banks' progressive withdrawal from the capital market.[130] Thus, the lack of exchange-rate flexibility produced an "adjustment inflation."[131] The Bundesbank thus felt itself forced to continue its restrictive policy into 1966 in response to fiscal "mismanagement" and the continued rise of prices. Higher interest rates abroad, and various capital-control-centered balance-of-payments programs, gave the Bundesbank some capital-account leeway for its policy.[132]

In mid-1966, however, the Bundesbank was forced to permit the payments inflows to have their full effect on bank liquidity.[133]

This inflow of liquidity was in fact very largely the result of the Bank's own high-interest policy. The Bundesbank's policy did not overtly change, however, until after the fall of the Erhard government and the conclusion of the Stability Law struggles in 1967.[134]

The ensuing recession was not moderated by a surge of exports, because the German business cycle, perhaps partly as a result of monetary-policy intervention, was out of line with those of its trade partners.[135] The payments surplus did not begin to grow until mid-1967, after the fiscal investment programs were under way. Bank lending also grew only slowly, and was diverted abroad as German interest rates fell.[136]

Recovery in 1968 did not bring a reduction of the export surplus, since the deep 1967 recession had widened international price-level differentials too far to be recovered cyclically.[137] This phenomenon helped precipitate speculative pressures over the succeeding months. The November 1968 border-tax measures were too little and too late. Despite progressively more restrictive monetary measures, speculation continued, and culminated in revaluation. Even after revaluation, monetary ease was delayed by massive capital outflows and by continued wage-price inflation, until international interest-rate differentials and renewed payments-balance surplus forced some ease as 1971 opened.

This outline history of German monetary policy reveals the limitations imposed on its by short-term capital movements (and so by foreign interest rates), and by business cycles (and so by international price-level differentials).[138] The former effect has been highlighted by the growing sensitivity of short-term capital to interest-rate differentials.

As instruments to palliate basic international disequilibrium, German credit policy measures were self-defeating.[139] First, liquidity restrictions could not offset the direct price-transmission effects on wages.[140] Then, because the export industries are largely financed by foreign demand, German investment is specially insensitive to interest rates. (On the side of demand for investible funds, also, the Council suggests that Germany's stationary labor force necessitates capital investment regardless of interest rates.) Growing inflationary expectations have also reduced the braking effect of interest rates. Finally, liquidity restrictions could discourage government borrowing only at the risk of crisis in the capital market.[141] Altogether, therefore, credit restrictions operated one-sidedly on private non-foreign-trade-oriented sectors, thus aggravating German income and growth biases.

In the light of German labor's long moderation, and the imported nature of German inflation, putting stabilization burdens one-sidedly on labor could be politically unbearable.[142] Events of the past two years revealed the radical potential within Germany's long-passive labor movement. Forcing government to bear the burden alone harms growth and social policy.[143]

Liquidity restriction cannot, in any case, be carried very far in Germany. As German incomes and prices lag and Germany's interest rates rise internationally, new funds in the form of payments-balance surpluses are received by exporters and capital markets.[144] Yet German prices and interest rates cannot be effectively sealed off from those of the world. Credit policy must thus vacillate between fostering "homemade" and provoking imported inflation. The resulting stop-and-go short-term-oriented credit policy is injurious to the long-term planning of firms, and constitutes an obstacle to consistent economic policy.[145] Monetary policy to combat the liquidity effect of the payments balance reaches definite limits in the volume of non-monetary assets available for placement by the central bank, in the "liquidity overhang" represented by most such assets, and in highly interest-elastic international capital movements.

The timing of credit policy shifts was further confused by the so-called wage lag.[146] Specific rounds of wage rises tend to "lag behind" price rises; in Germany this tendency is aggravated by the slow spread of wage leeway from the export industries to the remaining sectors.[147] Often the Bundesbank and others responded to each wage rises as if it were a new inflationary threat, when it was merely the lagged consequence of an inflationary movement already under way.[148] In theory, indeed, the Bundesbank recognized this lag.[149] These problems of timing and flexibility led the Council of Experts to characterize the payments-balance policy based on credit restriction measures as dangerous to both price stability and growth.[150]

POLICY DILEMMA AND POLICY MIX

The Nature of the Dilemma

There has been much written of Germany's policy "dilemma:" a restrictive financial policy will tend to lower German prices and raise German interest rates relative to the world's, and so to attract fresh liquidity from abroad through the balance of trade and the international capital accounts.[151] It is to be emphasized that this "dilemma" characterizes only non-adjusting financial policy measures

in an open economy under pegged exchange rates. It is not a dilemma
of balance-of-payments policy as such. Traditionally, balance-of-
payments policy, as the present study has envisioned it, is rather
faced with the choice between adjusting and non-adjusting strategies,
and among the tools available for these. As this study of the German
case re-emphasizes, any choice among these alternatives entails
both benefits and costs. To characterize this kind of situation as a
dilemma can be misleadingly superficial.

Given an open economy and pegged exchange rates, however,
financial policy does face a situation in which it must choose between
homemade and imported inflation. Hence that form of payments-balance
tactic here called non-adjustment through combating the liquidity effect
at the monetary-base level--but only that subdivision of balance-of-
payments policy--does face what could be called a dilemma. Neither
a restrictive financial policy nor an expansive one can in fact successfully combat the liquidity effect, so that the effort thus to avoid correction of more basic elements of the international disequilibrium
will eventually be frustrated.[152]

This much discussion indicates that the merely technical dilemma
is not the fundamental problem. The basic "dilemma" facing Germany
is that of weighing adjustment against non-adjustment in the light of
national goals. Adjustment seems to threaten the loss of some export
markets, the loss of financial prestige and power, and the abandonment
of the goal and slogan of absolute price stability in an inflationary
world. Non-adjustment appears to entail loss of financial and political
harmony in the Atlantic community, the domestic difficulties and
distortions of combating the automatic readjusting effects of disequilibrium, and the constant embarrassment of ultimately incurable
imported inflation. Further assessment of these alternatives and
their meaning for Germany will be attempted in Chapters 6 and 7.
Enough has been said here to indicate that the "dilemma" is basically
a choice.

Potential Resolution Through Policy Mix

Policy-Mix Theory

Some economists have advanced the notion of a constellation of
financial-policy tools designed to eliminate the dilemma of the financial-policy non-adjustment tactic.[153] It can be shown that any two
unrelated goals can both be achieved at once by appropriate application
of two independent tools, neither of which is constrained by any other
goal.[154] Domestic equilibrium (i.e., neither unacceptable inflation
nor unacceptable unemployment) and foreign equilibrium (i.e., neither

long-run gain nor long-run loss of international reserves) may be taken as goals, and fiscal policy (measured by the magnitude of the fiscal surplus) and monetary policy (measured by the height of interest rates) as tools.

Assuming constant exports and productive capacity, a reduction in fiscal surplus will raise income through the multiplier and decrease the trade-balance surplus through the multiplier times the marginal propensity to import. At the same time a rise in interest rates will lower income through the "marginal efficiency of expenditure" (or the interest-elasticity of expenditure) and increase the trade balance surplus through the marginal efficiency of expenditure times the marginal propensity to import. Therefore, every change in expenditure and trade balance brought about by a reduction in fiscal surplus can be exactly offset by an "appropriate" rise in interest rate (and vice versa). The appropriate mix of tools in each case is the arithmetic result of the given values of the functional relations mentioned just above. This suggests the existence of a schedule of various equilibrium combinations of tool settings.

However, a rise in interest rates will additionally increase the capital-accounts balance-of-payments surplus through the interest-elasticity of capital supply by increasing international interest-rate differentials. Thus the effect of a reduced fiscal surplus on the balance of payments could be offset by a smaller rise in interest rates than could the effect on domestic expenditure. Since changes in the two tool variables thus have differentiated effects on the two goal variables, the potential schedule of equilibrium tool combinations is reduced to a single full-equilibrium combination.

In this view the fundamental task of financial policy is to move from tool-variable combinations producing deflation and surplus, deflation and deficit, inflation and surplus, or inflation and deficit toward the single full-equilibrium policy mix. In the "easy cases" either tool or both can be used; in the "hard cases"--those of so-called "goal conflict" (which is really tool conflict)--the proper sequence and direction of tool applications, as well as the final settings, is unique. It is also, needless to say, difficult to discern.

Critique of Policy-Mix Theory

The highly formal policy-mix notions presented above are probably unworkable, for several reasons. By the schematic reasoning of the model, the interest rate required for the double equilibrium may be negative, which is absurd as it implies inflation or the equivalent as a precondition to price stability.[155] In any case, the interest rate is not free of the constraint of conflicting goals: virtually by definition, true interest rates serve the function of resource allocation. If the rate structure were forced away from the equilibrium dictated by the supply and demand of real capital, the cost of the policy mix would be high in terms of inefficiency.[156]

Again, the two tools presented are hardly sufficiently independent. The fungibility of money requires that this kind of policy mix be in essence a gigantic discriminatory "Operation Twist."[157] Can interest rates be manipulated by money-market operations while fiscal and capital-market operations of opposite tendency are being carried on? In economies sophisticated enough to be concerned with the policy "dilemma," this seems very doubtful.[158]

In Germany's real circumstances, the problem of how in fact to approach the double equilibrium from an initial position of balance-of-payments surplus and inflation must also be resolved. The superficial mechanics of the financial-policy "dilemma" ensure that, whichever tool is moved in whichever direction, the indicated distance and direction of motion of the other tool is changed from that indicated by the original situation. The problem is compounded, probably hopelessly, where various individual national inflationary tendencies have differential force. Reaching the right mix in these circumstances would seem to require an instantaneous and simultaneous jump to new policies whose correctness can be divined only by a kind of prescience. All of these problems are further compounded by ongoing shifts of the trade-offs among the domestic goals (Phillips-curve shifts, invention or innovation).

As a practical matter, too, the recommended policy-mix tool shifts for the German case--lower interest rates and fiscal restraint-- may tend to favor the established industrial status quo, by easing outside (capital-market) financing, which in Germany is dominated by banks and their institutionally related heavy-industrial customers, while reducing inside (sales-generated) financing, which is required if foreign demand is to be replaced by domestic.

Certain other assumptions of the formal policy-mix model are equally questionable, viz., that the interest elasticity of the international capital accounts is the same in both directions; that there is no concern anywhere for the composition of the payments balance; that no problems are raised by any degree of fiscal imbalance; that there are no Pigou effects; that exchange markets are perfect and without speculation; and that all the elements determining the functional relationships are themselves straight-line functions (or at least do not prevent an intersection point on a graph of equilibrium tool-setting combinations).

The formal policy-mix model does not offer a realistic escape from the dilemma of non-adjusting financial policy. The case of simultaneous boom and payments-balance surplus is, under the assumptions of the model common to both "dilemma" and "policy-mix" thinking, not only "hard" but "basically insoluble."[159] Despite this, a "new mix" was being applied vigorously in Germany in 1969.[160]

Policy-Mix Practice

The recommendations for "a better policy mix" that Germany has received from all sides,[161] and which the Bundesbank itself began to reiterate in 1967 and again in 1970, are in an entirely different logical class from the formal policy-mix model of Mundell, Cordon and Swan.[162] These recommendations simply referred, with rhetoric perhaps inappropriately borrowed from the current theoretical literature, to the impossible price-stabilization burden placed on the Bundesbank by the fiscal disorder of 1964-1966 and by the government's hesitations of 1970, and not to any hope that a combination of financial-policy tools could both stabilize price levels and balance international payments. The Bundesbank had been put into the position of overusing its restrictive tools; in the imagery of a former government: with blunt instruments, you must hit harder.[163]

Still another logical category is represented by the "mix" recommendations of the Council of Experts. Arguing that expenditures in Germany are not interest-elastic, the Council concluded that interest-rate policy can only be aimed at the capital accounts of the balance of payments.[164] Since the interest policy indicated in surplus is of inflationary tendency, domestic expenditures must then be regulated by an independent tool. Due to the fungibility of money, general fiscal measures are not such a tool. The Council therefore suggested that firms' investment be regulated by an administratively variable profit-tax rate (this had previously been suggested by Chancellor Erhard, and by the Government Economic Report of June 1964).[165]

It is conceivable that, through such a radical and even politically dangerous "discriminatory" measure, sufficient "twist" could be put on effective rates of return to achieve both economic-policy goals simultaneously. However, the Council itself found that investment was not sensitive to profits.[166] And it is not clear that even these two tools are really independent. In the case of low interest rates and high profit taxes, what is to become of the funds (impliedly available in the market) not invested by firms? Are they all to be absorbed by taxation? What then is the real meaning of the low interest rates? Again, what is to become of growth? What of the biases in favor of the outside-financed export sectors? Most recently, the Council of Experts has given increased emphasis to exchange-rate measures as the necessary second independent economic-policy tool.[167]

The experience of the past eight and a half years has wrought some changes in Germany's balance-of-payments tools. One-sided monetary price-stabilization was abandoned after the fiasco of 1966-1967. The drive to put the public sector "in its place" by the combination of monetary tightness and Stability-Law restrictions on government access to the capital market ironically increased the role of government by institutionalizing expansionary anticyclical fiscal policy in the final, recession-born version of the Stability Law.

The more recent pre-revaluation policy "mix" found the Bundesbank striving to perpetuate capital exports while fiscal policy bore the brunt of price stabilization.[168] This new tool combination certainly had more long-run chance to escape the dilemma of defending undervaluation than had the older "reverse mix." The capital export consisted too much of portfolio investment, sensitive to interest rates and security-price expectations. This means that merely maintaining low interest rates was insufficient to discourage repatriation. Again, a great part of Germany's defense of undervaluation lay, as noted above, in fiscal exports of capital, to absorb the liquidity effect at the "exchange level." The new fiscal price-stabilizing function could not be allowed to interfere with its capital-export function. Yet the two together might have proved even harder for the taxpayer to bear than was the earlier fiscal situation.

In 1970, the government heeded "policy-mix" warnings, although with some hesitation, and supported the Bundesbank's restrictive policy. An Economics Ministry spokesman referred expressly to the duty of mutual aid imposed on Bank and government by the Stability Law.[169] The Bank, in turn, was rather slow to ease its restraint in the face of the fiscal help. However, the rediscount-rate reductions of late 1970 were widely regarded as a true compromise in the policy-mix spirit.[170]

Faced with the "dilemma" of "imported" and "adjustment" inflation, fiscal and monetary tools are not sufficiently independent or specific. A distinctly different tool, such as exchange-rate flexibility, is needed.[171]

Neither at the international-exchange level nor at the monetary-base level has Germany succeeded in permanently offsetting the liquidity effects of the payments balance. Price and income effects of fundamental undervaluation continued, involuntary foreign lending through acquisition of international reserves continued, and the limits of monetary, fiscal and exchange measures were eventually reached. Thus adjustment measures were not consistently attempted and non-adjustment measures were not consistently successful. Was Germany's long-range policy nevertheless meaningfully characterizable? If so what was its strategy and its rationale? These questions form the theme of the following chapter.

NOTES

1. K. Blessing, Die Verteidigung des Geldwertes (Frankfurt, 1960), p. 235, 237.

2. Federal Republic of Germany, Sachverständigenrat zur Begutachtung der Gesamtwirtschaftlichen Entwicklung, Jahresgutachten (1968), Section 133.

3. JG (1964), Section 214; JG (1965), Section 191; JG (1966), Section 132; JG (1970), Section 100.

4. Minister Möller in Federal Republic of Germany, Bundesbank, Auszüge aus Presseartikeln (1971), #4, p. 4.

5. AP (1967), #53, p. 2.

6. See for example the list of subsidies, not to the restructuring of the coal industry, but to the use of coal in JG (1967), Section 88.

7. JG (1966), Section 117.

8. G. Gutman, H. J. Hochstrate, and R. Schüter, Die Wirtschafts-verfassung der Bundesrepublik Deutschland (Stuttgart, 1964), p. 419.

9. L. Erhard, The Economics of Success (Princeton, 1963), p. 268.

10. JG (1965), Section 155.

11. AP (1970), #74, p. 4.

12. AP (1970), #39, p. 8. The very existence of a CDU Chairman for Ways and Means during an SPD-dominated administration is revealing for the institutional problems of German policy formulation.

13. AP (1970), #74, p. 2.

14. JG (1966), Section 132.

15. JG (1965), Section 30.

16. JG (1967), Sections 134-137.

17. L. A. Hahn, "Die Grundirrtümer in Lord Keynes' General Theory of Employment, Interest and Money," Ordo-Jahrbuch, Volume 2 (1949), p. 171 ff.

18. AP (1970), #39, p. 8.

19. JG (1964), Section 214; JG (1965), Section 191; JG (1966),
Section 132.

20. JG (1964), Section 48.

21. JG (1964), Section 127; JG (1967), Section 110.

22. Federal Republic of Germany, Bundesbank, Monthly Report
(Sept 1970), p. 23; JG (1965), Section 103.

23. JG (1964), Section 201.

24. JG (1964), Section 213.

25. For details, see Federal Republic of Germany, Bundesministerium für Finanz, Finanzbericht (1969), p. 47.

26. JG (1964), Section 132.

27. JG (1968), Section 5.

28. Minister Möller, AP (1970), #39, p. 8.

29. JG (1968), Section 320 ff.

30. FR (1969), p. 129.

31. FR (1968), p. 33.

32. Federal Republic of Germany, Bundesbank, Annual Report
(1969), p. 73.

33. O. Veit, Grundriss der Währungspolitik (Frankfurt, 1961),
p. 322; JG (1964), Sections 48, 52, 54; JG (1965), Section 15; FR (1969),
p. 116.

34. German Economic Review (1964), #1, p. 80; GER (1963),
#4, p. 373.

35. JG (1966), Section 134 ff.

36. FR (1966), p. 234; K. Blessing, Im Kampf um Gutes Geld
(Frankfurt, 1966), p. 314.

37. AP (1968), #1, p. 1; JG (1966), Sections 12, 58; JG (1969),
Section 77.

38. FR (1967), p. 1.

39. JG (1967), Section 333.

40. AP (1967), #10, p. 10.

41. FR (1969), p. 196 ff. A remarkable gap in this arrangement was the exclusion of the communes (JG [1968], Section 320 ff.). The Public Authorities Cyclical Council did obtain the right to direct that up to three percent of state revenues remain unspent.

42. GER (1967), #2, p. 165n.

43. GER (1968), #3, p. 258.

44. AP (1966), #93, p. 6.

45. GER (1968), #3, p. 259.

46. FR (1969), p. 47; AP (1968), #43, p. 1.

47. GER (1968), #3, p. 269.

48. Federal Republic of Germany, Sachverständigenrat zur Begutachtung der Gesamtwirtschaftlichen Entwicklung, Sondergutachten (1967), Section 3.

49. JG (1970), Sections 322-358; JG (1968), Section 128. The Council ultimately selected a base year for measurement of changes in capacity utilization. See the explanation in JG (1970) above.

50. JG (1964), Sections 206-209.

51. Organization for Economic Cooperation and Development, Economic and Development Review Committee, Survey (Germany) (1968), p. 13.

52. JG (1967), Sections 66, 152, 149, 162, 167.

53. FR (1969), p. 24; Industrial Congress, AP (1967), #53, p. 2; Bundesbank President Blessing, AP (1967), #90, p. 3.

54. JG (1967), Section 110.

55. JG (1967), Section 160; JG (1969), Sections 160, 171.

56. Fr (1969), p. 27.

57. FR (1969), p. 89; and see JG (1969), Sections 112-118.

58. OECDS (1968), p. 10, 16.

59. FR (1969), p. 129; FR (1969), p. 317; OECDS (1968), p. 15.

60. JG (1968), Section 186.

61. AR (1969), p. 70; JG (1969), Section 134.

62. AR (1969), p. 71.

63. JG (1967), Section 312.

64. JG (1969), Section 108-109.

65. Minister Schiller, AP (1969), #56, p. 2.

66. AP (1969), #3, p. 3.

67. AR (1969), p. 11; FR (Aug 1970), p. 13.

68. MR (Jun 1970), p. 9-10.

69. AP (1971), #39, p. 11.

70. AP (1970), #43, p. 5.

71. AP (1970), #43, p. 4; AP (1970), #32, p. 2.

72. JG (1970), Section 192.

73. AP (1970), #85, p. 3.

74. AP (1970, #43, p. 1; AP (1970), #77, p. 5.

75. AP (1970), #91, p. 2.

76. Blessing, Verteidigung, p. 7.

77. JG (1964), Section 258.

78. JG (1965), Section 248.

79. JG (1964), Section 258; JG (1965), Section 195.

80. JG (1968), Section 280.

81. AP (1969), #51, p. 3.

82. W. Schmidt, "German Bundesbank," Bank for International Settlements, Eight European Central Banks (London, 1963), p. 88.

83. R. G. Hawtrey, The Art of Central Banking (New York, 1933), p. 265.

84. Schmidt, p. 69n.

85. MR (Apr 1965), p. 30, 33; Schmidt, p. 77.

86. Schmidt, p. 80.

87. The Bank has no obligation to lend to government (Schmidt, p. 80). On the contrary, its total credit to government was limited by law to 8.5 billion DM (including until 1971 all special credits for foreign debt and international-agency participation), of which cash advances to the federal government could not exceed three billion DM, until November 1967, when all these limits were doubled.

88. MR (Dec 1965), p. 5.

89. Schmidt, p. 79.

90. Schmidt, p. 89.

91. C. Fousek, Foreign Central Banking (New York, 1957), p. 48. It is also possible that the extensive inter-firm clearing arrangements which exist in Germany may have some effect on the force and direction of reserve requirements' impact.

92. R. Sayers, Central Banking since Bagehot (Oxford, 1957), p. 89.

93. AR (1969), p. 9; AP (1969), #58, p. 1.

94. AP (1969), #92, p. 2.

95. Schmidt, p. 67; MR (Apr 1965), p. 30. For the long list of items which are officially rediscount-eligible, see AR (1967), p. 64.

96. L. A. Hahn, Fünfzig Jahre zwischen Inflation und Deflation (Tübingen, 1963), p. 120.

97. JG (1964), Section 170.

98. OECDS (1968), p. 8; MR (May 1966), p. 3; FR (1967), p. 18; Blessing, Kampf, p. 292; AR (1966), p. 3.

99. MR (May 1966), p. 4.

100. MR (May 1966), p. 4, 5.

101. MR (May 1967), p. 5; The Economist, Quarterly Economic Survey (Germany) (1965), III, p. 4.

102. QES (1966), III, p. 4.

103. MR (May 1967), p. 6, 7.

104. AR (1969), p. 24-25.

105. AP (1970), #85, p. 7.

106. AP (1971), #4, p. 3.

107. Schmidt, p. 75.

108. Fousek, P. 95.

109. E. Brehmer, Struktur und Funktionsweise des Geldmarkts der Bundesrepublik Deutschland seit 1948 (Kieler Studien) (Tübingen, 1964), p. 114, 116.

110. H. W. Jenkis, Die Importierte Inflation (Schriften zur Wirtschaftswissenschaftlichen Forschung #15) (Meisenheim, 1966), p. 78.

111. Schmidt, p. 73.

112. AR (1967), p. 91 ff.; Schmidt, p. 94. For a full explanation of the mechanics of mobilization paper, see FR (1968), p. 370.

113. MR (Aug 1967), p. 5.

114. AP (1970), #85, p. 1; MR (Sep 1966), p. 12. In 1971, the Bundesbank made an effort to intensify its dealings with non-banks in the hopes of finding a more permanent placement for its open-market offerings.

115. MR (Sep 1966), p. 12.

116. MR (Sep 1967), p. 16.

117. AP (1968), #51, p. 2.

118. AP (1971), #5, p. 1.

119. Schmidt, p. 88.

120. MR (Jul 1967), p. 6.

121. L. A. Hahn, Ein Tarktat über Währungsreform (Tübingen, 1964), p. 187; AR (1970), p. 16.

122. Hahn, Jahre, p. 120.

123. Hahn, Traktat, p. 97-98; QES (1963), January·.

124. Blessing, Verteidigung, p. 123, 275.

125. Arbeitsgemeinschaft Deutscher Wirtschaftswissenschaftlicher Forschungsinstitute, Die Internationalen Währungsprobleme in der Weltwirtschaft der Gegenwart (Supplement to Zeitschrift für Angewandte Konjunkturforschung #14) (Berlin, 1967), p. 39.

126. JG (1965), Section 197; Blessing, Kampf, p. 317; O. Emminger, Währungspolitik im Wandel der Zeit (Frankfurt, 1966), p. 91; AR (1965), p. 23.

127. AR (1965), p. 2.

128. JG (1964), Sections 29-31.

129. JG (1966), Section 17.

130. OECDS (1965), p. 19.

131. JG (1969), Section 233.

132. JG (1966), Sections 7, 157, 158.

133. AR (1966), p. 5; JG (1967), Section 6.

134. JG (1967), Section 8.

135. JG (1967), Section 58.

136. JG (1968), Section 140.

137. JG (1968), Section 80; JG (1969), Section 233.

138. BR, AP (1970), #91, p. 7.

139. Hahn, Jahre, p. 113.

140. JG (1966), Section 285.

141. Emminger, Politik, p. 102; JG (1965), Section 196.

142. JG (1966), Section 213; JG (1965), Section 182; JG (1966), Section 285.

143. Blessing, Kampf, p. 275.

144. AR (1969), p. 11; JG (1966), Section 234; SG (1967), Section 8; JG (1968), Section 144.

145. JG (1966), Section 92; JG (1964), Section 255. The various "inside" and "outside" lags in the effectiveness of monetary policy recognized in the literature (H. G. Johnson, Alternative Guiding Principles for the Use of Monetary Policy [Essays in International Finance #44] [Princeton, 1963], p. 7) need not be discussed here. See H. Müller, "Die Bedeutung der Time Lags für die Wirksamkeit der Geld- und Kreditpolitik in der Bundesrepublik Deutschland," Weltwirtschaftliches Archiv (1968), p. 28; JG (1969), Sections 236-239.

146. JG (1965), Section 192; Hahn, Traktat, p. 99; JG (1968), Section 12.

147. JG (1967), Section 224.

148. JG (1966), Sections 204-205.

149. Blessing, Kampf, p. 275; AR (1966), p. 4.

150. JG (1968), Section 199.

151. P. Boarman, Germany's Economic Dilemma (New Haven, 1964), throughout; Blessing, Verteidigung, p. 108; Blessing, Kampf, p. 12, 28, 43, 156; L. Erhard, Wirken und Reden, 1952-1965 (Ludwigsburg, 1966), p. 255; O. Emminger, Währungspolitische Betrachtungen (Frankfurt, 1956), p. 16 and AP (1970), #8, p. 6; Gutman, p. 283; JG (1964), Section 48; Erhard, Economics, p. 348; Veit, Grundriss, p. 540; FR (1969), p. 89; AR (1960), p. 49; AR (1970), p. 21.

152. No review of the German balance-of-payments debate would be truly complete without some reference to the irresistible classicism with which German publicists have clothed the "dilemma"

as well as related policy problems. For example, the Federal Republic is pictured by Hahn (Traktat, p. 207) and Boarman (p. 282) as being in the position of Midas: every policy move turns to gold. Again, the Bundesbank's liquidity-absorption measures are compared by the same writers (Hahn, Traktat, p. 94) to the endless labors of the Danaids. Bundesbank President Blessing (Kampf, p. 26) has referred to the Bank's uncomfortable tergiversations as a "Janus policy." The Bank itself referred to non-adjustment financial-policy measures as "a labor of Sisyphus" (AR [1960], p. 5). The Council of Experts foresaw "Pyrrhic victories" for anticyclical policy without external safeguards (JG [1964], Section 257). Popular Bank Association President Baumann (AP [1969], #83, p. 5) described election promises as "Greek gifts," and Minister Schiller referred to the end-stage of European monetary integration as "Europe's Elysium" (AP [1970], #86, p. 4).

153. R. A. Mundell, "The Appropriate Use of Monetary and Fiscal Policy for Internal and External Stability," International Monetary Fund Staff Papers (March 1962); T. W. Swan, "Longer-Run Problems of the Balance of Payments," R. E. Caves and H. G. Johnson, eds., Readings in International Economics (Homewood, 1968); W. M. Corden, "The Geometric Representation of Policies to Attain Internal and External Balance," Review of Economic Studies, October 1960.

154. J. Tinbergen, Economic Policy: Principles and Design (Amsterdam, 1956), p. 53-55.

1   155. J. M. Fleming, "Targets and Instruments," International Monetary Fund Staff Papers (November 1968), p. 389.

156. G. N. Halm, International Financial Intermediation: Deficits Benign and Malignant (Essays in International Finance #68) (Princeton, 1968), p. 7, 9, 16-17.

157. Halm, Intermediation, p. 7, 16; J. M. Keynes, A Treatise on Money (New York, 1930), II, p. 319; United States Council of Economic Advisors, Economic Report of the President (Washington, 1962), p. 162 ff.

158. Hahn, Traktat, p. 48.

159. AR (1965), p. 2, 21 ff.

160. FR (1969), p. 89.

161. OECDS (1968), p. 5; OECDS (1969), p. 30; Emminger, Politik, p. 92; JG (1969), Sections 240-242.

162. MR (Jan 1967), p. 5, 7; MR (May 1967), p. 7; AR (1967), p. 30; AR (1969), p. 3, 22; AP (1970), #28, p. 6.

163. JG (1965), Section 129; JG (1965), Government Response, Section 6.

164. JG (1967), Section 310.

165. JG (1964), Sections 214, 258; JG (1965), Section 195.

166. FR (1968), p. 232; JG (1965), Section 248.

167. SG (1970), I.

168. Bundesbank Vice President Emminger, AP (1969), #15, p. 7; Minister Strauss, AP (1969), #65, p. 3.

169. AP (1970), #37, p. 6.

170. AP (1970), #86, p. 7-9; Minister Schiller, AP (1970), #85, p. 8.

171. JG (1969), Sections 243-244, 280.

CHAPTER

6

THE
POLICY RESPONSE:
GERMANY'S
PAYMENTS–BALANCE
STRATEGY

INDICATORS OF RECENT GERMAN
PAYMENTS-BALANCE POLICY

Germany's balance-of-payments situation, prescinding as far as possible from any given policy response, was presented in Chapter 1; Germany's leading national goals and interests were evidenced and linked to the balance of payments in Chapter 2; the various payments-balance tactics open to Germany were discussed in Chapters 3, 4 and 5, in terms of availability of tools and effect on goals. In the present chapter the conclusions of the previous chapters are utilized in an overall analysis of Germany's balance-of-payments policy in the sixties. On this analysis are based the predictions and prescriptions for the future in Chapter 7.

The present analysis has three major parts: a statistical description of German policy, its tools and its results; a discussion of the essence of the German policy in terms of its dynamics; and a review of the impact of these results on national goals and interests.

A statistical description of Germany's recent balance-of-payments policy requires first a defense of the indicators chosen, in the light of theory and of actual German experience; and then a brief commentary on the behavior of the indicators used, pointing out the policy tools employed and the results obtained.

Balance-of-Payments Indicators

In Chapter 1, the key variable representing the state of the balance of payments was identified as the surplus or deficit on those

235

international-payments accounts which cannot be directly manipulated
by the authorities, and which, in the absence of policy counteraction,
would confront them with an inflow or outflow of international reserves.
This policy-challenge variable, which has here been called surplus
or deficit on the "basic" or "autonomous" balance of payments, was
distinguished from the "overall" balance of payments, which is equivalent to the international reserve movements actually realized.

The basic balance of payments thus comprises the international
accounts upon which the monetary authorities can exercise an influence, if at all, only rather indirectly through the impact of their policy
tools on the money stock, and thence on incomes, prices and interest
rates. In principle these accounts include the merchandise and services balance, private transfers, and private long- and short-term
capital movements (Tables A).*

In fact the accounts cited all have "structural" elements (i.e.,
those very unresponsive to incomes, prices and interest rates) and
speculative elements (i.e., those responsive to political or economic
fears or hopes, rather than to present fundamental incomes, prices
and interest rates).** Since it is impossible to sort out these three
analytical components of the statistics satisfactorily, it is proposed
here to place them all together in the basic balance, showing, however,
a special subitem for the quite "inelastic" expenditures of foreign troops
(Tables A2). This arrangement is consistent with the conceptualization of the basic balance of payments as those accounts at any given
time constituting a datum for policy reactions.

*The residual item of the balance-of-payments document is
here included as a form of private short-term capital movement
(Tables A7), since it consists largely of such interest- and specu-
lation-sensitive items as leads and lags in trade payments, changes
in credit terms, and switches in the national origin of trade finance
(Federal Republic of Germany, Sachverstandigenrat zur Begutachtung
der Gesamtwirtschaftlichen Entwicklung, Jahresgutachten 1965 ,
Section 123; Federal Republic of Germany, Bundesbank, Supplements
to Monthly Report, Series 3: Balance-of-Payments Statistics Feb 1971 ,
Table 1 n. 5).

**The period under review was not lacking in exogenous events
which temporarily affected the whole basic balance, e.g., the Berlin,
Middle-Eastern, French and Czech crises, the two devaluations of
sterling, the devaluation of the franc, and the various speculative monetary crises.

basic balance of payments as those accounts at any given time constituting a datum for policy reactions.

The overall balance of payments (Tables C) was, however, often
almost equally significant for German policy during the period under
review. In other words, not only was the prospective degree of adjustment of autonomous accounts in succeeding periods considered
important, but also the degree of immediate overall balance in the
current period. This was so because Germany was under considerable
external political pressure throughout the sixties to eliminate "its"
balance-of-payments problem, which embarrassed Germany's trade
partners by reducing their international reserves.

The basic attitude of many Germans indeed was that the problems
of the deficit countries should serve as a signal for these countries
themselves to adjust;* yet, since the deficit countries' problems
were often presented as problems of the smooth working of the entire
international monetary system, which was endangered by "maldis-
tribution"and "poor composition"of international reserves, the
Germans--with their particular political position in Europe, NATO,
the Common Market and the OECD during this period, and with
their dependence on the openness of foreign economies--seemed to
be particularly sensitive to the urgings of foreign and international
entities. Thus, while the basic balance of payments itself ranks in
this study as the key balance-of-payments indicator, the overall
balance was also a primary policy target of the German authorities.

Policy-Response Indicators

Monetary Variables as the Appropriate Indicators of Policy

Chapter 1 recalls that the impact of liquidity variables on the
basic balance of payments is indirect and diluted by conflicting policy
goals, while the impact of the basic balance of payments on the
potential monetary base is immediate, automatic, and clear. So

----

*During the sixties the international payments situations of the
United States and Britain caused increasing concern. The substantial nature and causes of these difficulties have been widely canvassed,
without full agreement. From a German standpoint, however, the
view that these countries "lived beyond their means"and disregarded
"balance-of-payments discipline"is highly plausible, and it was
widely held.

intimate, immediate and obvious is the correspondence of potential
new monetary reserves to the basic balance of payments,* that the
authorities must be taken to have a contemporaneous policy with
regard to the current payments balance, viz., to what extent they will
permit or offset its direct impact on the monetary variables. A
lengthy lag in recognition by the monetary authorities, either of the
existence or of the expectable impact of an overall or basic imbalance,
can certainly be excluded from consideration. Thus the statistical
period selected for the present evaluation of German policy is the
quarter.

Movements in the monetary variables must therefore be considered either effects of or policy reactions to the roughly contemporaneous balance-of-payments variables, and not the reverse.

A policy is an intention with respect to possible intervention in
the expectable workings of market mechanisms. The official payments-balance policy is thus a decision with regard to engineering
changes in the basic payments balance which is presented to the

---

*In using the German figures to show this correspondence, an
adjustment must be made in the net movement of international reserves reported in the Bundesbank's balance-of-payments statistics.
In these tables the foreign-denominated items are valued in DM by
the parity rate, as prescribed by the International Monetary Fund.
In the Bundesbank's balance sheet, however, as prescribed by German
corporate law, these same items are valued in DM according to those
exchange rates occurring on the days of the respective transactions
which produce the lowest net asset values (SS3, [Feb 1971], Table 18a,
note*). Inter-quarter differences in this adjustment item were
labelled "transvaluation" in the tables of the present study (Tables D).
The DM difference between the overall balance of payments (Tables
C) and the sum of actual new reserve money (Tables G) and domestic
monetary operations of the monetary authorities (Tables E and F)
is in principle fully accounted for by this valuation discrepancy.
Although no detailed accounting of this "transvaluation" is available,
it can be exactly calculated for the gold and international securities
holdings of the Bundesbank. This ascertainable item generally
accounts for one quarter to three quarters of the total of item D of
the tables, depending on day-to-day exchange-rate experience. The
remainder of item D is accounted for by further, unidentifiable
"transvaluation" on various classes of foreign-exchange assets of the
monetary authorities, and by the effects of rounding. Item D is
rarely of any significance in judging balance-of-payments policy or
its instruments.

authorities as a datum by the market. The fundamental decision of balance-of-payments policy is therefore whether to raise, to lower or to leave untouched the existing (algebraic) basic imbalance. Since, as the discussions in previous chapters indicate, an imbalance in either direction has many theoretical and practical difficulties in the long run, it is common to call policies which tend to lower the imbalance "adjusting" and those which tend to raise it, "disadjusting."

It follows that current payments-balance policy will be indicated by movements in monetary variables as these affect the payments balance itself. Now, as outlined in Chapter 1, a basic balance-of-payments surplus will, abstracting from all policy responses, produce an automatic rise in the monetary variables, under a fixed-exchange-rate system. And, all other independent factors remaining constant, such a rise in the monetary variables eventually tends to produce a deficit in the basic balance of payments.

Therefore, a stance passive to the balance of payments on the part of the monetary authorities, permitting its full impact on the monetary variables, would favor payments-balance adjustment. Tactics aimed at offsetting or eliminating the domestic liquidity impact of the basic balance would be non-adjusting. Tactics which reinforce the impact of the basic payments balance on the monetary variables might be called forcing the pace of adjustment. Tactics which aimed at offsetting more than the total monetary impact of the basic balance could be called disadjusting. In terms of the final impact permitted on the monetary variables, thus, the overall balance-of-payments policy choice lies along the spectrum from forcing adjustment to disadjustment.

Since the basic challenge to policy posed by the balance of payments is couched in financial terms, it may be expected that the monetary variables are the best indicators of the entire payments-balance policy. It is true that the financial element is but one component of the overall international economic compatibility called balance-of-payments equilibrium. However, Chapter 3 has shown that adjusting measures in the real and market-structural areas were not significant in the period under review. In fact, there are few system-conformed market-interventions that are truly "direct": normally, intervention is through financial policy. It is equally true that the liquidity effect is but one of the mechanical results of basic international disequilibrium. However, as noted in Chapters 4 and 5, nonadjustment policies have done and can do little to retard effects other than the liquidity effect. Liquidity tactics are thus theoretically and practically dominant in German payments-balance policy: their effects override those of measures in other areas, whether in the direction of adjustment or of nonadjustment.

The results of liquidity, or financial-policy, measures can nearly all be reduced to purely monetary terms. Although some fiscal-policy measures have effects on income distribution and so on the velocity of money, nothing deliberate of this sort has been attempted in Germany. Hence the statistical reflection of Germany's balance-of-payments policy will be in terms of a monetary variable.

Changes in Effective Monetary Base as the Most Appropriate Indicator of Policy

To isolate the most significant monetary indicator of payments-balance policy, it will be helpful to recall the concepts developed in Chapter 1, and the specifically German situation. In seeking the variables most expressive of policy, indicators of intended rather than of realized goals must be sought. Since, for example, goal variables, reflecting national macro-economic objectives, are significantly affected by factors other than financial, it would be misleading to take the state of a goal variable as an adequate expression of policy.[1]

Similarly, since the financial authorities' intermediate targets-- deposit-bank liquidity, interest rates, the money stock--are affected by more than one monetary tool--rediscount rates, open market operations, reserve requirements--aswell as by other factors not immediately subject to control, no one tool's behavior can summarize the dominant policy. Again, since, even independently of shifts in general policy, individual tool settings can shift in response to changes in market factors, even the entire constellation of tool settings is an inadequate indicator of policy.

It is normal, therefore, to regard the target variables--deposit-bank liquidity, interest rates, and the money stock--as the key elements expressing the overall tenor of monetary policy. Whether bank reserves, money stock or interest rates are the most representative among these (and indeed the very terms in which their definitions are framed) depends largely on the specific institutions involved. Further refinement of the German policy indicators, therefore, requires briefly reviewing German conditions.

Interest Rates as Policy Indicators. Interest rates, like other prices, are in principle inadequate indicators of policy intentions in an open economy such as Germany's. Since financial capital is relatively free to move into or out of Germany in response to monetary ease or restraint, interest rates are subject to strong influences from abroad.

Additionally, the movements of the respective interest rates in Germany's money and capital markets are apt to be discoordinated.

The German capital market is thin, and deposit banks are its most significant single source of supply. Securities are, however handled by the banks speculatively or as volatile liquidity pools. Hence in periods of crisis or of policy turnround, no one set of interest rates can be considered properly representative.

Again, the government's interest-subsidization programs, and the changes in these programs, further invalidate interest rates as policy indicators. In the mid-and late sixties, too, capital-market interest rates depended very largely on special arrangements among borrowers to "nurse" the capital market. The banking system's own cartel-like arrangements further distort interest-rate patterns.[2]

Finally, many interest rates were tied to the rediscount rate through most of the period under review.[3] In periods of restriction, in which free rates rose while the rediscount-centered group remained tied to rates abroad, widespread evasion of the interest-rate controls was stimulated. The acute distortions and evasions of the 1966 restriction led to the abandonment of the tying rules in 1967. Interest-rate experience before and after this date is thus not comparable.[4]

For these reasons, interest rates have not in this study been used as primary indicators of overall policy intentions.

The Money Stock as a Policy Indicator. Institutional conditions also affected the meaningfulness of the money stock as an index to policy in Germany during the period under review.[5] Savings-deposit interest premiums were introduced in 1959 and by 1966 had risen to ten percent p.a. of the principal. Since there is little legal or operational difference between time and sight deposits in Germany, savings deposits doubled in the 1959-1966 period, while time deposits stagnated.[6] In 1969 a similar shift of time and sight elements in the broadly-defined money stock took place in response to the inflows of speculative international capital.[7]

Time deposits are in Germany felt to have significant liquidity, and probably influence expenditure plans more readily than is consistent with their total omission from money-stock figures. In spite of rather elaborate regulations intended to ensure bona fides, savings deposits of corporate bodies, too, are often operated much like demand deposits. For this reason, and also as a result of still-valid banking tradition and agreements against disintermediation, it is customary for firms to hold liquid funds in the form of cash rather than in money-market paper.[8] Bank's time deposits thus rise especially fast in times of economic slack.*

---

*Year-end crediting of whole-year interest earnings also

Loans extended by banks do not always represent real "money creation" by normal deposit-expansion mechanics, because the banks often merely transmit earmarked deposits from one firm to another.[9] German banks accordingly carry a unique category of liabilities: "medium- and long-term moneys taken from domestic non-banks."

The effect of time-deposit movements on money-stock statistics was increased in the latter part of the period studied by a progressive relaxation of deposit-interest ceilings between 1965 and 1967. The marked interest differentials which developed between time and sight deposits (probably six and a half percent in 1967)[10] caused a large shift of funds from the latter to the former. Later, short-term interest rates in some cases rose above those of longer-term deposits, further blurring the distinction between money and near-money assets.[11]

The progressive release, throughout the period, of legally blocked savings deposits stemming from the currency reform and from the "equalization of burdens" program also somewhat distorted the policy indications given by fluctuations of deposit moneys.

Observers such as the Council of Experts and the Bundesbank agree that shifts in the money and near-money components of liquidity in Germany have weakened the very concept of a "money stock."[*12] For on all these grounds, it appears that the three classes of deposits can neither be used in isolation one from another nor consistently combined to form a convenient index of monetary policy intentions.

Overall Bank Liquidity as a Policy Indicator. For these reasons, it would seem that net changes in the free liquidity of the banking system are a more significant monetary policy indicator for Germany. Free liquidity in principle includes both cash and claims immediately

_____

affects these statistics, as do the pronounced seasonal movements of funds from commercial banks to savings banks during the first two quarters and the reverse movement in the last two (MR [Jan 1963], p. 5; MR [Mar 1967], p. 7).

*Postwar German central-bank statistics have redefined the money stock several times. From 1948 to 1951 currency and savings, sight and time deposits entered into the money stock; after 1951, only currency and sight deposits were counted; after mid-1955, the "money stock" was not explicit carried in the statistics; in the sixties, the Bundesbank used several money-stock definitions alternatively or even conjointly (G. Schmölders, Geldpolitik [Tübingen, 1962], p. 10ln).

realizable in cash at the central bank, less those legally required
against existing deposits and debt to the monetary authorities. This
conforms to the OECD definition of net bank reserves.[13] The realizable assets are open-market-eligible paper, foreign exchange (under
a fixed-rate system) and rediscount-eligible paper (up to the rationing
quota within which the Bundesbank will rediscount passively) (Tables K).

The Bundesbank does not formally include unused rediscount
quotas in bank liquidity; by compensation, the Bundesbank does not
deduct existing rediscounts from bank liquidity.

However, only relative risks and rates of return dictate the
application of new free liquidity other than as reserves required
against new deposits. Such non-reserve applications therefore represent an overhang of potential reserves which may be called into
existence by the monetary authorities' attempts to raise money-market
interest rates. The liquidity figure which includes all these potential
reserves is thus important in assessing the longer-run effects of a
given monetary policy.

Effective Monetary Base as a Policy Indicator. However, since the
monetary authorities can and do deliberately vary the conditions for
cashing many of the "overhang" liquid assets, a second, narrower
figure--that of "bank-reserve money" or "monetary base"[14]--will in
the present study provide the measure of the actually existing and
substantively pursued monetary strategy, while the broader "bank
liquidity" figure will remain as an indication of the implications of
current strategy for future policy freedom.[15]

Changes in effective monetary base are changes in cash and
central-bank deposits not currently legally required against deposits.
These changes can be measured by

$$(V) \quad \Delta B = \Delta R + \Delta C + D \, \Delta l.$$

Where ΔB = change in effective monetary
base (newly available
reserve money)

R = reserve deposits of commercial banks

C = currency in circulation outside Bundesbank

l = average legally required
ratio of bank reserves
to monetary deposits
= L/D

D = monetary deposits of banks at
the end of the period over
which changes are observed

This measure and its components are given in the tables of the present study, Section F. That component representing reserve money newly freed by changes in the legal reserve ratio L/D is normally estimated by the Bundesbank on the occasion of reserve-requirement changes, by multiplying the total deposits existing after the change by the estimated total average required-reserve ratio before the change less that after it.

The figure for newly available reserve money thus constituted corresponds, through marginal deposit-expansion and cash-drain ratios, to the expectable changes in the money stock, defined as currency in circulation and commercial-bank demand deposits. (See Chapter 1.)

$$\text{(VI)} \quad \Delta B \left(\frac{1 + \Delta C / \Delta D}{\Delta C / \Delta D + \Delta E / \Delta D} \right) = \Delta M$$

$$\text{Where } M = C + D$$
$$D = \text{current monetary deposits in banks}$$
$$E = R - L$$
$$L = \text{legally required reserves of banks}$$
and other symbols as in Equation (V)

Since, moreover, the marginal cash drain from banks $\Delta C / \Delta D$ was sensibly stable over almost all of the period under review,* and since the ratio $\Delta E / \Delta D$ of banks' excess reserves to their deposits was throughout the period both stable and negligibly small,[16] effective changes in free reserve money were exactly proportional to expectable changes in the money stock, defined as above. These circumstances constitute further reasons for using the monetary-base figure as a policy indicator, and for leaving aside actual changes in the money stock, however measured.

Quarterly changes in effective monetary base (Tables G) will therefore in this study be taken as the most appropriate indicator of monetary policy with respect to the liquidity effects of the balance of payments, and hence of balance-of-payments policy in general. This figure has been called "decisive" by the Council of Experts.[17]

---

*In 1961, the introduction of a five-day banking week slightly raised cash drain (MR [Oct 1962], p. 4).

GERMANY'S PAYMENTS-BALANCE
POLICY IN FIGURES

In the light of the foregoing considerations, the statistically simplest test of Germany's ongoing payments-balance intentions is the quarterly difference between total potential additions to the monetary base due to the autonomous payments balance (Tables A) and the total actually realized effective additions to the monetary base (Tables G). Starting from Germany's situation of basic payments-balance surplus, if this difference is zero, the balance-of-payments policy may be pronounced adjusting. If the difference is less than zero, the policy was forced-pace adjustment. If the difference is more than zero, the policy was non-adjusting. The results of this calculation are presented in line H of the Tables. Excluding the second quarter of 1971 (for which complete data are not available), the period under review comprises forty quarters. In these forty quarters, Germany's basic balance of international payments showed a deficit only on three occasions, one of which was in fact a near-balance. Excluding these three instances, the concomitant change in monetary base was indicative of non-adjustment policy in twenty-seven of the remaining thirty-seven quarters. The pace of adjustment was forced in the other eleven quarters, seven of these being fourth quarters. Six of the relevant seven fourth-quarter surges in reserve money were clearly dominated by year-end central-bank aid to governments (Tables E12), and in all seven quarters the net increase in loans to government, as well as the overall adjusting movement, were fully compensated by the non-adjusting impact of corresponding contractions in the following first quarters.* The one fourth-quarter adjustment not entirely attributable to temporary year-end credit to governments occured during the 1961 adjustment boom.

---

*The German monetary authorities must reckon with sharp seasonal variations in the demand for credit (MR [Apr 1962], p. 16). The most pronounced seasonal shift in month-end figures (at each month-end the cash in circulation is several billion DM above that month's minimum--MR Feb 1963 , p. 24) occurs at year's end. A widespread tradition of window dressing of balance sheets, the long holidays and Christmas bonuses (under a largely cash-wage system), the surge of retail trade, year-end accountings, and a seasonal government demand for cash over the year's end, together raise the need for credit itself, the cash drain associated with granting it, and the desire for excess bank reserves for statement-day window dressing (MR [Dec 1962], p. 5). As a result, the monetary authorities must provide greater reserves in the fourth quarter or see a rise in interest rates and a repatriation of volatile foreign assets of banks,

TABLE 1

Selected German Payments-Balance-Related Data

(Nearest 100 Million DM)	61			62				63				64			
	II	III	IV	I	II	III	IV	I	II	III	IV	I	II	III	IV
A. Autonomous (Basic) Payments Balance	44	1	6	16	11	9	2	17	23	15	22	28	15	6	16
A1. Goods Receipts Net	17	17	13	6	9	10	10	8	12	12	28	24	20	7	10
A2. NATO Troop Receipts	10	9	10	10	10	10	12	11	11	10	11	10	10	10	12
A3. Services & Transfers Receipts Net	-9	-14	-13	-11	-14	-20	-18	-12	-16	-21	-9	-13	-12	-19	-16
A4. Aliens Remittances (shown as -)	-1	-2	-2	-1	-2	-2	-1	-2	-3	-3	-3	-3	-3	-3	-3
A5. Private Long-Term Capital Inflow Net	1	-1	-	4	-	2	3	7	9	9	5	5	-8	1	5
A6. Private Short-Term Capital Inflow Net	15	-2	1	-8	-2	8	2	1	5	1	4	-5	4	1	11
A7. Residual Receipts Net	11	-6	-6	13	5	-1	-6	3	3	-2	-14	10	4	8	-3
B. Total Payments-Balance Correction	59	8	-4	40	-	4	4	18	13	6	13	24	11	10	13
B1. Banks' Money Exports	16	-2	-18	22	-11	-6	-7	9	4	1	-11	11	-1	1	-3
B2. Official Transfers Outflow Net	9	9	10	10	10	7	11	10	9	8	7	7	10	7	6
B3. Off'l Long-Term Capital Outflow Net	35	3	4	3	3	3	3	2	3	2	5	3	2	3	5
B4. Off'l Short-Term Capital Outflow Net	-1	-1	-	1	-2	-	-2	-3	-3	-5	12	3	-	-1	5
C. Central Reserves Increase	-14	-7	9	-24	9	5	-1	-1	11	8	10	4	3	-4	3
D. Other Items	-	1	-1	2	-2	-	-	-	-	-1	-	2	-	-1	1
E. DM Effect of Bundesbank Non-Policy Ops	11	10	13	-17	2	-5	26	-27	-4	11	33	-34	8	-10	33
F. Monetary Base From Bundesbank Policy Ops	19	10	11	23	-1	4	7	3	11	-15	-12	9	-13	19	4
F1. Base Freed by Required-Reserve Change	16	7	6	10	-	-	-	-	-	-	-	-	-10	-13	-
F2. Bundesbank Credit to Commercial Banks	-4	10	-5	3	-1	1	5	9	6	-14	-2	11	-4	15	-8
F3. Bundesbank Net Open-Market Purchases	7	-7	10	10	-1	3	2	-6	5	-1	-10	-2	1	17	4
F4. Decrease in Anticyclical Deposits	-	-	-	-	-	-	-	-	-	-	-	-	-	-	-
G. Total New Effective Monetary Base	16	14	32	-16	8	4	32	-25	18	3	31	-19	-2	4	34
H. A Less G	28	-13	-26	32	3	5	-30	42	5	12	-9	47	17	2	-18

Table 1 is a synopsis of Table 2.

See sources and notes presented with Table 2, on pp. 304-313.

65-I	65-II	65-III	65-IV	66-I	66-II	66-III	66-IV	67-I	67-II	67-III	67-IV	68-I	68-II	68-III	68-IV	69-I	69-II	69-III	69-IV	70-I	70-II	70-III	70-IV	71-I	
11	4	-1	12	3	17	22	28	37	22	18	19	41	12	31	96	-45	116	71	-149	25	64	110	90	114	A
11	-	-5	6	8	14	23	35	43	44	38	43	43	34	42	64	28	39	40	49	29	33	43	51	37	A1
9	10	11	12	11	12	14	13	12	13	13	14	13	13	13	13	12	14	15	14	13	15	15	15	15	A2
-12	-21	-24	-16	-20	-20	-24	-16	-14	-15	-24	-10	-10	-15	-22	-10	-16	-15	-25	-17	-22	-21	-33	-25	-23	A3
-3	-4	-4	-5	-4	-5	-5	-5	-5	-5	-6	-6	-5	-5	-6	-6	-6	-7	-9	-8	-10	-10	-13	-13	-14	A4
5	6	5	6	6	5	6	2	-2	-5	-4	-5	-16	-25	-37	-23	-56	-41	-28	-85	-37	-2	10	9	4	A5
-12	-1	9	13	-8	6	8	6	-7	-4	-2	-10	-	-	28	64	-26	53	50	-5	26	18	53	43	12	A6
13	14	6	-7	8	5	1	-7	10	-6	4	-8	16	10	14	-6	19	73	28	-96	23	32	36	9	83	A7
15	17	-1	8	15	11	13	13	33	29	12	13	25	-2	21	65	26	40	-3	32	11	10	25	15	46	B
7	-1	-5	2	1	2	5	-9	20	13	7	-	16	-12	14	47	16	31	-19	5	2	-13	13	-4	26	B1
8	12	7	7	9	8	5	7	9	9	6	9	10	9	7	15	7	9	10	16	8	8	8	12	10	B2
2	3	3	4	3	18	3	12	2	3	4	5	2	3	4	6	2	1	7	9	2	10	6	6	4	B3
-2	3	-6	-5	2	-17	-	3	2	4	-5	-1	-3	-2	-4	-3	1	-1	-1	1	-1	5	-2	2	6	B4
-4	-12	-	3	-12	7	7	13	4	-9	5	3	16	14	10	31	-71	76	74	-181	14	54	84	76	79	C
-1	1	-	-1	2	-	1	2	-2	1	2	1	1	1	-	-	-3	-	-	-40	-4	-	1	1	-	D
-20	12	-13	24	-33	9	3	18	-26	3	-15	46	-54	-3	-15	33	-32	-	-23	99	-51	11	-22	40	-73	E
9	17	15	15	7	-3	-4	5	-5	32	-16	4	-2	10	-5	-10	63	-41	-34	121	27	-31	-28	-89	-26	F
-	-	-	15	-16	-	-	12	17	9	5	-	-	-	-	-4	-	-12	-9	16	-10	-	-19	-2	-	F1
13	9	13	-9	26	-2	-10	-6	-13	21	-18	-4	-3	4	4	-2	59	-25	-17	99	44	-18	12	-27	-3	F2
-4	8	2	9	-3	-1	6	-1	-9	2	-3	8	1	5	-9	-4	5	-4	-8	9	8	-2	-15	-47	-7	F3
-	-	-	-	-	-	-	-	-	-	-	-	-	-	-	-	-	-	-	-4	-14	-11	-7	-15	-16	F4
-17	18	2	41	-36	13	7	37	-29	27	-24	54	-39	23	-10	54	-45	35	18	1	-17	32	38	32	-20	G
28	-14	-3	-29	39	4	15	-9	66	-5	43	-36	81	-11	41	-42	*	81	53	-150	42	32	72	58	134	H

One of the four non-fourth-quarter adjustments also occurred during the adjustment action of 1961. A second of these non-fourth-quarter instances occurred during and because of (Tables F2) the reflation efforts of early 1967, and was very fully compensated in the succeeding quarters. The third adjusting quarter, 1965 II, represents no notable discontinuities in the tool variables themselves, but rather is explained by the (unique) disappearance of the goods surplus (Tables A) coupled with continuing moderate government credit needs.[18] The final adjusting quarter, 1968 II, is probably best explained by the sudden speculative reversal of short-term capital flows.

To the extent, therefore, that the foregoing analysis has justified the indicators used here, it may be concluded that the overall German policy intention in regard to the balance of payments in the period under review was consistently one of non-adjustment.

THE DYNAMIC-UNDERVALUATION STRATEGY

Summary of Experience

In the earliest years of the period, when basic surpluses tended to be relatively small following the 1961 upvaluation (Tables A), and when fiscal difficulties were as yet slight, correction of the payments balance at the international-exchange level was the favored tactic (Tables B and F).

Fiscal policy was passive in these years, and central-bank tools were manipulated so as to provide regular annual-rate increases in reserve money, with needed seasonal variations. As a result, free reserves of banks increased at a remarkably steady pace in the five years from April 1962 to April 1967 (Tables L).

As basic surpluses mounted in the more recent period, correction through capital export could not have been increased without severe strain on government's taxation and credit potential (i.e., without strain on Germany's savings rate or growth). In the slump from mid-1966 to mid-1968, deficit finance for recovery interfered both with government capital export and with liquidity absorption through monetary policy. Repayments of rediscounts, however, played a substantial role briefly as market interest rates fell below the rediscount rate. A major burden of combating the liquidity effect continued to be borne by money exports.

---

entailing a balance-of-payments surplus. In the ensuing first quarter, the extra reserves provided must be recovered by the authorities, unless more monetary ease is desired.

As the overhang of commercial-bank liquidity represented by open-market paper, foreign liquid assets and unused rediscount lines began to accumulate rapidly (Tables K), the leeway for combating the liquidity effect was narrowed. In 1968 the growing possibility of a German upvaluation, due to Germany's disaligned price level (itself created by the period of non-adjustment) and its liquidity overhang, added speculative inflows to the basic surplus, especially after the French and Czech crises.

The 1961 policy situation recurred: Germany was faced with the necessity of some form of adjustment, as the whole apparatus of non-adjustment through counteracting the liquidity effect was overborne in the crisis of November 1968. Neither full and real adjustment through flexible exchange rates nor controls on the flow of goods would have squared with German interests. Upvaluation was the only alternative. Yet only the partial and temporary surrogate of border-tax manipulation was carried out, under acute pressure from abroad. With this substitute for upvaluation, and the forward-rate "upvaluation" effected by the Bundesbank after the May 1969 crisis, Germany's basic problem was palliated until the elections of September 1969. At the same time fear of further surpluses forced Germany into a position of more monetary ease than its deficitary trade partners, stimulating a massive export of long-term capital and contributing to the disguising of the problem. Thereafter, an upvaluation was effected by floating and then restabilizing the DM.

Despite the nominal anti-inflationary "reserve" incorporated in the new exchange rate by pegging it above the current market quotation, numerous dynamic "cushions" on the real impact of revaluation allowed time for ongoing international disparities in inflation rates to dissipate the "reserve." As a result, the German trade balance was soon once again heavily in surplus. Much the same process, foreshortened in time and yet more exposed to international "hot money," took place between January 1970 and May 1971, eventuating in the openly guided floating of the DM (discussed in Chapter 7).

Analysis

The static non-adjustment tactics pursued by Germany in the sixties did not provide a true solution for its payments-balance disequilibrium. Offsetting the liquidity effect of the payments surplus at the international-reserves level produces either a boomerang effect or a liquidity overhang. Offsetting the liquidity effect at the monetary level entails an inescapable dilemma and eventual self-defeat. These measures can at best temporarily retard the liquidity effect, at the cost of further distributional biases from the income effect, and without eliminating either the income effect or the direct price-transmission effect.

Eventually, the progressive shifts of foreign relative to domestic price level must be faced. Such shifts redouble the trade-balance surplus and are the cause of speculative pressure on the balance of payments. The offsetting tactics cannot absorb the intensified liquidity effect, since capital-export and fiscal tactics have a limit in the tolerable savings rate, while monetary tactics and international window-dressing face a limit in the liquidity overhang. Both tactics will have been brought close to their respective limits by the preceding period of offsetting. Growing realization of these relationships stimulates yet more speculation in the exchange market. When exchange-rate expectations come to affect the great transactions balances financing world trade, not even international "recycling" operations can long defend the official exchange rate.

Speculative capital inflows can be reversed by ending the differential between actual and expected exchange rates; the trade-balance surplus can be ended by raising domestic relative to foreign effective price levels. When liquidity-offsetting tactics fail, therefore, either the exchange rate must be altered, reducing both speculative and trade-balance inflows, or border taxes and "bounties" must be altered, reducing the trade-balance surplus only. Fully flexible exchange rates present the means for the smoothest and closest adjustment of international price levels. Any measure, even when nominally adjustment-oriented, which deliberately falls short of this "yardstick" policy may from the more dynamic viewpoint be called non-adjusting, the more so if its manifest object is merely to reduce financial and political pressures toward full adjustment which can no longer otherwise be warded off.

In this light, the German revaluations and border-tax alterations can be described as periodic partial price-level realignments, recouping in each instance part, but not all, of the dynamically effective international price differential accumulated during the preceding period in which the balance-of-payments liquidity effect, but not the price-transmission effect, was offset. Thus the advantages of currency undervaluation were prolonged and protected from the threatened collapse of the very liberal-trade, fixed-rate system which makes undervaluation possible and advantageous. This policy, in which nominal adjustment steps are taken in order to combat the long-term adjustment-forcing effects of previous non-adjustment measures, may justly be called "dynamic undervaluation."

Even a full price realignment by such adjustment steps, if only periodic and not continuous, could serve the same non-adjustment purposes in Germany's case, where deeply structural psychological and political elements can be expected to foster a renewed price-level differential and where export-oriented industries are entrenched in a long-run perspective.[19]

can--or rather does--serve non-adjustment ends in Germany. And this was the actual sequence of events objectively necessitated by the government and Bundesbank policies.[20]

Thus, all indications are that, both in combating the liquidity effect and in periodically recouping the price-level effects of the balance of payments, German intentions were, at least until very recently, to perpetuate undervaluation. That is, upvaluation, border-tax manipulations and guided flexibility, while all nominally adjusting in nature, have in fact been seen as means to the same end as have capital exports and financial-policy restraint.[21] The indefinite floating of the DM in 1971 can more obviously subserve this strategy, since the float is subject to unilateral "guidance" by the Bundesbank.

The last element to be examined in this overall strategy is its officially presented rationale. If this rationale was the true intention of the dynamic undervaluation, stability export was Germany's ultimate strategic balance-of-payments goal; if this rationale was in fact merely a specious cloak, dynamic undervaluation was intended for its own sake, i.e., for the sake of its effects, reviewed below, on German national objectives.

STRATEGY, IDEOLOGY AND GOALS

Stability Export as Rationale
for Undervaluation

Ideology

Continued undervaluation entails imported inflation (Chapter 1). German policy was not able to escape this consequence (Chapters 3, 4 and 5). Yet in inflation-conscious Germany (Chapter 2), all public statements must deplore inflation, all public deliberations must seek to avoid it. In today's world, too, a permanently undervalued country must make periodic adjustment gestures. This is particularly desirable for Germany as a means of reducing political pressures from needed allies. Nor can undervaluation be allowed so to unbalance world payments as to endanger either free trade or the very monetary arrangements which in the first instance permit undervaluation.

The German policy of permanent undervaluation has very often been presented as one of "exporting stability" to payments partners, i.e., of forcing them to accept "balance-of-payments discipline": the adoption of less expansionary macrofinancial policies to avoid balance-of-payments deficits.[22] In all international bodies Germany

has repeatedly invoked these classic "rules of the game"as applied
to deficit countries.[23] In this way, Germany's policy has been represented both as fostering international adjustment by maintaining
pressure on others to accept the "burden"of adjustment, and as being
ultimately anti-inflationary at home by eliminating the foreign sources
of imported inflation. At the same time, this position afforded a
rationale for continued measures to combat the balance-of-payments
liquidity effect, even though some of these should permit and aggravate
the income-distribution effects of the payments balance. Finally, it
offered an excuse for creeping inflation and its effects, as being the
imported results of foreign errors. Hahn speaks in similar connections
of "an unholy alliance of market power and false theory."[24]

Logically considered, however, this was a far from merely
specious position. Balance-of-payments adjustment, as this entire
study has emphasized, is a matter of the relationships of many elements
in all countries. Purely logically, any element in any country could
be so shifted as to tend to restore adjustment. In this sense, the
relative contribution to adjustment made by manipulations in each
country is logically indifferent. Relative contributions are in fact a
matter of politics (i.e., who is strong enough to escape the adjustment
"burden") or of social philosophy (i.e., whose inflation rate shall be
assimilated to whose).

Furthermore, Germany had, in the principles of the social
market economy, a perfectly rational philosophy to justify its insistence on international "harmony"of policy at a low rate of inflation.[25] Nothing of equal cogency--and certainly nothing with equally
broad support--has yet been advanced to justify permanent creeping
inflation. Still further, even setting aside the "social philosophy"
aspects of relative inflation rates, Germany could claim that its
relative smallness, openness and isolation in an inflationary world
entitled it to make some special effort to retard the world inflation,
and to force its trade partners to come at least some way toward the
German outlook and to bear some part of the adjustment burden.[26]

Abstractly, all this is much more satisfying than its opposite.
The actual distribution of adjustment burdens is, however, largely a
matter of political and economic strength. Granted then that the
stability-export idea is both useful to German interests and logically
defensible, what are its real chances of success?

Reality

Germany's Financial Bargaining Position. Germany's bargaining
position from which to press its ideas of stability did not improve
over the period under review. An International Monetary Fund study

once called Germany the only country besides the United States which can detectably influence its trade partners' payments balances.[27] But Germany's power to do so has been roundly (and rightly) denied by German experts.[28] Beyond the payments balances of individual trade partners, German policy is also relevant to the recent concern over the distribution, "composition" and adequacy of world reserves. For some time, it appeared that an implicit threat to the world monetary system could be used as a club over Germany's trade partners.[29] In the most recent years, however, this has manifestly become a less reliable bargaining point.[30] The speedy issuance of Special Drawing Rights and their fast growth as a percentage of world official exchange reserves have much diminished the urgency of the reserves-adequacy and reserves-composition problems. Indeed, the implicit threat to world finance and trade has been wielded with increasing clarity, not by the "creditor" Germany but by the "debtor," the United States.

At least since the contretemps at Bonn in November 1968, moreover, France has been essentially estranged from the German concept of a Common-Market "island of stability."[31] The hope of forming such an international stability bloc, with greater stability-export potential, had been held out particularly by Minister Schiller, but was never considered very promising by the Council of Experts.[32] The "stability-bloc" elements in the latest efforts toward European monetary integration will be discussed in the following chapter.

Germany's Geopolitical Bargaining Position. For some time also, Germany could count on the stake that Germany's chief trade partners have in the economic and political stability of central Europe to deter any moves by them which might embarrass the Bonn regime. After 1968, however,--at least as far as international financial arrangements are concerned--Britain and France seemed to have become far more disposed to see Germany as rival than as ally, and to emphasize the strengths rather than the weaknesses of Bonn. Even in the United States, whose cold-war containment policy had reached an impasse, and whose relations with Russia have become somewhat ambiguous, the economic welfare of Germany is receiving a much lower policy priority. During and after the crisis of May 1971, the United States began an aggressive campaign to transfer to its allies, not merely the burden of international adjustment, but also many of the other economic burdens it had unilaterally accepted in the postwar era.

German Assessments of Stability Export. Germany's chances of success in exporting stability have been held minimal by many experienced observers: the 1968 Economics and Finance Ministers Conference at Rotterdam, the 1968 International Monetary Fund annual meeting, the Council of Experts, Hahn, Halm and Veit.[33] Among practitioners and theorists, few[34] other than those most closely

associated with the administration of policy continued to claim that
Germany could force policy changes abroad.[35] Even Vice President
Emminger of the Bundesbank has denied Germany's power to influence
the United States payments balance.[36]

One of the most striking indications of the bankruptcy of the
stability-export outlook came from Bundesbank President Blessing in
the last days of 1969. In his final official testimony before a Bundestag
committee, Blessing recalled that he had opposed upvaluation in the
past in order to promote Germany's export of stability. He then
declared that this possibility had been "a deceptive hope," since
social and structural difficulties prevented the United States and
Britain from responding to German pressures for stabilization.[37]
It is this sort of realization which has doubtless influenced the attitudes of the Brandt government.[38]

The Future of Stability Export

In spite of the foregoing, however, Germany achieved some
small measure of success in its stability-export drive. The United
States did initiate a "balance-of-payments program" consisting of
capital-account exchange control. (The resulting strength of the
Eurodollar market has, however, not been favorable to Germany's
own stability.) Yet the fact that this form of "adjustment" almost
carried over into the travel field makes it an ominous rather than an
auspicious beginning from the German standpoint. Further, President
Nixon's simultaneous efforts toward less inflation and more employment in the United States are not calculated to produce marked improvement in the United States balance of payments. Deep-rooted
social and economic structural problems probably forbid a radical
elimination of expansionary monetary measures in the United States
without danger to the economic-political system.[39] Several much
publicized United States studies of 1971 came to essentially similar
conclusions.[40]

German policy-makers are now equally aware of this situation,
and they also realize that the same United States social and psychological problems make any radical upheavals in the United States
highly dangerous for the world at large. It is now Germany's turn
to show solicitude for the social and political stability of North America.[41]

The British, French and other European responses to balance-
of-payments pressure are equally non-conformed to the liberal international system as it has hitherto been promoted.[42] A world of
growing international barriers is not the ideal outcome for German
stability-export tactics. World-wide realization of these impasses

has led to the call for institutionalized incomes policies in most industrial nations, and to the European drive for full monetary integration (discussed in Chapter 7).

In the light of its weakening bargaining position and the ambiguous outcome of its tactics, the German stability-export policy by 1969 appeared to be without substantial prospects of success in its general form. It is thus probably fair to characterize continued publicistic emphasis on the "world lack of liquidity" on the one hand and on "the national lack of monetary discipline" on the other, as "ideological weapons rationalizing political interests:" interests precisely in the distribution of the adjustment burden, and possibly also of domestic income.[43] Again, the recurrent and vocal worries on the part of all responsible German policy-makers over loss of export competitiveness, that have arisen whenever the German trade-balance surplus has shrunk, very emphatically belie the sincerity of the stability-export thesis. There is no point in "importing stability" from Germany, if Germany will react to this by "manufacturing" still more stability for export. This way lies the economic madness of competitive deflation, to which the Weimar experience should be more than sufficient deterrent.

In point of fact, if, as has been contended here, Germany's real problem is that its export-oriented industries cannot, politically or economically, be forced to adjust, then the "export of stability" is bound without fail to be aimed at competitive deflation abroad.

German policy-makers appear rapidly to have become more conscious of all these relationships. Yet there lingered a strain of moralism in German presentations of the stability-export thesis[44] which, coupled with the extremism in judgment noted by many observers, and perhaps also impelled by party-political or income-distribution considerations, could ultimately blind some influential German opinion to the dangers of intransigent stability export, and so force it into opposition to the present-day surrogate for stability export, viz., European monetary integration.

It has not been at all uncommon, even in the technical literature, to find the stability-export problem treated almost literally in terms of moral theology.[45] Bundesbank President Blessing himself either succumbed to or catered to this attitude sufficiently to provoke the criticism that he saw economic, social and political linkages in narrow moral categories.[46] Bundesbank spokesmen formerly made many comments on the "comfortable" position of key-currency nations which "live beyond their means."[47] Answers to such comments are probably feasible (but outside the scope of this study), in terms of the "responsibility" of key-currency nations not to jar the world monetary system

either by deflation or by devaluation, and in terms of Germany's
tendency to live "below its means," a state of affairs constituting, in
one view, the ultimate failure of financial policy.[48] These aspects of
the "moral" case for stability export have affinities with the desire to
protect the German social order against imports of or demonstration
effects of foreign welfarism and extravagance. Most recently, however,
Minister Schiller sharply dissociated himself from "moral-theological
appeals" in economic policy.[49] Schiller and his Ministry have in fact
stood at the center of the move away from stability export and toward
European monetary integration as Germany's primary international
economic goal.

In summary, therefore: at least until the beginning of 1970,
German policy-formulation motivation, policy-administration experience and policy-result statistics unite to suggest a deliberate intention to maintain a dynamic undervaluation of the DM; the export-
of-stability thesis is not a convincing rationale for this policy, if only
because it in actual fact serves no powerful interest in Germany and
has little chance of success.

The statements of German policy-makers and observers may be
adduced here to confirm this conclusion. Hahn wrote that real adjustment was excluded by mercantilistic power politics in Germany.[50]
Giersch confirmed that Germany was trying to hold on to its payments
surpluses.[51] Hahn pointed out that, in an export-prone economy, to
suggest capital exports is to suggest goods exports--and that the proponents of these suggestions knew this.[52] In its Position Paper of
June 24, 1964, the Council of Experts acknowledged the macroeconomic
equivalence of exchange-rate and monetary adjustment, but pointed
out the differences in their income-distribution effects. Meimberg
explained that, in spite of lip service to price stability, a very wide
circle would accept creeping imported inflation--among these the
opponents of upvaluation.[53] The Council of Experts on occasion raised
the not-altogether-rhetorical question whether price stabilization
was indeed really wanted, when the alternatives were so consistently
rejected as injuring specific interests.[54] Most recently, the Council
has stated that awaiting world agreement on stability is equivalent to
accepting imported inflation with all its consequences.[55] Again,
former State Secretary Klaus-Dieter Arndt of the Economics Ministry,
now President of the German Institute for Economic Research, accused
the Bundesbank of not really wanting price stability, since it refused,
on payments-balance grounds, to consider a third upvaluation.[56]

Observers such as Stützel in fact urge just such a course on
Germany, and explicitly plead for acceptance of some inflation.[57]
Emminger also holds out the hope that Germany's imported inflation
can at least lag behind those of other nations, and asks for concentration

of attention, not on foreign sources of inflation, but on domestic.[58]
Arndt, too, feels that relative stability is the best Germany can hope
for.[59] The Private Bank Professional Association agrees that internal
sources of inflation should be eliminated, whereupon the "residual
would be tolerable."[60] The very distribution of these remarks is
evidence for Clauss' statement that the actual course of German
policy favors industry and property interests.[61] In this light, it is
not surprising to find all the business associations consulted by the
Council of Experts strongly in favor of the export of stability as a
policy.[62] Even in these circles, however, evidence is strong that the
stability-export goal is giving way before its equally advantageous and
more comprehensive substitute, European monetary integration.

The implausibility of the stability-export rationale for Germany's
dynamic undervaluation prompts an attempt here to link this strategy
explicitly with the nation's most likely real goals and interests.

Dynamic-Undervaluation Strategy
and National Goals

Thus far in the present study, Germany's persistent undervaluation has been related to national goals mostly through the discussion
of its various tactics and tools. Here it will be convenient to summarize the impact of this policy on the goals reviewed in Chapter 2, both
objectively and as seen and voiced by policy-makers.

Macroeconomic Goals

Price-Stability Goal. Objectively, undervaluation does not foster
price stability. Rather its liquidity and price-transmission effects
directly foster inflation. However, in a relatively inflationary world
under fixed exchange rates, some degree of inflation is unavoidable
in any case. Thus, for example, it is not enough to find statistically
(with Boarman) that imported inflation is the chief cause of German
inflation;[63] when the alternatives are kept in mind, undervaluation
cannot be called the basic cause of inflation. The basic cause is
integration into an inflationary world. Nor is the basic question that
of Emminger: how much inflation will Germany accept in return for
integration?[64] Rather it is, will Germany accept the "standard"
distortions of inflation, or will it prefer distortions involving an ex-
port-bias? The latter may be preferred if other, non-price-stability
goals are considered.

The spectre of imported inflation, together with the stability-
export explanation of undervaluation, does serve to justify monetary
and fiscal restraint and explain a degree of inflation as due to foreign

errors. This kind of social understanding on inflation may be preferable in Germany to a disruptive, undisguised closed-system struggle
on Phillips-curve lines. Some confirmation of this possibility may
lie in the quick and sharp rejection by labor and business of the Council
of Experts' proposal of an income-distribution "peace treaty" in the
shelter of the 1969 revaluation.[65]

Growth Goal. It is difficult to make a final judgment as to the impact
of undervaluation on Germany's growth as such. Obviously, extraordinarily many other factors have been at work. It may be said on
the one hand that, since foreign demand readily substituted for domestic
demand whenever the latter faltered, German growth was correspondingly steadier than otherwise, and so arithmetically faster over time.[66]
But such a replacement of demand does not absolutely require persistent undervaluation, and demand fluctuations could more readily
be offset by financial policy, if the latter were not frozen in the effort
to defend the undervaluation. The experience of 1966-1968 weighs
against this viewpoint.

To the extent that defense of undervaluation required fiscal
measures which slowed infrastructural investment, growth may have
been slowed. The constant subsidy to export-oriented industry represented by the undervaluation, together with the harm done to the
capital market by the conflicting requirements of a net-capital-ex-
port policy and a monetary liquidity-absorption policy, may have
distorted German industrial structure sufficiently to slow growth
significantly through misallocations of resources.

The amassing of a relatively unproductive hoard of international
reserves represents "involuntary" abstention by Germany, while the
capital-export program probably has produced at the margin an export of desirable domestic growth. Yet it can be contended that, given
Germany's large marginal propensity to save and its poor capital
market which fosters monetary savings, incomes from production
must exceed expenditures for goods, so that a balance-of-trade
surplus is inevitable. The only remaining question in this case is
whether its counterpart should be a reserve hoard or deliberately
exported capital.[67] Assuming this rigid a financial structure, one
could assert with Emminger that it is not legitimate to regard the
financing of the payments-balance surplus as an alternative to the
financing of growth.[68] It is hard, however, to believe in quite such a
rigid financial-market structure, or in one which could not be amelio-
rated by better treatment than it has received during the defense of
undervaluation itself.

In fact the crux of the growth question lies in the question of
the rigidity, not of the capital market, but of the export-industries

themselves. If they are structurally rigid, undervaluation helps growth; if they are flexible, undervaluation almost certainly harmed growth.

Employment Goal. Undervaluation seems to be responsible for Germany's almost continuous overfull employment. Once again, judgment about this depends on knowledge of the degree of flexibility in German industrial structure. If this was low, undervaluation aided employment greatly; if it was high, undervaluation was of less use, particularly as the defense of undervaluation involved one-sided inflows of foreign labor.

Under the point of view adopted in the present study, German industrial structure was in itself economically inflexible and politically entrenched, and could in any case have been guided into a significantly greater domestic-market orientation only at cost of smaller-scale output, higher unit costs, and ultimate loss even of the home market to the nations operating with greater economies of scale.

Interests

Income-Distribution Interests. The same structural question has an important bearing on the income-distribution effects of undervaluation. It is likely that the continuance of an export surplus and the inflation necessarily associated with it, coupled with the Bundesbank's one-sided restrictive measures, transferred income from labor to property, especially favoring the export-oriented industries.[69] If the structure of German export industry is inflexible because of tradition, because of the need for large markets to dilute fixed costs, because of the treatment of recent market-winning costs for these purposes as "fixed," because of imperfections in the labor market, and because of the realization that international price-level differentials tend to favor Germany, then even the nominally adjustment-oriented attempts to realign international price levels through exchange-rate and border-tax manipulations will have in fact been ineffective in their long-run impact on income distribution.

Financial Technocracy. Continued undervaluation puts a far greater premium on official management of currencies and on the weight of the financial community's representatives in national and international policy-making than would either flexible-exchange-rate adjustment or monetary adjustment through the "rules of the game."

National Objectives

Social-Order Objectives. Undervaluation and the export of stability justify fiscal restraint and hence small government and less welfare expenditures than otherwise; they justify monetary restraint which puts stability burdens on labor; they explain the observed degree of inflation and its distorting effects as not the fault of the German system; and they underpin complaints about other nations which "live beyond their means."[70] All this corresponds to a widespread form of social-order-consciousness in Germany.

Geopolitical Objectives. It will have been noted that the basic meaning of undervaluation for several key German goals (growth, employment, social-order) is linked to the importance of those goals for an over-riding geopolitical objective. Thus, for example, the meaning of the impact of undervaluation on growth cannot be decided until the essentialness of export industry on other grounds is assessed.

Undervaluation has been helpful to the German geopolitical position.[71] Vis-à-vis the West the achievement of a hoard of international reserves has brought financial weight and prestige. In the western system, financial strength tends to be identified with economic strength and the latter in turn with geopolitical strength. The balance of payments is the one area in which a weakened postwar Germany could quickest regain influence, as it is an external manifestation of purely domestic policy. Despite its very low rate of return (under 1.5 percent in the mid-sixties),[72] and its susceptibility to inflationary losses (made visible in the Bundesbank's periodic revaluation losses), the international reserve hoard was therefore in itself an objective of German policy.[73]

The system of fixed exchange-rate parities was also viewed as a necessary precondition for European integration, or at least as a tool for enforcing "harmonization" of Common Market members' policies. It is interesting to note, however, that the 1969 upvaluation, with the consequent "disharmony" over agrarian policy, did nothing to prevent the Hague Conference of December from committing the Common Market to work for eventual economic and monetary union. The significance of this development will be further discussed in Chapter 7.

Among the more tangible benefits of undervaluation, surpluses afforded Germany protection against pressures from its allies based on their role as the military protectors of central Europe.[74] While Germany was able to "pay" for the troops on its soil, threats of their withdrawal were always negotiable.[75] Again, as long as Germany had a surplus over and above that provided by the troop income, Germany had both upward and downward flexibility in these negotiations. Germany is aware that fear of Russia was behind the postwar reversal of United States policy toward central Europe, and that this fear can be overshadowed by others.[76] Germany is also aware that the official

policy of Britain might never have changed, despite Britain's long-
standing fear of Russia, were not British policy tied to United States
policy, in part by debt. It is unlikely that Germany wishes to remain
economically dependent on this concatenation of political relations.

Germans often note the similarities of British and German
social and economic structure and export composition.[77] Germany's
undervaluation vis-à-vis this potentially dangerous rival (the Council
of Experts notes the statistical correlation of German surpluses and
British deficits), whose key-currency role makes it especially reluctant to devalue, forces Britain into a "competitive deflation race" with
France, a stop-go credit policy, lowered demand, and a continued
restricted use of capacity. These factors add up statistically to produce much of Britain's much-discussed postwar "inefficiency."[78]
The Germans are aware, and somewhat apprehensive, of British unhappiness over this situation.[79] Every speculative wave that sweeps
over the DM is blamed, even by quite responsible sources, on the
machinations of the British press and financiers.[80]

In other areas Germany may be enabled to "prescribe a dose,"
under the aegis of "multilateral surveillance," to recipients of inter-
central-bank aid.[81]

The maintenance of a large German export-oriented heavy industry gives Germany a strong position in Common-Market countries,
and so enhances its political influence in and through that bloc.[82] It
has also been speculated that the prestige of the DM would permit it
to assume a growing role as an international accounting unit, and so
eventually bring to the German capital market some of the strength,
influence and profits now enjoyed by New York and London.[83] In this
way, undervaluation practiced during the era of fixed exchange-rate
parities has provided Germany a useful springboard for leadership in
the coming era of European monetary integration.

Vis-à-vis the "third world," German export surpluses made
possible a high foreign-aid quotient and increased direct investment
in raw-materials sources.[84] Non-adjustment of German industry also
entails the importation of foreign workers. All of these trends enhance
the German world "presence." They also enable Germany to help
strengthen "a state-supporting middle class" in developing countries.[85]

Vis-à-vis the East, the independent position won by Germany
within the West increases its political flexibility in seeking an accom-
modation concerning reunification or, latterly, concerning East-
European markets. The new Brandt government in October 1969 began
talks with Poland and in December 1969 entered into negotiations with
the eastern German state.[86] In the meantime, the Federal Republic's

surpluses help to finance the officially-sponsored "eastern trade," designed to keep doors open to eastern Germany.[87]

The maintenance of a top-heavy industrial structure ensures that any eventual reunification would find a safe preponderance of all-German industry capitalistically organized. Such industry would also ensure a reunited Germany the per capita industrial production to play a role as a considerable world power.

Pending reunification, economic peace and social solidarity are fostered by steady growth little affected by cycles, and by Phillips-curve factors "short-circuited" by the economy's openness. The long refusal of Germany to make significant concessions on its stability-export stance pacifies both industrialists and extreme nationalists, whose alliance against the regime can be fatal.

The statistical evidence derived earlier in this chapter from the logic of Chapter 1 indicates that undervaluation was Germany's consistent policy intention in the period under review. The foregoing summary indicates how many of Germany's goals and interests (developed in Chapter 2) were served by undervaluation. The review of the actual application of policy tools in Chapters 3, 4 and 5 exposed a "dynamics of undervaluation" in which both adjustment and non-adjustment measures served the same end.

The accumulated circumstantial evidence is therefore clear. Faced with the classic case of divergence of international price levels, Germany has tried to steer a course between the Keynesian Scylla of revaluation and Charybdis of inflation.[88] The essence of its strategy has been to maintain currency undervaluation by offsetting some of the liquidity effects of balance-of-payments disequilibrium--chiefly by capital exports; absorbing the remaining liquidity effect in an imported inflation which was the vehicle of structural and income-distribution distortions; using its adjustment tools such as revaluation and border taxes only partially when accumulated price-level differentials made this unavoidable; and proclaiming stability export as a feasible goal. In many senses, Germany has "out-Bretton-Woodsed Bretton Woods."[89] Certainly, it is difficult to point to a more reasonable policy for Germany, given the constraints imposed by the post-war world.

Thus the strategy of dynamic undervaluation served many persistent German goals and interests born of the nation's inescapable historical and geopolitical position and of its undeniable character as a modern industrial society. Therefore, it may be assumed that future changes in German payments-balance strategy will be responses to the same underlying goals modified by changing tactical circumstances.

NOTES

1. See V. Argy, "Monetary Variables and the Balance of Payments," International Monetary Fund Staff Papers (July 1969); J. M. Fleming, "Targets and Instruments," International Monetary Fund Staff Papers (November 1968), p. 388; E. Brehmer, "Official Forward Exchange Operations: The German Experience," International Monetary Fund Staff Papers (November 1964), p. 106-107; L. Erhard, The Economics of Success (Princeton, 1963), p. 313.

2. Federal Republic of Germany, Bundesbank, Annual Report (1969), p. 26.

3. E. Brehmer, Struktur und Funktionsweise des Geldmarkts der Bundesrepublik Deutschland seit 1948 (Kieler Studien) (Tübingen, 1964), p. 41, 41n.

4. Federal Republic of Germany, Sachverständigenrat zur Begutachtung der Gesamtwirtschaftlichen Entwicklung, Jahresgutachten (1967), Section 200; K. Blessing, Im Kampf um Gutes Geld (Frankfurt, 1966), p. 292; G. Gutman, H. J. Hochstrate, and R. Schüter, Die Wirtschaftsverfassung der Bundesrepublik Deutschland (Stuttgart, 1964), p. 169.

5. Organization for Economic Cooperation and Development, Economic Policy Committee, Working Party Three, The Balance of Payments Adjustment Process (Paris, 1966), Section 3.

6. AR (1965), p. 58-59.

7. Federal Republic of Germany, Bundesbank, Monthly Report (May 1970), p. 6.

8. W. Schmidt, "The German Bundesbank," Bank for International Settlements, Eight European Central Banks (London, 1963), p. 75; MR (March 1967), p. 6.

9. AR (1965), p. 18-19.

10. MR (Feb 1967), p. 3.

11. AR (1969), p. 57; MR (May 1970), p. 6.

12. JG (1964), Section 66; AR (1966), p. 41-43; AR (1965), p. 47; AR (1970), p. 26.

13. Organization for Economic Cooperation and Development, Economic and Development Review Committee, Survey (Germany) (1968), p. 6n.

14. R. G. Davis, "How Much Does Money Matter: A Look at Some Recent Evidence," Federal Reserve Bank of New York, Review (June 1969), p. 124n; L. C. Andersen, and J. L. Jordan, "The Monetary Base--Explanation and Analytical Use," Federal Reserve Bank of St. Louis, Review (August 1968); M. W. Keran, and C. T. Babb, "An Explanation of Federal Reserve Actions (1933-68)," Federal Reserve Bank of St. Louis, Review (July 1969).

15. Many observers agree that (in varied contexts other than the German) bank reserves alone are most highly correlated with income in subsequent periods (G. Kaufman, "An Empirical Definition of Money," American Economic Review [March 1969]; R. H. Timberlake, Jr., and J. Forston, "Time Deposits in the Definition of Money," American Economic Review [March 1967]).

16. MR (April 1966), p. 30, 33; Schmidt, p. 77.

17. JG (1966), Section 152. By contrast with the approach presented here, M. Michaely (Balance-of-Payments Adjustment Policies [New York, 1968], p. 17) adopts the money stock and the rediscount rate as his monetary policy-indicator variables.

18. The Economist, Quarterly Economic Survey (Germany) (1965), III, p. 4.

19. L. A. Hahn, Ein Traktat über Währungsreform (Tübingen, 1964), p. 96; JG (1968), Section 217; K. Blessing, Die Verteidigung des Geldwertes (Frankfurt, 1960), p. 235; JG (1969), Sections 296-297; Federal Republic of Germany, Sachverständigenrat zur Begutachtung der Gesamtwirtschaftlichen Entwicklung, Sondergutachten (1969), III, Section 14; Federal Republic of Germany, Bundesbank, Auszüge aus Presseartikeln (1969), #86, p. 11; Veit, AP (1969), #98, p. 17; JG (1970), Section 287.

20. JG (1967), Section 264; H. W. Jenkis, Die Importierte Inflation (Schriften zur Wirtschaftswissenschaftlichen Forschung #15) (Meisenheim, 1966), p. 91n.

21. J. H. Williamson, The Crawling Peg (Essays in International Finance #50) (Princeton, 1965), throughout.

22. Blessing, Kampf, p. 93, 94, 102, 181, 199.

23. JG (1964), Government Response, Section 12.

24. Hahn, Traktat, p. 182.

25. Blessing, Kampf, p. 241.

26. AR (1966), p. 26.

27. Blessing, Verteidigung, p. 172.

28. Bundesbank Vice President Emminger, AP (1970), #8, p. 8; former Economics Ministry State Secretary Arndt in the Bundestag, AP (1971), #39, p. 3.

29. Blessing, Kampf, p. 183, 193.

30. JG (1969), Sections 276-279, 297.

31. O. Emminger, Währungspolitik im Wandel der Zeit (Frankfurt, 1966), p. 79.

32. Federal Republic of Germany, Bundesministerium für Wirtschaft, Wissenschaftliche Beirat, "Preisstabilität und Aussenhandel," Bundesanzeiger #244 (1967), p. 244; JG (1967), Section 411.

33. JG (1968), Section 98; JG (1964), Sections 237, 255; JG (1966), Sections 259, 265; JG (1967), Section 307; SG (1969), I, Section 19; L. A. Hahn, Fünfzig Jahre zwischen Inflation und Deflation (Tübingen, 1963), p. 123, 162; Hahn, Traktat, p. 45; G. N. Halm, International Financial Intermediation: Deficits Benign and Malignant (Essays in International Finance #68) (Princeton, 1968), p. 14, 16, 17; Veit, AP (1965), #80, p. 8.

34. W. Stützel, "Ist die schleichende Inflation durch monetäre Massnahmen zu beeinflussen?" (Beihefte zur Konjunkturpolitik #7) (Berlin, 1960); F. A. Lutz, The Problem of International Economic Equilibrium (Amsterdam, 1962), p. 56; Jenkis, p. 201n.

35. Bundesbank Vice President Emminger, AP (1968), #15, p. 2; AP (1969), #2, p. 7; Bundesbank Director Irmler, AP (1966), #96, p. 5; Blessing, Verteidigung, p. 200, 238; Kiesinger, AP (1969), #39, p. 5; Industrial Congress, AP (1969), #3, p. 4.

36. AP (1970), #8, p. 8.

37. AP (1969), #95, p. 1.

38. See Chancellor Brandt's "inaugural" address, AP (1969), #85, p. 3.

39. Hahn, Jahre, p. 201.

40. L. Krause, A Passive Balance-of-Payments Strategy for the United States (Brookings Papers on Economic Activity) (Washington, 1971); G. Haberler and T. Willett, a study prepared for the American Enterprise Association, Washington, 1971.

41. See Veit, AP (1969), #98, p. 15.

42. See a long catalog of recent worldwide restrictive measures in JG (1969), Section 98 ff.

43. F. Clauss, "Wirtschaftswachstum und Konjunkturpolitik in der bestehenden Währungsordnung," in Arbeitsgemeinschaft, etc., p. 67.

44. Clauss, p. 68.

45. Jenkis, p. 200; Chancellor Erhard, AP (1968), #44, p. 6.

46. Der Volkswirt (1968), #40, p. 27.

47. L. Gleske, "Die Finanzierung des Wachsenden Internationalen Handels," in Arbeitsgemeinschaft, etc., p. 117; H. Irmler, Discussion Contribution in Arbeitsgemeinschaft, etc., p. 102.

48. B. Moore, An Introduction to the Theory of Finance (New York, 1968), p. 209.

49. AP (1969), #69, p. 5.

50. Hahn, Traktat, p. 194.

51. AP (1968), #15, p. 12.

52. Hahn, Traktat, p. 167.

53. AP (1969), #46, p. 21.

54. JG (1965), Section 187; JG (1968), Section 228.

55. SG (1969), Section 19.

56. AP (1970), #72, p. 2.

57. AP (1969), #38, p. 10.

58. AP (1966), #90, p. 2.

59. German Tribune (15 Oct 1970), p. 10.

60. JG (1967), p. 224.

61. Clauss, p. 80.

62. JG (1967), p. 221-229.

63. P. Boarman, Germany's Economic Dilemma (New Haven, 1964), p. 54. Boarman (p. 18) sees international reserve movements, short-term capital movements and the payments-balance residual as representing the minimum imported inflation, and compares these with such other factors of inflation as government deficits and the wage-productivity gap.

64. Emminger, Politik, p. 80.

65. JG (1969), Sections 223-225; AP (1969), #97, p. 7, 12; AP (1969), #98, p. 5.

66. O. Emminger, Währungspolitische Betrachtungen (Frankfurt, 1956), p. 43; JG (1964), Section 35.

67. O. Emminger, "Practical Aspects of the Problem of Balance-of-Payments Adjustment," Journal of Political Economy (August 1967 supplement), p. 43.

68. Emminger, "Aspects," p. 28.

69. Hahn, Traktat, p. 29; JG (1965), Section 187.

70. Minister Schiller, AP (1968), #83, p. 7.

71. M. Friedman, Dollars and Deficits (Englewood Cliffs, 1969), p. 274.

72. JG (1964), Section 42.

73. JG (1964), Section 26; AR (1965), p. 38.

74. Emminger, Politik, p. 16, 22; Hahn, Traktat, p. 167.

75. JG (1964), Section 147.

76. Director Ponto of the Dresdner Bank, AP (1971), #5, p. 5.

77. JG (1966), Section 236; JG (1964), Section 2; JG (1967), Section 360; P. B. Kenen, British Monetary Policy and the Balance of Payments, 1951-57 (Cambridge, 1960), p. 198.

78. JG (1967), Section 434n; AP (1969), #15, p. 4; London Times, AP (1967), #32, p. 18; Clauss, p. 87, 90; D. C. Rowan, "Towards a Rational Exchange Policy: Some Reflections on the British Experience," Federal Reserve Bank of St. Louis, Review (April 1969).

79. Economist, AP (1968), #83, p. 18; Blessing, Verteidigung, p. 114.

80. Christian Democratic Union, AP (1969), #38, p. 5; AP (1968), #61, p. 3; Berlin Commercial Conference, AP (1969), #66, p. 11.

81. Blessing, Kampf, p. 96.

82. Emminger, Politik, p. 141 ff.

83. See C. P. Kindleberger, The Politics of World Money and World Language (Essays in International Finance #61) (Princeton, 1967).

84. Emminger, "Aspects," p. 51.

85. L. Erhard, Wirken und Reden, 1952-1965 (Ludwigsburg, 1966), p. 74.

86. Wall Street Journal (27 Oct 1969), p. 1.

87. JG (1967), Section 304.

88. J. M. Keynes, A Treatise on Money (New York, 1930), I, p. 356 ff.

89. Hahn, Jahre, p. 240.

FROM REUNIFICATION TO INTEGRATION

Chapter 6 summarized and characterized Germany's international economic policy through the most recent quarters. The present chapter attempts to assess both the continuity and the change in that policy during the past two to three years. On this basis an evaluation of future prospects is made. These assessments are perhaps most effectively introduced by examining the shifts that are taking place in Germany's national goals, due to the interaction of ongoing interests, changing external conditions, and the policy lessons of the sixties.

The most basic and widely influential of these shifts in goals concerns what has here been called Germany's geopolitical stance. Two phases of German geopolitical consciousness were distinguished in Chapter 2: the phase of public emphasis upon possible reunification with eastern Germany, and the phase of open striving for final integration with western Europe. This shift of policy approach has not in reality been abrupt; but it has been accelerated in recent years by several strong trends.

Although the Brandt government's overt change of approach to the East did not fail to arouse echoes of the "stab-in-the-back" legend in the West, and to put on guard all the vested interests in Middle-European tensions in both East and West, it must be recalled that it was Brandt's party which, after the German collapse of 1945, had for a decade advocated unification as the most immediate goal, and had deplored the policy of self-sufficiency for the more clerical-conservative southwestern parts of Germany.[1] In this light, Chancellor Adenauer's policy of consolidation on the three-zone basis can be viewed as in fact being a tacit policy of renunciation, behind a facade

269

of abstract legal claims to reunification. These rigid claims, indeed, were calculated to impede reunification with its dangers to the German capitalistic and western-oriented order.[2]

The crucial factors in the decisive shift of German policy emphasis included the undoubted (if bitterly paradoxical) consolidation of the German Democratic Republic after the erection of the Wall, the demonstrated disinterest of virtually everyone outside the Federal Republic in the reunification issue, and the need for an understanding with the East precisely in order to turn westward with comfort and dignity. The growing firmness of Germany's western commitment is itself not simply a pis aller; continental union has in its own right become a dire necessity for Europe's social-political-industrial order, as a means of protection from the economic and financial threat posed by the sheer size of the United States. (This necessity is discussed later in the present chapter.)

Thus Germany's eastern policy forms the logical and chronological hyphen between the two phases of geopolitical consciousness that have been distinguished here. During the first phase, the eastern policy sought to gain the maneuverability necessary for the drive to reunification. In the second phase, it seems calculated to secure Germany's "rear" and to pre-empt market positions, strengthening the Federal Republic in the hard negotiations with Britain and France over widening and deepening West-European integration. In this way, Germany need not seem geopolitically driven to hasten the western union, and will have existing trade (and perhaps also industrial-cooperation) connections with the East to offer to its partners in the West.[3]

For these reasons, the recent shift in policy emphasis toward integration in the West and understanding in the East is, despite all party-political carping, now in all probability permanent and effectively "bipartisan."

THE MOTIVES FOR EUROPEAN INTEGRATION

General Motives for European Integration

Certainly, the Federal Republic has, under Chancellor Brandt, been an avowed leader in the current integration movement, which envisages both "expanding" and "perfecting" the existing EEC.[4] The institutional end-state projected for about 1980 is to promote common social, technological, regional, structural, cyclical, monetary, fiscal and exchange policies on the part of the present EEC members and of an indefinite number of new additions. The EEC members have already agreed to wide-ranging policy consultations, to limited mutual exchange support and policy surveillance, and to some basic forms of overall indicative planning.

What advantages do the interested states foresee from this institutional and political consolidation? In this regard, the common interests of the EEC states, the individual interests of each of the states, and interests of groups within the individual states can be distinguished. The EEC as a whole is no longer motivated toward integration by fear of the East. Today's weapons make Europe the least, rather than the most, likely potential battlefield in an East-West war. Authoritative analysts accordingly speak of a sharp reduction in the felt threat from the East.[5] Germany's Ostpolitik and the prospect of an all-European security conference strengthen this impression.

Neither is textbook collective efficiency in terms of real adjustment, division of labor and welfare gains much more than a propaganda image. As noted in Chapter 1, imperfect modern markets require so much preventive and corrective intervention that governments necessarily redistribute around a third of most national incomes. This fact alone makes quite abstract the possibility of perfecting international division of labor and distribution of income through market mechanisms.[6]

It is rather the need for large-scale operations and wide markets felt by the concrete existing economic structures that lies at the root of the integration movement. With insufficiently large scale and with the consequent relatively high costs, Europe's industry will progressively lose even its home markets. Already the continental economies of the United States, the Soviet Union and even China (not to mention Japan) are in many ways outpacing Europe economically, and so reducing its international political weight.

European industries' access to their needed markets is today impeded in a rather special way by the international nature of these markets. This is not just a matter of the "natural" national differences in market conditions. Modern big business is quite competent to neutralize or even to exploit such differences. Nor is it only a matter of offical-style balance-of-payments problems and the related protective trade barriers, all of which must appear more and more irrelevant and impertinent to the managers of internationally-organized corporations. It is not even simply a matter of the growing technological and research gaps between Europe and the United States in agriculture, manufacturing and services alike.[7] The truly decisive problem for the monetary integration movement is that the smallness of the

European states makes each of them vulnerable, as it were "on the flank," to the international financial strength of the United States.

To understand this clearly, it is helpful to consider step by step the predicament of the EEC countries. In countries with small domestic markets, as repeatedly noted, the maintenance of a modern scale of industrial production requires outlets to international markets. This in turn requires the maintenance of free trade and of internationally competitive price structures. On this, according to Minister Schiller, depends Germany's "inner and outer security."[8] At the same time, the social and economic structure and the foreign-policy orientation of the United States make the United States payments balance incurable.[9] The attempted export of stability by the EEC has been a failure. Special Drawing Rights were activated not despite, but essentially because of, the United States disequilibrium and the threat it poses to the world system of trade and finance.

In these circumstances, the EEC as a whole will register net payments-balance surpluses and will accumulate international reserves. As long as Europe's individual currency areas are not comparable in economic weight to that of the United States, these net new international reserves will consist largely of United States dollars. The more successful a European country is in the primary aim of achieving a rationally-scaled industrial output, therefore, the more prone it is to finance the world activities of the United States, precisely as the latter may be buying up the European country's own industrial capacity and technological advances.

The European countries cannot refuse to accept these accumulating dollars, or even attempt to return many of them to the United States for gold, without destroying confidence in a large proportion of currently-held international reserves and so producing world financial chaos.* The European nations which depend vitally on exports of course cannot afford to do this.

The dollar has built up its commanding position as a key currency because it has been safe, convenient and necessary for traders to hold dollars and for central banks to intervene with them in exchange markets. The convenience and liquidity of the dollar rested very largely on the relative size and wealth of the United States market and its consequent overwhelming share of world trade. This led to

---

*This results from the fact that the official foreign dollar holders alone hold a multiple of the official value of the United States gold reserve.

the denomination of transactions among third nations in dollars and
to the necessity for traders to hold dollar working balances.

The inability to refuse the dollar as payment for surpluses
leaves smaller nations two choices: eliminate their net surpluses or
make forced loans of real exports to the United States. Governor
Guido Carli of the Banca d'Italia in 1970 estimated this kind of forced
lending by Europe to the United States at sixteen billion dollars in
two years.[10] Eliminating European surpluses would require either
(1) engineering the export of capital through artificially low interest
rates or through government capital movements, or (2) inflating at
the same rate as the United States, or (3) instituting discriminatory
trade controls, or (4) upvaluing in repeated discrete steps, or (5)
generally and permanently instituting flexible or floating exchange
rates. The German experience of the sixties has been discouraging
in each of these areas.

The limitations of artificial capital export have been discussed
in Chapter 4. Inflating at the dictate of the United States, coupled
with the loss of export markets, has no appeal to Europeans (Chapter
2). Discriminatory trade controls can today lead only to retaliation
and general protectionism. For reasons already made clear (Chapter
3), protectionism to avoid the embarrassment of payments surpluses
is the very opposite of desirable for exporting nations.[11] As concluded
in Chapter 3, repeated discrete exchange-rate upvaluations have been
extremely difficult and disruptive for Germany, international-financial-
ly and domestic-politically. It is precisely to avoid a threatened
further need for this defense that German policy leaders have moved
so swiftly on the European integration front.[12]

General flexible exchange rates, which would eliminate the need
for any form of official international liquidity, would thereby blunt
the financial flank attack by the dollar. But since today's key currency
is both a reserve currency and a vehicle currency, the dollar's
advantage would not by any means be ended with the obviation of
official exchange reserves. More importantly, it is in fact almost
impossible to imagine a world monetary system which would be able
to detect, distinguish and deter all forms of official intervention in
exchange markets. Even assuming such a system, most of the governments that are financially relevant would still have to operate in,
and so hold and try to accumulate, some form of internationally
acceptable asset. Again, it is not absolutely certain that flexible
exchange rates, as they would be operated by existing institutions,
would be more stable in the long run than pegged rates, or that they
would be less unsettling to world trade and finance. Finally, it is all
too certain that flexible rates would in the long run enforce real
international adjustment of industrial structures, which, in the present

world system of concentrated market and political power within and among nations, would be inacceptable and hence politically resisted. The only chance for carrying exchange-rate flexibility far enough to be effective would be to create economic systems with less concentrated market power. Reduction of domestic concentration is, however, for all practical purposes, politically and economically impossible.

By far the most feasible step in this direction, therefore, is to reduce relative concentration on the international level by increasing the financial and political integration of Europe. This move has the advantage (from the feasibility standpoint) of reinforcing, rather than countering, the technologically determined trend toward international economic concentration within Europe. This much balance to the financial weight of the United States could produce nearer-optimal currency areas between which flexible or officially guided exchange rates could operate with really functional effects.[13]

Creating a second currency area of nearly the market size of the United States would also relieve the dollar of its reserve-currency role more rapidly than the IMF Special Drawing Rights alone can do. It is important to note that a currency area, and not just a free trade area, is requisite for this. A free trade area, even without total real adjustment of industries, harmonization of social and economic structures, or coordination of economic policies, can be operated relatively smoothly through hidden trade barriers, compensatory international financing, and outright payments imbalances. A currency area, on the other hand, requires almost total real adjustment, harmonization, and coordination. Thus the fundamental impetus behind the European monetary integration movement is the realization that European nations in any case must eventually surrender their weakening monetary sovereignty. The question is simply whether to surrender it to the United States or to a common European authority.

A financially integrated Europe with a workably flexible external exchange rate could realistically hope to become a stability bloc, reducing the dangers posed by inflation for its social order, without the self-defeating payments-balance surpluses generated by the present system. Europe would in this way no longer be simply the passive adjuster to United States policies.[14] Such inner and outer strengthening would obviously allow Europe to play a larger role in world politics.[15] Thus, international finance is, today as never before, the primary battleground of international politics.[16]

Additionally, the present EEC member states may glimpse certain secondary advantages in a swift consummation of full monetary integration. Integration would for example facilitate a final regulation of the common agricultural-support program, which has repeatedly

been politically and technically lamed by exchange-rate problems.[17]
This in turn could better enable the original EEC states to direct
part of their net agricultural surpluses to the expected new members,
thus lowering their own contributions to the subsidy program.[18]

German Interests and European Integration

For Germany itself, there are numerous advantages in a speedy
completion of European monetary integration: advantages which do
not in every case fully overlap those available to the Community as a
whole. As the nation with Europe's highest absolute and per capital
industrial capacity, and probably also with Europe's weakest structural
tendencies to inflation, Germany can only gain from the full opening
of Europe's markets, and from the final renunciation of protective
devaluations. Even with insufficient preparatory harmonization of
national policies and structures (permitting inflationary pressure in
Germany and demands from Germany's deficitary partners for compensatory finance), circles close to Germany's decision centers may
see a net advantage in proceeding with full integration in Europe.
For, as the German experience of the sixties indicates, wide markets
are in the last analysis felt to be more imperative than price stability.
And as indicated in Chapter 2, both payments-balance surplus and its
alternative, adjustment inflation, in all probability favor property
income over labor income.

Again, German payments-balance gains can with some effort be
guided into direct investments in other lands. Progressive industrial
congestion on German soil can thus be relieved, at least relatively to
other lands, by growing German-owned production facilities elsewhere.*
In this way, Germany would assume the same role vis-à-vis the EEC
that the United States has hitherto played vis-à-vis the whole of
Europe. Increased German capitalization of far-flung projects might
also give the Federal Republic an improved chance to overtake the
City of London as Europe's leading financial center.[19]

If, after all, some international compensatory finance is required
from a prosperous Germany, this will be raised by fiscal means,
thus disproportionately affecting middle-income taxpayers and lower-
income purchasers of oligopoly products. Such compensatory payments would thus take much the same route and produce much the
same income-distribution effects as e.g., a foreign-aid program.
Flight of German labor from any resultant unfavorable tax-to-benefit

---

*Germany presently has the world's second-dirtiest air.

ratio in Germany would be discouraged by increased European social-
policy "harmonization" in these areas.

All in all, Germany can hope to gain world influence from full
integration in Europe, just as the Northeast of the United States has
more world importance within the fifty states than it would have as
one of, for example, six regional states in mid-North America. "No
European state is more vitally interested in the completion of the
European integration efforts. In a united Europe the German voice
has an incomparably greater weight, especially in the great political
life-and-death questions which affect our country."[20]

For the German governments which come to preside over the
process, European monetary integration can provide an excuse for
continued inflation as a "sacrifice" for integration, a necessary
"convergence" of Europe's national economic processes.[21] This
would enable them, if they wish, to claim credit for high employment
while refusing blame for rising prices.

For German industry as such, the key problem of assured large-
scale markets will be solved.[22] Additionally, the international and
domestic political spotlight will be removed from Germany's economic
and social structure. Again, full international integration and harmonization may well increase competition among labor more than it will
increase that among capitalist groups. Labor's movements are less
easy to hamper with hidden administrative restraints than are those
of products, yet labor may long retain its nationalistic mistrusts as
barriers to effective organization over against already existing international firms and financial groupings. These factors may therefore
increase labor's mobility on an individual level faster than its solidarity on the Community level whither incomes-policy negotiations are
to be transferred.[23] At any rate, full monetary integration and structural harmonization should contribute to the further reduction of the
German capital-to-labor ratio toward the general European level,
with a corresponding shift of incomes to property.

In other areas, European business as such may expect to benefit,
as has American business, from the weakness and competition among
the administrative units and political interests of a multiparty federal
state facing continental-scale firms. The speed of the decisions at
The Hague, and the very rapid pace of events since The Hague both
seem to indicate that, at least in Germany, industrial interests have
fully understood all these possibilities.

The European financial community also has specific interests
in European integration. Its rapidly increasing interest in incomes
policy has been noted, as has the ensuing debate concerning, in effect,

which was to come first, monetary or incomes-policy integration. Either way, the tendency has been to stress the expert over the politician. By definition, of course, integration turns away from traditional arms-length diplomatic and political relations. But the alternative envisioned here is not the impersonal market, but rather the narrow group of experts. The Germans, in particular, demand for Europe an eventual independent central bank like Germany's own, as well as confidential panels for setting common financial, social and structural policy.[24] Majority voting in these organs is apparently preferred, to prevent political vetos by individual nations.[25] At the same time, Germany would like to see oversight of the policy panels (but not of the central bank) by the European Parliament.[26] This body, even if directly elected, is apt to be far more divided than a normal national parliament vis-a-vis the European central bankers, the narrow panels staffed by financial-community experts, and the great internationally-organized firms. Yet France opposes even the direct-election proposal, fearing national isolation and wishing to retain a diplomatic style of political control.

If realized, therefore, the projected end-state of the integrationists would very likely be more technocratic, and more influenced by the financial community, than is the case in the existing national system of any industrialized country. This conclusion is somewhat confirmed by the recommendation of the ground-breaking Werner Committee that each nation create a formula for judging the impact of macrofinancial policy on its economy. That such a mechanistic and expert-bound device was accepted, despite its extraordinary difficulty (even without considering the upheavals of integration itself), and despite the previous general rejection of the logically analogous calculation of formula-based exchange-parity changes, suggests a determination by the financial experts to increase their own influence over national financial policies.

Germany's Common Market partners face these prospects with mixed reactions. France is certainly interested in a European counterweight to the dollar,[27] but is less enthused over, e.g., sharing atomic research with the Federal Republic.[28] Germany's partners are in fact worried by Germany's resurgent economic power and by its individualistic eastern policy.[29] At the same time, they hope to receive agricultural, social and structural aid funds from Germany and eventually from Britain. The candidates for EEC membership appear to have roughly the same hopes for gain from a common currency area as do the existing members, although the effect of joining the EEC agriculturally gives them pause.[30]

In the light of the foregoing discussion, it is fair to view the monetary integration movement as springing directly from continuing

interests, changing conditions, and the international financial lessons
of the sixties. The alternatives facing Germany in this movement,
and the prospects for the seventies, are discussed immediately below.

ALTERNATIVES AND PROSPECTS

Alternatives

Statically, completed European integration on the desired scale
is nearly equivalent to political union, involving, among much else, a
common cyclical policy.[31] Dynamically, the key question is whether
monetary integration logically presupposes political union, and so
presupposes an advance mutual adjustment of national economic
structures, or whether monetary integration can mechanically create
political union by forcing subsequent economic adjustment. It may
be remembered in this connection that European political community
based on military-defense exigencies foundered in the fifties.

The array of interests motivating integration, already presented,
foreshadowed the debate over procedures. It should be emphasized
that "only" procedures were, nominally at least, in dispute. All
European integrationists foresee essentially the same end state. On
the procedural question, there crystallized two main viewpoints,
respectively labelled the monetarist, chiefly represented by France,
and the "economist," chiefly represented by Germany.

The monetarist position favored freezing EEC exchange rates
at once, and narrowing their bands of permissible fluctuation rapidly
to zero. This would at once create a large de facto currency area
over against the United States and so permit the advantageous operation
of either fixed or flexible rates vis-à-vis the rest of the capitalist
world.

Such a rapidly built currency area would not yet have harmonized
its economic policies and structures, so that payments-balance disequilibrium among the members would persist. To assure common
exchange-market intervention, which could eliminate footholds for
the dollar as a key currency, the EEC international-reserves stock
would in this first stage be pooled. To ensure continued harmonization
efforts, even though this latter provision had removed much of the
stimulus to such efforts, the EEC's political executive, the Council
of Ministers, would issue binding directives on macrofinancial policy
to the national central banks. As these arrangements were expected
to exercise an influence toward real international adjustment, no
further decision-making bodies were held to be needed. Since there

was to be no politically-fostered advance harmonization of the economies, direct election of a European Parliament was not contemplated.

The "economist" position, on the other hand, called for very full
and reliable harmonization of national economic policies and structures
before any real macrofinancial or exchange-rate sovereignty was to
be surrendered to central EEC authorities.[32] "Economists" feared
that fixed exchange rates without detailed harmonization would require
either a pooling of all national exchange earnings or financial-compen-
satory and structural-aid payments by Germany, which would in turn
put pressure on Germany to adjust unilaterally to France, both in
real structure and through imported inflation. Even more, rigid
exchange rates could interfere with independent national interest-rate
policies, which themselves are necessary in order to work through
the differing national financial linkages toward price stabilization and
toward international adjustment itself.* Germans pointed to the temporary collapse and subsequent problems of the monetarily rigid EEC
agricultural program as evidence that merely monetary integration
will break down rather than force real adjustment of underlying structures and interests.[33]

In general, Germans tended to feel that France and Italy are not
only structurally prone to high inflation, but also apt to experience
abrupt socially-generated "wage explosions." Hence the German
spokesmen demanded prior agreement on "common denominators"
for European "social development" and for government expenditures.
In other words, Germany was trying to use its own economic strength
and perhaps its growing eastern ties--while these still remained
uncommitted--as bargaining counters to achieve a sort of "advance
adjustment" according to German ideas.[34] After the collapse of the
integration talks of December 1970, accordingly, Minister Schiller
hinted that Germany could use exchange-rate policy to put pressure
on France for agreement.[35]

As noted above, the "economists" favored the creation of a
series of small confidential bodies with strong powers to hasten

---

*Differing financial institutions and linkages dictate different
interest rates for the same stability-policy aims. Therefore, either
these institutions must be thoroughly harmonized or else even wider
exchange-rate bands are called for, in order to reduce interest-rate
speculation. Harmonization of financial structures is also advocated
in order to end "unfair advantages" of differing national financial
structures in competing for preeminence as the financial center of
the new Europe.

harmonization.[36] These groups would be made somehow responsive
to the European Parliament, which would itself be directly elected in
order to permit it to legitimate the wide and deep changes contemplated.[37] Despite this gesture, an aura of Hamiltonian "money-power"
manipulation hung over the entire German plan.

All measures other than the above were felt by the "economists"
to be "peripheral."[38] A pooling of international reserves, for example,
as suggested by France, was considered equivalent to recycling of
reserves, and so as making non-adjustment easier.

In the "economist" scheme, the progress of harmonization
according to a prearranged schedule was to be reviewed at several
stages, with the possibility of unilateral revaluation remaining open
until the last stage.[39] For the period after satisfactory harmonization,
finally, the "economists" insisted upon a strong, independent central
bank dedicated to price stability.[40] President Abs of the Bank Association, for example, pictured such central-bank independence as protecting it from control by interest groups.[41] Wide powers over the
major fiscal decisions of individual nations were similarly to be
lodged with the consultative bodies of experts.

The German stance was thus one of "readiness to accept the full
consequences of full union." Prescinding entirely from some rather
noisome moralizing over France's obstruction of "Europe,"[42] it
seems clear that the "consequences" of the German scheme would
nearly all have been welcome to Germany. France, on the other hand,
was not anxious to exchange the United States for Germany as dominant
partner.

The "economist" position has affinities with that of the rapidly
obsolescing Ordo-liberals. Muted now indeed are the latters' pleas
for competitive markets free of government intervention; for the
entire integration movement is motivated and carried by the interests
and needs of large-scale industrial and financial groups, which have
quite literally outgrown their domestic markets. In effect, indeed,
the rapid, even hasty, integration steps of the seventies constitute,
in common with the widespread price-wage freezes and the demands
for incomes policies, a form of open abdication by the old-liberal
order in the face of the technological imperative to large-scale production.[43] However, the German insistence on philosophical and
structural harmonization before real integration is still quite remi-
niscent of the Erhard-era Ordo-liberal dreams of a "formed society"
for all Europe. (See Chapter 2.)

In any case, continental monetary integration under the present
European social conditions is likely to represent a great step forward

in the development of post-competitive capitalism. In terms of its tendency to foster a closed socio-economic structure corresponding to large-scale concentrated production, such an integration would in a sense overleap the present United States stage of development.* If European decision-makers indeed reap from integration all the advantages that they hope for, an example may be set for the United States to follow, thus hastening the later stages of capitalist society world-wide.

This much discussion of the motives behind the European integration movement, and of the debate over the actual steps in the process, serves to indicate that integration under the "economist" format is for Germany a serviceable substitute for the stability-export strategy. It would maintain Germany's right to "undervaluation," with all its consequences, while eliminating the inconvenient international (or "inter-currency") nature of the resulting export surpluses. In short, since the international adjustment problem has proved intractable, the nature of the problem is to be redefined. The question which remains open is whether structures and interests which could not be adjusted economically can be compromised politically.

Prospects

Four kinds of possibilities face Germany on the road to European monetary integration. The first is full advance harmonization of individual national social and economic policies and structures, followed by integration based on a strong, independent central bank; in short, the "economist" program. This is in all probability too optimistic an expectation to be fulfilled in a useful period of time, considering the powerful interests opposing various elements of harmonization. After all, whatever may have been the case in the federating America of 1789, today's Europe has many already mature centers of economic and political power, which will not now abruptly surrender their economic functions. If indeed the social and industrial groups within nations were readily amenable to adjustment, and were not able to reach for political and discriminatory weapons of defense, the fixed-peg exchange rates proposed by France would be sufficient by themselves to force adjustment. In fact, full integration would already have taken place in response to the Bretton Woods system. When not merely social policy and structure, but also the shape of

---

*Naturally, the concept of social structure referred to here deals with power relationships, and not e.g., with consumption and entertainment standards.

the policy tools themselves, are candidates for harmonization, the
advance-harmonization project promises to be hopelessly slow.[44]
Predictably enough, EEC talks based on the Werner Report (according
to German spokesmen "a balanced compromise," but in fact embodying
the purest "economist" position) broke down over French resistence
in mid-December 1970. This resistence was overcome only with the
Brussels compromise of February 1971 (discussed below).

Germany's second possible prospect for the seventies is that
the integration scheme should stall at one point or another and subse-
quently fall apart. The experience analyzed in the entire present
study weighs against the possibility of Germany's accepting this outcome. The future of the present order in the Federal Republic hangs
fully on Germany's becoming, if possible the Prussia, but if necessary
(as it were) the Bavaria, of European integration.

Germany's third alternative is to accept an integration on the
monetarist exchange-market-intervention level only, without advance
adjustment of national economic structures adequate to prevent the
equivalent of continuing German payments-balance surpluses. On
the supposition that Germany then followed the international-financial
"rules of the game" to produce a post-integration adjustment, the
Federal Republic would have to accept a rise in its rate of inflation
sufficient to deny some German industry its normal export outlets.
This alternative would presumably leave Germany poorer in international reserves but richer in usable goods. It would also force a
shift in industrial structure away from heavy, export-oriented industry,
and a redistribution of real income down the income scale.

Germany's fourth alternative is the acceptance of integration on
the monetarist exchange-intervention level, again without adequate
advance international adjustment, but also without a subsequent adjustment inflation in Germany. In this case, Germany would have to
provide its EEC partners with some recycling of international reserves
and some financial aid toward performing the very adjustment being
refused by Germany itself. Germany would be poorer under this
formula than under the first alternative discussed above, but still
much richer than under the second. In all likelihood, too, the real
opportunity cost involved would be paid largely by the taxpayers in
lower-income groups.

The first two alternatives seem impossible. The one will be
rejected by France as surely as will the other by Germany. Of the
latter two alternatives, the third favors labor and the fourth capital.
Given the relative political strength and economic sophistication of
these two groups, and considering the lingering German fear of inflation, the politically most feasible solution for the Federal Republic

would seem to be to hold out for as much advance adjustment along German lines as seems possible, by maintaining some form of ex-change-policy option for several years to come, and only thereafter to accept finally the monetarist freeze on exchange rates. In doing so, Germany would have both to accept some inflation as a "sacrifice" for integration, and to give some perhaps fiscally-generated interna-tional compensation tied to "multilateral surveillance" of the recipi-ents' policies.[45] If more time, or increased pressure on EEC partners, were needed for the advance-adjustment process, Germany could threaten to exercise its option to upvalue. Upvaluation would theoreti-cally (i.e., from the static viewpoint) permit a quicker general ex-change-rate freeze without German compensatory payments. However, it would probably in reality further delay the final exchange-rate freeze for precisely this reason. This is because France could not accept a compensation settlement based on a momentary static analy-sis, until all the structural elements making for renewed German "dynamic undervaluation" had been eliminated. Illuminating for these possibilities is the swing of such influential personalities as President Hermann Abs of the Bank Association from the strict "economist" position to a more monetarist stance, under "the political and economic circumstances, which have since changed."[46]

Under the above strategy, it would not be excessively harmful to Germany to allow the EEC Council of Ministers to oversee the harmonization process, with the technical advice of the central-bank presidents.[47] Such an arrangement would indeed do no more than reflect the high-political, non-technical, and somewhat antagonistic and undemocratic haggling process to be conducted.

The package of compromises sketched here as Germany's politically feasible alternative constitutes an almost exact description of the EEC Council's Brussels agreement of February 9, 1971.[48] Stripped of much non-binding rhetoric borrowed from the Werner Report and from other "economist" documents, the agreement essen-tially provided for an experimental prior concession by Germany on the monetarists' exchange-bloc front, in the hopes of an eventual French quid pro quo on the "economists' " structural-harmonization front. Specifically, the compromise provided for common EEC inter-vention in the exchange markets, the narrowing (initally to 1.2 percent) of intra-EEC bands of fluctuation around exchange-rate parities, and the probable establishment of a European exchange-support fund largely financed from German sources. These three "action" items constituted the German "marriage-gift" to France. In return, Germany received rather promising statements of intent on the structural-harmonization and supranational-authorities issues, and an expiry clause that automatically ends the monetary cooperation after five years. The latter provision allows Germany to threaten a more or

less graceful retreat from the agreement in case it is not satisfied
with the progress of structural and policy harmonization. In other
words, Germany was still free to revalue without the onus of having
explicitly repealed an essential element of the European framework.

As it happens, it was no secret that German authorities were
less than satisfied with the Brussels compromise, and felt that Germany
had in fact been left with nothing more substantial than the escape
clause.[49] This attitude may have had some bearing on Germany's
approach to the crisis which broke in May 1971. In the long-run view,
however, it appears that the unbalanced compromise of Brussels
reasonably represents the basic European commercial, financial, and
geopolitical realities, and hence serves German interests better than
any feasible alternative. The real work of promoting international
adjustment, notably between the French and the German economies,
was indeed not convincingly provided for in the Brussels document.
Since in fact such work cannot effectively be carried out through
diplomatic-style political negotiations, however, Germany hardly
sacrificed overmuch in not insisting on legally formalizing the harmonization organs at this stage. If real harmonization is ever to come
to all under the umbrella of the Brussels text, it will in any case
come through small, confidential working groups in true "economist"
style. Thus, Germany gave up only the automatic, legally-enforced
execution of the working groups' decisions; and this latter was a
concession that was not to be expected of France at this stage.

On the other hand, even Germany's nominal option to permit
expiry of the concessions made to France in case of dissatisfaction
is itself somewhat lacking in credibility. Germany's real stake in
integration, the political onus that would (regardless of legalities)
attach to a German-fostered expiry, and the vested interests which
can be expected to form around any new monetary arrangements, all
make a full reversal of European arrangements at the end of five
years highly doubtful. On the other hand, Germany may legitimately
have hoped that the expansive logic of modern industrial society,
emphasized throughout the present study, would be working on the
German side to make France ever more amenable to real adjustment
concessions. This objective interest of a growing proportion of
Europe's industrial leaders is in the last analysis the best guarantee
of success for European integration efforts.

Second Quarter 1971

The seemingly logical development of the Brussels arrangements
was violently shaken by the events of May 1971. The causes, course,
and effects of the May crisis, while highly characteristic of the

present state of international monetary relations in general, displayed a number of unique aspects which mark the period as a turning point in European monetary development.

The general causes of the crisis have formed the themes of the present work as a whole. These include the incompatibilities of national aims, the disparities in national economic strength, the limping operation of the market system as a whole, and the vast growth of internationally-oriented short-term funds. The specific causes of the crisis may be discussed in two general categories, viz., Germany's internationally high interest-rate structure in the preceding year, and the exhaustion of Germany's means of absorbing the resultant inflow of liquidity. The most immediate occasions of the crisis will be noted in a further discussion.

The Bundesbank's high-interest-rate policy of 1970 was described in Chapter 5. The Bank explained this policy as being needed in order to reduce the astonishingly high long-term capital exports of 1969 and to help damp the inflationary boom.[50] Whatever the merits of the first of these reasons, the second is questionable on two chief grounds, both discussed at length in the preceding chapters. The first problem lies in the dilemma of restrictive monetary policy for a non-reserve currency under fixed exchange rates and convertibility: either foreign or domestic sources of liquidity will be made available to the increasing numbers of sophisticated borrowers, and hence to the economy as a whole. Both sources cannot be excluded. The second problem lies in the ability of large and sophisticated firms, entrenched in their market power and in the national economic-policy framework and possessed of vast internal sources of funds, to continue to pay increasingly high interest rates and hence to expand capacity, in the prospects of passing the extra costs on to the consumer in the long run.*

---

*Bundesbank President Klasen's ideas on the role of interest rates in the regulation of the economy seem to take some account of the growing interest-rate-immunity of the dominant firms. Touching on this problem in 1971, he asserted that firms will be influenced by interest rates if interest charges become a large fraction of their costs (AP [1971], #35, p. 2). To rely on this (rather unlikely) possibility is certainly to admit that the market-system-conformed impact of interest rates on firms, viz., their significance as the opportunity cost to be met by the business' overall rate of return, has been made obsolete by market power, artificial "normal profit rates," internally generated funds, and the lack of effective stockholder power.

The problematical aspects of Germany's interest-rate structure were sharply accentuated through most of 1970 by the rapidly progressing reversal of monetary policy in the United States. Euromarket rates, responding to the dominant economy's relaxation, moved from double Germany's to something over half Germany's. The resulting massive repayments of United States borrowings on the Euromarket, and the growing dissatisfaction with the Bundesbank's stance on the part of the Economics Ministry and of foreign central banks, have already been described.

The efforts of the United States to slow the stream of repayments have also been noted. In view of its need for domestic reflation, the United States was unwilling to go beyond the imposition of special reserve requirements, the large scale offsetting Eurodollar borrowings by the Export-Import Bank, and the brief attempt in April 1971 to raise the New York Treasury Bill rate. As has been noted also, influential non-official authorities were indeed de-emphasizing ad hoc manipulation of the payments balance, under the slogan "benign neglect." In any case, the United States effort to cooperate with the Bundesbank's high-interest policy could not produce a noticeable effect on the torrent of funds pouring into Europe. By mid-1970 these funds included repayments, new borrowings by European international firms, and some considerable speculation.

Germany's attempt to ward off the vast influx of funds while maintaining high interest rates has been described in detail in earlier pages. In essence, the Bundesbank first sought to discourage bank imports of funds by (in April 1970) imposing special reserve requirements on the growth of banks' external liabilities. Increases in liabilities on repurchase operations had also to be discouraged by deducting the equivalent amounts from banks' rediscount quotas. As a result, non-banks, and in particular large and foreign-affiliated firms, took on the role of international borrowers.[51] As has been explained, the mid-year rise of all reserve requirements by fifteen percent was designed to offset this new wave of liquidity. By July the need for some concession on the interest-rate front could no longer be ignored, and a 0.5 percent reduction (to seven percent) was undertaken. Instead of further rediscount reductions, the Bundesbank in September 1970, introduced (for the first time since 1960) reserve requirements on the growth of banks' domestic liabilities. At a scale descending from forty percent (on sight deposits), the measure was intended to end the profitability of increases in banks' reserve-carrying liabilities.[52] Favorably situated banks were able to respond to this measure with shifts of liabilities into long-term deposits, with the issue of bank bonds, and with increased international repurchase agreements. The scale, complexity and growing inequity of the reserve-requirement structure were indications of the Bundesbank's extreme difficulty in handling the inflow of funds.[53] By December, the domestic marginal reserve requirements were abolished in favor of an across-the-board rise in the average requirements, simplifying the system without reducing its absorption of funds.

In the meantime, as described in Chapter 5, the rediscount rate was reduced, step by step, in November and December 1970, and in April 1971, from seven percent to five percent. By early 1971, thus, the monetary-policy dilemma had once again worked itself out fully. Rediscount rate had ceased to affect domestic liquidity, and reserve requirements were strained to the limit, while foreign funds continued to enter Germany.

Other methods of reabsorbing or rerouting the inflows also became increasingly difficult. In open market operations the Bundesbank had already sold all its authorized mobilization paper and was for the first time offering so-called liquidity paper. As explained previously, however, these instruments are both far too liquid in their legal form to prevent expansion of bank credit at the descretion of the banks themselves. The relevant international interest-rate differential was felt to be far too favorable to Germany for convincing attempts to engineer bank money exports through manipulating the forward-market discount. European central banks were also becoming convinced that shoveling dollars out of their respective domestic markets into the Eurodollar market resulted almost automatically in a reflux of the funds from the market. The Bundesbank and the United States Federal Reserve did engage in direct buying of three-month dollars on the forward market, but that action could obviously only be undertaken on an indicative scale, and did not convince the market of the central banks' intention to maintain the DM parity for at least a few months to come.

Finally, the Brandt government's anticyclical fiscal policy was able to contribute relatively little to the absorption of excess funds. This was partly because of the government's contradictory policy stances, which promised structural and social reforms without more taxes, and price stability without danger to employment. Minister Schiller and Minister Möller's attempts to obtain budget freezes encountered opposition from the other levels of government in federal Germany and near-revolt from some within the federal cabinet itself. The latter problem eventuated in the dramatic resignation of Finance Minister Möller in mid-May and in the consequent "fusion" of the Economics and Finance Ministries under Schiller. In truth, the Brandt government could hardly be expected to cripple itself politically in order to support the unwelcome high-interest-policy of the Bundesbank.

The net result of these circumstances was reflected in Germany's short-term capital inflows and in the growth of its monetary base. From January 1, 1970, through May 3, 1971, Germany received the equivalent of almost forty-six billion DM in net short-term inflows, (including unrecorded transactions), over two thirds of which constituted foreign borrowing by non-banks. All other payments-balance items together showed a five-billion-DM deficit in the same period. Of the forty-one-billion-DM net inflow, fiscal surpluses absorbed about fifteen billion DM, an almost sixty-percent rise in absolute reserve requirements absorbed another twelve billion DM, open-market operations absorbed a further two billion DM, and around eleven billion DM was added to Germany's monetary base. The two trading days of May prior to the closing of the exchange markets accounted for fully seven billion DM of this inflow. Bundesbank President Klasen's optimistic hope that Germany could "somehow" handle the stream of funds had in fact been proven too optimistic even before May.[54]

Faced with these developments, the German authorities weighed the application of controls on international capital movements, as foreseen in paragraph 23 of the International Economic Law, and clearly intended in paragraph 4 of the Stability Law, which requires the application of available international economic-policy measures when domestic stability is threatened by disturbances from abroad which cannot be controlled by domestic policy measures or by international cooperation. This solution was rejected because the necessary exchange controls could not be effective in time to offset the tremendous speculative influx their announcement would set off; because elaborate exchange-control systems have had notoriously poor records both of effectiveness and of efficiency; and because it was desired to avoid direct affronts to the United States, especially in light of the delicate Berlin negotiations. In addition, Germany did not wish to raise the standard of capital-account payments-balance controls just as its own long-term private net "direct" export of capital had finally begun to be positive, and especially in view of the logical necessity of large German capital exports within the planned EEC monetary union. Germany might also have felt some reluctance in principle to infringe on any free market, although similar controls are fairly common within the EEC and elsewhere.

In these circumstances, the German authorities began to seek international cooperation, especially within the EEC, in avoiding the impending monetary crisis. At the EEC Ministerial Council meeting of March 22 and again at the Hamburg conference of EEC finance ministers and central-bank presidents, Germany sought both to forge a common EEC front against the dollar and to reaffirm the continuing legality of any possible unilateral steps by Germany.[55]   Several governments, however, having little sympathy for Germany's self-defeating high-interest policy, were ill disposed to rally to its defense.

At the Hannover Fair on April 29, Minister Schiller by implication told Europe that the time for reforms was running out and that, if no cooperation was forthcoming, Germany must act alone.* As it happens, the annual report of the Joint Working Group of the German Economic Research Institutes was dated on the same 29 April, a Thursday, but was made public only on May 3, a Monday. This report first pointed to the need for increased foreign price competition to damp the German inflation, and then openly stated that the German authorities must choose between their legal duty under the Stability Law to fight inflation and their implicit obligation under the Brussels compromise to maintain fixed parities. As this report was digested over the succeeding twenty-four hours, numerous saver- and consumer-oriented groups added their public appeals for upvaluation. On the Monday and Tuesday involved, close to two billion dollars were purchased by the Bundesbank. On May 5, therefore, Minister Schiller ordered the exchange markets closed. Switzerland, Austria, Holland, Belgium, Portugal and Finland also halted trading in dollars.

By May 7, the EEC Executive Commission had proposed four common measures toward ending the crisis without revaluations. The suggested measures were: a) restriction of EEC-based firms from the Eurodollar market, b) a concerted end to central banks' recycling of hot money into the Eurodollar market, c) reexpansion of the EEC bands of fluctuation around parities to two percent, and d) a negative interest rate on foreign investment in the EEC.[56] Virtually every part of these proposals seemed totally unworkable even had sufficient time to install them been available--to say nothing of their implications for transatlantic relations, for the market system as such, and for the immediate speculative atmosphere.

At noon on May 8, a special meeting of the EEC Ministerial Council opened in Brussels with an appeal by Minister Schiller for a common floating of all EEC currencies vis-à-vis the dollar. France and Italy opposed this. Neither country could float its currency upward with the DM except at grave risk to its exports, particularly

---

*Prophetically enough, the General Director of the Mannesmann firm, speaking after Schiller, clearly intimated that no one should discuss parities, that to do so was to try to prove oneself right through self-fulfilling prophecies, and that no imaginative additions to the existing monetary policy tools were needed. The relevance of each of these hints rapidly became clear in the sequel.

since Italy was experiencing a full-fledged recession. In a longer
view, also, these countries were unwilling to tie the EEC directly to
the DM alone, since intra-EEC exchange-market intervention in DM
(to maintain the EEC parities) would put Germany in almost exactly
the United States' present position vis-à-vis France.[57] After an
almost uninterrupted twenty-one-hour period of strained debate, the
Council promulgated its agreement on May 9. On the one hand, the
situation was held not to justify parity changes; on the other, flexible
exchange rates were declared incompatible with the proper functioning
of the EEC. However, the Council consented to temporary widening
of the bands of fluctuation around parity, for certain member nations.
Minister Schiller had to remain content with this awkward and in fact
inappropriate formulation, which in large part simply echoed his own
statements of April 22, emphasizing the lack of need for up-valuation
or flexibility, in view of Germany's state of fundamental international
equilibrium.[58]

The same day, the German cabinet "approved" the Brussels
result, asked the Bundesbank to cease intervention in the exchange
market upon the latter's reopening, announced compensation to farmers
for the effects of the float on the EEC agricultural-support prices,
and decreed expenditure freezes for the federal government.[59] Thus
began a period of de facto floating of the DM, officially denominated
as indefinitely widened bands of fluctuation around an unchanged
parity. The IMF duly "noted" the hasty German report of the decisions.
And, still on May 9, Switzerland and Austria upvalued their currencies
by seven percent. Holland allowed the guilder to float alongside the
DM, and Belgium introduced a split-exchange-rate system. In the
meantime, the Bundesbank directorate had in effect disapproved of
the floating DM by a vote of eleven to seven. Relying on paragraph 4
of the Stability Law, however, the Bundesbank did in fact abstain from
intervention in the reopened exchange markets on and after May 10.
On May 13 further agreements to pay interest on foreign-owned
deposits in German banks were forbidden.*

Germany's crisis was not ended by the de facto floating of the
DM. For, to Minister Schiller, the float represented the best possible

---

*The Council of Experts rightly pointed out (AP [1971], #44, p. 6)
the meaninglessness of this measure either for exchange-rate formation or for German bank liquidity, as long as the Bundesbank did not
intervene in the exchange market. A free market will form a forward
rate corresponding to the international interest-rate differentials;
and domestic liquidity cannot be reduced by exchange transactions if
the central bank is not in the market.

substitute for a swift upvaluation designed to brake German inflation through reduced foreign demand; while, in Bundesbank President Klasen's eyes, the float was primarily introduced to ward off the speculative inflows that had paralyzed and overridden the monetary and fiscal brakes on domestic demand. This difference in conception was not merely semantic or merely technical. Ultimately, the two emphases rested on differing views as to the function of the world monetary system and as to the domestic sectors which should be asked to bear the stabilization burden. Paradoxically, Schiller had pushed through a float whose speed and dimensions he could not control, although these factors had been central to his strategy, while Klasen had come to control a float that he in fact had not wished to see introduced.

In the circumstances, President Klasen's natural reaction was to move very slowly in ridding the Bundesbank of its many superfluous dollars. Accordingly the Bundesbank remained completely aloof from the exchange market. Slowness in upvaluing the DM would permit the differing national inflationary trends to ease the position of Germany's export industries.* This stance thus remained very much in the spirit of dynamic undervaluation. In his public utterances, also, Klasen was specifically denying that currency flexibility was a proper tool of domestic stability policy.[60]

Thus, Schiller was in danger of losing both the benefits he had hoped for from his management of the currency crisis. Brussels had not been stampeded into tying the EEC to the DM, and Frankfurt (i.e., the Bundesbank) had not been stampeded into wringing out the foreign demand facing German industry through rapid upvaluation of the DM. During the week following the floating of the DM, tension between Bonn and Frankfurt grew to the extent that rumors of President Klasen's impending resignation had to be publicly denied.

On May 18, Economics and Finance Minister Schiller travelled to Frankfurt bearing Chancellor Brandt's "clear and unequivocal instructions."[61] After a five-hour meeting, Schiller and Klasen appeared to have reached some agreement, although no overt action was then taken by the Bundesbank. Not even the federal cabinet was informed of the newly agreed-upon strategy, which seemed to be one of keeping the market guessing as to the length of the float and the

---

*The sizable upvaluations of Switzerland and Austria, and the parallel floating of the Netherlands guilder, also helped ease the competitive position of Germany's exports, over a fifth of which are normally sold in these three countries.

scope of any eventual revaluation. In any case, the Bundesbank remained aloof from the exchange market for a further two weeks, entering the market to sell dollars only on June 2, as a large contingent of the earlier forward-market dollar purchases matured. The net exchange-rate effect of such simultaneous release and acceptance of dollars was practically nil. As June ended, the Bundesbank's ultimate intentions were still officially unclear, despite the market's conviction that an effective revaluation of about five percent would be achieved by July, followed perhaps by a further period of guided floating which might approximately offset the trend of international inflationary differentials. Dynamic undervaluation thus seemed likely to assume the pure and undisguised form of guided flexibility.

As of the beginning of July 1971, almost all the liquidity created by the spring's speculative inflow of funds remained bottled up within Germany, perforce awaiting the Bundesbank's expected eventual massive sales of dollars. Neither the interest-rate reasons nor the exchange-speculation reasons for the original influx had been ended by the float. Since the unsupported exchange market continued to offer forward dollars at a substantial discount, German-based firms could still obtain relatively cheap foreign loans.

Reactions within Germany to the floating of the DM were predictable. Industrial and banking circles deplored the move as an unnecessarily costly way to shut off speculation;[62] savers, consumers, and labor welcomed the decision as a ready way to reduce overall effective demand, discourage price rises, and so protect the 1970 recovery of labor's share of the national income.*[63]

Outside Germany, official reaction was almost unanimously negative, shading from complaints of irresponsibility, both in the pre-crisis period and in the crisis itself, to hints of deliberate official fostering of speculation.[64] The timing of events from May 3 to May 10 seemed to some suspicious, to others incredibly inept. Germany indeed seemed to have brought the crisis on itself, if not with the week-long drumfire of upvaluation talk from circles close to the Economics and Finance Ministry, then certainly with the year-long extravagantly high-interest policy of the Bundesbank.[65] French authorities in particular repeatedly stressed the uncommunal, even anti-communal, effects of the situation. This point was further

---

*The Council of Experts confirmed that the so-called "wage explosion" of 1970 was simply a reaction to the "profit explosion" of 1969, which itself was made possible by the marked moderation of labor after 1967 (AP [1971], #44, p. 10).

emphasized by France's refusal to participate further, either in the EEC's monetary committee or in its committee of central-bank heads, in discussions of monetary union.[66] French opinion was naturally especially perturbed by the variable relation of the DM to the EEC's "green dollar" accounting unit. Since this system is one of France's prime benefits under the EEC, its periodic shattering by currency crises centering on Germany has become a sore point. French spokesmen and the French-influenced EEC Commission continually reiterated their irreconcilability to the principle of Germany's floating currency. The move was held up as a decision (or a capitulation) in favor of the dollar (i.e., against capital-account exchange controls) and against Europe (i.e., against the scheduled narrowing of EEC fluctuation bands).[67] French sources stressed the negative psychological impact of the EEC's first instance of retreat from an agreed forward step.[68] Christian Democratic critics in the Bundestag went so far as to suggest that Schiller's moves had been calculated to necessitate a "foreign adventure" because of the government's domestic economic-policy helplessness.[69]

If Minister Schiller had indeed decided to precipitate an already impending crisis (not of his own making) in order to force Europe to face up to the dollar problem--perhaps even to hasten Europe into a German-centered monetary union--and also to aid his domestic stabilization program without drastic internal measures, the balance sheet of the weeks of crisis must have appeared strongly negative. Neither effect was realized, while reawakened suspicions and hostilities threatened the European union which constitutes Germany's life-and-death long-run goal. Defiance of allies and of the Bundesbank was unprecedented for a postwar German government; yet nationalist feelings could not be invoked to invest the move with any real popularity at home. Abroad Germany's increased political isolation boded ill for attempts to shape Europe along "economist" rather than "monetarist" lines.*

On the more technical level, opinion appeared to be rather divided on the direction in which Germany should move after July. The Council of Experts Special Evaluation of May 28, 1971 contained several suggestions for positive exploitation of the new situation. Among these suggestions were guided floating of the DM, and a predetermined three-percent crawling peg.[70] One-time upvaluation was

---

*Britain, too, hoped for advantages in its entry negotiations from the political and doctrinal disarray of the EEC (AP [1971], #46, p. 9; AP [1971], #37, p. 18). The strong United States reaction has already been noted.

not recommended, since a return to a parity means a return to the direct international price-transmission effect, and to morally certain undervaluation in the medium run.[71] On the other hand, a pre-announced supplementary three-percent interest advantage for German-based firms' foreign borrowing has numerous domestic and international financial-policy disadvantages.*

President Klasen of the Bundesbank, on the other hand, definitely leaned to more unilateral administrative controls in order to maintain pegged parities internationally, and to avoid the blatant challenge Germany's stance was offering to the entire Bretton Woods monetary system. The unspoken fear behind such a choice of means is almost certainly that the end of fixed exchange rates entails the end of dynamic undervaluation and of the advantage this has long given Germany's exports. As President Klasen significantly pointed out, there is no such thing as a fully free exchange market and competitive manipulation of rates by governments is therefore almost certain to arise if meaningful flexibility is permitted.[72] Such a development would in a sense end Germany's practical European monopoly of exchange-undervaluation tactics, and so expose Germany's economy on its most vulnerable flank, that of its very high dependence on exports.

Accordingly, Klasen's post-crisis utterances fairly bristled with dirigistic hints. Basically, he pictured Germany as in need of economic-policy instruments that can brake the economy without breaking it.[73] His immediate suggestion appeared to be direct portfolio controls on bank lending. Again, Klasen warned large and foreign-affiliated firms against taking up credit abroad in times of monetary restriction in Germany, for fear that they might find no German bank ready to finance them on subsequent occasions. Klasen was elaborately careful to point out that this warning was "not in the least intended as a threat."[74] In connection with wages policy, Klasen used the perhaps intentionally meaningful phrase "the present constitution of the labor market." It is known that Klasen acknowledges the inevitability of a formal incomes policy, apparently to be based on the crude productivity-wage guideline, which he at one point characterized as "a simple economic law."[75]

It is worthwhile to note that both Schiller's proposal of a common European float and the administrative controls favored by Klasen and

---

*Professor Köhler of the Council of Experts made known his minority view that the former DM parity should be at once actively resumed with a view to rapid consummation of European monetary union. (AP [1971], #44, p. 9n.).

the EEC Commission betray the strong European desire to be free of the dollar incubus. In the hour of truth, unfortunately, the persistence of narrow national interests produced paradox and irony for European integrationists. Paradoxically, France could not face union with the DM without the latter's tie to the dollar. Paradoxically, Germany recoiled from union with the franc before the achievement of agree stabilization policies even while Europe's disarray was exposing both countries to an international inflationary infection. Ironically, France claims monetary union is needed to face the dollar successfully and thus control inflation, while Germany claims a harmonized end to inflation is needed for successful monetary union. And both are right.

The events of May and June 1971 seem both theoretically and politically opposed to European integration. These events, in the light of the major themes of the present work, illustrate the difficulty of reconciling, either by market "mechanisms" or by political negotiation, the fully matured industrial interests within individual capitalistic nations. It now seems that Europe needs to look hard and directly at this problem before any real progress toward integration can take place.[76] Such an examination has thus far not been attempted on the political level because of its very real ideological dangers.

In a more general view, as long as there are disproportionately powerful interests within nations and disproportionately powerful nations in the world, it is hard to see how any merely financial system can be truly binding.[77] Units in the system with great market power tend to break the system rather than be disciplined by it.[78] The world's social and political constitution must be improved before the financial system can really do the job it has (at least theoretically) been called upon to do.[79] The latter can be a complement to and a refinement upon the former, but cannot be a substitute for it.

Seen from the nation-state level, the monetary integration of the powerful European economies, with a corresponding dilution of powerful European interest groups, could in this sense contribute to greater balance in the world constitution. Seen from the social-interest-group level, integration could lend some stability to a deeply-roded economic system by tipping the balance of social power further toward the scale of property. This could set the stage for a rather lengthy period of "prosperity" without deep crises, either economic or political. It remains questionable, however, whether European integration can be accomplished fast enough or thoroughly enough to reverse the trend toward United States dominance. In the longer run, in any case, it hardly admits of doubt that the world system will again throw up virtually the same problems of rational scale, international payments, and domestic income distribution.

As a final word, it may perhaps be necessary here to emphasize that nothing in the present study should be--or, in the author's opinion, can be--construed as an adverse criticism of Germany's official policy, or of any interest group within Germany. On the contrary, it would be most difficult to indicate an alternative international financial strategy that could, under the existing social and political conditions, with any reasonableness be expected of Germany. By proceeding explicitly from the most basic underlying factors, indeed, the present study warrants the conclusion that Germany's recent international economic policy problems are simply acute and highly publicized examples of the general ills of our system in its present stage. Germany's case is, of course, particularly significant because of the nation's world-trading position; and particularly well articulated because of its unusually sophisticated and differentiated interest groups.

All the evidence of this study goes to show, moreover, how fully aware many contemporary German policy-makers are of the true nature of these problems, while none of this evidence indicates the slightest subjective ill will among the human actors involved. If the present study has therefore tended to highlight systematic and system-conditioned links of causality, this was simply in the hope of affording the existing good will some further slight leverage on reality.

NOTES

1. Süddeutsche Zeitung (6 June 1970), p. 4; German Tribune (16 July 1970), p. 4.

2. R. Alleman, Der Monat (Apr 1970), p. 20.

3. Federal Republic of Germany, Bundesbank, Auszüge aus Presseartikeln (1970), #85, p. 5.

4. AP (1970), #82, p. 1.

5. C. Gasteyger, W. Kewenig, and N. Kohlhase, "Europe and the Shape of Things to Come," Europa-Archiv (1970), p. 15-16.

6. Federal Republic of Germany, Bundesministerium für Wirtschaft, Wissenschaftliche Beirat, Gutachten (December 1952-November 1954) (Göttingen, 1955), p. 41.

7. The United States with its giant market is better able to exploit the "third industrial revolution" of automation and thereby to further extend its market. The vicious cycle of relatively small

markets, slow technological progress, and relatively shrinking markets has been called the "real crux of automation" for Europe. (W. Bittorf, Automation, Die Zweite Industrielle Revolution [Darmstadt, 1956], p. 159, 256-257). This has been specially damaging in the key future-oriented fields of aerospace and data processing. Also see Federal Republic of Germany, Sachverständigenrat zur Begutachtung der Gesamtwirtschaftlichen Entwicklung, Jahresgutachten (1970), Section 313.

8. AP (1970), #70, p. 39.

9. AP (1970), #43, p. 13; L. Krause, A Passive Balance-of-Payments Strategy for the United States (Brookings Papers on Economic Activity) (Washington, 1971); G. Haberler and T. D. Willett, a study prepared for the American Enterprise Association, Washington, 1971.

10. AP (1970), #37, p. 14; European Economic Community, Bulletin (Mar 1965), p. 637.

11. AP (1970), #75, p. 4; Emminger, AP (1970), #84, p. 3; President Abs of the Bank Association, AP (1970), #90, p. 5.

12. President Abs of the Bank Association, AP (1970), #90, p. 3; Minister Schiller, AP (1970), #36, p. 13; Arndt of Economics Ministry, AP (1970), #35, p. 2.

13. President Schmitz of the Austrian National Bank, AP (1971), #12, p. 11; Minister Schiller, AP (1970), #87, p. 5; President Pfleiderer of the Baden-Württemburg Central Bank, AP (1971), #12, p. 6.

14. Economics Ministry spokesman, AP (1970), #79, p. 5.

15. Chancellor Brandt, AP (1970), #82, p. 1.

16. AP (1970), #78, p. 9; J. Stohler, Wirtschaftliche Integration (Tübingen, 1958), p. 3.

17. AP (1971), #18, p. 14.

18. Agriculture Minister Ertl, German Tribune (11 June 1970), p. 10.

19. Bundesbank Vice President Emminger, AP (1970), #85, p. 5.

20. K. Birrenbach in P. Uri, Dialog der Kontinente (Berlin, 1964), p. 49.

21. Minister Schiller, AP (1970), #78, p. 8; German Tribune (11 June 1970), p. 10.

22. Bundesbank Vice President Emminger, AP (1970), #73, p. 13.

23. AP (1970), #79, p. 5; AP (1970), #41, p. 6; Former Belgian National Bank Governor, AP (1971), #20, p. 10; AP (1970), #85, p. 10; Spokesman of the Chancellor's Office, German Tribune (16 July 1970), p. 5. Also see JG (1970), Sections 234-237.

24. Minister Schiller, AP (1970), #78, p. 8.

25. AP (1970), #43, p. 11.

26. AP (1970), #80, p. 3.

27. French Finance Minister Giscard D'Estaing, AP (1970), #79, p. 4; AP (1970), #43, p. 15.

28. AP (1970), #80, p. 5.

29. Dutch Foreign Minister, German Tribune (18 June 1970), p. 2.

30. UK Europe Minister Home, AP (1970), #93, p. 15.

31. Minister Schiller, AP (1970), #37, p. 13; General Director of Swiss National Bank, AP (1970), #78, p. 5.

32. Minister Schiller, AP (1970), #78, p. 8; Federal Republic of Germany, Bundesbank, Annual Report (1969), p. 44; AP (1970), #85, p. 2.

33. AR (1969), p. 44.

34. Bundesbank Director Gleske, AP (1970), #43, p. 9; Aktions-gemeinschaft Soziale Marktwirtschaft, AP (1970), #80, p. 6; President of the Swiss Bankverein, AP (1970), #80, p. 5; Bundesbank Vice President, AP (1970), #29, p. 7.

35. Minister Schiller, AP (1970), #93, p. 12.

36. Werner Report, AP (1970), #88, p. 8.

37. Chancellor Brandt, AP (1970), #82, p. 1; AP (1970), #94, p. 15.

38. Bundesbank Vice President Emminger, AP (1970), #29, p. 6.

39. AR (1969), p. 44; Bundesbank Vice President Emminger, AP (1970), #29, p. 5; Minister Schiller, AP (1970), #86, p. 3 f. (six times).

40. Minister Schiller, AP (1970), #86, p. 3; Bundesbank President Klasen and Vice President Emminger, AP (1970), #93, p. 7.

41. AP (1970), #90, p. 4.

42. Die Welt, AP (1970), #82, p. 6 ff.

43. See the remarks of President Pfleiderer of the Baden-Württemburg Central Bank, AP (1971), #12, p. 7.

44. Bundesbank Vice President Emminger, AP (1970), #29, p. 4.

45. SPD spokesman in Bundestag, AP (1970), #74, p. 3.

46. AP (1970), #90, p. 4.

47. Bank Association, AP (1970), #75, p. 5.

48. EEC Council Release, AP (1971), #13, p. 1 ff.

49. AP (1971), #16, p. 5; Federal Republic of Germany, Bundesbank, Annual Report (1970), p. 41 f.

50. AR (1970), p. 62.

51. AR (1970), p. 14.

52. AR (1970), p. 46; AP (1971), #27, p. 6.

53. AR (1970), p. 47.

54. AP (1971), #26, p. 7.

55. AP (1971), #35, p. 12.

56. AP (1971), #46, p. 4.

57. AP (1971), #44, p. 14.

58. AP (1971), #39, p. 5.

59. AP (1971), #37, p. 1.

60. AP (1971), #42, p. 9.

61. AP (1971), #40, p. 6.

62. Hermann Abs, AP (1971), #39, p. 5; Die Welt, AP (1971), #35, p. 11.

63. AP (1971), #37, p. 9 f.

64. Neue Zücher Zeitung and Le Figaro, AP (1971), #37, p. 15; Le Monde, AP (1971), #35, p. 15.

65. Washington Post, 30 May 1971, p. Gl; AP (1971), #39, p. 2.

66. French Finance Minister Giscard-d'Estaing in cabinet, AP (1971), #38, p. 12.

67. AP (1971), #35, p. 15.

68. Le Monde, AP (1971), #37, p. 19; AP (1971), #46, p. 9.

69. AP (1971), #39, p. 2.

70. AP (1971), #44, p. 3 and 9.

71. AP (1971), #44, p. 4 and 6.

72. AP (1971), #43, p. 3.

73. AP (1971), #38, p. 5.

74. AP (1971), #43, p. 3.

75. AP (1971), #43, p. 2.

76. Treasury Secretary John Connolly, AP (1971), #41, p. 1. Also see notes 1, 2 and 3 to Chapter 2.

77. J. Vanek, "The Keynes-Triffin Plan: A Critical Appraisal," Review of Economics and Statistics (August 1961). In the words of Secretary Connolly (see note 76 above), it would be "unrealistic to anticipate workable monetary solutions for essentially non-monetary problems."

78. G. Haberler, Money in the International Economy (Cambridge, 1965), p. 11; R. Triffin, The World Money Maze (New Haven, 1966), p. 382.

79. Schiller, AP (1968), #84, p. 7; M. Friedman, <u>Dollars and Deficits</u> (Englewood Cliffs, 1969), p. 278.

TABLE 2

Recent German Balance-of-Payments Experience

(Nearest 100 Million DM)	61			62				63				64			
	II	III	IV	I	II	III	IV	I	II	III	IV	I	II	III	IV
A1 GOODS RECEIPTS NET	17	17	13	6	9	10	10	8	12	12	28	24	20	7	10
A11 Exports Total	.	.	.	.	.	.	.	.	.	.	.	.	.	.	.
A1111 Producers' Goods	.	.	.	.	.	.	.	.	.	.	.	.	.	.	.
A1112 Consumption Goods	.	.	.	.	.	.	.	.	.	.	.	.	.	.	.
A1113 Foodstuffs	.	.	.	.	.	.	.	.	.	.	.	.	.	.	.
A1114 Extractive Goods	.	.	.	.	.	.	.	.	.	.	.	.	.	.	.
A1115 Other	.	.	.	.	.	.	.	.	.	.	.	.	.	.	.
A1121 To Industrial Lands	.	.	.	.	.	.	.	.	.	.	.	.	.	.	.
A1122 To Socialist Lands	.	.	.	.	.	.	.	.	.	.	.	.	.	.	.
A1123 To Developing Lands	.	.	.	.	.	.	.	.	.	.	.	.	.	.	.
A12 Imports Total	.	.	.	.	.	.	.	.	.	.	.	.	.	.	.
A1211 End Products	.	.	.	.	.	.	.	.	.	.	.	.	.	.	.
A1212 Foodstuffs	.	.	.	.	.	.	.	.	.	.	.	.	.	.	.
A1213 Extractive Goods	.	.	.	.	.	.	.	.	.	.	.	.	.	.	.
A1214 Other	.	.	.	.	.	.	.	.	.	.	.	.	.	.	.
A1221 From Industrial Lands	.	.	.	.	.	.	.	.	.	.	.	.	.	.	.
A1222 From Socialist Lands	.	.	.	.	.	.	.	.	.	.	.	.	.	.	.
A1223 From Developing Lands	.	.	.	.	.	.	.	.	.	.	.	.	.	.	.
A2 NATO TROOP RECEIPTS	10	9	10	10	10	10	12	11	11	10	11	10	10	10	12
A3 SERVICES & TRANSFERS RECEIPTS NET	-9	-14	-13	-11	-14	-20	-18	-12	-16	-21	-9	-13	-12	-19	-16
A31 Transport & Insurance Receipts Net	7	7	7	6	6	6	6	6	6	6	6	7	7	7	7
A311 Gross Receipts	.	12	12	12	12	12	12	12	12	12	12	13	14	15	15
A312 Gross Outpayments	.	5	5	6	6	6	6	6	6	6	6	7	7	8	8
A32 Travel Receipts Net	-4	-8	-2	-3	-5	-12	-4	-3	-6	-11	-4	-3	-6	-11	-2
A321 Gross Receipts	.	7	5	4	6	7	5	4	6	9	5	5	7	9	6
A322 Gross Outpayments	.	15	7	6	11	19	9	7	12	19	9	8	12	20	9
A32a West-Mid-North Europe Net	.	.	.	.	.	.	.	.	.	.	-2	-3	-5	-11	-3
A32b Greece-Yugo-Turkey Net	.	.	.	.	.	.	.	.	.	.	.	-	-	-1	-1
A32c Iberia Net	.	.	.	.	.	.	.	.	.	.	.	-	-1	-1	-
A32d USA-Canada Net	.	.	.	.	.	.	.	.	.	.	1	1	1	2	1
A33 Government Services Receipts Net	-1	-1	-1	-1	-1	-2	-2	-2	-1	-1	-1	-2	-1	-1	-2
A34 Other Services Receipts Net	-8	-8	-11	-9	-10	-8	-11	-8	-10	-11	-6	-9	-8	-9	-10
A3411 Trade-Promotion Inflow	.	.	-	.	.	.	-	.	.	.	1	.	.	.	1
A3412 Trade-Promotion Outflow	.	.	2	.	.	.	2	.	.	.	3	.	.	.	3

65				66				67				68				69				70				71	
I	II	III	IV	I	II	III	IV	I	II	III	IV	I	II	III	IV	I	II	III	IV	I	II	III	IV	I	
11	-	-5	6	8	14	23	35	43	44	38	43	43	34	42	64	28	39	40	49	29	33	43	51	37	A1
.	174	173	196	190	196	199	222	208	219	207	237	233	228	247	287	256	285	285	309	287	311	309	346	331	A11
.	.	.	.	155	162	164	183	172	182	169	195	191	188	200	234	208	234	232	253	234	255	250	284	270	A1111
.	.	.	.	20	19	21	22	21	21	22	24	24	24	28	32	29	31	33	34	31	32	33	36	35	A1112
.	.	.	.	4	4	4	4	4	5	5	6	5	6	6	7	6	7	7	7	7	7	8	8	9	A1113
.	.	.	.	8	8	8	9	8	7	8	9	9	8	9	10	9	9	9	10	11	11	12	12	12	A1114
.	.	.	.	3	4	3	4	3	4	3	4	4	3	4	4	4	4	4	5	5	6	5	6	5	A1115
.	135	131	150	146	151	152	169	157	167	157	185	180	178	191	224	199	225	222	242	225	246	240	272	261	A1121
.	6	7	8	6	8	9	10	10	11	11	11	11	10	11	14	12	13	14	13	13	14	13	14	14	A1122
.	31	34	38	37	36	38	42	39	40	39	42	42	40	45	49	45	48	50	52	49	52	54	59	56	A1123
.	174	177	190	181	182	176	187	164	175	169	194	190	194	205	223	228	246	246	260	258	278	266	295	295	A12
.	.	.	.	79	81	75	83	71	77	70	81	82	85	92	98	106	114	115	127	128	140	131	150	157	A1211
.	.	.	.	44	43	42	46	39	42	40	45	39	41	42	48	45	52	47	49	48	51	50	60	54	A1212
.	.	.	.	57	57	57	56	52	53	57	65	66	65	68	73	74	77	80	80	79	84	81	81	80	A1213
.	.	.	.	2	2	2	2	2	2	2	3	2	3	3	3	2	3	3	4	3	4	4	4	3	A1214
.	130	131	141	132	135	129	136	119	130	123	132	137	143	153	165	169	188	185	196	196	215	204	227	226	A1221
.	6	8	9	7	7	8	9	7	7	8	9	8	7	9	10	9	9	10	12	10	10	11	13	10	A1222
.	38	38	40	42	40	39	42	39	37	39	41	45	43	43	48	50	49	50	51	51	53	50	55	58	A1223
9	10	11	12	11	12	14	13	12	13	13	14	13	13	13	13	12	14	15	14	13	15	15	15	15	A2
-12	-21	-24	-16	-20	-20	-24	-16	-14	-15	-24	-10	-10	-15	-22	-10	-16	-15	-25	-17	-22	-21	-33	-25	-23	A3
8	8	8	9	8	9	9	9	8	9	9	10	9	9	10	10	10	10	11	11	11	12	12	13	.	A31
15	15	16	17	16	17	18	18	17	18	20	21	19	20	22	22	20	21	23	22	22	23	24	26	.	A311
7	7	8	8	8	8	9	9	9	9	11	11	9	10	12	12	11	11	13	12	12	12	13	13	.	A312
-3	-6	-14	-4	-4	-7	-16	-4	-5	-6	-14	-2	-5	-7	-15	-3	-6	-9	-18	-6	-10	-12	-24	-12	.	A32
5	8	10	7	5	8	11	7	6	8	11	8	5	8	11	7	6	9	13	8	6	9	13	8	.	A321
8	13	24	11	9	15	27	12	11	15	25	10	10	16	27	10	12	18	31	14	16	22	38	20	.	A322
-3	-6	-13	-4	-4	-7	-14	-4	-4	-5	-13	-3	-4	-6	-13	-2	-5	-6	-15	-5	-7	-9	-19	.	.	A32a
-	-1	-1	-1	-	-1	-2	-1	-1	-1	-1	-1	-1	-1	-1	-1	-1	-1	-2	-1	-2	-2	-3	.	.	A32b
-	-1	-1	-	-	-1	-1	-	-	-1	-2	-1	-	-1	-2	-	-	-1	-2	-1	-1	-1	-3	.	.	A32c
1	1	2	1	1	1	2	1	1	2	2	2	1	2	3	-	-	-	1	1	-	1	2	.	.	A32d
-2	-1	-2	-3	-2	-2	-2	-2	-2	-2	-	-2	-1	-2	-1	-2	-2	-1	-2	-2	-1	-2	-2	-3	.	A33
-10	-10	-9	-10	-13	-9	-6	-6	-8	-8	-9	-9	-9	-8	-9	-10	-11	-11	-11	-12	-13	-10	-11	-14	.	A34
.	.	.	1	.	.	.	1	.	.	.	1	.	.	.	1	.	.	.	1	.	.	.	1	.	A3411
.	.	.	4	.	.	.	4	.	.	.	5	.	.	.	5	.	.	.	6	.	.	.	6	.	A3412

(Continued)

(Nearest 100 Million DM)	61			62				63				64			
	II	III	IV	I	II	III	IV	I	II	III	IV	I	II	III	IV
A35 Payments for Labor Net	.	.	.	.	.	.	.	.	.	.	.	.	.	.	.
A36 Private Transfers Receipts Net	-1	-1	-1	-2	-1	-2	-1	-2	-1	-2	-2	-2	-2	-3	-3
A37 Capital Earnings Net	-3	-3	-5	-2	-3	-2	-6	-3	-4	-2	-2	-4	-2	-2	-6
A371 Gross Receipts	.	3	2	2	2	3	2	2	2	3	2	3	4	3	3
A3711 On Equities	.	-	-	-	-	-	-	-	-	-	-	-	-	-	-
A3712 On Fixed-Rate Securities	.	-	-	-	-	-	-	-	-	-	-	-	-	-	-
A3713 On Financial Credits	.	2	1	1	2	2	2	2	2	2	2	2	3	2	2
A3714 On Direct Investments	.	-	-	-	-	-	-	-	-	-	-	-	-	-	-
A372 Gross Outpayments	.	6	7	4	5	5	8	5	6	5	4	7	6	5	9
A3721 On Equities	.	.	.	.	.	.	.	.	.	.	.	.	.	.	.
A3722 On Fixed-Rate Securities	.	.	.	.	.	.	.	.	.	.	.	.	.	.	.
A3723 On Financial Credits	.	.	.	.	.	.	.	.	.	.	.	.	.	.	.
A3724 On Direct Investments	.	.	.	.	.	.	.	.	.	.	.	.	.	.	.
A4 ALIENS' REMITTANCES (shown as -)	-1	-2	-2	-1	-2	-2	-1	-2	-3	-3	-3	-3	-3	-3	-3
AA AUTONOMOUS CAPITAL RECEIPTS NET	16	-3	1	-4	-2	10	5	8	14	10	9	-	-4	2	16
A5 PRIVATE LONG-TERM CAPITAL INFLOW NET	1	-1	-	4	-	2	3	7	9	9	5	5	-8	1	5
A51 Gross Inflow	.	.	.	.	.	.	.	.	.	.	.	.	.	.	.
A5111 Portfolio	.	.	.	.	.	.	.	.	.	.	.	.	.	.	.
A5112 Financial Credits	.	.	.	.	.	.	.	.	.	.	.	.	.	.	.
A5113 Direct Investments	.	.	.	.	.	.	.	.	.	.	.	.	.	.	.
A5114 Other	.	.	.	.	.	.	.	.	.	.	.	.	.	.	.
A512 From Developing Lands	.	.	.	.	.	.	.	.	.	.	.	.	.	.	.
A52 Gross Outflow	.	.	.	.	.	.	.	.	.	.	.	.	.	.	.
A5211 Portfolio	.	.	.	.	.	.	.	.	.	.	.	.	.	.	.
A5212 Financial Credits	.	.	.	.	.	.	.	.	.	.	.	.	.	.	.
A5213 Direct Investments	.	.	.	.	.	.	.	.	.	.	.	.	.	.	.
A5214 Other	.	.	.	.	.	.	.	.	.	.	.	.	.	.	.
A522 To Developing Lands	.	.	.	.	.	.	.	.	.	.	.	.	.	.	.
A6 PRIVATE SHORT-TERM CAPITAL INFLOW NET	15	-2	1	-8	-2	8	2	1	5	1	4	-5	4	1	11
A61 Gross Inflow	.	.	.	.	.	.	.	.	.	.	.	.	.	.	.
A611 To Firms	.	.	.	.	.	.	.	.	.	.	.	.	.	.	.
A612 To Banks	.	.	.	.	.	.	.	.	.	.	.	.	.	.	.
A62 Gross Outflow	.	.	.	.	.	.	.	.	.	.	.	.	.	.	.
A621 From Firms	.	.	.	.	.	.	.	.	.	.	.	.	.	.	.
A622 From Banks (without line B1)	.	.	.	.	.	.	.	.	.	.	.	.	.	.	.
A7 RESIDUAL RECEIPTS NET	11	-6	-6	13	5	-1	-6	3	3	-2	-14	10	4	8	-3
A. AUTONOMOUS (BASIC) PAYMENTS BALANCE	44	1	6	16	11	9	2	17	23	15	22	28	15	6	16

APPENDIX/TABLE 2

65				66				67				68				69				70				71	
I	II	III	IV	I	II	III	IV	I	II	III	IV	I	II	III	IV	I	II	III	IV	I	II	III	IV	I	
.	.	.	.	-2	-3	-2	-3	-2	-2	-2	-2	-1	-1	-1	-2	-1	-1	-2	-2	-1	-2	-2	-2	.	A35
-3	-3	-4	-3	-4	-3	-4	-4	-2	-2	-2	-1	-2	-3	-3	-2	-3	-2	-3	-3	-2	-4	-3	-2	.	A36
-2	-9	-3	-5	-3	-5	-3	-6	-3	-4	-6	-4	-1	-3	-3	-1	-2	-1	1	-2	-5	-2	-2	-1	.	A37
3	3	3	4	3	3	4	5	4	5	4	8	5	6	6	10	6	9	11	11	7	15	11	17	.	A371
-	-	-	-	-	-	-	-	-	-	-	-	1	-	-	-	1	-	-	-	1	-	-	-	.	A3711
-	-	-	-	-	-	-	-	-	-	-	-	-	-	-	1	1	1	1	2	2	2	2	2	.	A3712
2	2	2	3	2	2	2	3	2	3	2	4	3	4	3	5	4	4	5	7	3	9	3	10	.	A3713
-	-	-	-	-	-	-	-	-	-	-	2	-	-	-	1	-	-	-	-	-	-	-	2	.	A3714
5	12	6	9	6	8	7	11	7	9	11	12	6	9	9	11	8	10	10	12	12	16	14	19	.	A372
.	.	1	3	1	3	2	1	1	3	3	1	1	2	4	1	1	4	3	2	1	4	6	2	.	A3721
.	.	1	1	1	1	1	1	1	1	1	1	1	1	1	1	1	1	1	1	1	1	1	1	.	A3722
.	.	2	2	2	2	2	2	2	3	2	3	3	3	2	3	3	3	3	4	3	7	4	9	.	A3723
.	.	2	2	2	2	2	6	2	2	4	7	2	3	2	6	3	2	2	6	7	3	3	7	.	A3724
-3	-4	-4	-5	-4	-5	-5	-5	-5	-5	-6	-6	-5	-5	-6	-6	-6	-7	-9	-8	-10	-10	-13	-13	-14	A4
-7	5	14	19	-2	11	14	8	-9	-9	-6	-15	-16	-25	-9	41	-82	8	22	-90	-11	16	63	52	16	AA
5	6	5	6	6	5	6	2	-2	-5	-4	-5	-16	-25	-37	-23	-56	-41	-28	-85	-37	-2	10	9	4	A5
.	.	8	11	11	14	9	6	6	1	6	4	2	2	4	8	2	3	14	-11	-1	8	23	29	18	A51
.	.	2	4	1	7	-	-	-1	-2	-1	-2	-1	-1	2	-	-	-1	-1	-9	2	1	3	8	5	A5111
.	.	4	5	9	5	5	2	-	-1	-2	-2	-	-1	-1	5	1	4	6	-4	-1	6	15	15	9	A5112
.	.	3	3	2	2	3	4	7	5	9	7	5	4	3	2	1	10	3	-2	1	5	7	4		A5113
.	.	-	-	-	-1	-	-	-	-	-	-	-1	-	-	-	-	-	-	-	-	-	-	-	-	A5114
.	.	-	-	1	-	-	-	1	-	-	-	-	2	1	1	1	1	-1	2	-3	-1	-1	3	.	A512
.	.	3	5	6	9	4	5	7	7	10	9	18	27	41	32	58	44	42	74	35	10	13	21	15	A52
.	.	-	3	4	7	1	2	3	2	5	4	6	17	19	14	33	16	19	25	8	2	5	5	4	A5211
.	.	1	1	1	1	1	1	2	3	-	2	7	7	19	11	20	23	16	41	19	3	1	7	-	A5212
.	.	1	2	1	1	1	1	3	1	4	2	4	3	3	6	4	4	6	7	7	5	6	7	9	A5213
.	.	1	1	-	1	1	-	-	-	-	1	-	1	1	1	1	1	1	1	1	1	1	2	1	A5214
.	.	1	2	3	5	2	3	4	5	4	7	6	5	10	11	6	8	8	15	5	2	2	.	.	A522
-12	-1	9	13	-8	6	8	6	-7	-4	-2	-10	-	-	28	64	-26	53	50	-5	26	18	53	43	12	A6
.	.	7	14	-6	5	8	-3	-1	1	-	2	1	4	28	33	-23	56	56	-11	24	21	56	47	5	A61
.	.	4	3	5	4	7	1	10	-3	-4	-13	2	-3	4	3	7	22	31	-51	8	22	28	12	26	A611
.	.	3	11	-11	1	1	-4	-11	4	4	15	-1	7	24	30	-30	35	25	40	16	-1	28	35	-21	A612
.	.	-2	1	2	-1	-	-9	6	5	2	12	-	5	-1	-32	4	2	6	-6	-	3	1	4	-7	A62
.	.	-	-1	-	-	1	1	4	-	-	1	1	-1	-1	2	2	1	4	4	1	3	-1	4	-5	A621
.	.	-2	2	2	-1	-1	-10	2	5	2	11	-1	6	-	-34	2	-	2	-10	-1	-	2	-	-2	A622
13	14	6	-7	8	5	1	-7	10	-6	4	-8	16	10	14	-6	19	73	28	-96	23	32	36	9	83	A7
11	4	-1	12	3	17	22	28	37	22	18	18	41	12	31	96	-45	116	71	-149	25	64	110	90	114	A

(Continued)

		61			62				63				64				
	(Nearest 100 Million DM)	II	III	IV	I	II	III	IV	I	II	III	IV	I	II	III	IV
B1	BANKS' MONEY EXPORTS	16	-2	-18	22	-11	-6	-7	9	4	1	-11	11	-1	-1	-3
B2	OFFICIAL TRANSFERS OUTFLOW NET	9	9	10	10	10	7	11	10	9	8	7	7	10	7	6
B21	Gross Receipts	-	-	-	-	-	-	-	-	-	-	-	-	-	-	-
B22	Gross Outpayments	9	9	10	10	10	7	11	10	9	8	7	7	10	7	6
B221	Reparations under Treaties	3	2	2	2	2	-	-	2	2	1	-	1	3	1	-
B222	Individual Reparations	4	6	5	6	6	5	6	5	5	5	5	4	4	4	4
B223	To EEC Funds	-	-	2	-	-	-	3	-	-	-	-	-	-	-	-
B224	To Other International Orgns	1	-	-	-	1	-	-	1	1	1	-	1	1	1	-
B225	Other	1	1	1	1	1	1	1	1	1	1	1	1	1	1	1
B3	OFF'L LONG-TERM CAPITAL OUTFLOW NET	35	3	4	3	3	3	3	2	3	2	5	3	2	3	5
B31	Gross Receipts	-	-	-	-	-	-	-	-	-	-	-	-	-	-	-
B32	Gross Outpayments	35	3	4	3	3	3	3	2	3	2	5	3	2	3	5
B321	Development Aid	2	2	2	3	2	2	2	2	2	2	5	2	2	2	5
B322	London Debt Repayments	31	-	1	-	1	-	-	-	1	-	-	-	1	-	-
B323	To International Orgns	2	1	1	-	-	-	-	-	-	-	-	-	-	-	-
B4	OFF'L SHORT-TERM CAPITAL OUTFLOW NET	-1	-1	-	1	-2	-	-2	-3	-3	-5	12	3	-	-1	5
B41	Gross Receipts	-	1	-	-	-	-	2	-	-	-	-1	-	-	-	-1
B42	Gross Outpayments	-1	-	-	1	-2	-	-	-3	-3	-5	11	3	-	-1	4
B421	Arms-Purchase Prepayments	-1	-	-	-1	-2	-	-	-3	-3	-5	11	3	-	-1	4
B.	TOTAL PAYMENTS-BALANCE CORRECTION	59	8	-4	40	-	4	4	18	13	6	13	24	11	10	13
C1	LIQUID CENTRAL RESERVES RISE	-9	-17	4	-18	6	10	-1	-	10	7	9	1	2	-4	3
C11	Gold	11	5	1	-	-	-	-	3	-	-	3	4	5	3	4
C12	Non-Dollar Convertible Currencies	-20	-22	3	-18	6	10	-1	-5	7	4	3	-1	8	6	5
C13	U.S. Dollars	.	.	.	.	.	.	.	.	.	.	.	-6	-15	-17	-17
C14	Liquid U.S. Treasury DM Securities	-	-	-	-	-	-	-	2	3	3	3	4	4	4	4
C15	Genl-Arrangements-to-Borrow Position	-	-	-	-	-	-	-	-	-	-	-	-	-	-	7
C16	Special Drawing Rights	-	-	-	-	-	-	-	-	-	-	-	-	-	-	-
C2	LESS-LIQUID CENTRAL RESERVES RISE	-	-7	-	-	-	-1	-	-	-	-	-	-	-	-1	-
C21	Medium-Term US & UK Treasury Notes	-	-	-	-	-	-	-	-	-	-	-	-	-	-	-
C22	Short-Term IBRD Debt Certificates	-	-	-	-	-	-	-	-	-	-	-	-	-	-	-
C23	Earmarked Balances and Bills	-	-	-	-	-	-	-	-	-	-	-	-	-	-	-
C24	EPU Debt	-	-7	-	-	-	-1	-	-	-	-	-	-	-	-1	-
C3	IMF CREDIT POSITION RISE	4	11	-3	-3	1	-2	-1	-	-	1	-	4	2	-	1

65				66				67				68				69				70				71	
I	II	III	IV	I	II	III	IV	I	II	III	IV	I	II	III	IV	I	II	III	IV	I	II	III	IV	I	
7	-1	-5	2	1	2	5	-9	20	13	7	-	16	-12	14	47	16	31	-19	5	2	-13	13	-4	26	B1
8	12	7	7	9	8	5	7	9	9	6	9	10	9	7	15	7	9	10	16	8	8	8	12	10	B2
-	-	-	-	1	1	-	1	1	1	1	1	4	1	5	2	3	1	7	5	2	1	2	15	7	B21
8	12	7	7	9	8	5	7	9	10	7	10	14	10	12	17	10	10	17	22	10	9	10	27	16	B22
-	3	-	1	-	-	-	-	-	-	-	-	-	-	-	-	-	-	-	-	-	-	-	-	-	B221
5	5	4	4	5	4	4	5	5	5	4	3	5	5	4	4	4	4	4	3	4	3	3	5	5	B222
-	-	-	-	-	-	-	-	1	1	-	2	4	1	5	9	2	1	9	14	2	1	1	18	6	B223
2	1	1	-	2	1	1	-	2	2	1	1	2	2	1	1	1	2	1	1	1	1	2	1	1	B224
1	2	2	2	2	2	1	1	1	2	2	5	2	3	3	3	3	3	3	4	4	4	4	4	3	B225
2	3	3	4	3	18	3	12	2	3	4	5	2	3	4	6	2	1	7	9	2	10	6	6	4	B3
-	-	-	-	-	-	-	-	-	-	-	-	-	-	-	-	-	-	-	-	-1	-	-	-	-	B31
2	3	3	4	3	18	3	12	2	3	4	5	2	2	4	6	1	-	7	9	2	9	6	6	4	B32
2	2	3	4	3	3	3	5	2	3	3	5	3	2	4	4	2	-	3	5	2	3	3	2	2	B321
-	1	-	-	-	2	-	8	-	-	-	-	-	-	-	-	-	-	-	-	-	-	-	-	-	B322
-	-	-	-	-	14	-	-	-	-	-	-	-1	-	-1	2	-1	-	-1	1	-1	-	-1	1	1	B323
-2	3	-6	-5	2	-17	-	3	2	4	-5	-1	-3	-2	-4	-3	1	-1	-1	1	-1	5	-2	2	6	B4
-	-	-	-	-1	2	1	-4	1	-	-1	-	-1	-3	-4	5	-2	-3	-2	10	-1	-1	-3	2	-7	B41
-2	3	-6	-5	-	-15	-	-2	2	4	-6	-1	2	-1	-1	8	-3	-3	-1	9	-	-6	-1	-	-1	B42
-2	3	-6	-5	-	-15	-	-2	2	4	-6	-1	2	-1	-1	8	-3	-3	-1	9	-	-6	-1	-	-1	B421
15	17	-1	8	15	11	13	13	33	29	12	13	25	-2	21	65	26	40	-3	32	11	10	25	15	46	B
-4	-12	-5	1	-8	3	8	13	-	-9	5	2	7	7	7	19	-67	74	80	-170	28	50	79	76	78	C1
-	5	-	1	-	-4	-1	-	-	-	-	-2	-10	14	6	3	-	1	1	-19	-	-	-	-4	-	C11
4	-6	-2	-2	-5	-2	-3	-	-1	-	-	5	7	2	1	5	-5	18	1	1	-32	-3	-	-	1	C12
-8	-14	-3	2	7	9	12	13	1	-2	5	-1	10	-27	4	13	-56	56	74	-124	52	52	79	80	70	C13
-	-3	-	-	-10	-	-	-	-	-	-	-	-	-2	-	-2	-2	-	-8	-	-	-	-	-	-	C14
-	6	-	-	-	-	-	-	-	-7	-	-	-	18	-2	-2	-4	1	4	-20	-	-	-	-	-	C15
-	-	-	-	-	-	-	-	-	-	-	-	-	-	-	-	-	-	-	-	8	1	-	-	7	C16
-	-	4	1	-2	-2	-2	-	-	-	5	5	6	7	6	10	-2	5	1	-	-18	-	2	-	2	C2
-	-	-	-	-	-	-	-	-	-	5	5	5	7	5	10	-	5	-	-	-20	-	-	-	-	C21
-	-	-	1	-	-	-	-	-	-	-	-	1	-	1	-	-2	-	1	-	2	-	2	-	1	C22
-	-	5	-	-2	-2	-1	-	-	-	-	-	-	-	-	-	-	-	-	-	-	-	-	-	-	C23
-	-	-1	-	-	-	-1	-	-	-	-	-	-	-	-	-	-	-	-	-	-	-	-	-	-	C24
-1	-	-	1	1	5	-	2	-	-	-	-1	3	1	-	-	-2	-1	-	-22	-	3	11	9	2	C3

(Continued)

(Nearest 100 Million DM)	61 II	III	IV	62 I	II	III	IV	63 I	II	III	IV	64 I	II	III	IV
C31 Gold Paid in to IMF	-	-	-	-	-	-	-	-	-	-	-	-	-	-	-
C32 IMF Credit Position in DM	4	11	-3	-3	1	-2	-1	-	-	1	-	4	2	-	1
C4 MEDIUM-TERM IBRD DEBT CERTIFICATES	1	2	5	-	-	-	-	-	-	-	-	-	-	-	-
C5 INTERNATIONAL LIABILITIES FALL	-8	3	3	-2	2	-2	1	-1	1	1	1	-2	-	2	-1
C51 Inter-Central-Bank DM Paper	-1	-	-	-	-	-1	-	-	1	-	-	-2	-	1	-1
C52 Fall in Other Liabilities	-7	3	3	-2	2	-1	1	-1	-	1	1	-	-	1	-
C. CENTRAL RESERVES INCREASE	-14	-7	9	-24	9	5	-1	-1	11	8	10	4	3	-4	3
D. OTHER ITEMS	-	1	-1	2	-2	-	-	-	-	-1	-	2	-	-1	1
EE NET DM EFFECT OF PAYMENT BALANCE	-14	-6	8	-22	7	5	-1	-1	11	7	10	6	3	-5	4
E1 FALL IN NON-BANK CREDIT POSITION W/BB	11	12	15	-17	1	-7	32	-33	-5	11	39	-35	4	-9	40
E11 Private	-	-	-	-	-	-	-	-	-	-	-	-	-	-	-
E12 Public Authorities	11	12	15	-17	1	-7	32	-34	-3	16	29	-35	4	-9	40
E121 Federal	15	15	13	-6	4	-10	20	-22	-1	9	15	-31	3	-12	-33
E1211 Loans Rise	-1	-	-	-	-	-	-	-7	-	6	8	-17	-	-	11
E1212 Deposits Rise	-16	-15	-13	6	-4	10	-20	15	1	-3	-7	14	-3	12	44
E122 State	-4	-3	2	-11	-3	3	12	-12	-2	7	14	-4	1	3	-7
E123 Local	-	-	-	-	-	-	-	-	-	-	-	-	-	-	-
E124 Social Insurance Institutions	-	-	-	-	-	-	-	-	-	-	-	-	-	-	-
E2 BUNDESBANK CAP'L & RESERVE ACCT'S NET	-1	-	-	-	-1	-	-	-	-2	-	-	-	-3	-	-
E3 OTHER BUNDESBANK ACCOUNTS NET	1	-2	-2	-	2	2	-6	6	3	-	-6	1	7	-1	-8
E. DM EFFECT OF BUNDESBK NON-POLICY OPS	11	10	13	-17	2	-5	26	-27	-4	11	33	-34	8	-10	33
FF MONETARY BASE, NOT FROM BB POLICY OPS	-3	4	21	-39	9	-	25	-28	7	18	43	-28	11	-15	37
F1 BASE FREED BY REQUIRED-RESERVE CHANGE	16	7	6	10	-	-	-	-	-	-	-	-	-10	-13	-
F2 BUNDESBANK CREDIT TO COMMERCIAL BANKS	-4	10	-5	3	-1	1	5	9	6	-14	-2	11	-4	15	-8
F3 BUNDESBANK NET OPEN-MARKET PURCHASES	7	-7	10	10	-1	3	2	-6	5	-1	-10	-2	1	17	4
F31 Securities	-	-	2	-	-1	-	-	-1	-1	-1	-	-1	-	-	-
F32 Mobilization Paper	7	-7	8	10	-	3	2	-5	6	-	-10	-1	1	17	4

(This bibliography registers only material
cited in the notes.)

Aktionsgemeinschaft Soziale Marktwirtschaft. Stabiles Geld geht vor.
Ludwigsburg, 1963.

Alexander, S. S. "Effects of a Devaluation on a Trade Balance." International Monetary Fund Staff Papers, April 1952.

American Enterprise Institute. International Payments Problems.
Washington, 1966.

Andersen, L. C., and J. L. Jordan. "The Monetary Base - Explanation
and Analytical Use." Federal Reserve Bank of St. Louis, Review,
August 1968.

AP. (See Germany, Federal Republic. Bundesbank. Auszüge aus
Presseartikeln.)

AR. (See Germany, Federal Republic. Bundesbank. Annual Report.)

Arbeitsgemeinschaft Deutscher Wirtschaftswissenschaftlicher Forschungsinstitute. Die Internationalen Währungsprobleme in der
Weltwirtschaft der Gegenwart (Supplement to Zeitschrift für
Angewandte Konjunkturforschung #14). Berlin, 1967.

Argy, V. "Monetary Variables and the Balance of Payments." International Monetary Fund Staff Papers, July 1969.

Arndt, S. "International Short-Term Capital Movements: A Distributed
Lag Model of Speculation in Foreign Exchange." Econometrica,
January 1968.

Ball, R. Inflation and the Theory of Money. Chicago, 1964.

Bank for International Settlements. (See Schmidt, W.)

Barrett, M. "Activation of the Special Drawing Rights Facility in the
International Monetary Fund." Federal Reserve Bank of New
York, Monthly Review, February, 1970.

Bator, F. M. "The Political Economics of International Money."
Foreign Affairs, October 1968.

317

Baumol, W. J. "The Pure Theory of International Trade: A Survey." Economic Journal, March 1964.

_____. "Speculation, Profitability, and Stability." Review of Economics and Statistics, August 1957.

v. Beckerath, E., and H. Giersch. Probleme der normativen Ökonomik und des wirtschaftspolitischen Beratung (Schriften des Vereins für Sozialpolitik NF #29). Berlin, 1963.

Bell, P. W. "Private Capital Movements and the United States Balance-of-Payments Position." United States, 86th Congress, 2d Session, Joint Economic Committee, Subcommittee on International Exchange and Payments, Factors Affecting the United States Balance of Payments. Washington, 1962.

Benning, B. "Auslandskapital in der Bundesrepublik Deutschland." Schmollers Jahrbuch, 1966, p. 435.

Berliner Bank. Das Deutsche Zahlungsbilanzproblem: Diagnose und Therapie. Berlin, 1957.

Bernstein, E. M. "Strategic Factors in Balance of Payments Adjustment." International Monetary Fund Staff Papers, August 1956.

Bhagwati, J. "The Pure Theory of International Trade: A Survey." A.E.A. and R.E.S., Surveys of Economic Theory (Vol. 2). New York, 1965.

_____. The Theory and Practice of Commercial Policy: Departures from Unified Rates (Special Papers in International Economics #8). Princeton, 1968.

Bittorf, W. Automation, die zweite industrielle Revolution. Darmstadt, 1956.

Blessing, K. Im Kampf um gutes Geld. Frankfurt, 1966.

_____. Die Verteidigung des Geldwertes. Frankfurt, 1960.

Bloomfield, A. Monetary Policy under the International Gold Standard. New York, 1959.

Boarman, P. Germany's Economic Dilemma. New Haven, 1964.

Bombach, G. "Ursachen der Nachkriegsinflation und Probleme der Inflationsbekämpfung." Stabile Preise in wachsender Wirtschaft. Tübingen, 1960.

Bopp, K. R. "The Central Banking Objectives, Guides and Measures." Journal of Finance, March 1954.

BR. (See Germany, Federal Republic. Bundesministerium für Wirtschaft. Wissenschaftliche Beirat.)

BRD. (See Germany, Federal Republic.)

Brehmer, E. "Official Forward Exchange Operations: The German Experience." International Monetary Fund Staff Papers, November 1964.

_____. Struktur und Funktionsweise des Geldmarkts der Bundesrepublik Deutschland seit 1948 (Kieler Studien). Tübingen, 1964.

Briefs, G. "Der Unternehmer in Wirtschaft und Gesellschaft." Gesellschaftspolitische Kommentare, 1965, p. 171.

Bronfenbrenner, M., and F. D. Holzman. "A Survey of Inflation Theory." American Economic Review, September 1963.

Canada. Royal Commission on Banking and Finance. Report. Ottawa, 1964.

Carstens, R. Die Aufwertungsdebatte (Kieler Studien). Tübingen, 1963.

Chalmers, E. B. Monetary Policy in the Sixties: United Kingdom, United States, and West Germany. London, 1968.

Chipman, J. S. "A Survey of the Theory of International Trade, Part 3: The Modern Theory." Econometrica, January 1966.

Cicero, M. Tullius. De Re Publica (H. Schwamborn ed.). Paderborn, 1969.

Clauss, F. "Wirtschaftswachstum und Konjunkturpolitik in der bestehenden Währungsordnung." (See Arbeitsgemeinschaft, etc.)

Cooper, R. N. "The Balance of Payments in Revue." Journal of Political Economy, August 1968.

Corden, W. M. "The Geometric Representation of Policies to Attain Internal and External Balance." Review of Economic Studies, October 1960.

_____. Recent Developments in the Theory of International Trade (Special Papers in International Economics #7). Princeton, 1965.

Crouch, R. L. "The Inadequacy of 'New-Orthodox' Methods of Monetary Control." Economic Journal, December 1964.

Davis, R. G. "How Much Does Money Matter: A Look at Some Recent Evidence." Federal Reserve Bank of New York, Review, June 1969.

Despres, E., and C. P. Kindleberger. "The Dollar and World Liquidity - A Minority View." The Economist, 5 February 1966.

Deuss, H. "Die Geldanlagen der Geschäftsbanken im Ausland." Der Volkswirt, supplement to #43, 1961.

Deutsches Wirtschaftswissenschaftliches Institut (East Berlin). Berichte.

Dewald, W., and H. G. Johnson. "An Objective Analysis of the Objectives of American Monetary Policy, 1952-1961." D. Carson, ed., Banking and Monetary Studies. Homewood, 1963.

Dorrance, G. S., and E. Brehmer. "Control of Capital Inflows: Recent Experience of Germany and Switzerland." International Monetary Fund Staff Papers, December 1961.

The Economist. Quarterly Economic Survey (Germany). Quarterly.

EEC. (See European Economic Community.)

Einzig, Paul. A Dynamic Theory of Forward Exchanges. London, 1962.

_____. The Euro-Dollar System. New York, 1964.

Ellsworth, P. T. The International Economy. London, 1969.

Emminger, O. Die Herrschaft der Schlagworte in der jüngsten Währungspolitischen Diskussion (Kieler Vorträge NF #17). Kiel, 1961.

_____. "Kapitalexport als Mittel zum Ausgleich der Zahlungsbilanz." Zeitschrift fur das gesamte Kreditwesen, 1959, p. 814.

_____. "Practical Aspects of the Problem of Balance-of-Payments Adjustment." Journal of Political Economy, August 1967 supplement.

_____. "Reservewährungen und Reform der internationalen Währungssystems." Zeitschrift für die gesamte Staatswissenschaft, 1967, p. 630.

_____. Währungspolitik im Wandel der Zeit. Frankfurt, 1966.

_____. Währungspolitische Betrachtungen. Frankfurt, 1956.

_____. "Zahlungsbilanz und Kapitalexport." Neue Zürcher Zeitung, 3 August 1963.

Erhard, L. The Economics of Success. Princeton, 1963.

_____. Wirken und Reden, 1952-1965. Ludwigsburg, 1966.

Eucken, W. Die Grundlagen der Nationaleconomie. Berlin, 1950.

_____. Grundsätze der Wirtschaftspolitik. Hamburg, 1959.

European Economic Community. Bulletin. Monthly.

_____. Commission. Directorate General for Monetary and Financial Problems. The Instruments of Monetary Policy in the Countries of the European Economic Community. Brussels, 1962.

Fand, D. "Some Issues in Monetary Economics." Federal Reserve Bank of St. Louis, Review, January 1970.

Farrell, M. J. "Profitable Speculation." Economica, May 1966.

Federal Reserve Bank of New York. Monthly Review, December 1968.

Federal Reserve Bank of Philadelphia. Monetary Policy--Decision-Making, Tools and Objectives. Philadelphia, 1961.

Fellner, W., F. Machlup and R. Triffin, eds. Maintaining and Restoring Balance in International Payments. Princeton, 1966.

Fleming, J. M. "Domestic Financial Policies under Fixed and Floating Exchange Rates." International Monetary Fund Staff Papers, November 1962.

_____. Guidelines for Balance-of-Payments Adjustment under the Par-Value System (Essays in International Finance #67). Princeton, 1968.

_____. "Targets and Instruments." International Monetary Fund Staff Papers, November 1968.

Floyd, J. E. "International Capital Movements and Monetary Equilibrium." American Economic Review, September 1969.

Fousek, C. Foreign Central Banking. New York, 1957.

FR. (See Germany, Federal Republic. Bundesministerium für Finanz. Finanzbericht.)

Frankfurter Allgemeine Zeitung für Deutschland. Daily.

Friedman, I. S. "The International Monetary Mechanism--Part I: Mechanism and Operations." International Monetary Fund Staff Papers, July 1963.

Friedman, M. "The Case for Flexible Exchange Rates." M. Friedman, Essays in Positive Economics. Chicago, 1953.

_____. "The Demand for Money: Some Theoretical and Empirical Results." Journal of Political Economy, August 1959.

_____. Dollars and Deficits. Englewood Cliffs, 1969.

_____. "The Quantity Theory of Money - A Restatement." Milton Friedman, ed., Studies in the Quantity Theory of Money. Chicago, 1963.

_____. "Should There by an Independent Monetary Authority?" L. B. Yeager, ed., In Search of a Monetary Constitution. Cambridge, 1962.

_____, and D. Meiselman. "The Relative Stability of Monetary Velocity and the Investment Multiplier in the United States 1897-1958." Commission on Money and Credit, Stabilization Policies. Englewood Cliffs, 1963.

BIBLIOGRAPHY

_____, and R. V. Roosa. The Balance of Payments: Free vs. Fixed Exchange Rates. Washington, 1967.

_____, and A. Schwartz. "Money and Business Cycles." Review of Economics and Statistics, February 1963 supplement.

Furth, H. "International Monetary Reform and the 'Crawling Peg'-- Comment." Federal Reserve Bank of St. Louis, Review, July 1969.

Garvy, G. The Discount Mechanism in Leading Industrial Countries Since World War II. Washington, 1968.

Gasteyger, C., W. Kewenig and N. Kohlhase. "Europe and the Shape of Things to Come." Europa-Archiv, 1970, p. 15.

Gatz, W. "Gründe und volkswirtschaftliche Wirkungen der D-Mark-Aufwetung." Weltwirtschaftliches Archiv, 1963, p. 379.

Gerakis, A. S. "Effects of Exchange-Rate Devalutions and Revaluations on Receipts from Tourism." International Monetary Fund Staff Papers, November 1965.

GER. (See German Economic Review.)

German Economic Review. Quarterly.

Germany, Federal Republic. Bundesbank. Annual Report. Annual.

_____. _____. Auszüge aus Presseartikeln. Irregular, about thrice a week.

_____. _____. Monthly Report. Monthly.

_____. _____. Supplements to Monthly Report (Series 1: Banking Statistics; Series 2: Securities Statistics; Series 3: Balance-of-Payments Statistics; Series 4: Economic Indicators). Monthly.

_____. Bundesministerium für Finanz. Finanzbericht (officially: Die volkswirtschaftlichen Grundlagen und die wichtigsten finanzwirtschaftlichen Probleme des Haushaltsplans der Bundesrepublik Deutschland für das Rechnungsjahr [respective dates]). Annual.

————. Bundesministerium für Wirtschaft. Wissenschaftliche Beirat. <u>Gutachten</u> (December 1952-November 1954). Göttingen, 1955.

————. ————. ————. <u>Instrumente der Konjunkturpolitik</u> <u>und ihre rechtliche Institutionalisierung</u>. Göttingen, 1956.

————. ————. ————. "Preisstabilität und Aussenhandel." <u>Bundesanzeiger</u> #244, 1967.

————. ————. ————. "Report on Prices." <u>Bundesanzeiger</u> #32, 1968.

————. ————. ————. <u>Wirtschaftspolitische Problematik</u> <u>der deutschen Exportüberschüsse</u>. Göttingen, 1961.

————. Bundestag. Begründung zum Regierungsentwurf Bundesbank- <u>gesetz</u> (Drucksache 2781 A III, 2. Wahlperiode). Bonn, 1953.

————. ————. <u>Bericht über die Ergebnis einer Untersuchung</u> <u>der Konzentration in der Wirtschaft</u> (Drucksache 2320, 4. Wahl- periode). Bonn, 1964.

————. Press and Information Office. <u>The Bulletin</u>. Weekly.

————. Sachverständigenrat zur Begutachtung der Gesamtwirt- schaftlichen Entwicklung. <u>Jahresgutachten</u>. Annual since January 1965. (Each year's report has a different subtitle.)

————. ————. <u>Stellungnahme</u>, 24 June 1964.

————. ————. <u>Sondergutachten</u>, 1967 (March), 1968 (July), 1969 I (June), 1969 II (September), 1969 III (October), 1970 I (May), 1971 I (May).

Giersch, H. <u>Lohnpolitik und Geldwertstabilität</u> (Kieler Vorträge #50). Kiel, 1967.

Gilbert, M. "Reconciliation of Domestic and International Objectives of Financial Policy in European Countries." <u>Journal of Finance</u>, May 1963.

Gleske, L. "Die Finanzierung des wachsenden Internationlen Handels." (See Arbeitsgemeinschaft, <u>etc</u>.)

Goethe, W. Gedichte, Eine Auswahl (L. Kaim, ed.). Leipzig, 1949.

Goode, R., and R. S. Thorn. "Variable Reserve Requirements Against Commercial Bank Deposits." International Monetary Fund Staff Papers, April 1959.

Graham, F. D. Fundamentals of International Monetary Policy (Essays in International Finance #2). Princeton, 1943.

Grubel, H. G. Foward Exchange, Speculation, and the International Flow of Capital. Stanford, 1966.

_____, ed. World Monetary Reform. Stanford, 1966.

Gutman, G., H. J. Hochstrate, and R. Schüter. Die Wirtschaftsverfassung der Bundesrepublik Deutschland. Stuttgart, 1964.

Haberler, G. Money in the International Economy. Cambridge, 1965.

_____. A Survey of International Trade Theory. Princeton, 1961.

_____, and T. D. Willett. The United States Balance of Payments and International Monetary Reform: A Critical Analysis. Washington, 1968.

_____, and T. D. Willett. A study prepared for the American Enterprise Association. Washington, 1971.

_____, and others. "Round Table on Exchange Rate Policy." American Economic Review, May 1969 (Papers and Proceedings of the 81st Annual Meeting of the American Economic Association).

Hagemann, H. A. "Reserve Policies of Central Banks and their Implications for United States Balance-of-Payments Policy." American Economic Review, March 1969.

Hahn, L. A. Ewige Hochkonjunktur und kommandiertes Wachstum. Tübingen, 1967.

_____. Fünfzig Jahre zwischen Inflation und Deflation. Tübingen, 1963.

_____. Geld und Kredit. Frankfurt, 1960.

_____. "Die Grundirrtümer in Lord Keynes' General Theory of Employment, Interest and Money." Ordo-Jahrbuch, Volume 2 (1949), p. 171.

_____. Ein Traktat über Währungsreform. Tübingen, 1964.

Halm, G. N. The "Band" Proposal: the Limits of Permissible Exchange Rate Variations (Special Papers in International Economics #6). Princeton, 1965.

_____. International Financial Intermediation: Deficits Benign and Malignant (Essays in International Finance #68). Princeton, 1968.

_____. International Monetary Cooperation. Chapel Hill, 1945.

_____. Toward Limited Exchange-Rate Flexibility (Essays in International Finance #73). Princeton, 1969.

Hansen, Bent. Fiscal Policy in Seven Countries. Paris, 1969.

Harris, P. B. "Continuing Tensions within the European Community." South African Journal of Economics, December 1966.

Hause, J. C. "The Welfare Costs of Disequilibrium Exchange Rates." Journal of Political Economy, August 1966.

Hawtrey, R. G. The Art of Central Banking. New York, 1933.

_____. The Gold Standard in Theory and Practice. London, 1939.

Heckscher, E. "The Effects of Foreign Trade on the Distribution of Income." American Economic Association, Readings in the Theory of International Trade. Philadelphia, 1949.

Hein, J. "The Mainsprings of German Monetary Policy." Economia Internazionale, May 1964.

_____. "Monetary Policy and External Convertibility: the German Experience, 1959-1961." Economia Internazionale, August 1964.

_____. Monetary Policy and External Surplusses: the German Experience, 1955-1961 (Columbia University Dissertation). 1963.

Hendershott, P. H. The Neutralized Money Stock: An Unbiased Measure of Federal Reserve Policy Actions. Homewood, 1968.

Hendrickson, H. R. The Deutsche Bundesbank and West German Monetary Policies with Special Emphasis on 1955-1957 (University of Washington Dissertation). 1966.

Hitzinger, W. Die Europäische Automobilindustrie. Kiel, 1965.

Holms, A. R. The New York Foreign Exchange Market. New York, 1959.

Holtrop, M. W. Monetary Policy in an Open Economy (Essays in International Finance #43). Princeton, 1963.

Hudeczek, C. Geldprobleme der Europäischen Wirtschaft. Düsseldorf, 1961.

Ingram, J. C. "A Proposal for Financial Integration in the Atlantic Community." United States, 86th Congress, 2d Session, Joint Economic Committee, Subcommittee on International Exchange and Payments, Factors Affecting the United States Balance of Payments. Washington, 1962.

IMF. (See International Monetary Fund.)

International Monetary Fund. Balance of Payments Manual. Washington, 1950.

_____. International Financial Statistics. Monthly.

_____. International Reserves and Liquidity. Washington, 1958.

_____. Summary Proceedings, Annual Meeting. Annual.

Irmler, H. Discussion Contribution in Arbeitsgemeinschaft, etc., p. 104.

JEC. (See United States. Congress. Joint Economic Committee.)

Jenkis, H. W. Die importierte Inflation (Schriften zur Wirtschaftswissenschaftlichen Forschung #15). Meisenheim, 1966.

JG. (See Germany, Federal Republic. Sachverständigenrat zur Begutachtung der Gesamtwirtschaftlichen Entwicklung. Annual Evaluation.)

Johnson, H. G. Alternative Guiding Principles for the Use of Monetary Policy (Essays in International Finance #44). Princeton, 1963.

_____. "Towards a More General Theory of the Balance of Payments." In his International Trade and Economic Growth: Studies in Pure Theory. London, 1958.

_____. "The Welfare Costs of Exchange Rate Stabilization." Journal of Political Economy, October 1966.

Katz, S. I. External Surplusses, Capital Flows, and Credit Policy in the European Economic Community (Studies in International Finance #22). Princeton, 1969.

_____. Sterling Speculation and European Convertibility: 1955-1958 (Essays in International Finance #37). Princeton, 1961.

Kaufman, G. "An Empirical Definition of Money." American Economic Review, March 1969.

Kemp, M. C. "The Rate of Exchange, the Terms of Trade and the Balance of Payments in Fully Employed Economics." International Economic Review, September 1962.

_____. "Speculation, Profitability and Price Stability." Review of Economics and Statistics, May 1963.

Kenen, P. B. British Monetary Policy and the Balance of Payments, 1951-57 Cambridge, 1960.

_____. "International Liquidity and the Balance of Payments of a Reserve Currency Country." Quarterly Journal of Economics, November 1960.

_____. "Trade, Speculation, and the Forward Exchange Rate." R. E. Baldwin and others, eds., Trade, Growth, and the Balance of Payments: Essays in Honor of Gottfried Haberler. Chicago, 1965.

_____, and T. E. B. Yudin. "Demand for International Reserves." Review of Economics and Statistics, August 1965.

Keran, M. W., and C. T. Babb. "An Explanation of Federal Reserve Actions (1933-68)." Federal Reserve Bank of St. Louis, Review, July 1969.

Keynes, J. M. The General Theory of Employment, Interest and Money. New York, 1936.

_____. A Tract on Monetary Reform. London, 1923.

_____. A Treatise on Money. New York, 1930.

Kiesinger, K. "State of the Nation in Divided Germany" (Address, 17 June 1969). Federal Republic of Germany, Press and Information Service, The Bulletin (Supplement), 24 June 1969.

Kindleberger, C. P. Balance-of-Payments Deficits and the International Market for Liquidity (Essays in International Finance #46). Princeton, 1965.

_____. "Germany's Persistent Balance-of-Payments Disequilibrium." R. E. Baldwin and others, eds., Trade, Growth, and the Balance of Payments. Chicago, 1965.

_____. International Economics. Homewood, 1958.

_____. International Monetary Arrangements. St. Lucia (Australia), 1966.

_____. International Short-Term Capital Movements. New York, 1937.

_____. The Politics of World Money and World Language (Essays in International Finance #61). Princeton, 1967.

Klein, L. Finanzpolitische Instrumente der Konjunkturpolitik. Berlin, 1963.

König, H., and V. Timmerman. "An Econometric Model for the Federal Republic of Germany, 1950-1960." Zeitschrift für die gesamte Staatswissenschaft, October 1962.

Krause, L. A Passive Balance-of-Payments Strategy for the United States (Brookings Papers on Economic Activity). Washington, 1971.

Krelle, W. "The Consumption and Investment Functions in West Germany." Revue d'Economie Politique, 1963, p. 5.

Krueger, A. O. "Balance of Payments Theory." Journal of Economic Literature, March 1969.

_____. "The Impact of Alternative Government Policies under

Varying Exchange Systems." Quarterly Journal of Economics, May 1965.

Külp, B. "Der Einfluss des Aussenhandels auf die Einkommensverteilung." Weltwirtschaftliches Archiv, 1966, p. 116.

Kunz, H. "Swaptransaktionen und Geldexport." Zeitschrift für das gesamte Kreditwesen, 1964, p. 276.

Lanyi, A. The Case for Floating Exchange Rates Reconsidered (Essays in International Finance #72). Princeton, 1969.

Lederer, W. The Balance on Foreign Transactions: Problems of Definition and Measurement (Special Papers in International Economics #5). Princeton, 1963.

_____. "Measuring the Balance of Payments." United States, 86th Congress, 2d Session, Joint Economic Committee, Subcommittee on International Exchange and Payments, Factors Affecting the United States Balance of Payments. Washington, 1962.

Leontief, V. Input-Output Economics. New York, 1966.

Lindeman, J. "Political and Administrative Arrangements Affecting Foreign Financial and Credit Operations." Commission on Money and Credit, Fiscal and Debt Management Policies. Englewood Cliffs, 1963.

Linhardt, H. Kritik der Währungs- und Bankpolitik. Köln-Opladen, 1963.

Loehr, R. The West German Banking System. No place imprinted, 1952.

Lübbert, J. "Internationale Kapitalbewegungen als Problem und Instrument der Zahlungsbilanzpolitik." Weltwirtschaftliches Archiv, 1963, p. 61.

Lutz, F. A. The Problem of International Economic Equilibrium. Amsterdam, 1962.

_____. Towards an International Equilibrium System. Amsterdam, 1962.

Machlup, F. "Adjustment, Compensating Corrections and Financing of Imbalances in International Payments." R. E. Baldwin and others, eds., Trade, Growth, and the Balance of Payments. Chicago, 1965.

_____. Credit Facilities or Reserve Allotments? (Reprints in International Finance #7). Princeton, 1967.

_____. Essays in Economic Semantics. Englewood Cliffs, 1963.

_____. International Payments, Debt and Gold. New York, 1964.

_____. International Trade and the International Trade Multiplier. Philadelphia, 1943.

_____. Involuntary Foreign Lending (Wicksell Lectures 1965). Stockholm, 1965.

_____. The Need for Monetary Reserves (Reprints in International Finance #5). Princeton, 1966.

_____. Plans for Reform of the International Monetary System (Special Papers in International Finance #3). Princeton, 1962.

_____. Remaking the International Monetary System: The Rio Agreement and Beyond. Baltimore, 1968.

_____. "The Theory of Foreign Exchanges." H. S. Ellis and L. Metzler, eds., Readings in the Theory of International Trade. Philadelphia, 1949.

_____. "Three Concepts of the Balance of Payments and the So-Called Dollar Shortage." Economic Journal, March 1950.

_____, and B. G. Malkiel, eds. International Monetary Arrangements: The Problem of Choice. Princeton, 1964.

Madison, J. ("Publius"). The Federalist, #10, 1787.

Martell, H. "Kapitalmarkt und öffentliche Defizite." Konjunkturpolitik, 1967, p. 283.

McKenzie, G. W. "International Monetary Reform and the 'Crawling Peg'." Federal Reserve Bank of St. Louis, Review, February 1969.

McKinnon, R. I., and W. E. Oates. The Implications of International Economic Integration for Monetary, Fiscal, and Exchange Rate

Policy (Studies in International Finance #16). Princeton, 1966.

Meade, J. E. The Theory of International Economic Policy, Vol. 1: The Balance of Payments. New York, 1961.

Meigs, A. J. Free Reserves and the Money Supply. Chicago, 1962.

Meimberg, R. Zur Problematik des flexiblen Wechselkurses der Währung eines relativ preisstabilen Landes (Volkswirtschaftliche Schriften #96). Berlin, 1966.

Metzler, A. H. "The Demand for Money: the Evidence from the Time Series." Journal of Political Economy, June 1963.

Michaely, M. Balance-of-Payments Adjustment Policies. New York, 1968.

Mills, C. The Power Elite. New York, 1956.

Mills, R. H. "The Regulation of Short-Term Capital Movements." Board of Governors of the Federal Reserve System, Staff Economic Studies, May 1968.

Der Monat. Monthly.

Moore, B. An Introduction to the Theory of Finance. New York, 1968.

Mosse, R. "Die Messung der Zahlungsbilanzsalden mit besonderer Berücksichtigung der Kontroverse Bernstein-Lederer." Weltwirtschaftliches Archiv, 1968, p. 197.

MR. (See Germany, Federal Republic. Bundesbank. Monthly Report.)

Müller, G. Die Bundestagswahl 1969. München, 1969.

Müller, H. "Die Bedeutung der Time Lags für die Wirksamkeit der Geld- und Kreditpolitik in der Bundesrepublik Deutschland." Weltwirtschaftliches Archiv, 1968, p. 282.

Muller-Armack, A. Diskussionsbeitrag zu Stützels These der unmittelbaren Preiseffekte (Supplement to Konjunkturpolitik #7). Berlin, 1960.

_____. "The Principles of the Social Market Economy." German Economic Review, June 1965.

Mundell, R. A. "The Appropriate Use of Monetary and Fiscal Policy for Internal and External Stability." International Monetary Fund Staff Papers, March 1962.

_____. "Capital Mobility and Stabilization Policy under Fixed and Flexible Exchange Rates." Canadian Journal of Economics, November 1963.

_____. "Flexible Exchange Rates and Employment Policy." Canadian Journal of Economics, November 1961.

_____. "The Monetary Dynamics of International Adjustment under Fixed and Flexible Exchange Rates." Quarterly Journal of Economics, May 1960.

_____. "A Theory of Optimum Currency Areas." American Economic Review, September 1961.

New York Times. New York. Daily.

Norton, H. S. The Role of the Economist in Government Policymaking. Berkeley, 1969.

Nurkse, R. Conditions of International Monetary Equilibrium (Essays in International Finance #4). Princeton, 1945.

_____. "Domestic and International Equilibrium." S. Harris, ed., The New Economics. New York, 1947.

_____. International Monetary Experience. Geneva, 1944.

Oberhausen, A. "Zahlungsbilanzüberschüsse und Einkommensverteilung." Weltwirtschaftliches Archiv, 1964, p. 286.

OECDS. (See Organization for Economic Cooperation and Development. Economic and Development Review Committee.)

OECD3. (See Organization for Economic Cooperation and Development. Economic Policy Committee. Working Party Three.)

Ohlin, B. Interregional and International Trade. Cambridge, 1933.

Oppenheim, P. M. "Imported Inflation and Monetary Policy." Banca Nazionale del Lavoro Quarterly Review, June 1965.

Organization for Economic Cooperation and Development. Economic and Development Review Committee. Survey (Germany). Annual.

_____. Economic Policy Committee. Working Party Three. The Balance of Payments Adjustment Process. Paris, 1966.

_____. Ministerial Conference. Statement. Paris, August 1964.

_____. Study Group on the Creation of Reserve Assets. Report. Washington, 1965.

Ott, D. J., and A. F. Ott. "Monetary and Fiscal Policy: Goals and the Choice of Instructions." Quarterly Journal of Economics, May 1968.

Patinkin, D. Money, Interest and Prices. New York, 1965.

Phillips, A. W. "The Relation between Unemployment and the Rate of Change of Money Wages in the United Kingdom, 1861-1957." Economica, November 1958.

Predöhl, A. Das Ende der Weltwirtschaftskrise. Hamburg, 1962.

_____, and H. Jurgensen. "Europäische Integration." Handwörterbuch der Sozialwissenschaften Vol. 3. Stuttgart 1961.

Propp, P. Zur Transformation einer Zentralverwaltungswirtschaft sovjetischen Typs in eine Marktwirtschaft. Berlin, 1964.

QES. (See Economist. Quarterly Economic Survey [Germany].)

Rhomberg, R., and L. Boissoneault. "Effects of Income and Price Changes on the United States Balance of Payments." International Monetary Fund Staff Papers, March 1964.

Rittershausen, H. Internationale Handels- und Devisenpolitik. Frankfurt, 1955.

_____. "Swap als Steuerungsinstrument." Zeitschrift für das gesamte Kreditwesen, 1960, p. 954.

_____. "Das Swap-Geschäft als kreditpolitisches Instrument." Zeitschrift für das gesamte Kreditwesen, 1960, p. 813.

_____. Die Zentralnotenbank. Ein Handbuch ihrer Instrumente, ihre Politik und ihrer Theorie. Frankfurt, 1962.

Robertson, W. "The Finance of West Germany's Export Surplus, 1952-1958." Economia Internazionale, August 1960.

Robinson, J. "Exchange Equilibrium." Economia Internazionale, 1950, p. 400.

Ropke, W. Gegen die Brandung. Zurich, 1959.

_____. Geld und Kapital in unserer Zeit. Baden-Baden, 1964.

_____. "Der Kampf gegen die Inflation in unserer Zeit." A. Hunold, ed., Inflation und Weltwährungsordnung. Stuttgart, 1963.

_____. Währungspolitik in der Europäischen Integration. Baden-Baden, 1964.

Rowan, D. C. "Towards a Rational Exchange Policy: Some Reflections on the British Experience." Federal Reserve Bank of St. Louis, Review, April 1969.

Salant, W., E. Despres, L. D. Krause, and A. M. Rivlin. The United States Balance of Payments in 1968. Washington, 1969.

Samuelson, A. La Banque Centrale de l'Allemagne de l'Ouest: ses Institutions, ses Techniques, et sa Politique de 1948 à 1960. Paris, 1965.

Samuelson, P. "International Factor Price Equalization Once Again." Economic Journal, 1949, p. 181.

_____. "International Trade and the Equalization of Factor Prices." Economic Journal, 1948, p. 163.

Sayers, R. Central Banking in Europe. Oxford, 1962.

_____. Central Banking since Bagehot. Oxford, 1957.

_____. Modern Central Banking. Oxford, 1958.

Schacht, H. Schluss mit der Inflation! Berlin, 1960.

_____. "So kann unser Geld gerettet werden." Quick, #49, 1964.

_____. "Der Staat betrügt uns um unser Geld." Quick, #48, 1964.

Schiller, K. Der Ökonom und die Gesellschaft. Stuttgart, 1964.

_____. Preisstabilität durch globale Steuerung der Marktwirtschaft (Vorträge and Aufsätze aus dem Walter-Eucken-Institut #15). Tubingen, 1966.

_____. Stabilität und Aufstieg (Wirtschaftspolitische Tagung der SPD). Bonn, 1963.

_____. "Stability and Growth as Objectives of Economic Policy." German Economic Review, September 1967.

Schmidt, W. "The German Bundesbank." Bank for International Settlements, Eight European Central Banks. London, 1963.

Schmölders, G. Finanzpolitik. Berlin, 1965.

_____. Geldpolitik. Tübingen, 1962.

_____. Die Politiker und die Währung. Frankfurt, 1959.

_____. Psychologie des Geldes. Reinbeck, 1966.

_____. Vergleichende Finanzpsychologie. Mainz, 1968.

Schneider, E. Vorschläge zur Überwindung unserer Zahlungsbilanzkrise. Düsseldorf, 1957.

_____. Discussion Contribution in Arbeitsgemeinschaft, etc., p. 163.

Scitovsky, T. Money and the Balance of Payments. Chicago, 1969.

Scott, I. O. "Imported Inflation and Monetary Policy." Banca Nazionale del Lavoro Quarterly Review, December 1964.

Seeck, H., and G. Steffens. Die Deutsche Bundesbank. Frankfurt, 1959.

Sen, S. N. Central Banking in Undeveloped Money Markets. Calcutta, 1952.

SG. (See Germany, Federal Republic. Sachverständigenrat zur Begutachtung der Gesamtwirtschaftlichen Entwicklung. Special Evaluation.)

Siegert, W. Währungspolitik durch Seelenmassage? (Schriftreihe zur Geld- und Finanzpolitik #7). Frankfurt, 1963.

Simons, H. C. "Rules vs. Authority in Monetary Policy." Journal of Political Economy, February 1936.

Smith, W. L. "Are There Enough Policy Tools?" American Economic Review, May 1965.

_____. "On the Effectiveness of Monetary Policy." American Economic Review, September 1956.

Sohmen, E. "Fiscal and Monetary Policies under Alternative Exchange Rate Systems." Quarterly Journal of Economics, August 1967.

_____. Flexible Exchange Rates: Theory and Controversy. Chicago, 1961.

_____. Internationale Währungsprobleme. Frankfurt, 1964.

Sozialistische Partei Deutschlands. Report of the Proceedings of the Annual Convention. Bonn, 1958.

Der Spiegel. Weekly.

SS3. (See Germany, Federal Republic. Bundesbank. Supplements to Monthly Report, Series 3.)

v. Stein, Hans Joachim. "Keine Deutsche Mark in Bar." Entwicklungspolitik, 1965, p. 11.

Stein, J. L. The Nature and Efficiency of the Foreign Exchange Market (Essays in International Finance #40). Princeton, 1962.

Stigler, G. The Theory of Price. New York, 1952.

Stohler, J. Wirtschaftliche Integration. Tübingen, 1958.

Stucken, R. Deutsche Geld- und Kreditpolitik 1914-1963. Tübingen, 1964.

Stutzel, W. "Ist die schleichende Inflation durch monetäre Massnahmen zu beeinflussen?" (Beihefte zur Konjunkturpolitik #7). Berlin, 1960.

Süddeutsche Zeitung. Daily.

Swan, T. W. "Longer-Run Problems of the Balance of Payments." R. E. Caves and H. G. Johnson, eds., Readings in International Economics. Homewood, 1968.

Tamagna, F. Central Banking in Latin America. Mexico, 1965.

Teschner, M. "Global Growth Control Through 'Concerted Action.'" Konjunkturpolitik, 1966, p. 58.

Timberlake, R. H., Jr., and J. Forston. "Time Deposits in the Definition of Money." American Economic Review, March 1967.

Tinbergen, J. Economic Policy: Principles and Design. Amsterdam, 1956.

Triffin, R. "The Adjustment Mechanism to Differential Rates of Monetary Expansion among the Countries of the European Economic Community." Review of Economics and Statistics, November 1962.

_____. The Evolution of the International Monetary System: Historical Reappraisal and Future Perspectives. Princeton, 1964.

_____. Gold and the Dollar Crisis. New Haven, 1960.

_____. "National Central Banking and the International Economy." Postwar Economic Studies. Washington, 1947.

_____. Our International Monetary System Yesterday, Today, and Tomorrow. New York, 1968.

_____. The World Money Maze. New Haven, 1966.

Tumlir, J. Taxes, Public Expenditures and the Balance of Payments: Germany 1954-1958 (Yale University dissertation). 1962.

UK. (See United Kingdom.)

United Kingdom. Committee on the Working of the Monetary System (Radcliffe Committee). Report (U. K. Command 827). London, 1959.

United States. Bureau of the Budget. Review Commission for Balance-of-Payments Statistics (Bernstein Commission). The Balance of Payments of the United States. Washington, 1965.

_____. 88th Congress, 1st Session. Joint Economic Committee. Subcommittee on International Exchange and Payments. Guidelines for Improving the International Monetary System. Washington, 1965.

_____. 90th Congress, 2d Session. Joint Economic Committee. Subcommittee on International Exchange and Payments. Next Steps in International Monetary Reform. Washington, 1968.

_____. Council of Economic Advisors. Economic Report of the President. Washington, 1962.

_____. Department of Commerce. The Balance of Payments of the United States, 1949-51. Washington, 1953.

Uri, P. Dialog der Kontinente. Berlin, 1964.

US. (See United States.)

Vanek, J. International Trade: Theory and Economic Policy. Homewood, 1962.

_____. "The Keynes-Triffin Plan: A Critical Appraisal." Review of Economics and Statistics, August 1961.

Veit, O. Grundriss der Währungspolitik. Frankfurt, 1961.

_____. Reale Theorie des Geldes. Frankfurt, 1966.

Viner, J. International Economics. Glencoe, 1951.

_____. Studies in the Theory of International Trade. London, 1955.

Der Volkswirt. Monthly.

Vorwärts. Daily.

Vosshall, G. W. The West German Banking System (New York University dissertation). 1965.

Wall Street Journal. New York. Daily.

Wallich, H. Mainsprings of the German Revival. New Haven, 1965.

Waterman, A. M. C. "Some Footnotes to the 'Swan Diagram.'"
Economic Record, September 1966.

Whitman, M. v. N. International and Interregional Payments Adjustment:
A Synthetic View (Studies in International Finance #19). Princeton,
1967.

Williams, D. "The Development of Capital Markets in Europe."
International Monetary Fund Staff Papers, March 1965.

Williams, J. H. "The Theory of International Trade Reconsidered."
Economic Journal, June 1929.

Williamson, J. H. The Crawling Peg (Essays in International Finance
#50). Princeton, 1965.

Wirtschaftswissenschaftliches Institut der Gewerkschaften. Berichte.

Yeager, L. International Monetary Relations. New York, 1966.

Zeitel, G. "Über die Beziehungen zwischen Währungs-, Finanz- und
Zahlungs-bilanzpolitik." Finanz-Archiv, 1964, p. 369.

WILLIAM P. WADBROOK, Associate Professor in the College
of Business Administration at Boston University, specializes in
international finance, which he has taught at several colleges and
universities. Dr. Wadbrook has done consulting work for major banks
and banking organizations. He has traveled extensively in Europe
and elsewhere and is now residing in Germany, carrying on intensive
research on Germany's role in European monetary integration.

Professor Wadbrook was formerly on the staff of the Bureau
of International Programs, United States Department of Commerce,
and of the First National City Bank. He has written many articles
in the Commerce Department's periodical, International Commerce,
and several pamphlets for its World Trade Information Service.

Dr. Wadbrook studied international economics and finance at
Georgetown University's Walsh School of Foreign Service and at
Tufts University's Fletcher School of Law and Diplomacy, as well
as at the Universities of Bonn and Munich as a Fulbright graduate
grantee.